eb 2018 - SIP
Oct 2019 - SIP
nar 2023 - SIP, new ed avail

D0757583

5/3/

Advanced
CRIME SCENE PHOTOGRAPHY

Second Edition

Advanced
CRIME SCENE
PHOTOGRAPHY

Second Edition

Christopher D. Duncan
Crime Scene Investigator
Houston, Texas, USA

CRC Press
Taylor & Francis Group
Boca Raton London New York

CRC Press is an imprint of the
Taylor & Francis Group, an **informa** business

CRC Press
Taylor & Francis Group
6000 Broken Sound Parkway NW, Suite 300
Boca Raton, FL 33487-2742

Printed and bound in India by Replika Press Pvt. Ltd.

Printed on acid-free paper
Version Date: 20141021

International Standard Book Number-13: 978-1-4822-1186-3 (Hardback)

Visit the Taylor & Francis Web site at
http://www.taylorandfrancis.com

and the CRC Press Web site at
http://www.crcpress.com

For my loving wife, Rhonda

Contents

Preface

Advanced Crime Scene Photography developed from my personal challenges and experiences as a crime scene investigator in a large metropolitan police department. Like in any major city, violent crime is quite prevalent and has offered numerous opportunities to learn, create, and develop tools and skills needed to properly document a crime scene. Working an active crime scene is so much different than working in the pristine world of a photography studio. Evidence is commonly found in some of the most difficult to access and photograph locations. Possessing the knowledge and skills necessary to photograph evidence in less-than-accommodating environments is certainly advantageous. The ability to thoroughly and accurately photograph a crime scene is a mandate for all investigators, regardless of the time of day, weather conditions, and/or confines within which a piece of evidence is concealed.

Crime scene photographers are not tasked with proving a person's guilt or innocence. They are not responsible for *proving* the prosecutor's case. Crime scene photographers and crime scene investigators are required to find and testify about the truth found at the crime scene and about the evidence. Testifying is another skill that does not just happen. It develops over time and through experiences: some good and some bad. When the time to testify comes, some of the first pieces of evidence shown to a jury will be the crime scene photographs. If those photographs are out of focus, poorly exposed, or fail to show the evidence, then the whole body of work by an investigator may be questioned by the jury. Investigators will certainly benefit from putting their best foot forward by showing the jury a photographer's skill and dedication to his craft. Consequently, from start to finish, the value of quality crime scene photographs cannot be emphasized enough, and this text is written to help photographers achieve the goal of capturing the best possible image in all kinds of environments and conditions.

Anyone with a camera phone can take a photograph in perfect lighting, with the subject sitting out in the open and already positioned for the best composition. The goal of this text is to help give crime scene photographers the skills to record those same beautiful photographs in adverse condition, surrounded by tragedy, and with the tools available to the investigator. The greatest tool a photographer has is their brain. Cameras cannot be relied upon to calculate exposures in every situation. Furthermore, cameras are not able to compose an image within the viewfinder. As a result, photographers must take control of their photographic endeavors, identify the challenges, design a plan to capture the image correctly, and execute that plan.

Another goal of this text is to help readers solve those difficult photographic challenges and impress upon them the importance of recording accurate and quality photographs. Readers should have a base knowledge of basic photographic concepts, such as exposure and depth of field. *Advanced Crime Scene Photography* hopes to build upon a photographer's basic skill set and move them to a level where nothing is impossible. If one can see a subject, then one can photograph it. In addition, even if an investigator cannot see a piece of trace evidence, one may still be able to photograph it.

The first edition of *Advanced Crime Scene Photography* has been quite well received and, specifically, has been popular with college forensic programs. One of the major additions to the second edition is the inclusion of review questions and photography assignments at the end of each chapter. This text is meant to provide guidance and ideas on how to record those difficult-to-capture images, and all photographers should practice their craft, whether they are actively working cases or are just beginning their careers. Providing guidance to the next generation of crime scene photographers is certainly a true honor.

A second significant change to the text is the addition of a chapter on fire investigations and photographing fire scenes, which was a direct request from the Harris County Fire Marshal's Office and the Houston Fire Department's Arson Division. Presented in this chapter, like in many areas of the book, are the common challenges faced by fire investigators and a variety of solutions to solve those challenges. As with any crime scene photographic endeavor, the recording of quality photographs at the scene of a fire is extremely important.

To conclude, I hope that *Advanced Crime Scene Photography* provides students, photographers, and investigators with the knowledge and skills necessary to record meaningful photographic images. Quality crime scene photographs do not just happen. They must be planned by a detail-minded photographer. Taking the time to plan and execute a photographic task is extremely important. *Point and shoot* is not an effective philosophy for crime scene photographers. Investigators should be telling the camera how to record an image, not the other way around. I am confident that readers will find *Advanced Crime Scene Photography* helpful in achieving their photographic goals.

Acknowledgments

Maturing into a confident and valuable crime scene investigator and/or photographer occurs over time and through training, education, and experience. The process of improving one's skills is made much easier with the help of investigators who preceded the novice. Lieutenant Alton "Glen" Riddle preceded me and has been my inspiration by setting the bar so high. I could not have had a better role model. Today that bar is set by my peers. Two of the finest investigators I know are Christine Ramirez and Celestina Rossi, crime scene investigators with the Montgomery County (TX) Sheriff's Office. Christine has also provided me countless opportunities to teach all around Texas through our positions with Texas A&M University. Not only do investigators need a role model, they need support as well. My support comes from my current lieutenant, Ronald Walker. Lieutenant Walker supports all the investigators assigned to our unit by encouraging their continued growth and knowledge in the field of crime scene investigations.

A single investigator cannot do it all. It takes a team to be successful and the team I work with at the Houston Police Department is truly outstanding. My first on-the-job trainer was Jay Hammerle. Jay is about to finish up his 28-year career this summer and we all wish him the best in his retirement. I could not have completed this book nor do my full-time job without the assistance of my coworkers: Andrew Taravella, Ernest Aguilera, Daniel Nunez, Alton Holmes, and Mike Perez. I am truly blessed to work with some of the sharpest and knowledgeable crime scene investigators anywhere around.

I have been a member of the International Association for Identification (IAI) since 2001 and I have been blessed with the opportunity to serve the association in a number of capacities. A superior photographer in his own right, past IAI president Phil Sanfillipo, has always supported my efforts, and I appreciate the confidence he has in me. Longtime IAI member Laura Tierney also has been a huge supporter for my work. In fact, she was the first one to encourage me to offer a presentation at one of our yearly educational conferences. It was those teaching experiences that initially led to being asked to write the first edition of *Advanced Crime Scene Photography*. Therefore, I owe Laura a great deal of appreciation and gratitude. Another recently retired friend and colleague, Curtis Klingle, was a big help in the writing of this text. Curtis and I have exchanged a number of techniques and photographic solutions over the years, as well as having worked together on forensic-related writings.

Taking on the challenge of completing the second edition of this work was monumental and much more than I expected. Finishing all the rewriting and editing of the text could not have been completed without the support of my loving wife, Rhonda. She worked just as hard, if not harder, taking care of the home and our two wonderful children, Wynn and Miranda. The second edition was certainly a team effort, all the way around. And that team would not be complete without the folks at CRC Press. I must thank Taylor & Francis Group for having the confidence in my work to ask for a second edition. Of course, none of this writing would ever have come to light without Becky McEldowney Masterman, senior acquisitions editor, and David Fausel, project coordinator.

My ultimate goal is to encourage investigators to make the extra effort necessary to capture truly outstanding crime scene photographs and to avoid permitting arbitrary computer chips or checklists to determine what, which, and how photographs are recorded. I hope this book starts the creative juices flowing in all of us and that investigators seek out new techniques to record difficult evidentiary subjects. *Advanced Crime Scene Photography* should not be taken as a singular guide for crime scene photography, but as an invitation to crime scene photographers and investigators to take a more active role in their current photographic work. I hope that the readers will find this book informative and encouraging. I further hope that every investigator continues to seek the truth in all that he or she does.

Author

Christopher (Chris) D. Duncan is a senior police officer with the Houston Police Department and has been assigned to the Identification Division, Crime Scene Unit, since 1997. Prior to transferring to the Identification Division, he was assigned to patrol duties, including spending two years as a Gang Task Force Officer. He began his career with the Alexandria Sheriff's Department just after graduating from George Mason University with a BA in history. In 2007, he earned his MA in criminology from the University of Houston–Clear Lake. In regards to crime scene investigation, he has over 2100 hours of training specific to the documentation, collection, and processing of physical evidence. As part of his professional education, he attended and graduated from the National Forensic Academy (Knoxville, Tennessee) in 2003.

Chris is a member of the International Association for Identification (IAI), which is the premier organization of crime scene investigation specialists. He is board-certified by the IAI as a Senior Crime Scene Analyst, a Bloodstain Pattern Analyst, and a Forensic Photographer. He is currently a member of the IAI's Editorial Review Committee for the *Journal of Forensic Identification* and serves on the Science and Practices Committee for Bloodstain Pattern Analysis. Chris previously served the IAI as a member of the board of directors and the Science and Practices Committee for Forensic Photography. He is recognized as a *distinguished member* of the IAI and has won the yearly Forensic Photography contest five times. He is also a member of the Chesapeake Bay Division and the Texas Division of the IAI. Chris is a member of the International Association of Bloodstain Pattern Analysts (IABPA). He has written a number of articles, mostly on photography, for the IAI, IABPA, and several of the state IAI organizations. He has also taught at numerous educational conferences hosted by these organizations, at numerous police and sheriff academies, and currently instructs for the Texas Engineering Extension Service, a member of the Texas A&M University System.

Introduction

1

The complete and accurate photographic documentation of crime scenes is the cornerstone of any criminal investigation. The faithful portrayal of a crime scene demands that investigators and photographers thoughtfully and purposefully record true and accurate depictions of the location and evidence. Photographs provide a link between evidence recovered at a crime scene and the identification of a defendant in a court of law. The systematic and complete photographic recording of all aspects of an investigation helps bridge the gap between an individual piece of evidence and the processing of that evidence, which can lead to the identification of a suspect. Consequently, crime scene photography is an important and required task that must be accomplished with dedication and skill.

All too often, investigators feel they must operate in a robotic or automated mindset, which requires them to record a specific set of images, all with the camera set to the *Program* mode and recorded as if to checkmark some hypothetical box on some crime scene to-do list. Investigators who operate in such an automated mode, with rigid parameters, miss the opportunity to inspire and excite the photographic images' viewers. Not only should investigators document a scene as true and accurately as possible, they should also strive to create a lasting impression with the viewers, especially those viewers charged with deciding between guilt and innocence in a jury's deliberation room. Creating powerful evidentiary images that make a statement and have the greatest impact on the viewers should be a goal of all crime scene photographers. Documenting a crime scene is so much more than fulfilling the requirements found on some arbitrary checklist. It is an opportunity to show one's dedication and professionalism to the jury, prosecutors, and other investigators. Creating a lasting impression with a jury will go a long way during their deliberations. Typically, the first pieces of evidence seen by a jury are the crime scene photographs recorded by the investigator. If those photographs are poorly exposed, out of focus, or poorly composed, then the rest of the investigator's testimony may be questioned by a jury. On the other hand, by starting off one's testimony with professional looking, quality photographs, one's body of work will only serve to support the investigator's testimony and credibility on the witness stand.

Frequently, the fear of venturing too far away from a camera's *Program* or automatic mode settings comes from a lack of confidence. Investigators are afraid of making mistakes in exposure or composition and therefore rely too heavily on the camera to make all the decisions. The mistake actually being made is relying upon the camera to do all the work. One can possess the latest and greatest camera, having all the bells and whistles imaginable, but if the command dial is never moved off the automatic mode, one may as well be documenting the scene with a disposable point-and-shoot camera. The photographer, not the camera, is responsible for taking the picture. Cameras can be easily fooled into capturing under- and overexposed images. A photographer must learn to recognize what the camera is looking at and know how to compensate for difficult compositions, something even the best of photographic equipment cannot do. In addition, composing and orienting a subject with the camera are just as important to obtain a proper exposure evaluation, and cameras are not able to make compositional decisions.

Advanced Crime Scene Photography is designed for those crime scene investigators and photographers comfortable with the operation of their cameras and who have a basic understanding of apertures, shutter speeds, ISO values (film speed), *stops* of light, and basic exposure calculations. Countless books and general photography classes cover basic photography concepts. Applying those fundamental concepts to the thorough documentation of a crime scene is the next step in a photographer's maturation and is one goal of this text.

Basic light evaluation and camera operation is all based on combining an ISO value, an aperture, and a shutter speed. Because everything in photography is about give and take, photographers must decide which exposure variable is most important for each composition and which exposure value can be sacrificed. The ISO value sets the camera's sensitivity to light, and lower ISO values offer the best color and image sharpness (Figure 1.1). The choice of aperture is primarily about depth of field. Larger apertures limit the image's zone of sharp focus, while smaller apertures extend the depth of field (Figure 1.2). The final variable is shutter speed and shutter speed control motion. The motion can come from subject movement, as well as the photographer's movement. Crime scene photographers should be comfortable with long exposures, just as much as they are with quick exposures (Figure 1.3). Quality photography begins with taking control of the process, which will most likely require the camera to be moved off of the *Program* mode. By moving to the *Manual* mode or one of the *Priority* modes, the photographer can choose the exposure value or values most important to them and record better overall compositions. This concept of selecting exposure variables for a specific purpose will be a key theme throughout this text.

The photographic skills of an investigator will naturally improve with time. Common failures among investigators include developing tunnel vision and failing to record a sufficient number of photographs in order to connect individual pieces of evidence with the overall crime scene. Subjects need to be oriented within the entire crime scene, shown in relationship to other pieces of evidence, and be properly photographed in close-up detail. Simply recording one or two images prior to an item's recovery is not conducive

Figure 1.1 Lower ISO values provide the sharpest images, with the best color. The ISO value of 100 is often recommended for any evidentiary photograph that is used for comparison and analysis. This composition was recorded at ISO 100, f/8, for 30 s.

Figure 1.2 Apertures primarily affect a composition's depth of field. The zone of sharp focus extends throughout this entire composition and was achieved with an aperture value of f/22 (ISO 100, 4 s).

(a)   (b)

Figure 1.3 Shutter speeds can be just a fraction of a second to several minutes long; (a) was recorded at 1/2500th of a second and was able to stop the explosive action of a bomb. (Photographed by Ernest Aguilera, Crime Scene Investigator, Houston Police Department, Houston, TX); (b) was recorded over the course of 45 min and recorded the movement of stars across the nighttime sky.

to achieving a full understanding of the evidence and its meaning within the context of the crime scene. Taking a thoughtful approach and actively participating in the crime scene photographic process will result in more stunning photographs and more valuable evidentiary images. When in doubt about a composition's success, always record another photograph. The cost of film (or digital image storage space) never outweighs the value of completeness.

Review of Basic Photographic Concepts

A fundamental understanding of basic photographic concepts is necessary in order to appreciate the ideas presented in this text. Therefore, a review of the general concepts of light evaluation and exposure principles is appropriate to ensure that everyone is speaking the same language. Capturing photographic images is all about the recording of light onto film or a digital imaging chip. A photographer can set his or her camera up in a completely dark room, open the shutter for hours, and not capture a single piece of information. However, a photograph can be taken during the daytime in a 1000th of a second under the right circumstances. Finding the correct exposure between a fraction of a second and an extended time exposure is based upon the amount of light illuminating a subject and the camera settings (ISO value, aperture, and shutter speed) chosen by the photographer. At times, the range of camera settings may be limited by the equipment, but the fundamental concepts remain the same regardless of whether one is using an older, fully manual film camera or the latest and greatest digital single-lens reflex (SLR) camera.

The photographic principles and concepts an investigator might have learned in order to use his or her film camera are just as applicable in today's world of digital imaging. Although film photography is not dead, digital cameras have become the primary recording media for law enforcement and the world as a whole. Film will still have its place in the art world and for photography purists, but the benefits offered by digital imaging to the law enforcement community from capture and processing to the dissemination of images are too great to ignore. Digital imaging will continue to improve with time, and the cost of digital equipment will become more and more affordable. In addition, digital imaging continues to provide tremendous advantages to the science of photography as the capabilities of digital photography continue to expand. The benefits of immediate gratification, simplicity of distribution, and the ease of image processing make digital photography especially favorable for crime scene investigators. However, whether an agency or individual photographer is using film or digital capture, the concepts of light, exposure, and composition are largely the same.

To begin, all cameras evaluate light, and light is broken down into *stops* or fractions of a stop. A full stop of light is equal to one-half or twice as much light as the next full stop. Therefore, if one increases an exposure by one stop, then effectively twice as much light is added to that particular composition. If one decreases an exposure by one stop, then one-half the amount of light is subtracted from the composition. The idea or concept of a stop allows one to compare apples to oranges. In regards to the camera, the apples and oranges refer to the camera's settings for ISO values, apertures, and shutter speeds (the exposure triangle). By breaking light down into stops, the photographer is able to compare equal amounts or values of light among ISO values, apertures, and shutter speeds. Eventually, these values can be adjusted in order to fine-tune an exposure by making reciprocal changes in an exposure's calculation. As an example of reciprocity, if an accurate exposure can be made with the camera set to ISO 100 (sensitivity of media to light), f/8 (aperture or lens size), for 1/250 of a second (shutter speed) and one desires to increase the depth of field by decreasing the aperture's size to f/16, then a reciprocal change(s) in the other values must be made to balance the two-stop loss of light (f/8 to f/11 to f/16). Possible adjustments in the exposure could include the following:

- ISO 100 (constant), f/16 (−2 stops), at 1/60th of a second (+2 stops)
- ISO 400 (+2 stops), f/16 (−2 stops), at 1/250th of a second (constant)
- ISO 200 (+1 stop), f/16 (−2 stops), at 1/125th of a second (+1 stop)

The basic principle of light and stops of light should already be understood by the reader before progressing any further into this text. A multitude of books explain light evaluation, but anyone with a camera should already own such an explanatory text—it is the camera's instruction or owner's manual. The instruction manual does offer most readers a basic understanding of how one's camera evaluates an exposure and how their particular camera model breaks down light into stops. Commonly, cameras are able to break down light evaluations into half-stops or third-stops. As a refresher, full stops of light are typically identified as follows, although this list is far from all inclusive:

- ISO values
  - 100, 200, 400, 800, 1600, 3200, 6400
- Apertures
  - f/1.4, f/2.0, f/2.8, f/4.0, f/5.6, f/8.0, f/11, f/16, f/22, f/32
- Shutter speeds
  - 1/1000, 1/500, 1/250, 1/125, 1/60, 1/30, 1/15, 1/8, ¼, ½, 1 s

The ISO value is determined by the choice of film inserted into the camera or by the digital camera's particular ISO range. The choice of an ISO value will set the camera's sensitivity to light and will be the base from which the aperture and shutter speed choices will combine to create an exposure. The range in aperture choices is determined by the particular lens attached to the camera. Therefore, not every photographer will have the same flexibility in exposure adjustments because of the variety of lenses and their capabilities. If one is using a point-and-shoot style of camera, then the aperture range is likely to possess a very narrow gamut of available apertures. The range of available shutter speeds typically offers the greatest flexibility or greatest range of available values and will be determined by the camera's capabilities. SLR cameras typically have a range of shutter speeds from 30 s to 1/4000th of a second. Point-and-shoot cameras may or may not have as much versatility. Crime scene photographers are much more likely to employ slower shutter speeds, especially when working in low-light conditions. Therefore, the faster shutter speed values are not used as frequently. Crime scene investigators should also possess a camera capable of B (bulb) or T (time) exposures. This feature allows the camera's operator to keep the lens open for as long as the photographer desires. Understanding exposure evaluations and how one's camera meters light must be possessed by the photographer in order to get the most out of *Advanced Crime Scene Photography*.

It does not require a PhD (*push here detective*) to operate a camera. Crime scene photography may not be as easy as aim and shoot, but it certainly is not rocket science. Fortunately, cameras provide the photographer with a plethora of information, and the user simply has to become accustomed to what the camera is seeing and what the camera is saying about a composition. The vast majority of electronic SLR cameras (film or digital) can be operated in a number of different modes capable of adapting to a photographer's particular style. The basic operating modes of modern SLR cameras are as follows:

- *Program* mode—camera selects aperture and shutter speeds.
- *Shutter Priority*—user selects shutter speed and camera selects aperture.
- *Aperture Priority*—user selects aperture and camera selects shutter speed.
- *Manual*—user selects aperture and shutter speed.

Photographers are also likely to find custom modes and *creative modes*, as well as the basic exposure modes, on their camera's command dial. However, for crime scene photographers, these modes are less likely to be used. Becoming familiar with the camera's functions and how to read the information contained within the viewfinder are vitally important toward understanding what is occurring within the camera and to the composition itself.

Comprehending the information contained within the camera's viewfinder or displayed on its liquid crystal display (LCD) screen is vitally important for photographers. Failure to recognize when the camera is having difficulties with a particular exposure is likely to produce poor photographs, which may cause the jury to have less respect for the investigator and his or her body of work. The camera's instruction manual is a photographer's best resource for information on his or her camera. However, technical manuals and books are published about the specific use of higher-end SLR model cameras, and these materials can help photographers utilize their cameras to their maximum potential. In many police departments, cameras are issued to investigators and the manuals have been long since lost. Fortunately, many camera operation manuals can be found on the individual manufacturer's website and downloaded for free. Prior to progressing further in this text, one may wish to review their camera's operation manual.

In the end, obtaining a proper exposure is not a difficult proposition. All crime scene photographers have to do is know how their cameras work and what the cameras are telling them about the compositions in the viewfinder. Exposures are easily calculated by the camera and they can even make the reciprocal changes to the ISO, aperture, and shutter speed values when necessary. However, there will be times when photographers must recognize conditions that can fool their cameras' light meters. For example, any photographer who attempts to photograph a backlit composition or gunpowder residue on black clothing will need to understand what the camera is using to calculate an exposure. A camera's light meter is searching for an 18% gray evaluation of light, which means that bright-white or jet-black subjects can cause severe under- and overexposures in photographs. Operating in a *Manual* mode allows for changes to be made easily to exposures that are outside the camera's ability to accurately meter the scene. Photographers must be capable of compensating for such evaluation problems caused by difficult compositions. Understanding how the camera operates and how it meters light will only improve a photographer's overall body of work.

Creating a Lasting Impression

Being able to operate one's camera in the *Manual* mode goes a long way toward creating powerful and valuable pieces of photographic evidence. Crime scene photographers should take control of the photographic process and not let the camera make every decision as far as exposure and composition are concerned. The light metering systems in modern cameras are quite adept at calculating a vast majority of exposure evaluations correctly, but that does not mean that they can be relied upon in every situation. Bracketing exposures, which is recording the same image with different combinations of apertures and shutter speeds, is one sure way to capture the most impressive images and ensure the best possible image from which to testify. Even slight changes in exposure can refine the richness of color, make visible important details otherwise hidden in the highlights or shadows of an image, and create significant changes in an image's depth of field. Prior to the advent of digital imaging, bracketing of exposures was a staple of crime scene photographers. However, the art of recording multiple images for any particular composition has seemingly lost its appeal due to the ability to immediately review one's images on the back of the camera. This immediate gratification is a double-edged sword. True, this enables the photographer to correct for major compositional or exposure errors, but he or she can also fail to correct for minor problems, believing that an image is *good enough*. It is also a major mistake to believe that all corrections can be made with postcapture editing programs on the computer and that this voids the requirement to capture the best image possible while at the crime scene. Crime scene photography is about image capture, not editing. A crime scene photographer needs to strive to capture the best possible image at the point of capture and not rely on a computer's ability to improve an image that could have and should have been recorded properly at the crime scene.

The one thing a camera cannot do on its own is compose or orient the subject to the camera. This aspect of crime scene photography can only be done by the photographer, and a subject's composition makes the difference between just another *snapshot* and a truly awe-inspiring photograph. Not only is composition a way to distinguish oneself as a thorough and professional investigator, it is also of paramount importance in recording accurate and informative photographs. Software programs, such as Adobe Photoshop®, cannot correct for poor focus and poor camera-to-subject orientation. Out-of-focus photographic images cannot be put in focus through any amount of postcapture editing. Subject-to-camera positioning can also be critical to the accurate portrayal of evidence. A number of subjects commonly encountered by crime scene investigators must be recorded with the camera's lens perpendicularly aligned with the subject, and when that alignment is not correct, no amount of editing will correct for the errors made at the point of capture. Always remember: crime scene photographers must not be content with capturing an image *close enough* to the desired outcome. Photographers must strive to record the absolute best images at the point of capture.

A crime scene photographer can also create an impact with the jury by creating images that display a little artistic flair. There is nothing wrong with adding a bit of pizzazz to a composition. Certainly, the documentation of a crime scene needs to have specific images recorded so that it is thorough and complete. However, photographers can still add a little bit of themselves within some of their compositions. By using perspective, depth of field, and light, crime scene photographers have the opportunity to capture images that can affect and even move their viewers. Think of those iconic, Pulitzer Prize–winning images by Sal Veder, Nick Ut, and Joe Rosenthal and how they moved a nation, much more than a small body of citizens deciding upon the guilt or innocence of a defendant. Not every image recorded by a photographer will be utilized in court, only the very best. Some images may not even be allowed by the court due to their graphic or repetitive nature, but those images entered into evidence may include something that helps convince the jury of the investigator's commitment and dedication to the complete and accurate investigation of a crime scene. At the beginning of an investigator's testimony, the prosecution will seek to establish the investigator's credibility with the jury by reviewing his or her education, training, and experience. How much more impact will that testimony have when bolstered by providing the jury with a set of crime scene photographs that are well illuminated, properly exposed, precisely focused, and meaningful to the investigation? The documentation of a crime scene should not be considered trivial nor should it be thought of as some inconvenient necessity, but rather as an opportunity to demonstrate the investigator's skill and talent.

Thinking Outside of the Box

Far too often, investigators can become stuck in a rut when it comes time to document and process a crime scene. Although the photographic documentation of crime scenes has a great number of similarities from one location to the next, every scene will have its own distinctive features. In regard to photography, the main variable is most often the lighting. Obviously, the contrast between daytime and nighttime lighting is drastic, but so is the lighting from one daytime (or nighttime) scene to another. One day it can be cloudy and the next day the sun can be shining brightly. Not only is the intensity of light completely different, but so is the presence of shadows and the harsh contrasts between a composition's shadows and highlights. Lighting differences found at nighttime crime scenes can be just as strikingly dissimilar because the light can be provided by a number of different sources and each source has its own intensity, color, and directionality. As a result of these variables, photographers must be aware of the lighting conditions at each scene and examine each composition for not only subject content but also proper illumination. The photographer should evaluate and examine each individual crime scene, then create a plan designed to meet the challenges each scene presents. When studying a photographic composition, thinking about how to adjust for a subject's stark contrast is an important aspect of crime scene photography. Frequently, this requires the photographer to step away from the camera's *Program* mode feature and assert more control over the recording of images. Working in the *Manual* mode allows the photographer the ability to more easily adjust exposure values in conflict with what the camera's light meter suggests.

Depth of field is another characteristic of quality crime scene photographs. Capturing images with deep depths of field is frequently required in crime scene photography, and many times, cameras tend to seek a middle ground for the selected apertures and shutter speeds, thereby shrinking an image's zone of sharp focus. Once again, investigators should be cognizant of what the camera is actually recording and not just what is visible in the viewfinder. Improving a composition's depth of field will be referred to frequently throughout this text.

Composing a photograph that will create a lasting impression is necessary not only at the scene of the crime but also back in the laboratory where many macro- or examination-quality photographs will be recorded. Many times, photographing smaller subjects is more difficult than larger, more-expansive subjects. Small pieces of evidence can be singular in color, have reflective surfaces, and/or possess undulating surfaces that create distracting shadows. Crime scene photographers must recognize these difficult situations and, thinking unconventionally, come up with solutions. There is no one correct way to solve any particular problem, but as long as the end result develops as desired, the solution succeeded. Not every attempt will end in a success, but as long as one great photograph is captured, the photographer should feel good about their work. For example, in low-light situations, he or she may have to add light to a scene in order to illuminate evidence hidden in the shadows. Light can be added to the composition in a number of ways, including lengthening exposure time, adding light with electronic flash, or adding light with a flashlight. Each of these solutions can dramatically improve a nighttime's composition, and photographers will determine their favorite ways of supplementing and compensating for poor lighting. Think creatively and try different solutions to problems. Remember, one does not have to solve a problem on the first attempt or even the second.

A little creativity and ingenuity can actually begin long before arriving at the scene of a crime. Creativity can also go a long way toward saving investigators' money. Crime scene and photographic supply companies sell all kinds of tools, gadgets, and instruments meant to make the life of an investigator a little easier. However, these items can often be fabricated from supplies and contraptions purchased at home improvement, hobby, or craft stores for far less money than purchasing the items fully assembled from a retailer. Everything from alternate light sources to the construction of light boxes can be purchased in whole or in part from local stores or from Internet resources. Investigators simply need to examine the parts and/or features of a particular piece of desired equipment and search through their local discount, tool, and/or hobby stores in an effort to replicate the piece of desired equipment. Pretty much anything with a *forensic* label attached will cost an investigator three times as much as it should. For example, fluorescent-tube black lights that are sold as forensic light sources cost between $30 and $40. However, those same lights are sold during the Halloween season as toys for less than $10. Investigators and photographers can save a great deal of money by applying a little ingenuity and creativity to the building of their photographic studio and equipment kits.

Thinking outside the box sometimes involves the simple matter of examining a photographic problem, developing a set of solutions (not always just one solution) that could potentially solve the problem, and then attempting each solution until a successful result emerges. This process is similar to conducting experiments to answer crime scene reconstruction questions. When evaluating a scene or composition, one must evaluate the ambient light and decide if supplemental light needs to be added, as well as how the image will be framed and where the focus should be set. As an example, review Figure 1.4. The composition was complicated by the bright high-pressure sodium lamp shining in the background of the image, thereby causing a drastic difference in light intensity between the front and back sides of the scene. As a result, there was a need to balance the lighting between the two sides. Adding supplemental light to the darker foreground was chosen as the solution to the lighting problem. The next question needing to be answered was the decision on which source of supplemental light to use. An electronic flash was used

Figure 1.4 The bright light observed in the background was metered and a proper exposure was found to be ISO 100, f/4.0, for 2s. In order to provide the time necessary to paint the unilluminated statue in the foreground with light, reciprocity was used to adjust the exposure to ISO 100, f/16, for 30 s. As a result, the background was not overexposed and the time was available so that an electronic flash could be cast across the foreground in order to complete a balanced exposure.

to paint the statue with light. The next task was to meter the ambient light. As will be described later, metering of light took place in the brightest part of the scene (underneath the high-pressure sodium lamp). The supplemental light was added to the areas of shadow in order to match the bright area underneath the security lamp. The light was metered underneath the security light and found that an exposure of ISO 100, f/4.0 at 2 s would provide a proper exposure. However, 2 s was not enough to paint the shadows with light. Using reciprocity, an equal amount of light could be recorded with the exposure settings of ISO 100, f/16, for 30 s. The 30 s offered plenty of time to paint the scene with light and obtain a well-balanced photograph. As this example shows, crime scene photographers simply have to examine the scene, identify the challenges, and come up with a plan to tackle those challenges. Understanding what the camera is seeing, thinking, and saying is the key to quality photographic documentation. There are many photographic conditions unique to crime scene photographers, and some of those conditions discussed in this book include the low light photography challenges like the one seen in Figure 1.4, but also the challenges created by infrared, ultraviolet, bloodstain, and shooting incident photography.

Digital photography has made crime scene photography a little less difficult and certainly enables photographers to make exposure adjustments with more confidence. The assurance provided by the ability to immediately review one's images has tremendous value. The photographer is able to adjust for lighting and shadows and to correct for common errors found while performing more advanced photographic techniques. The crime scene photographer simply has to identify any detrimental artifacts in an image and determine the best way to eliminate them. In the end, preparation and the ability to adjust for difficult lighting conditions and/or compositional problems will only serve to improve the impression left by a crime scene photographer's body of work.

Sometimes, finding solutions to different photographic problems requires a little thinking outside of the box, and frequently these challenges occur even before heading out to the crime scene. Preparation is an important key for investigators. For example, the documentation of a crime scene and/or individual pieces of evidence frequently requires a pointer device or evidence marker in order to indicate the object's location. A variety of pointers can be purchased from crime scene supply companies. However, they might just as easily be made from one's own computer or altered for use from everyday objects found around the house. A number of examples of such evidence pointers will be provided later in this book. The idea here is that a photographer's task of completely and accurately documenting a crime scene begins long before his or her arrival to a crime scene. Preparation for the job results from understanding what is expected of a crime scene photographer, being prepared, and organized. However, equally important is the ability to adjust on the fly in order to take advantage of the unique photographic opportunities that can set one photographer apart from the next.

Advanced Crime Scene Photography

Techniques, tips, and suggestions illustrated in *Advanced Crime Scene Photography* are meant to assist crime scene investigators in accurately documenting a criminal event with skill and style. This book does not contain a checklist of photographs to be taken because the photographic documentation of a crime scene should not be limited in any way. The basic principle that the cost of film does not outweigh the value of completeness should be a guiding principle for all photographers. Investigators should also not worry if a photograph fails or does not produce a desirable result. Not every photographic endeavor will succeed, but that should never prevent the photographer from attempting to capture difficult subjects or create innovative compositions. Whether a subject is hidden from view because of its physical location or its imperceptible nature does not matter. What does matter is that the photographer makes an attempt to permanently record the evidence prior to its recovery or processing. And who knows, he or she may even develop a new technique for capturing latent evidence. Ultimately, the goal of crime scene photographers and investigators alike is to develop enough confidence in their work so that they are able to look at problems and mentally prepare plans to find a solution to photographic challenges. Sometimes, the solutions work and sometimes they do not. However, the photographer should try each and every time.

Maturing from a point-and-shoot mentality of crime scene photography to one of more deliberation and purpose is an important step in the photographer's growth. Experience is certainly a tremendous part of the maturation process, but that experience does not necessarily have to be at actual crime scenes. Crime scene photographers should become familiar with their equipment prior to working actual crime scenes. They should be cognizant of how their cameras function under different lighting conditions and environments. Any camera, even a disposable camera purchased at a convenience store, can easily photograph a vehicle on a bright but cloudy day (lack of deep, contrasting shadows). However, lighting conditions can change by the minute and investigators must be ready to compensate for shadows at one point and a complete lack of light at another. Possessing a camera that is capable of the versatility needed by crime scene investigators is one important factor in the successful documentation of a crime scene. However, feeling comfortable with what the camera is seeing and what it is using to make an exposure evaluation is equally important toward obtaining well-illuminated photographs on a consistent basis. Being confident and consistent in one's photographic documentation of crime scenes is the sign of a professional photographer.

Exposure issues are just part of the photographic process. Composing a valuable image by filling the viewfinder, maximizing the depth of field, and framing the image with style is also invaluable for the true and accurate documentation of a crime scene. Being able to deliver high-quality, professional images on a consistent basis will create a positive, lasting impression with the viewer. What else could one ask for? And hopefully, the readers will find that *Advanced Crime Scene Photography* will help them achieve the goal of leaving a lasting impression.

Basic Photography Concepts–End of Chapter Questions

1. What does the "B" setting found on the camera's command dial allow the photographer to do?
   a. Record flash exposures
   b. *Blocks* light from entering the camera
   c. Keeps the shutter open as long as the shutter button is pressed
   d. Is the exposure compensation button

2. With all else equal, which shutter speed is better able to stop motion?
   a. 4 s
   b. ¼ of a second
   c. 1/40th of a second
   d. 1/400th of a second

3. The photographer accurately meters an exposure at ISO 200, f/5.6, for 1/500th of a second. The photographer wishes to bracket the exposure by adding one stop of light. What would be the new exposure values?
   a. ISO 400, f/5.6, for 1/500th of a second
   b. ISO 200, f/4.0, for 1/500th of a second
   c. ISO 200, f/5.6, for 1/250th of a second
   d. All of the above

4. Depth of field extends _____ to the front and _____ to the rear of the point of focus.
   a. ¼ to the front–¾ to the rear
   b. ⅓ to the front–⅔ to the rear
   c. ½ to the front–½ to the rear
   d. 1 to the front–1 to the rear

5. An aperture of f/8 allows twice as much light as f/16 to enter the camera.
   a. True
   b. False

6. Which ISO value is the most sensitive to light?
    a. ISO 100
    b. ISO 400
    c. ISO 800
    d. ISO 3200

7. What is a *stop* of light?
    a. Aperture value
    b. "f" number
    c. One-half or twice the next full value of light
    d. Exposure compensation

8. Which value is one stop less light than provided by an aperture f/8?
    a. f/2.0
    b. f/4.0
    c. f/11
    d. f/16

9. Which value allows three more stops of light into the camera than provided by an ISO 100 setting?
    a. ISO 300
    b. ISO 800
    c. ISO 1200
    d. ISO 1600

10. A photographer accurately meters an exposure at ISO 400, f/16, for 1/500th of a second. A minus ten (–10) stop neutral density filter is added to the camera's lens. What are the resulting exposure values to record an equal or reciprocal exposure?
    a. ISO 100, f/2.8, for 1 s
    b. ISO 400, f/16, for 2 s
    c. ISO 800, f/16, for ½ of a second
    d. All of the above

11. Which shutter speed is five stops slower than 1/60th of a second?
    a. ½ of a second
    b. 1/20th of a second
    c. 1/300th of a second
    d. None of the above

12. A camera's light meter attempts to find a/an _____ gray value as a light-balanced exposure.
    a. 18%
    b. 25%
    c. 33%
    d. 50%

13. Which aperture allows three stops more light into the camera than f/16?
    a. f/2.8
    b. f/5.6
    c. f/11
    d. f/32

14. An ISO value of 400 allows twice as much light as ISO 800 to enter the camera.
    a. True
    b. False

15. What does the camera search for when autofocusing?
    a. The center of the composition
    b. The point allowing the best depth of field
    c. The first subject identified in the composition
    d. Brightest part of the composition

16. Which aperture allows the most light into the camera?
    a. f/1.8
    b. f/5.6
    c. f/16
    d. f/32

17. A photographer accurately meters a nighttime exposure at ISO 100, f/4.0, for 1 second. However, the photographer needs to stop motion with a faster shutter speed. Which would be an equal or reciprocal exposure?
    a. ISO 400, f/22, for 1/60th of a second
    b. ISO 800, f/8, for 1/15th of a second
    c. ISO 1600, f/4, for 1/500th of a second
    d. ISO 3200, f/2.0, for 1/125th of a second

18. An investigator is photographing in black and white and wishes to adjust the contrast by lightening the composition's red background. Which colored filter would work best?
    a. Red
    b. Green
    c. Blue
    d. Any of the above

19. Which piece of equipment must be used when photographing nighttime crime scenes?
    a. A film camera
    b. Tripod
    c. Polarizing filter
    d. All of the above

20. When the shutter button is depressed, what is the camera going to do?
    a. Focus
    b. Meter the light
    c. Record the exposure
    d. All of the above

21. With all else equal, which aperture provides the best depth of field?
    a. f/2.8
    b. f/8
    c. f/11
    d. f/22

22. A photographer is recording a black-and-white image and wishes to darken the blue background found in the composition. Which colored filter would be the best choice?
    a. Yellow
    b. Orange
    c. Red
    d. Blue

23. A photographer accurately meters a composition's light to be ISO 400, f/4.0, for 1/60th of a second. However, the photographer wishes to record a longer exposure. What would be an equal or reciprocal exposure and allows for a longer exposure?
    a. ISO 100, f/22, for 2 s
    b. ISO 200, f/1.8, for 4 s
    c. ISO 400, f/22, for 4 s
    d. ISO 400, f/16, for 8 s

24. Which ISO possesses the most distracting noise or grain in an image?
    a. ISO 100
    b. ISO 400
    c. ISO 800
    d. ISO 3200

25. A shutter speed of 1/250th of a second allows twice as much light as 1/500th of a second to enter the camera.
    a. True
    b. False

26. What are the variables of exposure that the author compares to *apples and oranges*?
    a. Apertures, shutter speeds, and ISO values
    b. Apertures, ISO values, and white balance
    c. Shutter speeds and EV (Exposure value) compensation
    d. Brightness and reflectance

27. What are the basic operating modes of modern digital cameras?
    a. Automatic and *Manual*
    b. *Program, Aperture Priority, Shutter* (time) *Priority,* and *Manual*
    c. Automatic, *Manual,* and TTL (through the lens)
    d. Portrait, landscape, action, and close-up

Photography Assignments

Required Tools: General photography equipment will be necessary for these photographic assignments, such as a digital camera (preferably an SLR), various lenses, tripod, and cable release. Photographers can use only what they possess, but using all one's available resources is likely to produce the best results.

Photography Subjects: General photographic subjects

I. Demonstrate one's ability to select an exposure variable (ISO value, aperture, or shutter speed) for a particular purpose and adjust the remaining variables in order to record a properly illuminated composition:
  A. ISO values (controls sensitivity to light and affects the image's quality):
    1. Record a pair of photographs, one with the ISO value set as high as possible and one of the same composition with the ISO value set as low as possible:
       a. Record one pair of images in the daytime.
       b. Record one pair of images in the nighttime (the lower ISO value composition will likely need to be recorded with the camera supported by a tripod).
       c. Compare the images for color, sharpness, noise, and overall quality.
    2. Photograph an indoor composition (gym, classroom, living room, etc.) while hand-holding the camera. The image should be free of camera shake or motion:
       a. Hand held with the use of a flash.
       b. Hand held without the use of a flash.
    3. Photograph a pair or more of photographs using the camera's flash, either the pop-up flash or an external flash:
       a. Set the camera to *Manual.* The shutter speed and aperture values should be held constant for each photograph. The flash can be set to automatic (TTL) or in the *Manual* mode, depending on the photographer's skill and comfort level.
       b. Set the ISO value to 100 and record an image.
       c. Set the ISO value to 400 and record an image.
       d. Record any other ISO values as desired for comparison.
       e. Record one set of images indoors and another set outdoors during the nighttime.
       f. Compare the images and observe how the choice in ISO value affected the recorded photographs.

    B. Shutter speeds (controls motion and movement in an image):
1. Record a set of photographs recording motion:
   a. Choosing a fast shutter speed, photograph moving subjects (passing car, bouncing ball, pedestrian, etc.).
   b. Choosing a slow shutter speed, photograph moving subjects (passing car, bouncing ball, pedestrian, etc.).
2. Record a set of low-light or nighttime photographs:
   a. Record a longer exposure (approximately 20–30s) and during the exposure, walk in front of the lens and across the composition.
   b. Record the same composition, but changing the camera settings, record an image of just a few seconds in length. Once again, walk in front of the lens and across the composition.
   c. Compare the two images.

    C. Apertures (controls light intensity and primarily affects an image's depth of field):
1. Record a set of images showing variable depths of field:
   a. Record a pair of images, changing the aperture from wide open to completely closed down. The subject should be distant from the camera (>30 ft away from the camera). Compare the images for any differences in focus (depth of field). For example,
      i. Photograph a skyline.
      ii. Photograph a large field, parking lot, or courtyard.
   b. Record a pair of images, changing the aperture from wide open to completely closed down. The subject should be a close up subject, where the first subject is within 18″ of the camera. Compare the images for any differences in focus. For example,
      i. Photograph a car's vehicle identification number (VIN number found on the driver's side dashboard) at an oblique angle and fill the viewfinder with the VIN plate.
      ii. Photograph a sign, book cover, or any posted wording by getting as close as possible and setting the camera at an oblique angle to the lettering. Photograph the image with a large and small aperture and compare the resulting images.
2. Record a nighttime composition with the smallest aperture available, such as an f/22:
   a. Record one image by adjusting ISO value to compensate for smaller aperture.
   b. Record one image by adjusting shutter speed to compensate for smaller aperture.

II. Record a set of photographs utilizing the different command dial settings:
  A. Record an image of the same composition, but set the command dial to
1. *Program* mode (notice what the camera chose for the exposure settings)
2. *Aperture Priority* (the photographer selects a desirable aperture)
3. *Shutter* speed *Priority* (the photographer selects a desirable shutter speed)
4. *Manual* mode (the photographer selects all the exposure variables)

B. Record several images in the full *Manual* exposure mode:
  1. Take a daytime exposure.
  2. Take a nighttime exposure.
  3. Take an indoor exposure.
  4. Review the images and ensure that one understands how the camera's light meter works and that the resulting images resulted in properly exposed photographs.

Photography Equipment

2

As investigators gain experience through the years, they will naturally collect a large assortment of camera accessories in order to help them document crime scenes more thoroughly and accurately. Some of these attachments and accoutrements will be used repeatedly, whereas others will be placed on a shelf where they collect dust. The choice of what to carry and have readily available is an individual decision and dependent upon the investigator's specific job assignment and duties. There are a few items that are necessities, including the camera itself. The cost of photography equipment and the financial resources available often play a major role in determining what kinds of photographic accessories are available for use at crime scenes. Fortunately, some expenses can be lessened through purchasing used equipment, using a little creativity, and occasionally thinking outside the box. Because this text is designed for those with a basic understanding of photography, none of the equipment discussed in this chapter should be unheard of. However, due to the expense of such equipment, less-expensive alternatives will be introduced that should also be of value to photographers.

The cost of photographic equipment is always a concern for both photographers and the agencies they work for. Many times, the type of camera carried by an individual investigator is based solely upon what the department or agency has issued or what the individual can afford. One word of warning, an expensive camera does not necessarily guarantee a quality end product. A photographer using a very expensive single-lens reflex (SLR) camera, but only knowing how to photograph in an automatic mode, may not be able to produce images any better than someone capturing images with a point-and-shoot style of camera. On the other hand, a skilled and knowledgeable crime scene photographer can work with an older, fully manual film camera and capture outstanding and accurate photographic images that have the capability of leaving a positive and lasting impression with the viewer. There are ways to help reduce the cost of expensive accessories with a little creative thinking. Creativity and artistry are not just a compositional issue occurring at the crime scene but can also be part of the planning and preparation process prior to arrival at the scene.

Cameras

Before any scene documentation can begin, the investigator must choose a camera. The choices among the different makes and models of cameras are too numerous to list here. However, cameras come in some general forms from which an investigator may then select a manufacturer and a particular model with the features they deem more desirable. Predominantly, crime scene investigators use SLR cameras. SLR cameras gain their name through the use of specifically arranged mirrors contained within the SLR housing, allowing the photographer to view the subject through the camera's lens. During the actual exposure, the mirror flips up and out of the way, allowing the focused image to be recorded on the digital sensor or film plane. Consequently, the image observed in the viewfinder is largely the same image recorded. The recording of an image may be captured by a digital imaging chip or onto a roll of film. However, digital imaging is now the primary recording media for police agencies, as well as the public as a whole.

The main advantage that SLR cameras have over more user-friendly, point-and-shoot styles of camera is their extreme versatility. SLR cameras have interchangeable parts and nearly an unlimited amount of attachments and accessories. The variety of accoutrements may include external flashes, filters, and specialty lenses that can be interchanged in order to create truly outstanding photographs. As a result of this inherent versatility, SLR cameras can be used in a variety of situations and scenarios. They are equally at home in the laboratory as they are working nighttime crime scenes. In addition, the SLR camera's body style has been around since 1936 when Karl Nuechterlein and the Ihagee Company invented and produced the Exakta camera, the world's first single-lens mirror reflex camera. The SLR camera body will remain in use for a very long time to come, regardless of the media used to record the photographs. In fact, older SLR cameras are just as useful to an investigator as the more modern, state-of-the-art cameras found today. The newer generations of SLR cameras all have *Program* or *automatic* modes to assist those users not confident in their abilities to meter ambient light, calculate flash exposures, or sharply focus their cameras. In these automatic modes, the camera's use is just as easy as a point-and-shoot camera. However, SLR cameras allow for the growth of the photographer's ability by providing the opportunity of working in a more *Manual* mode of operation.

Cameras can be quite expensive, but an individual can save a little money by buying used equipment. In the past, purchasing fully manual film cameras could occur without a great deal of risk. However, with all the electrical and computer components incorporated in modern SLR cameras, especially digital cameras, one may desire to forego purchasing a used digital camera. Cameras typically come with a shutter-life expectancy (total number of shutter actuations) and with used equipment, there is always the risk of potentially buying an expensive, camera-shaped, paper weight. Most communities have at least one used camera store where good deals on photographic equipment can be had. Any reputable camera store will give a money-back guarantee on its used equipment, giving the purchaser an opportunity to run the camera through its paces in order to determine if it will meet their needs. The decision to purchase new or used equipment is a personal decision, but the option does provide the photographer with greater latitude in choices of cameras and equipment. Cameras are not the only used equipment available for purchase. Used electronic flashes, various types of lenses, and other camera attachments may be found cheaper, rather than purchasing them new. Used equipment can always be found on the Internet, but buyers should be cautious when dealing with an unknown seller.

SLR cameras come in every size and shape imaginable and have a seemingly unlimited number of choices among features, specifications, and benefits. Choosing the right camera may seem a daunting task at first, but one merely has to determine his or her photographic needs, consider their crime scene responsibilities, and match or determine which camera and accessories will fulfill those needs. Most crime scene investigators find the SLR camera more advantageous because of its ability to adapt to the various needs and responsibilities of the crime scene investigator. Furthermore, the SLR camera's platform is completely flexible when it comes to recording photographs in a variety of environments. This flexibility is enhanced by the various camera attachments that will be discussed in this chapter and used throughout this text.

All SLR cameras have the same basic controls, but how those controls are operated and the ease of their use differ among not only the manufacturers but also between the different models produced by the same company. Consequently, an individual should visit his or her local camera store and actually get the feel of a particular camera model by physically working the control dials, buttons, and switches. Photographers may find one camera too cumbersome, another camera's aperture control dial inconvenient, or even find that camera settings keep changing because the photographer's nose continuously bumps into the control buttons. As a result, getting an idea of how a camera feels in one's grip is an important aspect of camera selection.

In addition to the actual controls of the camera, the way the viewfinder displays exposure information may be different as well. Some displays are easier to understand, while others may provide more information and offer more assistance to the photographer. In the end, remember that the most important camera accessory is the owner's instruction manual. If photographers do not know how to manage the camera's controls or understand what the viewfinder is telling them, then the camera merely becomes a glorified point-and-shoot camera.

Point-and-shoot cameras are another popular style of camera. They have a number of advantages, including being easily portable and operated. Point-and-shoot cameras can be an effective camera choice for patrol officers and for those simply taking photographs as a way of recording notes about a crime scene. Other point-and-shoots may have as many manual operation settings as an SLR camera but lack the adaptability offered by an SLR. The point-and-shoot genre of cameras is found in both digital and film formats. In the end, point-and-shoot cameras are acceptable for novices and patrol officers, but should not necessarily be utilized by professional investigators conducting the thorough documentation of a crime scene.

The one exception to the suggestion that SLR cameras are a better choice for investigators is when photographers need to go underwater. There are certainly expensive underwater housings for SLR cameras that are designed for divers and those that work extensively in underwater environments. These expensive camera housings and lighting systems would certainly be of great assistance at times. However, for those investigators that only once in a blue moon will need to recover evidence from underwater, then a point-and-shoot camera designed for such environments is an excellent option. These underwater cameras are easily operated in the *Program* mode, with all the exposure and focus adjustments automatically accounted for. Figure 2.1 illustrates just such a composition. It was easily recorded in the automatic mode and shows a well-focused, properly illuminated underwater image. In lieu of purchasing a more expensive underwater camera, a one-time use or disposable camera encased in plastic for photographing underwater can be found at almost any pharmacy or department store. These waterproof cameras can be used during the time of monsoon-rain conditions or when it is necessary to photograph evidence or a body in a swimming pool. Waterproof cameras are not able to photograph in extremely murky water or at any severe depths, but they are effective for swimming pools or extremely wet conditions. Fire investigators might find them useful as well because of the conditions they must work in.

In general, SLR cameras are the cameras of choice for crime scene investigators. Point-and-shoot cameras have many limitations regarding focus, depth of field, and flash capabilities. Accepting that each and every camera will have its own set of advantages and disadvantages, a photographer considering the purchase of a point-and-shoot camera should be fully aware of the individual camera's features and specifications. Understanding

Figure 2.1 On occasion, evidence may be found in underwater environments or needing documentation during heavy rain events and the use of an underwater camera can be advantageous. This image was recorded with a Nikon AW100 digital camera and the exposure settings were ISO 125, f/4, for 1/30th of a second.

the limitations of an investigator's equipment is just as important as understanding the photographer's own limitations. Not trying to go beyond a photographer's skill level or their equipment's capability can help prevent poor photographic images.

One of the specifications that is important to police investigators includes the ability to close focus. Point-and-shoot cameras may have a minimum focus distance of only 3–4 ft. Such a limitation would seriously hamper a crime scene investigator's ability to do any macro or identification quality photography. Some digital cameras have a *macro* setting, but the macro setting may not provide a true *optical* image. The digital camera may record a normally viewed image and during the image's processing, the camera crops the center portion of the image out. The center portion is then interpolated to an expanded size, creating a *close-up* image. This image could be problematic in court because it is not a true-optical image and was created using the digital process of interpolation during its resizing. Another severe limitation of these cameras is the limited range of their apertures. Without a broad range of apertures, the crime scene investigator will not be able to control an image's depth of field. The most severe limitation of point-and-shoot cameras is in the area of low-light photography. The point-and-shoot genre of cameras does not always allow for extended or timed exposures. In addition, the flash capabilities of the point-and-shoot camera may be limited to a simple pop-up flash. A pop-up flash is a convenient tool to have in limited situations, but it should never be considered as an all-purpose flash for crime scene work. On the positive side, a photographer that uses a point-and-shoot camera within the camera's limitations can still capture just as sharp-focused and valuable images as with an SLR camera. However, it is these limitations that prevent the point-and-shoot camera from being an appropriate choice for crime scene investigative work.

Digital versus Film

The decision to photograph crime scenes with a digital camera or a film camera is seldom made by the investigators. Most often that decision is made by the department or someone higher up in the agency's chain of command. Although film cameras are still available, both in new and used condition, today's photographic world is dominated by digital imaging. However, film cameras should not be disposed of all together. They still have a place in criminal investigations. Regardless whether a digital or film camera is utilized, a camera should not be selected for crime scene use because some command staff member's brother-in-law took *outstanding* pictures of his vacation to the Grand Canyon with a particular camera. A camera's ability to record a beautiful image of an iconic landmark does not necessarily make it an acceptable choice for law enforcement purposes.

With literally hundreds of digital cameras on the market, the final choice in a chosen model of camera should be a compromise between cost and features. One characteristic that should be maintained is that the camera should really have an SLR body style. Unfortunately, fiscal responsibility and constraints in this day and age are a reality. It would be great if every department could have an unlimited budget for the purchase of crime scene investigative tools. However, that is never going to occur and the cost of any camera outfit will always have to be balanced against the agency's financial constraints. Fortunately, entry-level SLR cameras are not much more expensive than some higher-quality point-and-shoot cameras. The cost of outfitting a photographer does not stop with the camera. Photographers will need a host of other tools, everything from cable releases, special lenses, external flashes, various scales, tripods, etc. The cost of these accoutrements should not outweigh the ability to achieve the ultimate goal of photographing crime scenes accurately, professionally, and with style and creativity.

Conveniently, most digital cameras have parts that are interchangeable with film cameras from the same manufacturer. Therefore, if an agency's previous film-imaging system was Canon or Nikon, by converting to the same manufacturer for digital photography, the agency or individual may not have to purchase all new lenses, flashes, cable releases, etc. However, do not be surprised if one or two accessories will need to be updated and replaced. The complete conversion to the digital world of photography can be an expensive proposition, but it will need to be made at some point.

Many crime scene photographers are excited about the potential of digital photography, especially when it comes to the ability to immediately review their captured image for exposure, focus, and composition. The immediate gratification offered by the review screen on the back of the camera has tremendous benefit, but it should not be routinely used as the final word in whether or not an image has value. The tiny review screen is not a substitute for viewing a printed or full-screen computer-generated image. Crime scene photographers need to develop confidence in their work without constantly examining the review screen. The review screens are simply too small to accurately examine the quality of an image's depth of field and lighting. Review screens have their advantages, such as checking for composition and basic lighting conditions. In the end, even when photographing with a digital camera, bracketing one's exposures is still an important task that remains the responsibility of the crime scene photographer.

Another argument made to encourage the switch to digital photography is that faults in an image can be easily corrected by image-enhancing software such as Adobe Photoshop®. However, one must remember the *garbage-in, garbage-out* philosophy of image enhancement. Having the ability to manipulate and enhance an image on a computer screen is not the same as being a good crime scene photographer. Crime scene photographers must make an effort to capture a quality image using good lighting, controlling an image's depth of field, and showing creativity in the captured images. Photographers must not rely on a computer program to do what should have been done at the point of capture. Furthermore, image enhancement programs cannot fix a poorly focused or badly composed image.

Digital imaging is the primary means by which today's crime scene photographs are recorded. The capture of any image is simply a process of image composition, the metering of light, and the proper selection of exposure values (ISO value, aperture, and shutter speed) in order to achieve one's intended outcome. Those factors do not change because one has switched from film to digital capture. This text is not wholly about *digital photography*; it is about the accurate, complete, and professional documentation of crime scenes and evidence regardless of the media used to make the image. Granted, there are differences between the two formats including exposure latitude, focal length multipliers, and digital artifacts. However, the basic image capture concepts learned over time and presented in this book are completely applicable to both film and digital photography.

Film can sometimes be a better choice of recording media, over digital imaging. For example, when a photographer needs to record an extremely long (timed) exposure, film can be a better recording media. Digital cameras, especially those with an imaging sensor smaller than 35 mm film format (24 mm × 36 mm), suffer significantly from *noise*. Noise is an artifact that develops in digital images and appears as blown pixels within the recorded image. Another benefit that film cameras have over digital cameras is that film suffers from *reciprocity failure*. Reciprocity failure is discussed in more detail in Chapter 5. However, for now, it is enough to say that reciprocity failure is not necessarily a negative attribute and allows film photographers much more exposure latitude or room for error during longer, nighttime exposures. Film can also be a better choice when recording an image through a Wratten 18A filter, which is used in reflected ultraviolet (UV) light photography. This topic is discussed in greater detail in Chapter 10. The 18A filter prevents visible light from entering the camera and allows UV light and infrared light to pass. Because film does not record infrared light, the reflected UV light photography technique works quite well. However, digital imaging chips can record infrared light, which prevents the recording of a quality UV image. For these two reasons alone, film cameras should not be thrown in the trash, but retained for specific crime scene photographic tasks.

Digital imaging also comes with a few added responsibilities and evidence control requirements. Many digital imaging recommendations and requirements are set forth by the Scientific Working Group on Imaging Technology (SWGIT). SWGIT is a group of law enforcement and photography professionals who organized to provide leadership and guidance to the law enforcement community by developing guidelines and recommendations for best practices in the training, capture, and archiving of digital images within the criminal justice system. Those entering into the digital world of crime scene photography must be knowledgeable about digital compression, RAW data files, and the current 1000 pixel-per-inch standard for latent print photography. Digital photographers simply need to be aware of the guidelines provided by SWGIT and their own agency's procedures and protocols when it comes down to the digital recording of crime scene photographs.

In conclusion, the true and accurate documentation of crime scenes and evidence is the responsibility of the crime scene investigator, regardless of the media on which the images are recorded. Furthermore, agencies should be fully cognizant of the additional requirements that accompany the conversion to digital imaging in the law enforcement community.

Lenses

A camera cannot take a photograph without a lens. Light is focused by the camera lens as it makes its way to the recording media. Lenses come in a variety of styles and are intended or designed for different photographic tasks. The cost of any particular lens depends upon the lens' features and the quality of its glass elements. The more expensive the lens, typically the better quality and the sharper the final image will end up being. Lenses can be quite expensive, especially professional quality lenses. Rather than saving money by purchasing inferior products, photographers could consider buying used lenses. Used equipment should be purchased in person and not necessarily over the Internet. One needs to evaluate the lens' condition by checking for the presence of mold inside the lens or scratches on the focusing elements. Regardless of how expensive an individual lens is, a photographer should always safeguard the exterior glass elements with a protective filter, such as a Skylight or Wratten 1A filter. It is much less traumatic to replace a damaged filter than it is to replace a very expensive lens.

Because lenses come in so many forms and for so many different purposes, the lenses discussed here will be those lenses of particular value to crime scene investigators. There are two main varieties—zoom lenses and fixed focal length lenses. Zoom lenses allow the photographer to capture images at a variety of focal lengths, while a fixed focal length lens only has one focal length or field of view at which to record a photograph. A fixed focal length lens will generally record a sharper image from corner to corner in comparison to a comparable zoom lens, because the fixed focal length lens has fewer variables (focal lengths) to adjust for. On the other side of the coin, due to their versatility, a zoom lens offers the investigator more adaptability and flexibility. The zoom feature will prevent the need to constantly change the camera's lens in order to alter the image's perspective. A 28–80 mm zoom lens (35 mm film format) is an excellent choice for crime scene investigators. There are variable focal length lenses that can expand the zoom capability into the 200 or 300 mm range, but the overall image quality may suffer because the lens is being asked to do too much in regard to focal length. Lenses are also graded in regard to the size of their maximum aperture. A lens with an aperture of f/2.8 will be more expensive than a similar lens that merely has a maximum aperture of f/4.0. The f/2.8 lens has better light-gathering ability and can be more useful in low-light conditions. Other features that may be of value to crime scene photographers include lenses with a macro capability or an image stabilization feature. These two features assist investigators in close focusing on subjects and helping eliminate camera shake from images. In the end, the quality of the lens is a primary factor responsible for an image's sharpness, and photographers should seek to use the best quality lens available.

Lens Filters and Attachments

Filters that are attached to the end of a camera's lens are accessories that can be quite beneficial to photographers. Filters can compensate for lighting and color or simply be used to protect the outer lens element. A UV blocking or *Skylight* (1A) filter should always be attached to protect the lens from accidental scratching or other damage. Most filters are identified by their Wratten number. Frederick Wratten was a British inventor who produced filters for Kodak and the Wratten identification numbers have remained in use to this day. Crime scene investigators will eventually collect their own set of filters that they find most useful. Listed below are some of the more commonly used filters in crime scene photography. Their specific uses will be detailed throughout this book:

- #1A—protective filter (reduces UV effects on image)
- #8—yellow filter (B&W photography and alternate light photography)
- #18A—UV band-pass filter (reflective UV photography)
- #21—orange filter (alternate light photography)
- #25—red filter (color separation and alternate light photography)
- #47B—blue filter (color separation)
- #58—green filter (color separation)
- #80A and 80B—blue tinted filters (color compensation for tungsten and incandescent lighting)
- #87 and 89 series—infrared band-pass filters (reflective IR photography)
- FLD (Fluorescent to daylight)—pink colored filter that compensates for fluorescent lighting
- Neutral density (ND) filters (reduces amount of ambient lighting)
- Polarizer—eliminates plane waves of light, cutting glare from reflective surfaces
- Diopters—magnification filters (increases close-focusing ability)

All these filters can dramatically improve one's photographs in one way or another. A filter's cost varies with its specialization and size of the filter itself. For example, a 1A Skylight filter may cost approximately $15, while an 87 infrared filter may sell for as much as $100. In addition, even among 1A or UV filters, the quality of the filter's glass can vary. More expensive filters can prevent unwanted lens flair or reflections from developing in the recorded image. Compare the two photographs in Figure 2.2. Figure 2.2a was recorded through an inexpensive (approximately $10) 1A filter. Figure 2.2b was recorded through a more expensive (approximately $100) 1A filter. The variety of filtration is both diverse and beneficial to crime scene photographers in a number of applications and will be detailed throughout this text.

(a)   (b)

Figure 2.2 (a) was recorded through an inexpensive, consumer quality 1A filter. Notice the creation of a large circular lens flair. (b) was recorded through a more professional quality 1A filter and in the same composition; the lens flair was eliminated.

Tripods and Other Camera Supports

While tripods are one of the most overlooked and left behind pieces of equipment in the crime scene investigator's arsenal, every nighttime crime scene should be photographed, at least in part, with the camera mounted upon a tripod. Time exposures, capturing the crime scene in its natural light, are mandatory and this feat is impossible without the use of a tripod. Even daytime exposures may require a tripod-mounted camera at times, for example, photographs recorded with extremely small apertures or when close focusing on a single piece of evidence frequently requires the camera to be stabilized. Much like camera lenses, tripods come in a variety of shapes and sizes and with a variety of features (Figure 2.3). The choice of tripod is up to the individual photographer and the size of his or her wallet.

Weight is a major factor in the ultimate selection of a tripod. The heftiness of the camera support can be extremely important when photographing in windy conditions or when an artificial wind is created by a passing semitractor trailer along a busy freeway. The heavier the tripod, the more stable it will be in these adverse conditions. If one is given or issued a tripod of limited mass, weight can be added by draping sandbags or beanbags across a tripod's leg supports. This will add additional stability to the camera platform. Unfortunately, heavier tripods are often left behind in the crime scene investigator's vehicle because they are too burdensome. This is a huge and all too common mistake of crime scene photographers. Lighter weight tripods are easier to transport from place to place and around a crime scene, and what they lack in mass, they make up for in convenience. There is nothing wrong with encouraging investigators to have a pair of

Figure 2.3 Tripods are a necessity for all crime scene photographers. They come in many forms and having a choice of tripods for different situations can be invaluable.

tripods available, one more sturdy and another for light duty. The heavy-duty tripod can be used for scenes found along busy roadways, in inclement weather, or for longer exposures. The lighter weight tripod can be used for scenes that may need to be reached by trekking over an extended distance or for indoor settings in which the space to extend the legs of a large-frame tripod is limited. In addition, there are times when two tripods are necessary such as when reconstructing shooting scenes with lasers. One tripod is used to support the camera and the second tripod is used to support the laser in the position of a fired weapon.

Other factors to consider in the purchase and use of a tripod are the maximum and minimum heights the tripod can reach. There are times when a tripod is needed to photograph impression evidence on the ground or when the crime scene investigator must lift a camera over an obstruction, such as a fence. A tripod must be flexible in order to accommodate such diverse situations. As for impression evidence, the ability to attach a side arm is beneficial. A sidearm attachment or a columned neck capable of being mounted horizontal to the ground can help a photographer capture those hard-to-reach subjects or to record a footwear or tire wear impression on the ground, while helping prevent the tripod legs from being a distraction in the captured image.

Quality tripods are frequently purchased without a mounting head. These heads are purchased separately and come in a variety of styles, including pan and tilt, ball, and ball-grip heads. A tripod head with a quick-release plate is a time-saving feature well worth the extra cost. Quick-release plates allow a photographer to expeditiously remove and replace the camera from the tripod without having to manipulate the mounting screw each time. By far the easiest style of tripod head to work with is a pistol-grip head with a quick-release plate. The pistol-grip head is operated by squeezing the locking mechanism, moving the camera into the desired position, and releasing the locking grip. Once again, the size of a photographer's wallet may be the determining factor for the type of tripod head selected. Typically, the easier the head is to maneuver and the more features the mounting head possesses, the more expensive it will be.

Regardless of the type of tripod one uses, here are a few simple suggestions that will help guarantee a sharper image, because even images captured with a tripod-mounted camera can still be blurry due to camera shake. Tripods are collapsible and they typically are enlarged by extending the tripod's legs and/or center column. When extending the legs, always extend the upper sections first. In this way, the lower portion of the legs will be denser and provide greater stability. The lower portions of the tripod legs can be extended next. Absolutely, the last portion of the tripod that should be extended is the neck. It may be easier just to slide the neck up in order to get the camera to a proper height, but then the neck can act more like a fulcrum and the camera can sway during a long exposure. The neck should only be used for fine-tuning the height of the camera. Additionally, the mounting screws that attach the camera to the tripod's head typically come as a pair of interlaced locking rings that encircle a ¼″ screw. The bottom locking ring is the smaller of the two rings and should be tightened first. The upper rotating ring of the pair is a locking ring that firmly secures the camera to the tripod head or mounting plate. Rotating these locking rings in an incorrect order may cause the camera to pivot upon the threaded screw. If an investigator notices camera shake in their recorded images, even with the camera firmly mounted upon a tripod, then the cause could be the lens' *image stabilization* or *vibration reduction* feature. These features should be switched off for any tripod-mounted recordings. The stabilization feature is meant to dampen camera shake (causing a blurry image) from handheld exposures, but can actually cause camera shake to develop in securely fastened, tripod-mounted images.

Another time-saving and extremely convenient camera support is known as an articulating or Magic Arm, manufactured by Bogen–Manfrotto (Figure 2.4). One end of this device clamps to nearly any surface and the other mounts to the camera. The articulating arm is flexible enough to position the camera in any orientation within the arm's reach.

(a)

(b)

(c)

Figure 2.4 The Bogen–Manfrotto Magic Arm® is extremely versatile and applicable to crime scene photography. It allows photographers to stabilize their cameras in the narrowest of confined spaces, as well as ensure a perpendicular alignment with a subject. (a) illustrates how effective the Magic Arm is by clamping onto the edge of a door in order to maintain a perpendicular alignment for a fingerprint impression. The Magic Arm can also be used in combination with a tripod (b) in order to photograph subjects such as footwear and tire wear impressions when a photographer's tripod does not have a side arm or boom. (c) shows a tripod with just such a side arm or boom assisting in the photographing of a bullet strike to the underside of a vehicle.

Figure 2.5 This figure illustrates the benefits of possessing a small minitripod in order to capture photographs of evidence resting close to the ground. Getting close to one's evidence, regardless of its location, is not only vital for the recording of accurate photographs but also will help create resourceful and important pieces of evidence. (Photographed by Mike Perez, Crime Scene Investigator, Houston Police Department, Houston, TX.)

This feature can be vitally important when it is necessary to position the camera perpendicular to a piece of evidence in a confined or difficult to reach space. The articulating arm can also be clamped to a tripod, allowing the support to act as a sidearm attachment that makes photographing footwear and tire wear impressions much easier. A word of warning when utilizing a magic arm: a photographer should use a cable release or the camera's self-timer to trip the shutter in order to avoid the potential for camera shake.

Minitripods can also be used in a variety of situations and should be part of any crime investigator's equipment arsenal. Minitripods (Figure 2.5) are inexpensive and can help stabilize a camera for low-profile photographs, such as documenting bloodstains along a wall's baseboard. Beanbags or even tube socks filled with rice or beans can replace a minitripod as a camera support (Figure 2.6). Beanbags are also used to stabilize lightweight tripods and can be laid across the camera's body, where it joins with the lens, during exposures when *mirror slap* might be an issue. Mirror slap may occur in exposures between 1/20th of a second and a couple of seconds and occurs when the mirror flips up inside the camera's body causing vibration within the camera. This can create a blurry image. When photographing with a minitripod or a beanbag support, it is a good idea to use a cable release. If a cable release is not available, use the camera's self-timer. The cable release or self-timer will help eliminate the vibration that may be caused by the actual depression of the exposure button.

Identification Markers

Evidence comes in every conceivable size, shape, and form. It can be microscopic or as big as a truck. Regardless of its size, the crime scene investigator has a duty to document the evidence and that documentation must be sharp, in focus, and identifiable. Without clear, sharp images, one cannot create a lasting impression with the jury. When one is able to create a good impression with a jury, the rest of an investigator's courtroom testimony is much

Figure 2.6 Small beanbags, even homemade ones created by filling a tube sock with rice such as pictured here, will help stabilize cameras at ground level. Creating such low-profile photographs can help create artistic and captivating photographs. They can also be used to help accurately document evidence requiring perpendicular orientation between the camera and subject matter that is found on and/or along low-level surfaces.

more credible. Poorly composed and blurry images diminish a jury's opinion of the investigator, and the overall weight given to the investigator's testimony may suffer severely. In that regard, identifying and pointing out what information or evidence is important within an image are critical to the jury's understanding of the case being tried before them.

An investigator should possess a broad range of evidence markers, flags, and pointers. The numerous crime scene supply companies in business can provide investigators with a varied assortment of photographic aids. These devices aid viewers of crime scene photographs by pointing out everything from very small pieces of evidence to larger items hidden within expansive locations, such as an overgrown field of weeds. The most common style of evidence marker, as frequently seen in television crime dramas, is the numbered tent marker. Tent markers are folded pieces of plastic with large visible numbers or letters imprinted upon them. Commercially purchased tent markers and pointer arrows are probably one expense that is worth the money due to the professional look they provide in the final recorded images. However, alternatives are available for cash-strapped agencies and investigators.

One inexpensive alternative is to build your own evidence markers and pointers. A replacement for tent markers can be as simple as filling plastic film containers with sand or caulk and using adhesive numbers or letters to mark the sides of the film containers. The sand or caulk is used to prevent the evidence markers from rolling away with a sudden gust of wind. Reflective tape can be added to canisters to aid in their visibility. A crime scene investigator may also choose to create his or her own markers by laminating numbered pieces of cardstock folded into tent-shaped evidence markers.

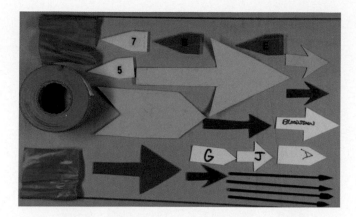

Figure 2.7 The photographer does not have to purchase expensive evidence markers in order to create powerful photographic images. An assortment of arrows and pointers can be created in a number of ways, including those made from empty plastic detergent bottles, plastic coffee stirrers, and from arrows printed off a personal computer and laminated or printed onto self-adhesive address labels.

Pointer arrows cut from an empty liquid detergent bottle can also be created for far less than what it would cost to purchase them commercially (Figure 2.7). Companies use different colored plastics to create their packaging and, as a result, investigators can cut out different styles of arrows in a number of colors. Arrows help point out the smaller pieces of evidence such as blood drops and bullet strikes. In addition, the plastic is extremely durable and can be washed with bleach if it falls into a pool of blood. Arrows can also be cut out of colored paper and laminated. Although the laminated arrows are not as durable, they can be created on a computer and are easier to cut out. Consequently, they will look more professional in the crime scene photographs.

For evidence found on vertical surfaces, Sharpie® or other permanent markers can be used to bring attention to a particular subject or piece of evidence. Adhesive address labels can be preprinted with arrows and/or scales for adherence to vertical surfaces unable to hold other types of markers. Crime scene photographers should never go anywhere without their permanent marking pens. These pens are extremely useful for making notations on surfaces where traditional evidence markers cannot be placed, such as vertical surfaces or in small, confined spaces.

In grass fields or vacant weed-covered lots, tent markers and arrows are not likely to be visible. An easy solution is to use small flags purchased from the local home improvement store. These small fluorescent colored flags are mounted on a stiff wire and are most commonly used to identify gas or phone lines during construction projects. They are also perfect for marking the location of evidence in an investigator's crime scene photographs. Regardless of the manner in which an investigator identifies a piece of evidence, the scene photographs will be much improved through the use of identification and/or orientation markers. Furthermore, the cost for such evidence markers can be greatly reduced with a small amount of creative thinking. By examining what is commercially sold for the forensic community, investigators may be able to fabricate their own items by shopping at tool, hobby, and general department stores, thereby saving quite a bit of money.

Electronic and Strobe Flashes

Electronic flash is a necessity in crime scene photography. Flash photography has many benefits, but it also has a number of disadvantages. These advantages, disadvantages, and the use of electronic flashes are covered in Chapter 6. When selecting which flash to purchase, one must choose among a host of available styles, all with a variety of features, found on the market. Many cameras come with a built-in *pop-up* flash, but this flash is extremely limited and should not be considered as the primary light source for low-light situations. An off-the-camera flash is much better suited for crime scene work.

Flashes are graded by their power, which is referred to as a *guide number* (GN). A GN is equal to the aperture multiplied by the subject's distance from the flash unit and is routinely quoted in relation to an ISO value of 100. The higher the GN, the more powerful the flash. However, power is not everything when trying to evaluate and choose among the numerous flashes for sale. More beneficial aspects of the flash include whether or not the flash can bounce light, diffuse light, create a strobe effect, or allow for rear or high-speed synchronization. In addition to the sheer power of the flash, these other features should also be included in a flash's evaluation. Some of these *extra* flash features that might be found beneficial include a built-in diffuser.

The strobe feature allows the flash to fire multiple times during an exposure and can be quite helpful when painting with light. Rear synchronization photography is not often needed at crime scenes, but may be beneficial in other areas of photography. During a standard exposure, the shutter opens, the flash immediately fires, the length of the exposure continues, and the shutter closes. This sequence can cause moving objects to appear as if they are moving backwards in the photograph. Rear synchronization flash enables the camera to delay the flash exposure to the end of the overall exposure, thereby placing any subject blur into correct sequence within the image (Figure 2.8). High-speed synchronization is also not frequently required by crime scene investigators, but may be useful in some aspects of reconstruction photography, when the investigator wishes to stop the action or

Figure 2.8 A rear-synchronized capable flash is able to accurately capture the direction of travel for moving subjects. The image was recorded at ISO 400, f/11, for 8 s.

motion of experiments being conducted. High-speed synchronization allows photographers to adjust their shutter speeds to faster settings. Crime scene investigators are more likely to record flash exposures with the shutter left open for several seconds rather than several hundredths of a second. Oftentimes, electronic flashes possessing the most features will likely have greater power; therefore, one will not necessarily have to choose between features and illuminating power. Electronic flash and GN calculation, flash operation, and painting-with-light techniques are discussed in detail in Chapters 6 and 7.

A synchronization cord is another piece of equipment that is a must for any crime scene investigator. A *sync cord* is a coiled wire that connects the flash to the camera and allows the flash to communicate with the camera while separated from the camera. Being able to separate the camera from the flash enables the photographer to change the direction of lighting projected onto or across a subject. For a few extra dollars, there are wireless flash units that eliminate the need for a physical connection between the flash unit and camera. Flash diffusers are also invaluable. One of the more effective flash diffusers available is known as a soft box. Soft boxes come in a variety of styles, but basically they are coverings placed over the flash head to soften and disperse the light in order to help eliminate shadows and create the appearance that light is illuminating the subject from different angles. A couple of the more popular soft boxes are the *Sto-Fen*® and *Gary Fong*® diffusers. Photographers can actually make their own soft boxes by using a clear or white plastic food or butter container and thus eliminate the need to purchase one. Simply cut a hole in the lid so that it fits snugly over the flash head (Figure 2.9). Upon sliding the two pieces together, the homemade diffuser disperses light more effectively and creates a well-balanced and illuminated image.

Cable Releases

In order to capture sharp images without any camera shake visible in the photograph, the remote firing of the camera's shutter is recommended. Several types of cable releases are available. Older cameras use a mechanical, plunger style of cable. These cable releases are inexpensive and are threaded into the shutter-release button and operated through the pressing of a thin metal rod into the shutter-release button, setting the camera off. These cables work well, but because the operation applies force to the camera, the recorded image may still show vibration if the photographer is not careful. Newer model cameras utilize an electronic shutter-release cable. These cables fire an electronic signal to the camera. Therefore, no matter how hard the cable's shutter-release button is depressed, that energy is not transferred to the camera and the image does not suffer from camera shake. The third type of remote shutter release is an infrared remote. Although these remotes are excellent for some aspects of photography, they may not be as useful in extended time exposures or painting-with-light exercises. Some (not all) infrared remotes require the photographer to remain within 15 ft of the camera in order to keep the button depressed during bulb exposures. Being tethered to the camera and having one hand tied to the remote limit the photographer's ability to move through a crime scene during painting-with-light projects. Some of the electronic remotes can be rather costly and although their use is extremely convenient, the camera's self-timer can always be used as the remote firing feature. Unfortunately, an actual cable release is necessary with painting with light. Without a cable release, the photographer will be at a great disadvantage.

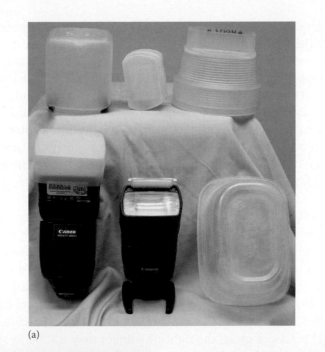

(a)

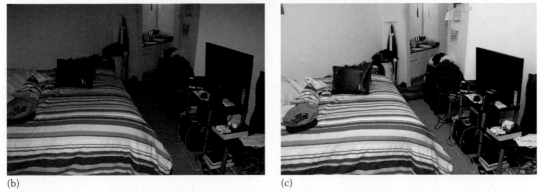

(b)   (c)

Figure 2.9 A soft box, even a homemade soft box, is capable of diffusing light emitted by an electronic flash and allows the light to filter into the darker recesses of a composition. (a) shows a series of diffusers, including a built-in, homemade, Sto-Fen® and Gary Fong® diffusers. (b) was captured with the flash pointed directly at the subject. The camera metered the light reflecting off the bed in the foreground, thereby causing an underexposure to the background. The same subject was photographed in (c), but recorded with a Sto-Fen flash diffuser. Although the two images are not drastically different, the light was able to reach into the back of the composition and better illuminate the environment around and behind the bed.

Lens Attachments

When composing identification quality photographs, one needs to get up close and personal with their subject. The minimum focus for standard camera lenses will not always allow photographers to get as close as they need to be. Therefore, extension tubes or diopters (magnification filters) may be the solution. Extension tubes and diopters work with a photographer's own lenses. Extension tubes separate the camera from the lens, thus altering the focal point of the lens. Because extension tubes do not have any glass elements and record the image through the lens' glass elements, the resulting pictures are extremely sharp. The tubes can be combined in order to extend the focal point, thereby enlarging the image even further. Extension tubes are sold individually and in groups. A lens bellows is another type of lens extension that can increase the size of a subject in the viewfinder. Bellows units are far more expensive and better suited for controlled environments, such as a laboratory. A less-expensive alternative is the use of diopters or magnification filters. These glass filter elements thread onto the end of the camera lens and magnify the subject. The diopters can be stacked upon one another for greater magnification, but the image's sharpness will deteriorate with each additional glass element that light must pass through on its way to the camera.

Another lens attachment that can be placed between the camera body and the lens is known as a teleconverter. Teleconverters multiply the focal length of the attached lens. For example, a 50 mm lens with a 2× teleconverter would now photograph a subject at the equivalent focal length of 100 mm. Teleconverters are designed to help a photographer capture distant subjects, but they can even help enlarge a nearby subject as would an extension tube, although not with the same quality. Teleconverters have glass elements and, as a result, the image may suffer in its overall sharpness. Because light must pass through additional pieces of glass, the light or subject may not be as sharply focused as it would be through a set of extension tubes or a dedicated macro lens. Teleconverters should be used for their designed purpose, which is to extend a lens' focal length and bring distant subjects into better view.

Hard Cases, Soft Cases, and Backpacks

Crime scene investigators and photographers invariably collect an assortment of photographic accessories as they travel through their careers. Some equipment will be highly regarded and rank second only to the invention of the wheel, while other accessories will be sold in a garage sale for pennies. As the collection grows, investigators need a safe and convenient way to transport their equipment from scene to scene. Hard cases, soft cases, and backpacks specifically designed for photographic equipment are all available for purchase. Hard cases provide the most protection and are preferable to softer camera cases. However, backpacks, one form of soft camera cases, can be quite beneficial and extremely convenient when having to transport camera paraphernalia across longer distances. Hence, having both styles of camera cases available for use during different times and tasks may be an appropriate solution. Either way it is important to protect the equipment because evidence found at a crime scene will have limited value if it cannot be fully documented photographically.

Conclusion

No two crime scenes are ever exactly the same. Lighting conditions, the size and location of evidence, and environmental factors will vary greatly from scene to scene. Because of this, a crime scene photographer must be prepared to document evidence in a variety of conditions. Consequently, investigators need a variety of photographic equipment and tools. Whether photographers purchase equipment new, used, or build their own, the ultimate goal should still be the same: to truly and accurately document a crime scene with sharply focused and vivid photographic images. Furthermore, a crime scene photographer does not have to spend a fortune on equipment. Thinking outside of the box and doing a little research can result in money saving purchases. As a final note, the Internet is a great resource for cost-saving purchases and ideas for better photographic techniques.

End of Chapter Questions

1. What is the recommended style of camera for crime scene investigators?
   a. Point-and-shoot camera
   b. SLR camera
   c. Medium format camera
   d. Any automatic or *Program* camera

2. Who developed the first SLR camera?
   a. Carl Zeiss
   b. Matthew Brady
   c. Karl Nuechterlein
   d. Ansel Adams

3. According to the author, what is the most important camera accessory?
   a. Owner's instruction manual
   b. External flash unit
   c. Remote shutter/cable release
   d. Focus prism

4. In what environment may *point-and-shoot* cameras provide an advantage?
   a. When greater depth of field is required
   b. When evidence is found underwater
   c. When using an alternate light source (ALS)
   d. None of the above

5. Which filter is recommended for all camera lenses?
   a. ND
   b. Average density
   c. Wratten
   d. 1A, Skylight, or UV

6. What can cause blur or camera shake in an image recorded with the camera securely mounted upon a tripod?
   a. Lightweight tripod
   b. *Image Stabilization* or *Vibration Reduction* feature set to *On*
   c. Fully extending the tripod's neck before extending the tripod's legs
   d. All of the above

7. Evaluating electronic flash units is solely based on the power of the unit or amount of light that the unit can produce.
   a. True
   b. False

8. When should photographers utilize a remote shutter-release cable?
   a. For UV or infrared photography endeavors
   b. For flash photography endeavors
   c. For extended time exposures
   d. All of the above

9. Which lens attachment can provide a magnified image of a subject?
   a. Extension tubes
   b. Bellows unit
   c. Diopters
   d. All of the above

10. What type of lens attachment can assist in capturing distant subjects?
    a. Macroconverters
    b. Teleconverters
    c. Light amplifiers
    d. Teleamplifiers

11. What type of *point-and-shoot* camera may be an appropriate substitution for an SLR at certain times?
    a. Macrocamera
    b. Underwater camera
    c. Depth of field camera
    d. Polaroid camera

12. Which composition would be better recorded by film than digital media?
    a. Depth of field images
    b. Surveillance photography applications
    c. Reflected UV light images
    d. Bloodstain photographs

13. Which electronic flash feature assists photographers in representing moving objects to be traveling in the proper direction?
    a. Rear synchronization
    b. Front synchronization
    c. Timed synchronization
    d. Slow synchronization

14. High-speed flash synchronization is an important feature to possess for crime scene photographers.
    a. True
    b. False

15. Both film and digital images suffer from noise during extremely long exposures.
    a. True
    b. False

16. What is the main advantage of using an SLR camera?
    a. It looks professional.
    b. SLR cameras are easier to use than point-and-shoot cameras.
    c. SLR cameras are more versatile than point-and-shoot cameras.
    d. They are so similar that there is no clear advantage.

17. Zoom lenses
    a. Allow the photographer to capture images while bracketing exposures
    b. Can only be used on video or cine cameras
    c. Are a historic type of lens that is no longer in use on modern cameras
    d. Allow the photographer to capture images at a variety of focal lengths

18. Which filter(s) is most commonly used to reduce glare when photographing evidence behind glass or underwater?
    a. #8 Yellow, #21 Orange, #25 Red
    b. ND
    c. Polarizer
    d. Diopters (+1, +2, +4)

19. Which filter reduces ambient lighting and is most commonly used to take a photograph using a slower shutter speed or wider aperture than would normally be possible under identical lighting conditions?
    a. #8 Yellow, #21 Orange, #25 Red
    b. ND
    c. Polarizer
    d. Diopters (+1, +2, +4)

20. Remote activation of the camera's shutter can help reduce blur caused by the camera shaking during the exposure. Which of the following devices are mentioned for this purpose in Chapter 2?
    a. Filters and other lens attachments
    b. Mechanical and electronic cable releases
    c. Infrared remotes and self timers
    d. Both B and C

21. A photographer using an expensive SLR-style camera will always get better results than a photographer using a point-and-shoot camera, regardless of his or her photographic abilities.
    a. True
    b. False

Photography Assignments

Required Tools: General photography equipment. Cardstock, permanent-ink markers, clear or white plastic container, colored (empty) plastic detergent bottles, and similar household items

Photography Subjects: General photographic subjects

I. Students should create a set of evidence placards or tent placards for use in photographing mock crime scenes:
   1. Placards can be created from folded card stock, small weighted containers, or surveyor flags.
   2. Markers should have clearly visible numerical or alphabetical identifiers.
II. Students should create a set of individual evidence pointers:
   1. Evidence pointers can be cut out of old plastic containers, laminated card stock, or any other medium that is available.
III. If not in possession of a professional flash diffuser, students should create one for use in their photographic endeavors:
   1. Using a clear or white food container, cut a hole into the lid that allows one's flash head to fit snugly inside.
IV. Record a series of photographs using the various markers and pointers created by the individual. Observe how shadows are formed if the evidence markers are reflective and how they react with the camera's flash unit.
V. Photograph an indoor composition with and without a flash diffuser. Compare the two images, so that the photographer will know which he or she prefers at a real scene:
   1. Use the flash diffuser in photographing the overall view of a room.
   2. Use the flash diffuser in photographing a close-focused (macro) subject.

Additional Readings

Busselle, M. (1992). *Complete 35 mm Sourcebook*. New York: Mitchell Beazley Publishers.

Davies, A. and Fennessy, P. (1998). *Digital Imaging for Photographers*. 3rd ed. Worburn, MA: Reed Educational and Professional Publishing, Ltd.

Davis, P. (1995). *Photography*. 7th ed. Boston, MA: McGraw Hill.

Grimm, T. and Grimm, M. (1997). *The Basic Book of Photography: The Classic Guide*. New York: Penguin Books.

Hyypia, J. (1981). *The Complete Tiffen Filter Manual*. New York: American Photographic Books.

Landt, A. (1993). *The Kodak Workshop Series: Lenses for 35 mm Photography*. Rochester, NY: Silver Pixel Press.

McDarrah, F.W. and McDarrah, G.S. (1999). *The Photography Encyclopedia*. New York: Schirmer Books.

Stensvold, M. (2002). *The Complete Idiot's Guide to Photography Like a Pro*. 3rd ed. Indianapolis, IN: Alpha Books.

www.swgit.org, Retrieved January 15, 2014, from http://www.swgit.org.

Crime Scene Photography

3

Crime scene photography is vitally important to the overall documentation of a crime scene. The photographs must be material, relevant, accurate, and without prejudicial bias. These are the typical standards crime scene photographs must meet in order to be accepted as evidence in a court of law. Because the art and science of photography is not always well understood, many times the photographic documentation of a crime scene has turned into just another annoying task that must be checked off a *to-do* list. Crime scene photography should be thought of as an opportunity to impress all those who view the photographer's work and especially as an opportunity to educate and inform the jury. By impressing the jury with his or her photographic skill and ability, a crime scene investigator creates the opportunity to dramatically influence the outcome of a trial. Furthermore, the opposite is also true. Failure to capture quality evidentiary photographs can cost the prosecution dearly. Crime scene photography must be regarded as a primary responsibility and duty of investigators, because everything done subsequently has little value without a proper photographic foundation.

Preparation and General Photography Tips

Any effort to photograph a crime scene begins prior to arriving at the location. In addition to making sure that all the necessary equipment is available, photographers must ensure that batteries are charged and that the equipment is in good working condition. Some agencies have enough camera equipment so that all investigators have their own gear. However, other agencies do not and investigators are forced to share equipment. Sharing photography equipment presents so many potential problems that it is recommended investigators belonging to cash-strapped agencies invest in their own photography gear. The headaches avoided by possessing their own gear will far outweigh the cost.

Regardless of whether investigators share equipment, the next step is to ensure that the starting camera settings are correct. Every subject's composition has the potential to be different. One photograph may be recorded in monochrome, while the next photograph demands the smallest possible aperture, followed by a timed exposure of a luminol reaction. There is nothing worse than when an investigator believes he or she is photographing in an automatic exposure mode, not worrying about reading the exposure meter, only to realize later that all the photographs are over- or underexposed because the camera was not set as originally thought. This can easily occur when equipment is shared between investigators or photographers.

Photographers should get into the habit of checking a digital camera's settings for no other reason than the fact they can be easily changed unintentionally. On some camera models, it is quite easy to accidentally push a button or bump a dial without immediately recognizing that it had some effect on the recorded photograph's outcome. Some (not all) of the more important settings to make sure are properly set prior to working a crime scene include the following:

- Image quality, compression, and RAW capture settings
- ISO setting
- White balance, monochrome, or color selections
- Exposure (capture) mode
- Exposure and flash compensation settings

One good habit to develop is to reset all settings to some type of default like, *Program* mode, so that if an unexpected photo opportunity presents itself the camera can be quickly accessed and fired without having to reset previous settings.

Digital cameras can pose more difficulties for the photographer because of the numerous additional settings compared to film cameras. For example, film cameras have DX coding that tells the camera what type of film has been loaded into the camera. However, the film speed or ISO setting is one of the many choices found in a digital camera's menu, and this setting must be chosen and confirmed before any forensic photographic documentation of a crime scene is begun. It is a good habit to routinely check all camera settings prior to beginning a photographic venture. For example, the ISO value is an extremely important value to set properly because it fixes the playing field in which all photographs are taken and that the camera uses to combine with shutter speed and aperture to record a properly exposed image.

Even more valuable than the gratification of immediately reviewing photos offered by the digital camera is the ability to change one's film speed from image to image. A photographer can use an ISO 100 value when recording colorful bloodstains on clothing, immediately switch to an ISO 400 setting to capture a flash exposure of the bedroom where the clothes were found, and switch again to ISO 800 or 1600 to document latent bloodstains treated with luminol. However, while the frequent changing of ISO settings can enhance one's overall documentation of a crime scene, the photographer must double check the ISO values from time to time to ensure that they are recording the scene as intended.

White balance is another setting often forgotten about while capturing images with a digital camera. To eliminate the yellow stain caused by high-pressure sodium streetlights, an investigator can set the white balance to incandescent lighting. However, failing to reset the camera to a daylight setting and then capturing images in natural sunlight or with electronic flash will create a very distracting blue staining on the recorded image. This staining cannot always be completely removed by computer enhancements and may not be discernible in the small review screen on the back of the camera. Therefore, the photographer must check the white balance setting prior to beginning every new photographic assignment.

Digital cameras are now the primary means of recording images in the forensics field, as well as in the civilian world as a whole. However, along with every technical advance in crime scene photography come additional responsibilities or impediments. For example, digital cameras come with a number of custom functions that can be hidden deep inside a camera's menu system. For those unlucky crime scene photographers who must share their equipment with other investigators, it is even more important that all camera settings from exposure compensation, film speed, white balance, auto exposure bracketing, flash exposure compensation, etc., are set exactly as desired. Fortunately, these functions can easily be reset to factory defaults from the camera's menu. If one finds their camera's settings causing composition or exposure problems, every camera will have a *reset to factory default* setting somewhere in the menu system. This menu feature resets the camera to how it originally came from the factory. Once again the value of completely reading and understanding how the camera works is paramount to preparing for actual scene work and obtaining quality crime scene photographs. Please read the camera's instruction manual completely and thoroughly.

Beyond the necessity of reading and comprehending the manual for each individual camera, an investigator must *listen* and feel how the camera is performing in order to realize when something is not working properly. For example, it should be routine to check the exposure meter and the information displayed in the viewfinder while photographing even when using an automatic exposure mode. Investigators should also listen to their cameras to ensure they are working properly. The most obvious audible information the camera provides the photographer is when proper focus and exposure is achieved. Cameras typically *beep* or provide some sort of visual clue inside the viewfinder when a proper exposure and/or focus is obtained. Investigators should be constantly aware of these alerts in order to record the best photographs possible. Obviously, the operator should feel the camera advance the film from frame to frame or that the digital camera's recording light illuminates after an exposure is taken. In fact, digital cameras should be set so that photography without an imaging chip is impossible. This feature is found in the menu system and will prevent wasted effort or worse, a complete loss of a scene's photographic documentation. Although it would be too time consuming to review every single image on a digital camera, photographers should periodically examine the photographs they have taken. Film photographers are not able to review their images at the scene, and that makes it even more important that they make sure their cameras are operating correctly.

In addition to listening to and looking at one's camera, the photographer should feel for the camera's shutter activation. The rule of thumb when hand holding the camera is that the shutter speed should be faster than one over the focal length of the camera lens. For example, if a 28 mm focal length camera lens is used to capture an image, the minimum shutter speed should be 1/30th of a second if the camera is being handheld. Longer lenses require even faster minimum shutter speeds: a 200 mm telephoto lens should have a minimum shutter speed of 1/200th–1/250th of a second. The photographer should always round an exposure toward a faster shutter speed to be sure of a sharp, nonblurry image. The faster shutter speed requirements may be difficult to maintain even during the daytime when the sun is blocked by clouds and lower ISO settings are chosen. It is important that photographers listen to and carefully feel the camera's operation in order to ensure they do not hear or feel the distinctive double-click of the shutter opening and closing. While hand holding the camera, the photographer should only feel one quick shutter actuation. If two distinct clicks (shutter opening and then closing) are felt, then the recorded photograph may possess camera shake or blur in the image. The shutter's action should feel and sound like just one instantaneous event. As stated, this is just a rule of thumb, and some individuals may be able to push the envelope a little, but very little, maybe half a stop. Other photographers may find they need to keep their shutter speed one or two full stops faster than this rule of thumb. Experience will help identify a comfortable zone for the photographer to work in. For those who do not have a steady hand and who find themselves in need of faster shutter speeds to ensure sharp images, there are a couple of solutions. A monopod support may be helpful to stabilize the camera. Another solution is to purchase a vibration reduction or image stabilization lens. These specialty lenses can compensate for minor camera movement or shake.

Another suggestion for better photographic documentation is that crime scene photographers critically examine their work from previous scenes and/or training exercises. Critical evaluation of one's own work is recommended because it enables the photographer to see where his or her photography can be improved through lighting, composition, depth of field, etc. Also, this evaluation can also help identify problems with cameras and equipment and help prevent compromising other crime scenes. As cameras get older, shutter curtains can fail, light meters can become unbalanced, and door seals can become damaged allowing light into the camera, all of which can impact the quality of a photograph.

One important way in which investigators can prepare to be better crime scene photographers is to train and practice with their personal equipment. No one should just be handed a camera, told to set the camera to an automatic mode, and then be advised to go forth and conquer. In the past, this was a standard practice. However, in today's forensically knowledgeable world, processing a crime scene taking shortcuts or in an automatic mode is just not acceptable. Training is an important first step. The investigator does not need a photography degree to be a crime scene photographer, but should be comfortable and confident in operating his or her photography equipment in a fully *Manual* mode. It is not that every photograph must be taken in the *Manual* exposure mode, but when a challenging composition confronts the photographer, taking full control over the camera is an important skill to possess. The reading of the camera's instruction manual is an obvious and important first step. Second, the reading of textbooks on general photography and crime scene photography is quite advantageous. Last but not least, training courses on crime scene photography are extremely beneficial. Quality training courses are not only informative, they also provide the student with opportunities to practice different photographic techniques and to visualize in a concrete way the hypothetical models presented by the instructor.

The practicing, experimenting, and testing of photographic techniques should occur both in and out of the classroom. For example, anytime new equipment is purchased, it should be tested to be sure it works correctly and to determine how it will affect the photographic process. This is especially true in low-light and alternate light photography. Because the intensity and quality of the numerous light sources available are so different, the photographer needs to experiment and practice taking photographs in both situations prior to working an actual crime scene. In addition, these variable light sources react differently in various environments, such as an enclosed bathroom or a vast open field. Therefore, testing and practicing with the equipment that will be used in these environments and conditions are strongly recommended. A little practice and the knowledge gained from experimentation with any equipment will help engender confidence and result in improved crime scene photographs.

Capturing the Impossible Shot

When the photographer is facing a challenging photograph to capture, it is a good idea to step back from the camera, examine the scene, and identify what features of the subject are making the image a challenge. These features might include items such as

- Light intensity and light sources
- Direction of lighting
- Depth of field issues

- Deciding on the focus point
- Camera to-subject orientation
- Exposure values

A photographer is tasked with composing the image, evaluating the light intensity (obtaining a proper exposure) and ensuring that the direction of lighting captures the subject and that the subject is in sharp focus throughout the composition. Sometimes these tasks can be difficult, but this is where the photographer can shine and demonstrate their skill and ability to the image's viewer. Crime scene photography is so much more than a simple *point-and-shoot* endeavor.

One excellent way to impress others with one's photographic skill is to photograph those pieces of evidence thought to be impossible to capture. In situations when it would be easier to give up photographing a piece of evidence such as latent footwear impressions or fired projectiles imbedded inside walls, investigators can take the initiative and create the opportunity to have others ask, "How did you do that?" Difficult to capture photographs are often formidable merely because they challenge the photographer to properly cast light onto or into the subject. Thinking outside the box, utilizing different types of light sources, and composing the image's capture in a way to optimally record the photograph will help captivate viewers and demonstrate one's dedication to their duties.

Fired projectiles found inside walls, car tires, and other surfaces offer photographers priceless opportunities to distinguish themselves. As fired bullets pass through walls or other surfaces, they can become tangled within insulation, shred through ductwork, or become lodged in wood studs. After the exterior of the perforation is documented, the interior of the impact can be photographed. The investigator must cut out a large enough section around the impact site so that he or she can insert a hand into the wall and retrieve the projectile. Consequently, because a camera lens is not much wider than a person's hand, the opening makes a perfect spot in which to slide the camera lens. If needed, a smaller hole can also be cut into the surface but slightly to the side of the camera lens so that a flashlight or other lighting device can be positioned to shine into the environment. Peering through the viewfinder, the photographer can adjust the light so that a balanced illumination inside the structure is achieved. Additionally, vehicle tires can also be photographed in a very similar way. It is just easier to cut through sheetrock rather than tire rubber. As far as cutting into tires, it is easier to slice into the sidewall than to cut through the surface area that comes into contact with the roadway. Tire treads are likely to have steel belts and cords that make cutting through them arduous. Unique and powerful photographs like these add credibility to the investigator on the witness stand by creating a lasting impression of professionalism and dedication on the jury (Figure 3.1).

Lighting is the crucial element for capturing images in hard-to-reach areas, and these areas are seldom conducive to flash photography. While it is possible to remove larger sections of walls to create a more open area so that a flash exposure can be recorded, victims and their families usually do not appreciate the additional damage to their property. Nor is there any reason to add insult to injury by destroying a victim's property. Replacing flash photography with flashlight photography is one option to help avoid the further destruction of someone's home. Flashlights come in many sizes, intensities, and styles. Keeping a variety of options available can be of tremendous benefit to an investigator (Figure 3.2). Many investigators possess the typical policeman's SL-20 (equivalent to four D-cell batteries) flashlight, and it is wonderful in larger environments but can be too

(a)   (b)

Figure 3.1 (a) A photograph of a fired bullet, found resting on top of insulation, lost its momentum following its passage through two walls and fiberglass insulation. A hole was cut in the wall and the camera lens was placed inside. Light was provided by an external flash also placed inside the hole. The recording was made at ISO 400, f/11, for 1/60 of a second. Notice that a small plastic evidence pointer was utilized to help identify the subject of the photograph. (b) Car tires are another difficult but commonly encountered subject. In this figure, a bullet perforated the tire. The side of the tire was cut out to illustrate the path of the bullet's travel as well as recover the bullet's jacket as it separated passing through the tire.

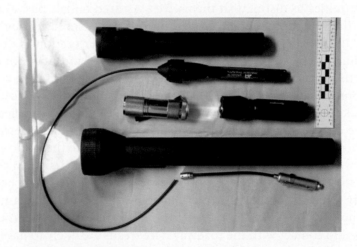

Figure 3.2 Possessing an assortment of flashlights and light sources will assist photographers in photographing hard-to-reach subjects. This figure shows several options available to investigators including police-style, LED, and penlight flashlights, as well as fiber optic cable attachments that fit onto the ends of these lights.

powerful for smaller endeavors. For getting into small nooks and crannies, an investigator needs a smaller light source. Dollar store penlight flashlights make excellent alternatives. Additionally, discount tool supply businesses carry ingenious fiber optic cables that can be attached to the end of small penlight flashlights. These cables can be inserted into the narrowest of openings and will then provide enough light to illuminate a myriad of hidden or secluded subjects. Another alternative frequently sold at discount tool stores is the flexible-head light emitting diode (LED) flashlight. These small flashlights are useful for

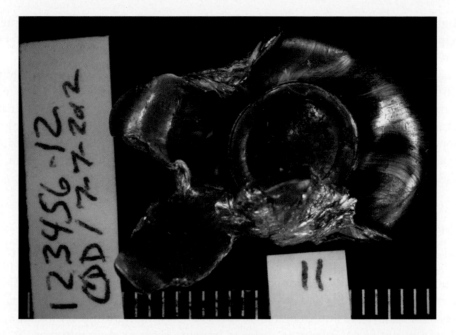

Figure 3.3 This photo is of a fired projectile recorded at ISO 100, f/22, for 56 s and was recorded using a penlight flashlight to illuminate the ballistic evidence. The low-power flashlight created a need for a longer exposure, which gave the photographer more time to add light onto the small subject by painting the subject and allowing light to reach into the small crevices created by the expanded bullet.

reaching into remote areas. In addition, these flexible-head lights or fiber optic cables can illuminate the interior of a subject without causing the glare or harshness to appear on the exterior. The subject can just as easily be a bullet strike as the barrel of a firearm or other hollow subject (Figure 3.3).

The use of flashlights to illuminate close-focused subjects does pose a couple of problems, but fortunately, the problems can be overcome with a little ingenuity. Flashlights characteristically leave a *hot spot* in the center of their illumination. This hot spot can be diffused by placing fingerprint tape over the flashlight's lens or by sliding a thin piece of white paper between the subject and the light. If the hot spot remains, the light will need to be painted much like one would paint an outdoor crime scene. The photographer can close down the aperture to a smaller opening, thus creating a need to extend the image's exposure time. During the exposure, light can be swept back and forth across the subject improving the evenness of light recorded in the final image. This technique is explained and demonstrated further in Chapter 4.

Another drawback in using flashlights is that because they are typically incandescent, they will stain an image yellow. This yellow stain can be compensated for with a Wratten 80A or 80B blue-tinted filter. The choice of filter will depend on the color temperature of the particular light source. Digital cameras provide an easier fix because the photographer can simply set the white balance for incandescent lighting. LED flashlights are becoming more common and generally possess a more color-correct, white light. Some LED lights may actually create a blue hue in the final recorded image. As a result, photographers should take test photographs with any new flashlight or any other light source in order to be aware of any shift in color. Testing one's equipment can also help with determining the light source's intensity and how that may affect one's exposure.

In conclusion, crime scene investigators should seek out those opportunities to photograph difficult-to-capture subjects at every opportunity. Not only is it mandatory for quality documentation purposes and a thorough scene investigation, but it will also instill the photographer's professionalism and dedication into the minds of the viewers—especially the jurors. Mastering control over a subject's lighting is the most difficult part of capturing problematic pieces of evidence. However, with a little practice and determination, a photographer can create stellar evidentiary images.

Kodak's Top 10 Tips for Better Photographs

Applying artistic and popular photography recommendations to the business of crime scene photography can only help improve one's photographic skill and ability. Imitation is the sincerest form of flattery, and investigators can review popular photography magazines and books for innovative and imaginative ideas concerning lighting, composition, depth of field, and inventive equipment in order to improve their photographic results. George Eastman and his Eastman Kodak Company first introduced the public to snapshot photography in 1888 with the slogan, *You press the button, we do the rest.* Since then, Kodak has led the way in popular and professional photography with cutting-edge developments in everything from cameras and film to image development. In a continuing attempt to improve the results of photographers around the world, Kodak offers its *Top Ten Tips* for better pictures. The following tips can be applied to crime scene photography just as easily as to popular photography:

1. *Get down on the subject's level.* When taking pictures of children and animals, the photographers should get down on the level of their subjects and look them in the eyes in order to capture more interesting compositions. This is easily applied to crime scene photography (Figure 3.4). Evidence is often found lying on the ground or along baseboards and can be captured quite effectively if the crime scene photographer is willing to get down to its level. Some investigators are blessed with an abundance of equipment and specialty lenses that can improve the quality of most photographic endeavors. Unfortunately, many investigators are given only the basics and may only have one zoom lens, typically a 28–80 mm (18–55 mm with cropped-sensor digital cameras) focal length lens. When a small piece of evidence, such as a fired cartridge case, is resting on the ground, photographing it from a standing position will create a rather boring and uninformative picture. Even with the camera's lens zoomed out to the 80 mm focal length, the size of the cartridge case may only make up a very small proportion of the overall image. When 90% of the image is merely the floor or ground upon which the subject rests, what kind of priority does this image portray about the evidence depicted? The viewer may also question whether the real subject of the image is the ground. Even without having a macro lens, a basic 28–80 mm lens is capable of capturing a quality image, where evidence is identifiable and can be placed into context within the crime scene. A photographer must make the most out of his or her equipment and fill

Figure 3.4 Getting down at the same level as the evidence adds creativity into one's photographs. In addition, important and informative background information can be added to the image. This figure illustrates how a small change in perspective can enhance and multiply the amount of detail contained within a photograph. (Photographed by Andrew Taravella, Crime Scene Investigator, Houston Police Department, Houston, TX.)

the camera's viewfinder with the subject, even if it is from a difficult position. By following Kodak's first suggestion and positioning one's camera at the same level as the evidence, more creative and informative images can be captured.

Photographing evidence from different perspectives will also provide investigators the best opportunity to understand the crime scene and give prosecutors the opportunity to select the most optimum image to illustrate the crime scene to the jury. Although a selection of images can be recorded with a little artistic creativity, one should not eliminate the classic *eye viewpoint* positioning of the camera in documenting the crime scene. Additionally, providing a selection of photographs for the prosecutor to choose from will help alleviate any issues that may arise in court as far as prejudicial bias.

2. *Use a plain background.* Having a distracting background can ruin what otherwise would be a good picture. There are times when the background is more confusing than it is illuminating. When the goal of an image is to bring the viewer's eyes directly to a single subject or piece of evidence, the background should be out of focus and/or plain (Figure 3.5). Large apertures and longer focal lengths help cause the background of an image to become unrecognizable (shallow depth of field). When photographing evidence in a laboratory setting, it is much easier to control the background than when operating in the field. When at the crime scene, investigators, patrol officers, and *rubbernecking* onlookers will routinely be found in the background, and it can benefit the final photographic product if these parties are removed from in and around the crime scene.

If the distractions cannot be physically removed, one way to blur the background of an image and make it more plain is to narrow one's depth of field. This is easily accomplished by opening the lens' aperture, choosing a longer focal length, and getting in close to the subject. All three depth-of-field reducing actions do not necessarily have to be applied to a single image, but the background will be less recognizable and less distracting with each action selected.

Figure 3.5 Using a plain background eliminates distracting elements. Individual pieces of evidence can be placed on paper or fabric backgrounds as demonstrated here. Individuals should also be photographed against generic, plain backgrounds. Distracting backgrounds reduce the value of evidentiary photographs.

When working in the controlled-lighting environment of a laboratory, creating a plain background for individual pieces of evidence is rather easy. Place the evidence on butcher paper, against a photographic backdrop, or even on paper evidence bags that might be available. By removing distractions caused by equipment, scene notes, other pieces of evidence, or any distracting material from being visible in the photograph, the evidentiary value of the image is dramatically improved. Another common mistake by photographers is to hold evidence being photographed. This practice is not recommended because it opens up the evidence to attack in court. The evidence should be recovered and processed in a manner that preserves its integrity, and excessive handling of the evidence may cause that important principle of crime scene investigation to be in question. The close-up photographing of individual pieces of evidence is covered more thoroughly in Chapter 4.

Using a plain background is extremely important in the photographing of individuals, especially suspects. A bare wall, of a solid color, is preferable; however, the photographer needs to be sure that there is neither gang graffiti on the wall nor any other signs indicating a police presence. For example, crime scene tape, police officers, and marked patrol cars should be excluded from any part of the image's background. A defense attorney will have no problem showing bias toward his client and have the images excluded from evidence, if any photo arrays incorporate these items.

3. *Use a flash outdoors.* The use of a flash during outdoor and daytime exposures is one of the greatest tips a photographer can receive. Just because a camera's light meter tells the photographer an image has a proper exposure, the photographer should remember that the camera is attempting to find an exposure average (18% gray) and will not necessarily recognize areas of shadow that need added illumination. One aspect of capturing a quality photograph is the balance between shadows and

Figure 3.6 Shadows can be caused by any number of objects, from tent markers to vehicles. Daytime exposures will require flash from time to time. This figure illustrates the need to supplement daytime illumination with electronic flash even though the camera's metering system did not give an underexposure warning. Adding fill flash to a composition is about creating a balance between the shadows and highlights. The photograph was metered for the sun-exposed portion of the composition, and flash was added to the shadows in order to illuminate the hammer now visible underneath the dog house. (Photographed by Andrew Taravella, Crime Scene Investigator, Houston Police Department, Houston, TX.)

highlights. Filling in shadows with electronic flash, known as *fill flash*, is an excellent way to improve one's photographs (Figure 3.6). The first step is to recognize the presence of shadows or those areas that need additional illumination. A strobe flash typically will not be able to outproduce the sun in light production. Therefore, overexposing an image should not be of great concern. However, when in doubt, bracket the exposures by recording one with and one without supplemental flash.

The need for flash photography in the daytime is frequently underestimated. For example, merely photographing a person standing underneath a noontime sun may require fill flash. The overhead sun can cause small shadows in the eye orbits and beneath the nose, and these shadows can eliminate the visibility of a person's eyes and mouth. Wearing a hat can exacerbate problem shadows, creating large areas of blackness on the subject's face. In addition to photographing people, fill flash is extremely useful in general crime scene photography as well. Shadows can be caused by a number of things ranging from the actual subjects being photographed to the tent markers placed next to the subject by the crime scene investigator. It is imperative that investigators recognize the presence of these shadowed areas and compensate them by filling in the area with supplemental light (Figure 3.7).

Photographing evidence found on clear glass surfaces can also present problems for the camera's light meter and cause an image's capture to be underexposed. As an example, photographing a bullet strike to a glass window can create exposure problems for the photographer. Imagine a bullet strike to a window being photographed from the inside of a building or vehicle toward the outside. A scale ruler that is placed next to the impact site and a daytime photograph captured from an outward-facing perspective can cause an underexposure even though the camera's viewfinder indicates a proper exposure. The sun's light will tell the camera

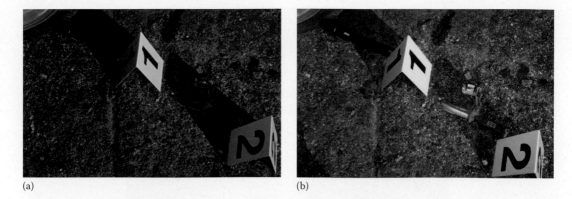

(a)   (b)

Figure 3.7 Even evidence markers can create unwanted shadows as observed in (a). (b) The image illustrates the need for fill flash to be added in some compositions in order to fill in the shadows and illuminate important subjects.

that no flash is needed to capture the image, but the sun is not going to be striking the scale or the glass window's interior surface. Consequently, additional light needs to be added to the composition in order to record a more informative image (Figure 3.8). Failing to add flash illumination is an example of how photographing in a full automatic or *Program* mode can seriously impede an investigator's photographic documentation process, because *Program* mode exposures do not account for the need to add fill flash.

4. *Move in close.* While working through a crime scene, photographs have a natural progression from an overall perspective to a close-up view of the evidence. The importance of getting in close and capturing in detail even the smallest piece of evidence or information is extremely important (Figure 3.9). In fact, the

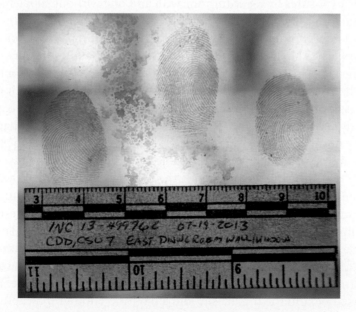

Figure 3.8 Adding flash to backlit subjects is extremely important to crime scene photographers. Fill flash was added to illuminate the scale and fingerprint visible on a glass window.

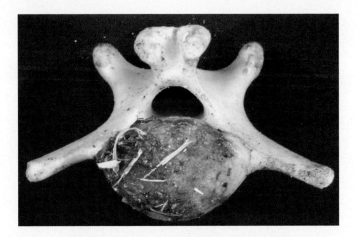

Figure 3.9 Quality close-focused images will enhance any case presentation. The keys to a distinctive image include a stable camera, proper illumination, and a desirable depth of field. Crime scene investigators responding to *found bone* calls for service are frequently required to determine whether the bones are human or animal. This photograph is of an animal's vertebrae and was recorded at ISO 100, f/36, for 6 s.

importance of capturing close-focused images is so great that Chapter 4 is solely devoted to this particular subject. Just as Eastman Kodak recognizes the value of close-focused images, their value is even greater for crime scene investigators.

Of primary importance is filling one's viewfinder with the subject or piece of evidence. Many times getting in close proximity to the subject causes issues with lighting and/or camera shake. A lack of proper macrophotography equipment might also be an impediment to investigators trying to record close-up images. Fortunately, there are solutions to each of these problems and they are addressed in much more detail in Chapter 4. For now, remember to capture as much detail as possible in the close up documentation of a crime scene's evidence. These images can be very helpful to jurors, especially if the evidence in question is bloody or reeks of body decomposition odors. Jurors may not want to handle some pieces of evidence, especially nauseating and putrid items. A sharp-focused, close-up image of the item will serve as an excellent substitute.

5. *Take some vertical pictures.* All too often, crime scene photographers get locked into only one way of capturing an image. The camera is always set to *Program* mode, each piece of evidence is photographed three times (overall, midrange, and close-up), and the camera is always held in the classic horizontal or *landscape* position for each and every photograph. However, thinking outside the box and adjusting to the crime scene's environment is very important in order to record the very best crime scene images possible (Figure 3.10).

One main objective is to fill the viewfinder with as much information as is practical. Many circumstances commonly encountered dictate a vertical or *portrait*-oriented camera. Rotating a camera to match the orientation of doorways and staircases is a common example (Figure 3.11). These passageways have a natural vertical orientation and should be captured as such. Investigators will often find themselves needing to orient their cameras in a vertical orientation simply to capture all the evidence within a single composition. This is especially useful when

Figure 3.10 The environment or location of the evidence should dictate whether a camera is held horizontally or vertically. This figure illustrates how evidence aligned in a vertical manner is enhanced by capturing the image in a similar orientation. Photographers should strive to fill the camera's viewfinder with the subject. This photo was recorded at ISO 400, f/22, for 1/20th of a second. Electronic flash was added to complete the exposure.

capturing midrange photographs and showing the relationships between different pieces of evidence. Relationship photographs require the composition of multiple pieces of evidence in the same image, and the photograph can sometimes be enhanced by rotating the camera 90°. For example, evidence from a car crash can be scattered down a long roadway and one should orient the camera to match the scene. Although Kodak's goal is to put variety into the photographer's work, crime scene investigations can actually dictate the photographer's need to change the camera's orientation.

6. *Lock the focus.* Most modern cameras have multiple focus points from which the camera will seek the nearest subject visible in the viewfinder on which to lock its focus upon (Figure 3.12). This can be problematic in crime scenes that are cluttered with furnishings, cars, evidence, etc. For example, one may want to focus on the body of a deceased person lying beneath a vehicle. However, the camera selects the rear quarter panel as the nearest object and the resulting image is ruined because the body is not in sharp focus. This occurs all too often. Locking the focus on the true subject is the photographer's responsibility. The photographer must not rely on the camera to establish the point of focus or the most important aspect of an overall image.

One way to lock in the focus is to preselect only one focus point in the viewfinder, instead of using the camera's entire range of focusing reticules. Optimally, the middle focal point should be selected simply because it is the easiest point in

Figure 3.11 Doorways present a challenge to photographers for a couple of reasons. First, the camera should be oriented in the portrait orientation. Secondly, lighting can be difficult. Frequently the lighting on either side of the threshold is different. This image was recorded with exposure settings of ISO 100, f/16, for 12 s. The doorway was illuminated with the one flash, while the middle room was painted with a second flash. Ambient light illuminated the room visible in the background.

Figure 3.12 Cameras with autofocus features will always seek out the first subject in order to set the focus. However, that may not always be the best choice. As in this image, focus should be locked onto the true subject of the photograph, which is located in the background.

the viewfinder to locate visually. Wherever that single point is placed is where the point of focus for the image will be. Just because the viewfinder's center reticule is chosen as the focal point does not mean that the center of every image must be the center of focus. *Locking the focus* refers to finding what the photographer wants in focus and locking that point into focus while he or she recomposes the image. Locking the focus in most cameras is done by simply pressing and *holding* the shutter-release button halfway down at the desired point of focus. The whole body of the camera can then be shifted or adjusted to a more desirable position and orientation. When the composition of the image is determined, depressing the shutter can be completed and the photograph captured. It is important to remember that a camera's autofocus feature always tries to identify the subject closest to the camera as its point of focus. Understanding this basic fact will help crime scene photographers recognize what their cameras are *seeing* and focusing upon during their operation. Manually focusing the camera is another way to ensure that the resulting image develops as planned. Be aware that in some cases, pressing the exposure button halfway not only locks the focus but also the exposure settings. This may cause exposure problems if the photographer is not careful.

Knowledge and control over an image's depth of field is another way to control the depth and the location of an image's focus. *Zone focusing* is an approach to focusing the camera by extending the depth of field over a predetermined range, incorporating the composition's subjects. At a given lens' focal length and chosen aperture, the depth of field's width will have a specific and known distance for the area of sharpest focus. This enables photographers to take their pictures with confidence and without worrying themselves about focus, as long as the subject(s) is within that span of sharp focus. This style of focusing can be extremely useful when your subject lacks contrast and the autofocus lens has difficulty zeroing in on a particular subject. Because focus is about distance, the crime scene investigator can also find a subject in the same focal plane or distance from the camera as the actual subject. The focus can then be locked in, the camera reoriented, and the image recorded. Whatever focusing technique chosen, it is the responsibility of the photographer to ensure that the image's focus is accurate and true.

7. *Move it from the middle*. The premise of *move it from the middle* is self-explanatory, move subjects away from the center of the composition. Crime scene investigators that treat photography more as a chore than as an opportunity typically take a minimum number of pictures, rely on automatic modes, and routinely place every subject square in the middle of their viewfinder. The impression created by a better composed image will elevate the crime scene investigator in the eyes of the image's viewers. By putting a little creativity into one's compositions and varying the subject's placement around the photograph's perimeter, an investigator's work will create more interest (Figure 3.13).

The *rule of thirds* is another popular photography technique that can be applied to crime scene photography. This photographic precept asks photographers to draw imaginary lines through the composition that divides the viewfinder into thirds, both horizontally and vertically. The image's primary subject should be positioned approximately where these imaginary lines intersect. In crime scene photography, evidence or subjects can be moved around to these four points in an image and still leave plenty of room for background information. Small apertures

Figure 3.13 Crime scene photographers are not required to have the evidence locked into the middle of every image. Moving the subject into the corners of a composition will create variety, interest, and lend innovation to one's images. Moving one's subject, in this case a Winchester 12 gauge shotgun shell, to a corner of the composition enables the photographer to incorporate more information about the surrounding area into the photograph.

assist in keeping a deep depth of field and protecting this connective bond between the image's foreground and background. The previous tip from Kodak, locking in one's focus, is an important prerequisite for moving subjects around the perimeter of the viewfinder while still maintaining a sharp-focused photograph.

8. *Know the flash's range.* Flash photography is really not as difficult as many people believe. Of prime importance is knowing the range (strength) of the flash (Figure 3.14). In other words, photographers need to know how far their flash

Figure 3.14 Photographers must know the capabilities and limitations of their electronic flash, including exactly how far it can reach into a composition. In this photo, a flash was used to only illuminate the side of the police car found in the foreground. The background vehicles were illuminated by ambient light. Using the flash to illuminate the background would have caused a severe overexposure to the foreground. Instead, the flash was cast from the side of the camera and perpendicular to the police car in order for the light to have just one target to illuminate.

will reach in order to properly illuminate a subject. This is a major problem with point-and-shoot cameras when investigators attempt to use them at nighttime crime scenes and do not recognize that pop-up-style flashes may only be able to illuminate a subject 10–15 ft away. The distance a flash can operate depends on the ISO setting and aperture chosen by the photographer. An ISO setting of 400–800 will be able to record light from greater distances than an ISO setting of 100 or 200. However, one must be careful not to overexpose the foreground when trying to reach something in the far background of an image. In addition to faster ISO speeds, more powerful external flashes can reach farther out into a scene, but overexposing the foreground is still quite possible. General flash photography techniques and avoiding problems such as overexposing the foreground are discussed in Chapter 6.

One common photographic error that illustrates this photographic tip occurs at every major sporting event, whether it is the Olympics, the Super Bowl, or at a ballgame when some baseball slugger is setting another steroid-enhanced milestone. Shutterbugs sitting in the upper decks of colossal stadiums routinely try to capture the activities on the playing field from hundreds of feet away using a flash exposure. Although the flashing of thousands of lights appears impressive on television, the only thing reached by the flash illuminations is the bald-headed spectator 10 rows in front of the camera. If an image is recorded, it is not because of the flash exposure but rather due to the stadium's ambient lighting.

9. *Watch the light.* A photographic image cannot be recorded without light. Therefore, light is everything to a photographer, and all of its characteristics and attributes must be understood and appreciated so that exceptional crime scene images are recorded. When evaluating a crime scene for lighting, a photographer should observe how light falls onto a scene and, specifically, how it falls onto individual items of evidence. The photographer should also observe not only where the light falls but also where it does not, that is, the shadows. Be aware that shadows are not only an issue in daylight, they are present in nighttime environments as well. Light has many properties, including
    a. Color
        i. Color of the light source
        ii. Color balance setting on camera (or filtration)
    b. Directionality
        i. Angle of light (oblique or direct lighting)
        ii. Single source of light, possibly creating shadows
        iii. Multiple light sources alleviating shadows
    c. Intensity
        i. Distance from source
        ii. Focused beam or broad casting of light
        iii. Contrast between highlights and shadows

Because of light's importance to photographers, the properties and characteristics of light will be discussed repeatedly throughout this text.

Light consists of a multitude of colors and crime scene investigators must understand the relationship between the primary colors of light: red, blue, and green. The color of the light becomes important during nighttime crime

Figure 3.15 This image is of a red-colored M&M® bag. The photograph was recorded in B&W and through a Wratten # 25 red filter. The red filter lightened the color of the red M&M so that the powdered fingerprint was visible through the dark red–colored candy icon.

scenes, photographing with alternate light sources, and when using colored filters to enhance black-and-white images (Figure 3.15). The intensity of light also plays a part in nearly every photograph taken. The intensity is controlled by the combination of apertures and shutter speeds because these allow more or less light into the camera. Becoming comfortable with the reciprocal relationship between these two variables will greatly improve a photographer's work. Of course, these two variables combine with the camera's ISO value (camera's sensitivity to light) in order to determine the total amount of light used to create an image.

The direction in which light is cast onto a subject also plays a number of important roles in crime scene photography. Photographing impression evidence and painting with light exercises at nighttime crime scenes will be made much easier through an understanding of how the directionality of the light affects the final recorded image. Purposefully directing light into or across a crime scene or individual piece of evidence from multiple angles can help remove distracting shadows from concealing evidence (Figure 3.16a and b). On the other hand, purposefully casting a single direction of light across a piece of indented-impression evidence can create shadows that help identify that piece of evidence (Figure 3.17).

10. *Be a picture director.* A crime scene investigator typically cannot return to a crime scene and find it in the exact condition as it was when first examined. This fact has been and will continue to be a basic principle of crime scene investigation. As a result, the initial photographic documentation of crime scenes is of utmost importance and a major responsibility of crime scene investigators. This responsibility should not be taken lightly. If the pictures are out of focus, poorly exposed, or if specific photographs of evidence were forgotten, the responsibility lies in only one person. Therefore, the obligation of being a *picture director* belongs to the scene investigator. It is not uncommon for other investigators, patrol officers, and/or

(a)   (b)

Figure 3.16 (a) The image shows how valuable information can be hidden by compositions recorded by casting a single flash into a crime scene. (b) The image was recorded of the same composition. However, the light was cast across the subject from multiple directions, illuminating hidden evidence. Both images were recorded at ISO 100, f/16, for 15 s.

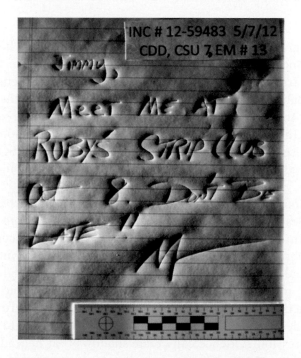

Figure 3.17 Oblique lighting is beneficial when trying to improve subjects that would profit by creating detail through shadows, such as the impression evidence. Light was painted across the indented writing sample by skimming the light across the paper's surface. The exposure was ISO 100, f/16, for 15 s.

family members to attempt to speed up the investigative process. However, it is essential that the scene is properly documented and processed, and this far outweighs the inconvenience to or for the accommodation of others. In conclusion, just as crime scene investigators need to take command and control of the crime scene, they must also take control of the true and accurate photographic documentation of the crime scene.

Figure 3.18 The documentation of a crime scene must establish the location and the evidence in the minds of those that have never visited the area. Establishing the scene with the image's viewers requires the photographer's ability to compose a quality image, as well as take control over the camera's controls. This image was recorded at ISO 100, f/7.1, for 30 s. The ISO value (100) was chosen to capture the sharpest, most colorful image. The shutter speed (30 s) was chosen so that the water would appear to be moving in the image, and the aperture was suggested by the camera in order to record an accurate light balance.

In addition to the compositional responsibilities of the crime scene investigator, he or she must also give the camera *direction* by choosing the exposure values that record an image in the best possible light, literally and figuratively (Figure 3.18). Photographers need to decide which exposure variable is most important to control for each composition and which variable is least important. Whether it is the image's color (ISO value), depth of field (aperture), or a photograph's motion (shutter speed) that is most important is up to the photographer, and once two of the three variables have been chosen, then the camera's light meter can assist in determining the third unknown value in order to capture a well-exposed photograph.

Bracketing

The cost of film should never outweigh the value of completely documenting the crime scene. And with the ever-increasing employment of digital imaging in the documentation of crime scenes, no one should limit the number of photographs recorded during any investigation. Bracketing is a crucial step in the complete documentation of a crime scene. Two pictures are always better than 1, and 10 pictures are better than 2. Although digital cameras provide the instant gratification of knowing whether or not an image appears well illuminated and in focus, the small review screens cannot always provide the type of accuracy one demands in the final printed image. Bracketing occurs across a number of variables found in photography. Lighting is first and foremost. In fact, most new model cameras have an autobracketing feature that makes it easier to photograph a subject at different exposure levels. However, this only scratches the surface of image bracketing.

Bracketing helps ensure that the best possible image is captured. When presented in court, bracketed photographs not only help the jury understand the dynamics of the crime scene but also help them see and appreciate the professionalism and dedication of the crime scene investigator's work. Because very few subjects outside of the laboratory are perfectly illuminated by studio lighting, bracketing is an absolute necessity in order to find the right balance between shadows and highlights. Automatic modes try to find a balance, but it is only what the camera believes to be a proper exposure. The camera is not perfect and can make exposure evaluation errors. Capturing one image in the automatic mode or with the camera's meter set to *zero* (18% gray) is a great place to start. However, this is only the beginning, especially for those important or key photographs. At least two additional photographs of the same subject should be captured, one picture should add light to the image and one should subtract light. The amount of light added or subtracted is up to the photographer and largely depends on the subject. On bright, sunny days where there are many shadows, a two-stop correction may be needed to ensure that both the highlights and shadows are accurately recorded. On the other hand, cloudy days have much less contrast and may not require such a drastic compensation. A one-stop change in exposure may be all that is needed. The bracketing for lighting may not always involve ambient light. Bracketed images can include the addition of fill flash or some type of painting with light technique in order to improve the image. Bracketing exposures will help ensure a quality captured image. It bears repeating that one should not always rely on the camera's light meter or the image review screen to guarantee that an accurate photograph was recorded.

The media on which the image is recorded is another factor that affects how much bracketing is required. Color-print film has an exposure latitude of approximately two stops of light. Black-and-white film can have an exposure latitude as much as three stops of light. Ultimately, this means that a photographer can underexpose or overexpose an image by as much as two stops and still obtain a quality image. Therefore, bracketing exposures by two full stops in either direction of what the camera shows as 18% gray is an excellent way to ensure that the absolute best photograph is recorded. However, digital cameras recording in the JPG mode do not have as much latitude as print film. Metering exposures with digital cameras is more like photographing with slide film, in that the latitude for exposure errors is typically between one-half to one full stop of light. Therefore, bracketing with a digital camera may actually require that more photographs be taken of an important subject than what might be required if film was the recording media. For example, when photographing a subject with a great deal of contrast with a digital camera, a series of five images might be necessary. The first image would be the 18% gray or zero-balanced exposure as suggested by the camera, but then a pair of exposures with plus and minus one stop and plus and minus two stops of light should be recorded to ensure a complete range of exposures is recorded. Not until the images are printed or viewed full size can the best image be selected. Granted, image enhancement programs such as Adobe Photoshop® can correct minor errors in exposure, but the goal of the crime scene photographer should be to capture quality images, not create them with a computer.

In addition to the bracketing of exposures for light, it is important to bracket for items such as the point of focus within the image and the orientation of the camera to the subject. As will be discussed later in this chapter, control over an image's depth of field separates a snapshot from an exceptional crime scene photograph. Unfortunately, there will be times when circumstances make it impossible or impractical to get every piece of evidence in sharp focus within a single photographic image. When those times present themselves, bracketing the points of focus is the most efficient solution to the dilemma. Photographing from the same perspective or position, set the camera's focus on each level or at different depths across the crime scene and record a series of images with the point of focus placed at different points throughout the length of the location. By recording a series of images with the *zone of focus* or depth of field adjusted through the series of recorded images, the photographer guarantees that the entire scene or subject is in focus in at least one of the images. This will ensure a complete and accurate recording of the crime scene and help viewers of the images observe how the pieces of evidence relate to one another. One can also change the camera's viewpoint or relationship to the subject in order to help capture a full series of sharp-focused images. Adjusting perspective is another way in which to bracket exposures. Changing the physical location of the camera, whether by climbing onto a rooftop or lying on the ground while taking a picture, will also enhance the overall documentation of a crime scene. Furthermore, important subjects should be photographed at different angles in order to show the different relationships between the item and its environment.

Overall Crime Scene Photography

Before attempting to close focus on individual pieces of evidence, the entire crime scene should be fully documented with photography. This may seem an unnecessary or redundant statement, but far too often investigators zero in on the evidence found at a crime scene and fail to document its relationship to the overall scene or other pieces of evidence. Overall scene photography is often overlooked and undervalued as a step in the scene's documentation process. The photographer must always remember that the juror was not at the crime scene and needs to be shown the layout of the entire site. Therefore, photographic documentation of the crime scene must be complete and thorough, including a comprehensive view of the location.

Working crime scenes in a consistent and organized pattern will help prevent the accidental omission of valuable pieces of photographic evidence. Photographing a crime scene from a general to specific manner is logical and recommended. A crime scene's *overall* or *long-range* photographs are meant to establish the location in a concrete manner for the viewers. When photographing the area surrounding a crime scene, the investigator should look for *scene identifiers* that definitively place the crime scene within the jurisdiction in which the investigator works. Obviously the most common scene identifier is a street sign. Hopefully, the street signs are still present and facing in the correct direction (Figure 3.19).

Other items routinely disregarded in the overall crime scene photographs are subjects that can help investigators and prosecutors with their investigations. Photographing scene identifiers such as street signs is clearly an important aspect of documenting a crime scene, but photographing the location's identification information is just as important. For example, information from business and property signs can be of value at a later time during the investigation. Questions that arise during a probe into criminal activity can be quickly answered if the name of the property's management, alarm company, or other property information is readily available in photographic form. Other items of value are the maps of properties found at the entrances of apartment complexes, warehouse districts, and commercial shopping centers. Photographs of these maps can be enlarged for testimony and used to point out the locations of witnesses, routes of travel by fleeing suspects, etc.

In order to record a complete 360° view of the location, a minimum of four photographs should be taken. The street sign or other scene identifier should be placed along one edge of the camera's viewfinder in each of the four photographs, and these photographs should then be captured facing the four points of the compass: north, south, east, and west.

Figure 3.19 It is important to record all aspects of a crime scene and specifically where it is located and any nearby landmarks.

By so doing, a complete 360° view is obtained along with a common reference point from which to connect the images. The number of photographs taken at a crime scene should never be limited, and it is conceivable that while investigating more involved incidents, this 360° panoramic capture might be taken at a number of points along the location's perimeter. Furthermore, a 360° series of photographs should be recorded from the crime scene's focal point (i.e., point of entry, location of the body), and these photographs should be looking outward across the scene. These can become valuable when a witness surfaces after the scene is released and investigators want to confirm or refute if the witness had a clear line of sight and could actually see what they claim to investigators.

In the end, the photographer should avoid tunnel vision by zeroing in or focusing in on particular pieces of evidence. Even though small pieces of evidence might not be clearly visible in the *big picture*, the establishing nature of the photograph is still valuable. For example, a violent crime may have occurred inside an individual apartment's bedroom. Investigators must still photograph the exterior of the apartment and points of access, including access into the apartment complex itself. In other words, think big and progress small. Documenting the scene from general to specific will assist investigators in keeping a logical progression of the photographic documentation of the crime scene. One should not ask whether or not a photograph *should* be recorded; rather, one should always take the picture and the only question to be asked is whether or not enough photographic images were recorded of a particular subject. Ultimately, the photographer should think of the investigator, prosecutor, and/or jury member that were not at the crime scene and photograph the overall and entire location for them.

Panoramic View Compositions

Another effective way to document the overall crime scene is to create a panoramic view of the location (Figure 3.20). This is easily done by connecting a series of photographic images to form one larger image. Software that can effortlessly connect different images together in such a manner is available and many times is bundled with the digital camera's software.

Figure 3.20 This figure is a compilation of eight digital images recorded and *stitched* together to form one panoramic image. Photographs can be automatically merged and stitched together by a number of different computer programs available to investigators. The camera should be tripod mounted, and approximately one-third of each photograph should be overlapped to aide in a smooth transition between individual images. The actual pixel size of this photo is 11,586 × 3,557 pixels.

However, even photographic prints can be pinned together on a bulletin or poster board in a way to give the viewer a better understanding and overall connective view of the location. As is the case with much of crime scene photography, photographing a panoramic view of a location requires a little planning and forethought. Preferably, the camera should be mounted upon a tripod in the approximate center of the crime scene's outside perimeter. The tripod helps ensure a stable platform from which to record the scene and helps prevent camera shake or blurring. A tripod-mounted camera also assists in keeping the images aligned and in maintaining the same perspective. Although digital images can be easily cropped, printed images pinned to a board can be somewhat disorienting if their borders fluctuate up and down across the final presentation.

Because panoramic photographs are taken at a distance, depth of field is typically not a major issue. Therefore, an advantageous aperture choice would be one in approximately the middle of the lens' range of apertures. An aperture of f/8 or f/11 is typically a safe and beneficial choice. Additionally, it does not matter whether it is daytime or nighttime as to the choice of aperture. Since the camera is mounted on a tripod, one only needs to increase the length of exposure time in low-light conditions. Ambient light photographs are better than flash exposures when trying to connect several nighttime images. Also, the individual pictures should overlap by approximately one-third in order to ensure a smooth transition from one photograph to the next. Therefore, when compiling a set of panoramic images, two neighboring images should have about one-third of their images in common with each other. If at all possible, movement from vehicles and/or individuals should be eliminated before the photographs are taken. If an individual is present in more than one location of the final stitched image, that event can distract the viewers from the intent of the photograph, which is to show the overall composition of the location.

Midrange or Evidence Establishing Photography

The goal of midrange crime scene photography is to illustrate and document the relationship between different pieces of evidence and between the evidence and the crime scene itself. It is in these relationship photographs that crime scene investigators can separate themselves from other shutterbugs. Depth of field plays a crucial role in capturing quality relationship images. By relying too much upon a camera's *Program* mode, a photographer is prevented from utilizing the full range of benefits afforded by smaller apertures. Cameras operating in an automatic mode tend to keep apertures large so that shutter speeds remain fast. The faster shutter speeds help prevent camera shake during the exposure, but can seriously limit an image's zone of sharp focus. This bias toward larger apertures and faster shutter speeds is especially true in low-light conditions. In addition, a little artistry and creativity is more easily included in these midrange photographs when the photographer is capable of utilizing their complete range of apertures. Quality photographic images will only serve to impress a jury with the photographer's ability, professionalism, and dedication.

Single lens reflex (SLR) cameras, especially those manufactured more recently, have a number of *Program* and automatic modes that make picture taking an uncomplicated task. Unfortunately, operating in this automatic mode prevents photographers from taking control of their work, and they might as well be using a point-and-shoot camera purchased at the neighborhood department store. SLR cameras operated in a *Manual* mode offer the advantage of allowing the photographer greater control over their depth of field and exposure values. As a result, better compositions and recordings will be available to investigators, prosecutors, and jurors alike. At times, a quality photograph requires the minimizing of distracting backgrounds but more often requires an increase in the depth of field so that two pieces of evidence or information are both in the zone of sharp focus. This text is targeted for those with at least a basic understanding of photographic concepts, and consequently, control over one's depth of field should not be a foreign subject. However, as a review, depth of field and a composition's focus are discussed in the next section.

Depth of Field

Depth of field is a basic concept that should be understood by all crime scene investigators. This text is meant to expand the understanding of depth of field as well as to demonstrate ways in which a photographer can improve his or her efforts. As a review, depth of field is defined as the area of sharp focus surrounding a subject (Figure 3.21). This area or zone of sharp focus extends approximately one-third in front of the point of focus and two-thirds to the rear. This becomes important when photographing a series of subjects over an extended distance. Three key factors affect a photographer's depth of field or zone of sharp focus:

- Aperture
- Focal length of the lens
- Subject-to-camera distance

Aperture is the most straightforward factor affecting depth of field. The smaller the aperture, the greater the depth of field. The larger the aperture, the more shallow the depth of field. A deeper zone of sharp focus occurs with smaller apertures because the rays of light are more finely focused on the recording media as they pass through the narrower opening of the camera's lens. Remember that smaller apertures have larger f/stop (aperture) value numbers and vice versa.

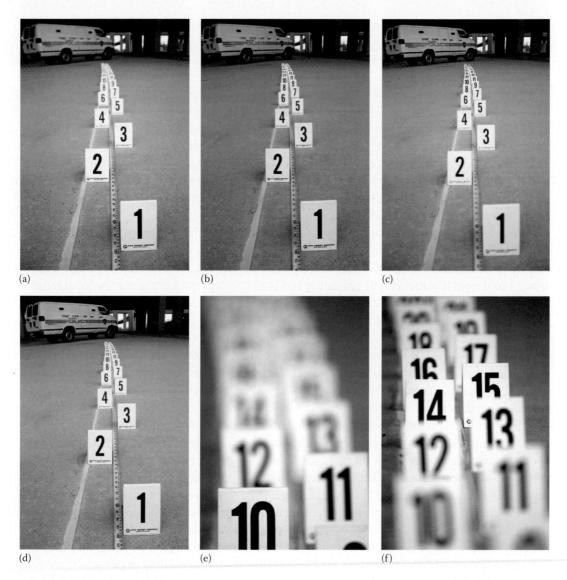

(a)   (b)   (c)

(d)   (e)   (f)

Figure 3.21 Depth of field is defined as the zone of sharp focus. Depth of field is affected by aperture, focal length, and the distance between the subject and camera. In (a) and (b), evidence markers were placed in 1 ft increments from the camera and recorded with a 28 mm focal length lens. The focus for these images was on evidence marker # 1. (a) This image was recorded with an aperture of f/3.5 and (b) with an aperture of f/22. Observe the difference in the sharpness of the evidence markers as they get further and further away from the point of focus. (c) and (d) These images were recorded in the same manner as (a) and (b), but the point of focus was moved 10 ft away from the camera and placed on evidence marker # 10. (c) This image was recorded with an aperture of f/3.5. (d) This image was recorded with an aperture of f/22. Notice how the depth of field extended much more to the rear for both images but still suffered toward the front when the image was captured with the larger f/3.5 aperture. Longer focal lengths and subjects physically closer to the camera lens will significantly decrease the zone of sharp focus. (e) and (f) These images were both recorded with an aperture of f/2.8 and with a 325 mm focal length lens. (e) This image was focused on evidence placard # 10, while (f) this image was focused on placard # 15. Observe how the zone of sharp focus is slightly better in the image focused 5 ft further away from the camera's lens, but the depth of field in both images is significantly reduced because of the longer focal length used to capture the images.

Everything in photography is about give and take. Aperture selection is so important in depth of field considerations, because the trade-off is time. And time does not have any effect on an image's focus. Some photographers may substitute a change in the ISO value instead of a change in time, and ISO values also have no effect on depth of field and focus. On the other hand, a lens' focal length and subject-to-camera distance are related to each other and both factors have an effect on depth of field. For example, if a photographer uses a wide-angle lens (28 mm) in order to increase the composition's depth of field, then the photographer may have to get closer to their subject in order to create the composition. Moving in closer to the subject will decrease depth of field, effectively cancelling out the benefit of using a wide-angle lens. Again, the trade-off with apertures is time, which does not affect depth of field and therefore is a very important feature of the camera to comprehend and use to one's greatest benefit.

One word of warning about very small apertures is that although they provide the best depth of field, they will require longer exposure times, which may necessitate securing the camera to a tripod or other stable platform. The rule of thumb is that one should never hand hold a camera if the shutter speed is any slower than one over the focal length. For example, if a photographer is capturing a subject with an 80 mm focal length lens, the shutter speed should be no slower than 1/90th of a second for a handheld capture. Some photographers may be able to push this limit slightly, while others may need to increase their shutter speeds in order to ensure a sharp image capture. This rule is and will be repeated because it is that important to remember. Because this rule of thumb is only a guide, photographers must critically evaluate their work in order to determine their individual capabilities and limitations.

The focal length of a lens will also affect an image's depth of field. With all else equal, longer focal lengths decrease a picture's zone of sharp focus, while wide-angle lenses increase it. One effective way to create an undistinguishable background is by creating a shallow zone of sharp focus with telephoto lenses. Because of their longer focal lengths, 200 and 300 mm lenses can effectively blur and eliminate a subject's background. Limiting depth of field and background helps draw the viewer's eyes directly to the subject of the photograph. This may be desirable when the background is distracting, such as when spectators are milling around and gawking outside the crime scene's barrier tape. At times, investigators may use the zoom feature in order to enlarge a subject in the viewfinder instead of physically moving closer to the object. Isolating the subject and bringing it to dominate the image is made easier by controlling one's depth of field and in this case making it quite shallow (Figure 3.22).

Getting up close and personal with the subject can have a detrimental effect on an image's depth of field. By shortening the distance between the camera and subject, depth of field is negatively affected. The zone of sharp focus shrinks as the camera gets closer to the subject. When the camera is only a few inches from a subject, depth of field can be as small as a few millimeters. Dealing with such extremes is covered in detail in Chapter 4. Smaller apertures can help offset the shrinking of the depth of field due to the close-focusing nature of macrophotography.

On the opposite end of the focus spectrum, every camera lens reaches a point where depth of field ceases to be an issue. Most every lens has an infinity (∞) mark on its focusing ring. At this point or distance from the camera and beyond, all subjects will be in sharp focus. This is not to say the foreground will be in the zone of sharp focus, but everything beyond the point of infinity and just before it will be in focus. Many camera lenses have a distance scale printed on the focus ring that tells the photographer at what distance infinity is

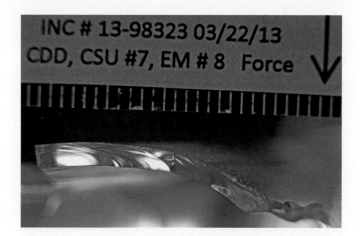

Figure 3.22 This figure is of the stress markings (Wallner lines) on the edge of a fractured piece of glass. The image was recorded with an aperture of f/4.0 in order to isolate the visibility of the fracture lines. An aperture of f/22 allowed for a deeper depth of field but obscured the visibility of the fracture lines because the focus extended through the glass and not just the Wallner lines on the top edge of the glass.

reached. If the infinity distance is not present on the lens, the information should be found in the owner's manual for that particular lens. Being aware of how distance affects one's depth of field and knowing how to compensate with proper aperture and focal length choices makes the difference between a simple snapshot and a valuable crime scene photograph.

Finding the right combination between camera-to-subject distance, focal length, and aperture is the artistic part of crime scene photography. Anyone can take snapshots of a cartridge case, but it is the artist who is able to include the legible image of the cartridge's head stamp in the image yet still have its relationship to the crime scene clearly visible. Out-of-focus images do not impress anyone, especially the jury, and it does not matter what caused the blurry nature of the photograph. The jury will judge the investigator by the careless, out-of-focus photographs they are shown. The investigator can explain in court about the depth of field and why something is not focused as sharply as it should be, but excuses should not be the lasting impression left with a jury. A sharp-focused image is of primary importance to the crime scene investigator, and control over a photograph's depth of field will go a long way toward improving the focus and overall quality of the final image (Figure 3.23).

Adding Artistic Flair

Midrange photographs can be improved with a little imagination, invention, and a touch of artistic flair. The perspective from which a photograph is taken can greatly improve the viewer's response to the image. Most often photographs are taken from eye level, and frequently that viewpoint is from a standing position. Unfortunately, that may not necessarily be the best way to capture the most informative and engaging image. A single piece of evidence lying on the ground and photographed from a standing position will only include a small portion of the overall scene because of the downward angle of the camera. This is especially true when a longer focal length is chosen, which further decreases the

Figure 3.23 The cartridge's head stamp is observed in the foreground as well as the ammunition box in the background. The photograph's depth of field was extremely limited because it was photographed through a 50 mm lens, with a 12 mm extension tube attached to the lens. Only a couple of inches separated the lens from the cartridge. An aperture of f/22 was chosen in order to extend the zone of sharp focus as far as possible.

angle of coverage by the camera's lens. However, the amount of background information can be significantly enhanced by changing one's perspective (Figure 3.24). Many times this requires the crime scene investigator to get down and dirty with the evidence during the scene's investigation. Kneeling or even lying on the ground to capture the subject from the same level as the evidence can create exceptional and captivating images. Not only can particular pieces of evidence be enlarged in the viewfinder and ultimately the final image, but also the photograph's background can be added to the composition in order to increase the informative value of the photograph. The image's main subject can

Figure 3.24 Changing the perspective from which a photograph is recorded cannot only add valuable information to the image's composition but can also increase the interest and impressiveness of the overall photograph's composition. Photographing from on top of structures, bridges, and balconies is one way to document the crime scene from different perspectives. Photographing from the ladder of a fire department's ladder truck and photographing from helicopters are other ways to record images from elevated positions.

Figure 3.25 Another way to enhance the scene's documentation is to get on the same level as the evidence, choose a small aperture (f/22), and show the relationship between the sharp-focused subject (fired cartridge case) and the background (nightclub). Furthermore, just because the sun goes down does not mean that small apertures cannot be chosen. The exposure settings for this image were ISO 400, f/22, for 8 s.

be magnified because one is not positioning the camera 5 ft away from the subject during capture as happens when standing upright and photographing something lying on the ground. The background is also enhanced because instead of a single piece of evidence being surrounded by boring asphalt or flooring, the change in perspective allows the crime scene to become the backdrop for the subject. Furthermore, since the purpose of midrange photography is to show relationships between pieces of evidence and the crime scene, the value of these types of images becomes much greater (Figure 3.25).

In conclusion, investigators should strive to record midrange photographs with smaller apertures. Smaller apertures are most often preferred because they are better able to show relationships between evidence and the crime scene. Naturally, smaller apertures require longer exposure times with all else being equal. The longer exposures may require that the camera be supported in some manner other than by just the photographer's hands. Even the simple depressing of the shutter-release button can cause the camera to shake or move during an exposure. Therefore, in order to ensure a sharp-focused image without camera shake, a tripod-mounted camera and a remote shutter or cable release are recommended. A crime scene photographer will greatly improve midrange image capture through the control of the aperture, camera orientation, and image composition.

Close-Up Photography

Before the collection of any evidence from a crime scene can take place, investigators must document all exhibits from an overall to a close-up perspective. There are several levels of close-up photography that occur during a crime scene investigation (Figure 3.26). The first begins at the physical crime scene. The next commences after the investigator departs the immediate crime scene and involves his or her capturing images in a more controlled environment. The final level of close-up photography is known as *examination quality* imaging. Examination quality photographs can be taken at either the physical location where

Figure 3.26 Close-up photographs are imperative to achieving the complete and thorough documentation of a crime scene. Keys to capturing quality photographs are a stable camera, filling the viewfinder with the subject, and providing the viewer with some sort of identification for the evidence. This photo demonstrates the use of pointer arrows to highlight the small blood spatter stains found on the jacket.

the evidence was found or in a controlled environment, such as a laboratory. Examination quality photographs are those intended for comparison purposes or other detailed analysis. Because the recording of these more refined images requires additional care and planning, they are discussed in Chapter 4.

Close-Focused Images Recorded at the Crime Scene

The complete and thorough photographic documentation of a crime scene should not be limited by the fear of taking too many photographs. It may seem redundant to photograph individual pieces of evidence repeatedly, from different angles, with a variety of light sources, and at different camera settings for aperture and shutter speed, but the value will become clear when it is time to testify in front of a jury. Do not worry; not every single picture will be paraded in front of 12 bored jurors. Prosecutors will only show a select number of photographs to the jury, but those images must be the absolute best possible recordings. It is easy for an investigator to envision a complicated crime scene in his or her mind having physically been there. However, other investigators, prosecutors, and viewers of the crime scene photographs may not have been at the physical location of the crime, and they need to have a comprehensive grasp of both the incident, layout of the crime scene, and the recovered evidence. From that standpoint, close-focused images cannot be overlooked due to some false sense of security created by the fact that the overall and midrange photographic documentation of evidence is complete.

Two important elements go into making a good close-up photograph: filling the viewfinder with the subject and a sharp-focused image. These aspects may seem elementary, but sadly, they are often overlooked or ignored by crime scene investigators.

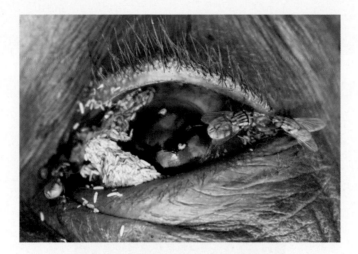

Figure 3.27 This image is of freshly deposited maggots in the eye socket of a recently deceased person. Although the subject matter is difficult, it is important to get in close and personal with a composition's subject.

Getting close to the subject may be difficult at times. In fact, it can be downright disgusting, especially when trying to photograph a fired cartridge case lying in a pile of brain matter or attempting to document flies and maggots crawling across a decomposing body. However, as nauseating as such photographs can be to record, the image must be photographed (Figure 3.27). These two examples also illustrate the frequent requirement to rephotograph pieces of evidence in a controlled environment. The cartridge case resting in brain matter may have its head stamp covered in blood and the information obscured. One picture needs to show the condition in which the casing was found, and a second picture should identify the ejected cartridge case, for example, identifying it as a Remington-Peters 9 mm Luger. Likewise, maggots and flies are photographed crawling across rotting flesh in order to show the environment in which they were found, but there is also a need to photograph them in greater detail so that entomologists can identify the species. Forensic entomologists may not necessarily make specific identifications from photographs, but at least when it comes to testify in court, they will have a better piece of demonstrable evidence to explain their scientific determinations. An 8 × 10 glossy photograph of a *Chrysomya rufifacies* (hairy maggot blow fly) is an effective piece of demonstrative evidence that jurors can use to understand the fly species' characteristics being testified about (Figure 3.28).

Filling the viewfinder with the subject may be difficult for some investigators merely because they do not have the appropriate equipment. Financial realities and fiscal responsibilities abound in the public sector, especially when working with government agencies. Compounding the problem, command staff personnel unfamiliar with the duties and requirements of crime scene investigation often are the ones who make decisions on what equipment will be purchased. These decisions are frequently based solely on the cost, not what would work best for investigators, with the result that a majority of investigators are likely to be limited to a basic 28–80 mm lens for film cameras or a comparable lens for digital cameras (18–55 mm). Consequently, investigators often must purchase their own photography equipment or construct less-expensive alternatives. Standard lenses can only get so close to the subject. One may be able to record an adequate photograph but not a

Figure 3.28 A quality close-focused image fills the camera's viewfinder and has sharp focus throughout the subject. This image was recorded at ISO 400, f/22, and the exposure lasted for 85 s as light was painted onto the subject with a small (single-bulb) LED flashlight.

spectacular photograph. Using diopters and extension tubes are less-expensive alternatives to costly macro lenses and will allow photographers to capture quality close-focused images. Diopters are glass elements or filters that are threaded onto the end of a camera lens and decrease the minimum focus distance of the lens, thereby increasing the size of the subject in the camera's viewfinder. Diopters or close-up filters can be individually purchased but are commonly sold as a set of three: +1, +2, and +4. The filters can be stacked to increase the magnification; however, because the elements are glass, they tend to soften the focus of the subject if all three elements are used for an enlargement.

Extension tubes are a little more costly but are an excellent way to get in close and photograph sharp, undistorted images. Extension tubes fit between the camera and the lens. These tubes can also be purchased individually or as a set. The elements can be stacked to increase magnification, but since they do not have glass elements, they do not negatively impact the recorded image. Although extension tubes are slightly more expensive than diopters, they are typically less expensive than a macro lens. As stated earlier, there is always a trade-off in photography. The use of extension tubes does produce sharper images over diopters, but will require more time during the exposure because of the reduction in light reaching the imaging chip or film plane.

The second element involved in recording quality, close-focused images is a stable camera. Camera shake or movement during an exposure can severely affect an image's crispness and frequently occurs when the shutter speed is set too slow for the focal length of the lens. Remember, the shutter speed needs to be equal to or faster than one over the focal length of the lens when hand holding the camera. Furthermore, smaller apertures are needed in order to offset the loss of depth of field caused by the shorter distances between subject and camera. Small apertures also will naturally require longer exposure times, and any lengthening of the exposure's time allows for more opportunity for camera shake to develop in the recorded image. The photographer must be aware of this possibility and be willing to support the camera in some manner. Tripods, minitripods, and beanbags are all tools that help stabilize cameras.

A more humorous approach to crime scene photography is presented by the investigator who bends over at the waist to photograph a piece of evidence lying on the ground. This unnatural position may keep his or her uniform pants clean, but it seriously jeopardizes the quality of the photograph. Furthermore, the camera is not being firmly supported and camera shake may develop in the image. In addition, the presence of the photographer's feet in the picture can be a problem. Although it may be uncomfortable to kneel or even lie down next to a subject, the value gained by a stable, blur-free image cannot be overemphasized.

Close-up photographs of the crime scene are obviously important. Less obvious is the necessity to include orientation and identification notations and markers in the recorded images (Figure 3.29). Although the midrange photographs should provide viewers with a general location of the evidence within the scene, close-up photographs can be enhanced by including additional orienting information. This is especially true with smaller pieces of evidence, such as bloodstains, bullet holes, and fired cartridge cases. Orientation markers and notations might include one or more of the following notations:

- Direction of north
- Direction of travel
- Height above floor or ground
- Evidentiary pointers
- Evidentiary scales and rulers
- Case number and date
- Photographer's identification

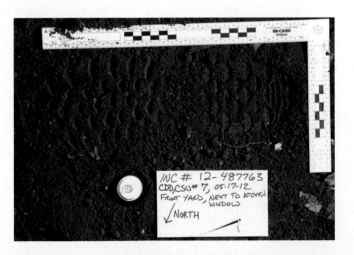

Figure 3.29 This photo illustrates the advantages of providing orientation to a subject within the scene. Not only is the direction of north clearly indicated, but the location of the footwear impression has also been documented in the photograph. As always, the more information included into a photograph the better.

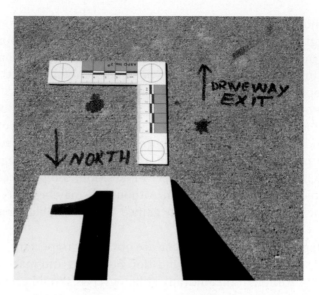

Figure 3.30 Sharpie markers are extremely useful and can assist viewers in recognizing the value and positioning of evidence as shown here.

Photographers can purchase commercially available products to add information to an image, but one of the best tools is a Sharpie® indelible marker (Figure 3.30). Scales, rulers, and other orientation markers are discussed in Chapter 4. Simply be aware that small, close-up photographs can suffer without orientation information included in the image's composition.

In conclusion, capturing superior close-focused images results from a combination of filling the viewfinder with the subject, having a stable camera, and controlling the image's depth of field. Although crime scenes can be dirty, blood-soaked environments, investigators must be willing to get close to and focus on the evidence. Photographers have a number of tools available to record captivating images; however, the primary tool is simply the desire to examine the subject and purposefully compose the image for a quality outcome. Specific close-focusing techniques found in Chapter 4 can be applied to both photographs recorded at the crime scene and those recorded in a laboratory.

Close-Up Images Captured after Leaving the Crime Scene

Documenting evidence found on crime scenes requires that it not be disturbed during the photographic process. Therefore, the subjects must be photographed as they are found, and because of this guiding principle, not all facets of smaller pieces of evidence may be observed due to their positioning. Evidence can be caked in mud or blood, or it can be half-buried in a wall or floor or merely oriented in a way that makes photographing it from an informative angle impractical. When this occurs, it becomes necessary to recover the item and, prior to submitting it into evidence, to take a more detailed photograph. This is another opportunity for a crime scene investigator to demonstrate his or her talent because photographs taken in a controlled environment allow the photographer to more easily adjust the lighting and composition of an image. Even the investigator who does not

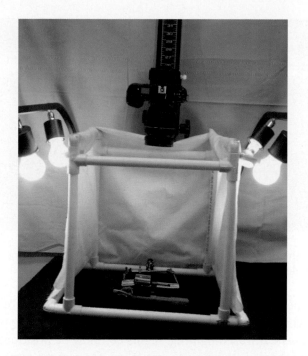

Figure 3.31 A homemade light box or cube can be constructed from parts costing approximately $25.

have a fully equipped laboratory or an evidence processing station to work with can still capture captivating and informative pictures. Crime scene investigators simply have to create their own controlled environments.

Professional light studios can cost upward of a thousand dollars but are extremely beneficial when photographing smaller subjects. Even portable light studios and light boxes can cost hundreds of dollars. Most publicly funded agencies do not have access to high-priced equipment and must consider less-expensive alternatives. A common theme among agencies is *do more with less*, and with a little imagination and creativity, photographers can build their own light boxes/studios for far less than a purchased one would cost. A light box (Figure 3.31) is basically a skeletal box frame covered with a monotone, translucent material. A box frame is easily created with PVC (polyvinyl chloride) pipe. A PVC-framed light box can be easily and cheaply constructed with the following list of materials:

- Two 10 ft lengths of pipe (¾″ or ½″)
- Eight "T" connectors
- Eight 90° connectors with one end tapered to fit the "T" connectors
- Two cubic yards of fabric in white, black, and gray
- Four or more clothespins

The tubing can be either ½″ or ¾″ pipe. The ¾″ is more rigid and costs a little more. The ½″ pipe is lighter and a little more flexible but is sufficient to support the fabric. Attach each 90° angle to one end of the "T" connector. These eight connectors become the corners of the cube or light box. Cut the PVC pipes into 12 equal lengths. The 12 lengths of pipe will constitute each edge of the cube, and the length at which they are cut depends on

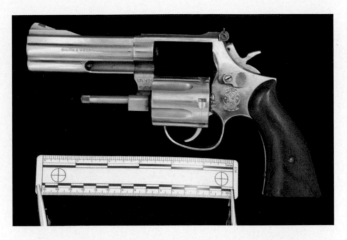

Figure 3.32 Soft lighting and a contrasting background provide the perfect combination to capture exquisite evidentiary photographs.

the photographer's needs and available space. However, 12″ lengths of pipe provide a very nice sized cube in which to position evidence for imaging. The white fabric can be draped around the box to create diffused lighting. Lights can now be positioned to the side of the light box and shone through the translucent fabric for a more even and balanced light presence. The black and gray fabric can be used to create the plain background for the photograph's subject (Figure 3.32). For items that are wet or saturated in blood, place butcher paper or some other form of barrier into the light box instead of the cloth.

Sheets of plain fabric can be used as alternatives to expensive backdrops that are purchased from photo supply businesses. These backdrops can be used inside the photo cube, but they can also hang up on a wall and used as a backdrop for the photography of people. At a cost of $2–$3 a square yard, different colored linens and cloths found at craft stores are inexpensive yet effective alternatives. Three basic colors are recommended: black, white, and gray. Additional colors can be purchased for specific photographic needs, but these three colors will provide contrast to any subject that may need to be photographed. The gray fabric should be consistent with an 18% gray color but does not have to be exact.

A photo cube as described earlier can help image pieces of evidence with reflective surfaces such as jewelry, silverware, or anything with a reflective surface (Figure 3.33). These types of surfaces can be difficult to photograph because cameras, tripods, and other distracting backgrounds might be visible in the object itself. The fabric-covered PVC frame will eliminate much of the distracting background. Unfortunately, the camera and its support structure may still be visible. An easy, inexpensive solution is to purchase two pieces of foam core board, one black and one white. Cut the foam core to fit over the PVC cube and then cut a lens-sized hole into the middle of the board. Place the camera lens into the hole and focus on the subject. As a result, only the camera's lens should be visible in any reflections.

Lighting Close-Focused Subjects

Investigators must first understand and remember that cameras seek to capture images at 18% gray. The proper reciprocal relationship between aperture, shutter speed,

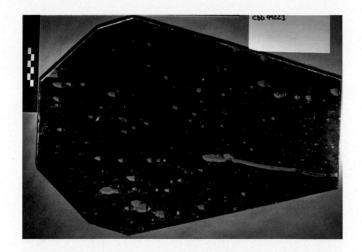

Figure 3.33 One cannot get much more reflective than a mirror. The bloodstains photographed on this mirror were recorded with light cast obliquely across the surface.

and the ISO value is found at 18% gray, and largely black or largely white subjects may cause the camera difficulty in determining an appropriate exposure. Although the camera will meter any subject and inform the photographer of the proper aperture and shutter speed combination based on the chosen ISO value, it may not always be accurate. For a vast majority of subjects, the camera's light metering system works extraordinarily well. However, the photographer may discover that an image is under- or overexposed. In difficult metering situations, it is important to bracket exposures. It is far better to have too many photographs of one subject than too few.

One way to ensure a quality light evaluation is to use a *gray card*. A gray card is a commercially available piece of plastic or cardboard that represents 18% gray. After the subject and camera are positioned for the best possible composition and focus, the gray card is placed just above the subject. Ideally, it will fill the camera's viewfinder. If the viewfinder is not completely covered by the gray card, an inaccurate exposure determination may occur. If the gray card cannot fully cover the viewfinder, the photographer should select the spot metering feature on the camera so that the camera will only meter the light falling in the very middle of the viewfinder. The light falling on the gray card can now be metered and the ISO value, shutter speed, and aperture set. Once the gray card is removed, the camera may tell the photographer that an image is going to be over- or underexposed. However, the image captured will have a more precise light evaluation because the camera previously evaluated the light value from the gray card. This technique is best accomplished in the *Manual* capture mode, because when photographing in the *Program* mode, one risks the chance of the camera reverting back to an incorrect exposure once the gray card is removed.

The manner in which light is cast onto a subject is also important. Diffused or softened light can improve many photographic endeavors, but there will also be times when light must be projected across, through, or into a subject. For example, indented writings, footwear, and tire wear impressions need to have light cast on them at an oblique angle so that shadows create contrast, which allows details to be more clearly visible. In other situations, light might need to be projected into or through a subject, such as a gun barrel or US currency in an attempt to photograph a watermark (Figure 3.34).

Figure 3.34 Transmitted light is light that passes through a subject. Transmitted light was used to image the watermark present in a US $20 bill. The camera metered the light without any compensation (ISO 400, f/16, for 1 s).

There will be times when light is needed to reach into dark recesses and cavities. Gun barrels are an excellent example of this concept. Any number of items can be found down inside the barrel of a gun: blood, hair, gunpowder, dust, etc. In addition to documenting these findings in a written report, it is also possible, although somewhat challenging, to photograph something lodged deep inside a firearm's barrel. The first problem is the lighting. A gun barrel has two ends; light can be shone through one end and the photograph can be taken through the other. Because semiautomatic gun barrels can be removed and photographed apart from the weapon's frame, semiautomatic pistols are slightly easier to photograph than revolvers and rifles. However, revolvers, rifles, and shotguns can be photographed in a similar manner. To do so, align the camera's lens perpendicular to the muzzle end of the barrel. This is one image where manual focusing on the exact point of interest inside the barrel is suggested. Light can now be shone through the opposite end of the barrel. Because gun barrels are typically small in diameter, a small light source is necessary. A penlight flashlight may be adequate, but a flexible end, single-bulb LED flashlight is ideal. If the barrel is extremely long like those belonging to rifles, a larger light source may be necessary.

Once the light source is selected, the photographer needs to peer down the weapons' barrel through the viewfinder and set the focus on the trace evidence observed inside the barrel. The camera should be as close as possible to the barrel, using a macro lens, extension tubes, or diopters. The camera's aperture should be set to the smallest opening possible to compensate for the shortened distance between the subject and camera and to ensure the broadest zone of sharp focus. Once the camera's focus and aperture are set, the photographer needs to determine how best to position the light source. A light shining straight up the barrel toward the camera lens is not always the best alignment, especially with the shorter barrel lengths found on pistols. Directing the light down the barrel by bouncing it off the interior walls of the barrel is often the most effective. These bouncing techniques work best with chrome, light-colored, or polished barrels. Flat-black or matted-surface barrels can present more difficulty. However, trying various angles and repositioning the light source should provide at least one combination of light and subject that will enable the photographer to capture a true and accurate representation of the trace evidence found inside the weapon. The light used to illuminate the inside of a barrel can also be *painted*. Due to the smaller apertures necessary to increase the depth of field, the corresponding shutter speed (length of exposure) will be considerably longer than standard photographs of the weapon's exterior. Photographing with an ISO 100 or 200 setting will also require longer exposure times but is recommended so that the sharpest photograph is recorded. During the extended time the lens is open and the image is recording, the light source can be traced around the edge of the barrel opposite the camera. This results in more even lighting on all sides of the barrel and helps create a more accurate image. Bracketing the exposures for different lighting techniques is a must. Furthermore, the techniques for illuminating the inside of a gun's barrel can be applied to any difficult, hard-to-reach subject.

With the light source positioned, aperture selected, and the ISO set, the last variable is the shutter speed. With the light source stationary, the camera's meter can be used to provide an approximate length for the exposure. Bracketing is important because of the number of exposure variables involved. In addition to the close focusing and critical illumination of subjects such as these, bracketing should be done in one-half to one-full-stop increments. If painting the subject with light is necessary, additional bracketed exposures may be required. Having a steady hand in such a finely tuned endeavor is difficult, and the light may flash across the camera lens by accident, causing a hot spot or lens flair. There is always the opportunity for human error in these types of difficult compositions. Therefore, bracket, bracket, bracket the exposures. This mandate also applies to photographers utilizing digital cameras. Digital cameras have less exposure latitude than film, and contrary to popular belief, digital cameras frequently require bracketing more often than film cameras.

Photographing trace evidence found inside a gun barrel is just one example of a problematic photographic situation (Figure 3.35). Others will present themselves time and time again. However, whether it is a bullet strike found inside a wall, skin tissue stuck to a car's undercarriage, or bloodstains found in a sink's drain, the crime scene photographer is responsible for photographing every piece of evidence prior to collection. This basic principle of crime scene investigation is not negated because a particular photograph is too difficult or too inconvenient to capture. Remember, if something can be seen (and even if it is not visible), it can be photographed. Think through the problem. Determine how the camera can best be positioned, how best to illuminate the subject, and how to determine the proper exposure settings. Finally, bracket the exposures and be proud of the final results.

Conclusion

The complete photographic documentation of a crime scene requires effort, dedication, and innovative problem-solving abilities. The number of photographs taken should never be limited. When in doubt, take the picture. In fact, take a number of images, changing camera settings, lighting, perspective, etc. The photographer should never hesitate or fear taking photographs that may not develop into quality images. Through bracketing,

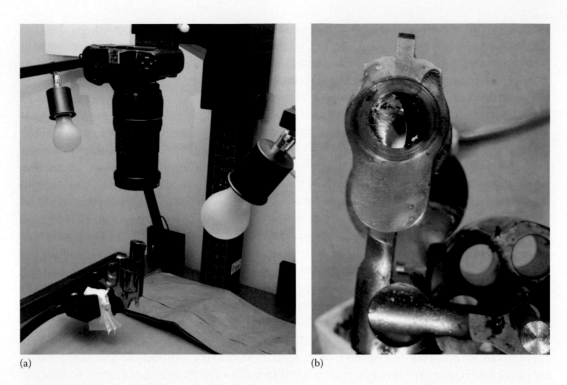

(a)   (b)

Figure 3.35 (a) This image shows how the camera was set up to take the photograph in (b). (b) This image was taken at ISO 100, f/36, for 1.3 s and shows the interior of a gun's barrel. This close-up photo shows the blood drawn back into the barrel after the weapon was fired while in contact with the victim. The light source used to illuminate the interior of the barrel was a single LED flexible-head flashlight.

a photographer is simply looking for that one, single image from a series of photographs that will be shown to a jury or used by investigators to put the pieces of a criminal puzzle together. This one image will demonstrate the crime scene investigator's knowledge, dedication, and professionalism to all who view it. This is especially important with jurors. The *CSI effect* has had a profound impact on the forensic community. Juries and the general public expect crime scene investigators to be able to find a pubic hair in a haystack. In addition, they expect to see perfectly exposed photographs depicting the crime scene and recovered evidence. These expectations must be met if an investigator wants to make a positive, lasting impression on the jury. The complete and professional photographic documentation of a crime scene is the best way to leave this lasting impression.

End of Chapter Questions

1. Which value is selected first in an exposure evaluation and combines with shutter speed and aperture to record a quality image?
   a. Exposure mode
   b. Light value
   c. f/stop
   d. ISO (film speed)

2. What is an audible sound photographers should be aware of when recording an image?
    a. *Beep* or *Beep-beep* sound when the proper focus is achieved
    b. *Beep* or *Beep-beep* sound when the proper exposure is achieved
    c. When a distinctive *click-click* of the shutter is heard
    d. All the above

3. What is the rule of thumb in regards to handheld photography?
    a. Two hands should hold the camera at all times.
    b. The shutter speed should not be any slower than one over the lens' focal length.
    c. The aperture should be the largest available.
    d. The camera should always be held in *landscape* orientation.

4. Which of the following is *NOT* conducive to improving one's photographic skill?
    a. Reading literature on general photography
    b. Attending educational courses in photography
    c. Utilizing the camera's full-automatic mode
    d. Reviewing past photography endeavors and assignments

5. What is the crucial element in photographing subjects in difficult areas of access?
    a. Desire
    b. Choice of shutter speed
    c. Choice of aperture
    d. Getting light onto the subject

6. Which of the following is *NOT* one of Kodak's *Top Ten Tips* for better photography?
    a. Use a plain background.
    b. Maintain shutter control.
    c. Take some vertical pictures.
    d. Lock the focus.

7. It is not necessary to use a flash during outdoor photography assignments as long as the sun is shining on the subject.
    a. True
    b. False

8. What does a camera's autofocus feature seek?
    a. Subject of composition
    b. Light
    c. Depth of field
    d. To focus on the closest object to the camera

9. What are the three primary colors of light?
    a. Red, blue, and green
    b. Red, blue, and yellow
    c. Cyan, magenta, and yellow
    d. Red, white, and blue

10. *Bracketing* one's exposures (photographs) refers to
    a. Proper grip and hand placement onto camera
    b. Recording multiple exposures of the same subject but in different ways
    c. Recording images in grayscale
    d. Ensuring 18% gray is achieved throughout the image

11. Which of the following is *NOT* necessary to photograph at a crime scene?
    a. Alarm permits.
    b. Property maps.
    c. Street signs.
    d. None of the above, all should be included in the scene photographs.

12. *Depth of field* is defined as
    a. The composition's area of sharp focus
    b. The distance from the foreground to the background in the image
    c. Infinity focus
    d. The camera's range of apertures

13. Which of the following is a factor affecting an image's depth of field?
    a. Aperture
    b. Focal length
    c. Subject-to-camera distance
    d. All of the above

14. What can help enhance a close-up photograph?
    a. Increased exposure
    b. Decreased exposure
    c. Orientation notations included in the image
    d. Higher ISO value

15. What is the camera seeking to achieve in calculating an exposure for light?
    a. A 50/50 balance between white and black
    b. 18% gray
    c. 33% gray
    d. Two stops above or below a *balanced exposure*

16. Which does *NOT* have an effect on an image's depth of field?
    a. Shutter speed
    b. Point of focus within the image
    c. How far away (or how close) the photographer is standing from the subject
    d. f/stop

17. Which camera company came up with the slogan, *You push the button, we do the rest.*
    a. Canon
    b. Eastman Kodak
    c. Nikon
    d. Polaroid

18. Which is *NOT* one of the aspects of quality crime scene photograph?
    a. Accurate
    b. Material
    c. Relevant
    d. Biased

19. Some camera light meters search for an 18% gray evaluation of light. What does this mean?
    a. The meter evaluates 18% of anything appearing in the viewfinder.
    b. The meter evaluates light in order to find 18% of reflected light in the composition.
    c. The meter evaluates light in order to find 18% of absorbed light in the composition.
    d. After evaluating the light, the meter increases the exposure by 18%.

20. Slight changes in exposure can
    a. Refine the richness of contrast, make visible objects not appearing in the viewfinder, and eliminate focus problems
    b. Never affect depth of field or color rendition because these are unrelated to exposure
    c. Refine the richness of color, make visible details that are hidden in highlights and shadows, and create changes in the depth of field
    d. Cause the camera to malfunction

21. Which of the following statements is true?
    a. Use of an automated camera mode improves the depth of field in crime scene photos.
    b. Use of an automated camera mode can eliminate the depth of field in crime scene photos.
    c. Use of an automated camera mode can degrade the depth of field in crime scene photos.
    d. Use of an automated camera mode never impacts the depth of field in crime scene photos.

22. Which of the following items appearing in a suspect's photo can cause a photographic lineup to be excluded from introduction into evidence in court?
    a. Gang graffiti
    b. Police personnel and patrol cars
    c. Crime scene tape
    d. All of the above

23. A benefit of working in *Manual* mode is that this mode allows the photographer to easily adjust exposure values in conflict with what the camera's light meter suggests.
    a. True
    b. False

Photography Assignments

Required Tools: General photography gear

Photography Subjects: Supplies for a mock crime scene, including replica weapons, replica ballistic evidence, and anything that might be found at a crime scene (be creative). Have an assortment of evidence markers or placards, even if they are simply folded pieces of cardstock with identifying numbers/letters on them.

I. Depth of field exercise
   A. Demonstrate the photographer's ability to record an image with a shallow depth of field.
   B. Complete a series of photographs that isolate a subject from its surroundings.
   C. Demonstrate the photographer's ability to record an image with a deep depth of field.
   D. Complete a series of photographs that demonstrate the relationship between a subject and its surroundings.

II. Mock crime scene project
   In order to complete these photographic assignments, the photographer should set up a small mock crime scene with several different pieces of evidence. The mock evidence should be of variable sizes (large and small) and randomly dispersed across the *scene* so that the recording of the *scene photographs* offers a challenge to the photographer. The photographer should concentrate on the following:
   A. Full scene documentation
   B. Bracketing exposures to ensure quality image capture
   C. Ensure quality lighting
   D. Ensure sharp focus, utilizing depth of field
   E. Change of perspective
      1. Record a complete set of *overall* or *scene establishing* photographs, including a quality 360° view of the location.
      2. Record a complete set of *midrange* or *evidence establishing* photographs, recording photographs that concentrate on depth of field and ensuring the connective link between the overall and close-up photographs.
      3. Record a set of *close-up* photographs of the evidence found in the scene.
      4. Record a set of *close-up* or identification photographs of the evidence after its *recovery*.
      5. Critically examine the recorded images and review them for
         a. Comprehensive coverage of scene
         b. Sharp focus
         c. Quality depth of field
         d. Proper exposure (light)
         e. Ability to identify individual subjects

III. Photographing challenging subjects
   A. Photograph the VIN plate found on a vehicle's dashboard.
   B. Photograph a US penny or US dime (substitute for a serial number).
   C. Photograph the watermark found on a US currency paper bill.

D. Photograph the interior of a hollow tube, garden hose, or pipe (substitute for a gun barrel).
E. Photograph a 3D (indented) footwear impression.
F. Photograph an indented writing sample.
G. Place an object underneath the edge of a vehicle during a sunny day and photograph the car and shadowed object so that both are properly illuminated (fill-flash exercise).
H. Photograph a backlit subject.

Additional Readings

Burnie, D. (2000). *Light*. New York: Dorling Kindersley Publishing, Inc.

Davis, P. (1995). *Photography*. 7th ed. Boston, MA: McGraw Hill.

Eastman Kodak Company. (1990). *How to Take Good Pictures: A Photo Guide by Kodak*. New York: Ballantine Books.

Editors of the Time-Life Books. (1970). *Light and Film*. New York: Time, Inc.

Fisher, B. (2005). *Techniques of Crime Scene Investigation*. 7th ed. Boca Raton, FL: CRC Press.

Gardner, R.M. (2005). *Practical Crime Scene Processing and Investigation*. Boca Raton, FL: CRC Press.

Geberth, V.J. (1996). *Practical Homicide Investigation: Tactics, Procedures, and Forensic Techniques*. 3rd ed. Boca Raton, FL: CRC Press.

James, H.J. and Nordby, J.J. (2005). *Forensic Science: An Introduction to Scientific and Investigative Techniques*. 2nd ed. Boca Raton, FL: CRC Press.

Lee, H.C., Palmbach, T.M., and Miller, M.T. (2001). *Henry Lee's Crime Scene Handbook*. Burlington, MA: Burlington Press.

Miller, L.S. (1998). *Police Photography*. Cincinnati, OH: Anderson Publishing Company.

Robinson, E. (2007). *Police Photography*. Burlington, MA: Academic Press.

Examination Quality Photography

4

A special set of close-up photographs that can be absolutely critical to an investigation are known as examination quality photographs. These images may be analyzed and/or compared to real evidence to make an identification. However, examination quality photographs are not just for comparison or analysis purposes. They can also be considered as any close-up composition where important, detailed information needs to be documented. Sometimes, recorded photographs are used for comparison to other close-focused images and may actually be used to individualize a piece of tangible evidence. Consequently, the photographic evidence can become the lynchpin in a criminal trial. Therefore, the importance of capturing a sharp-focused, well-illuminated, accurately composed image is crucial. As with other forms of crime scene photography, lighting, depth of field, and especially perspective play a critical role in the close-focusing efforts of comparison photographs.

In midrange and overall crime scene photography, the perspective from which a picture is captured can add artistic flair and creativity to the image's aura. However, perspective plays a more important role in photographing pieces of evidence destined for closer examination or comparison with real items of evidence. These images must be captured in a perpendicular alignment between the camera and the subject (Figure 4.1). Perpendicular alignment can be difficult when dealing with images such as bloodstain patterns found along the baseboard of a wall or a footwear impression located on an inclined surface. Although these situations create difficulties, an attempt must be made to obtain a perpendicular alignment. Even a small deviation from a 90° alignment can create difficulties for examiners attempting to make comparisons. Scales are used in nearly all examination quality photographs and the appearance of the measured increments present on the scale will appear unequal or out of focus if the scale is not perpendicular to the camera's lens. An accurate scale graduation from one end to the other is critical to everything from developing one-to-one scale prints of the evidence to the actual measurement of a particular piece of photographed evidence. If the ruler is canted even a little, the measured increments on the part of the ruler closest to the camera lens will be shorter than those increments further away from the camera. It is easy to imagine how such an inconsistency in the measuring device could cause some irritability and annoyance among examiners viewing or developing the images. Consequently, photographers should strive to maintain a proper perpendicular subject-to-camera alignment in all their close-focusing work.

Raw and Digital Imaging

The Scientific Working Groups (SWGs) are forensic practitioners that collaborate to improve forensic practices, build consensus standards, and develop best-practice protocols for the different forensic disciplines, including digital imaging. The SWG for Imaging Technology (SWGIT) has developed a number of documents available for examination and

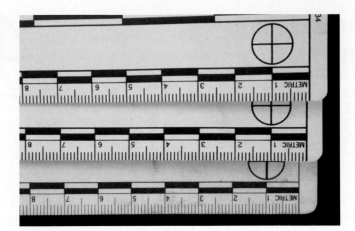

Figure 4.1 The camera and subject must be perpendicularly aligned at 90°. Even an error of 1° or 2° can create problems with focus, along with any potential comparison efforts. Observe how small changes in alignment or perspective create a difference in the appearance of the scales pictured in this figure. The three 15 mm scales were evenly aligned at the 15 mm mark, but they were raised at the opposite end by approximately 2 mm. Notice the amount of error created at the "0" increment point by such a small distortion.

that can be used as a guide for digital imaging in the law enforcement community. These documents can be found on the www.swgit.org website. As of the writing of this text, there are currently 24 documents available to the public, including, but not limited to,

- Overview of SWGIT and the Use of Imaging Technology in the Criminal Justice System
- Field Photography Equipment and Supporting Infrastructure
- Guidelines and Recommendations for Training in Imaging Technologies in the Criminal Justice System
- General Guidelines for Photographing Latent Impressions Using a Digital Camera

Specific to the photography of any evidence that will be compared to a known exemplar or analyzed in any manner, the recommendation from SWGIT is that these images be photographed in the *raw* (unprocessed and uncompressed) or *lossless* image file formats. *Raw* image files are the digital equivalent of a film negative. Tagged Image File Format (TIFF) and Bit Map Picture (BMP) are examples of lossless image files. Joint Photographic Expert Group (JPEG) images use *lossy* compression and lossy compression actually removes some originally recorded information from the image's data. JPEG images are not acceptable for any image that has the potential to be used for analysis or comparison. Examples of comparison and analysis photographs would include, but not limited to,

- Fingerprint, footwear, tire wear, or any other impression evidence
- Bloodstain documentation
- Bullet strikes and impacts
- Tool marks and bite marks
- Reconstruction photographs

Recording all one's photographs in *raw* is not necessary. JPEG images are utilized in crime scene photography. They are used for any photographs involving time, place, or event. Therefore, JPEG images are allowed for a vast majority of crime scene photographs, but when it comes time to photographing close-up/examination quality images, recording the images in *raw* and converting them to TIFF so they can be viewed is the recommendation. Using a lossless compression for examination quality photographs helps eliminate any possible challenges in court as to the accuracy and validity of the photographs.

Raw files are unprocessed and uncompressed image files. The digital files are just a bunch of ones and zeros strung together in a binary code. The *raw* files have to be converted to an image file, such as JPG (JPEG) or TIF (TIFF), in order for them to be viewed. In regard to *raw* files, every camera manufacturer has its own proprietary *raw* file formats. In addition, different cameras made by the same company can have different *raw* file structures. What this means to the photographer is that general software programs meant to process, enhance, and/or read image files will not be able to read *raw* files without an *add-on* or *plug-in* provided by the camera's manufacturer.

Digital cameras come with the software to read and convert *raw* captured files. *Raw* files should be converted to a *lossless* compressed file format, such as TIFF or BMP. Lossless compressed or TIFF files do not throw away pieces of the image like a JPEG or lossy compressed file. As a result, TIFF files can be used by examiners to make comparisons between known and unknown pieces of evidence. Although JPEG images are easy to share between different computers and are small enough to quickly send across the Internet, they can be challenged in the courtroom. Just to be clear, any evidence that is destined for comparison or analysis needs to be captured in the unprocessed, uncompressed *raw* format and converted to a lossless-compressed image for viewing. Most of the more recently manufactured digital cameras will have a recording setting that records an image twice, once as a *raw* file and once as a JPEG file. This allows a photographer to share or view the image with any computer but still possess a copy of the image saved as a *raw* file for any subsequent enhancements, comparisons, and/or courtroom testimony.

In addition to recording comparison evidence in the *raw* format, there are other specific requirements for digital recordings. Fingerprint evidence should be captured with a 1000 pixel per inch (ppi) ratio. In order to find this ratio, one needs to know the size of the imaging chip. The size of an imaging chip is given not only as an overall megapixel count but also in the number of pixels that run along the horizontal and vertical edges of the chip. Take the values for the horizontal and vertical pixel counts and divide each one by 1000. The result will provide the investigator with the maximum image capture size in inches. The result is likely to be a fraction of a whole number and converting the capture area size from inches to millimeters is recommended. Since there are 25 mm in each inch, multiply the horizontal and vertical values by 25 and the end result will give the image capture area in millimeters. As an example, the Canon 6D Digital SLR is a 20 megapixel camera and has an imaging chip that measures 5472 pixels by 3648 pixels. The following steps are necessary in order to determine the maximum dimensions for the image capture area:

- Size of imaging chip = 5472 × 3648
- 5472/1000 = 5.42″ (Horizontal length)
- 3648/1000 = 3.64″ (Vertical height)
- Converting horizontal length to millimeters: 5.42 × 25 = 135 mm

- Converting vertical height to millimeters: 3.64 × 25 = 91 mm
- Maximum size of capture area equals 135 mm by 91 mm

The size of the image's capture area is the maximum amount of space visible in the view-finder and therefore recorded by the camera. Unlike the film capture of fingerprints where the photographer merely has to get as close as possible to the print, the digital capture of fingerprints requires a specific capture area. One can have a greater than 1000 ppi ratio, but they must maintain the minimum standard. Instead of measuring the perimeter of the capture area for every photograph, the photographer can make a template. This template can be made out of almost anything. Foam core or cardboard is not the most durable of templates and wood can be a little too thick and cumbersome to be practical. A good compromise between durability and thickness is plastic. The photographer should make another visit to the local home improvement store and purchase a thin sheet of plastic. Cut a rectangular hole in the middle of the plastic that matches the size of the predetermined capture area. The template can then be placed over the fingerprint and either a pen or pencil can be used to draw on the surface and delineate the image capture area. If the surface is horizontal, another option is simply to leave the template in place and take the photograph. The final step to capture a 1000 ppi image is to fill the viewfinder with the interior of the template. With the camera focused on the print, the drawn periphery of the template or the template itself should *not* be visible in the viewfinder. Remember both the fingerprint, fingerprint identification information, and the scale must be included inside the template's perimeter. The final result is a 1000 ppi photograph captured in *raw*, which will be acceptable in any court (Figure 4.2).

Squeezing a palm print, footwear, or tire wear impression inside the small capture areas resulting from the 1000 ppi requirement is difficult at best. Fortunately, palm prints, footwear, and tire wear impressions only require a 500 ppi ratio. An investigator can create a second template doubling the size of the fingerprint template. Most palm prints should fit in a 500 ppi template. Footwear and tire wear impressions are a slightly different story.

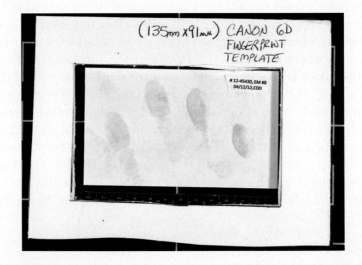

Figure 4.2 This is a template for the Canon 6D digital camera that has a 5472 × 3645 pixel imaging chip. When photographing with this template, the print and scale must fit inside the template and the edges of the template should not be visible in the photograph.

It is recommended to record these images at 500 ppi, but if nothing else, the impressions should be photographed in sections. Footwear impressions have a natural break in the arch region of the foot. After photographing the entire print, the shoe print should be photographed again filling the viewfinder with the forefoot and the heel separately. If there are image details in the region of the arch, that section can also be photographed separately. There is a potential that as many as nine identification photographs or more are recorded of a single footwear impression. Images created with flash are best recorded in a series of three, which is detailed later in this chapter and that means three overall photographs, three photographs of the heel, and three photographs of the toe box, for a total of nine images. Clearly, there are a few more steps to photographing pieces of impression evidence with a digital camera. However, the added burdens are a small price to pay for a job well done and the benefits digital photography provides today's crime scene investigators.

Tire wear impressions can range from a few inches to several yards in length. Preservation of this evidence requires breaking the entire length of the impression down into segments. The entire length of the impression needs to be photographed in relation to the scene and then the impression can be photographed in segments from one end to the other. The length of each segment will depend on the size of the camera's imaging chip. Using the previously calculated example, a 500 ppi image capture area for the Canon 6D would be 272 mm × 182 mm or 10.9″ × 7.28″. Therefore, the tire impression needs to be broken down into segments approximately 10″ in length. In addition, it is recommended that a 1″ overlap be made between each successive image. As the size of digital imaging chips continues to improve, the photographing of print evidence will become easier because the individual segments will become longer.

Scales

Photographs destined for close scrutiny by laboratory examiners, crime scene reconstructionists, and other experts require that scales, rulers, or other measuring devices be included in the photograph. The choice of scales belongs to the individual photographer. Scores of different photographic rulers are available from crime scene supply companies. These rulers are made from a variety of materials, come in a variety of colors, and are shaped into numerous lengths and forms, making it too tedious to list them all. Regardless of the type of scale selected, one should avoid using *scales of desperation*. Scales of desperation are commonly held items such as dollar bills, coins, and pens, which, in a pinch, photographers might lay into the frame of a picture in order to show scale. Although it has been advised that the submission of the desperation scale into evidence along with the photograph would adequately serve as a substitute for a true-measure scale, the professionalism of the crime scene investigator could be severely questioned in court. Therefore, utilizing standard rulers, scales, and measuring devices is truly the best course of action.

Scales, rulers, and other measuring devices come in a number of shapes and sizes and possess a number of unique features (Figure 4.3). There are a few standard features that investigators might find beneficial. The color of a scale is one such important feature. Scales come in a number of colors, including black, white, and fluorescent colors designed for alternate light sources (ALSs). White scales with black printing are common and useful for the majority of crime scene photographs. However, black scales with white printing are extremely beneficial with flash photography. Casting a flash's light across a white scale can

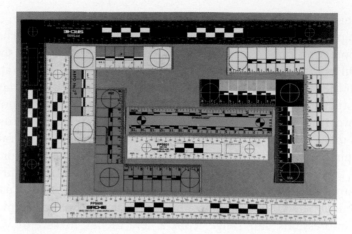

Figure 4.3 The ABFO #2 scale is perfectly suited to crime scene investigations. The finely graduated ruler, leveling circles, and two-sided construction help create both a practical and professional photographic images.

cause an overexposure to a white-colored scale and the printed graduations could vanish. Therefore, black-colored scales are extremely useful when electronic flash or other light sources are added to the composition. Rulers with 18% gray backgrounds were originally designed to assist image developers in calibrating the photograph's correct color and tonal value. However, while modern photographic processing methods and automated processors have largely eliminated the need for an 18% gray scale to be present in an image, the subdued tone of the gray scale is less distracting in some images and therefore still useful. Fluorescent-colored rulers are not as subdued but are especially valuable when using ALSs, such as ultraviolet (UV) light or colored light.

Rulers should also be flat both in their rigid shapes and in their colorings or coatings. A flat rigid shape is preferred for several reasons. Metal retractable tape measures often have edges that curl up and these can create a multitude of problems. They can cast shadows across an image from light projected at oblique angles. The curled-up edges are typically where the increment markings are located, which can create difficulties for examiners trying to make a measurement or comparison. Additionally, with the increment markings curled away from the surface on which the subject is located, the correct perspective may be lost. Furthermore, if the photograph is close focused and the depth of field is shallow, measured increments on the tape measure may not even be in focus. Metal retractable tape measures typically have glossy or reflective surfaces and these can create additional problems, especially when a flash is used. The bright light added to the image can create hot spots on the ruler, washing out the marked scale. As a result, thin, flat, and matte finish scales are recommended.

An individual's choice of photographic rulers is personal, but more than one type of ruler is typically needed for different tasks. Investigators tackle everything from footwear impressions and bite marks to bloodstain patterns. The environments and surfaces on which evidence is found vary just as greatly. For example, the crime scene photographer may need to photograph an arterial gush pattern projected over an entire wall or document a small semen stain under UV light. One ruler or scale will simply not be capable of fulfilling every possible need. The American Board of Forensic Odontology (ABFO)

#2 scale should be a part of any crime scene photographer's arsenal. This L-shaped ruler is both versatile and practical. It has a millimeter scale on both sides, and the nonreflective coating is excellent for photographing under a variety of lighting conditions, including electronic flash. The leveling circles located on its three corners assist developers with alignment problems when the photographer was not able to orient the camera perfectly perpendicular. Although automated developing *minilabs* may not be able to adjust for perspective issues, hand processing can result in correctly oriented photographs that enable an examiner to make an accurate comparison.

Rulers need to be placed on any number of surfaces and used in a number different of environments. For that reason, specialty and disposable rulers can be convenient. Scales with adhesive backings are useful for affixing them to vertical surfaces where a ruler will not remain in place due to gravity. An inexpensive alternative to the more expensive adhesive scale tapes is *plumber's putty*. Plumber's putty is an inexpensive, reusable, and tacky material that can be placed onto the back of a ruler and will allow it to adhere to a vertical surface. For use on surfaces such as car doors and fenders, commercially available magnetic rulers can be purchased. Inexpensive magnetic rulers can also be created by combining a plain scale with magnetic tape purchased at a craft or hobby store.

Although these reusable alternatives are effective in some situations, other circumstances may dictate the need for a completely disposable measuring device. Surfaces saturated with blood or contaminated with brain matter may not be environments in which an investigator will want to place an expensive measuring scale. Most scales are made of washable plastic and therefore can be washed with a bleach solution. However, the convenience of using adhesive scale tape and leaving it behind after the photograph has been taken is a time- and effort-saving benefit. As one can see, adhesive, magnetic, and disposable rulers, scales, and tape measures can all be useful to investigators at some point.

Companies that supply crime scene investigators with tools and equipment inundate the market with proclaimed time-saving devices and gadgets meant to make the life of an investigator a little easier. Many of the various measuring devices used during the investigation of crime scenes can be found at local hardware stores at much cheaper prices than those that are marked up ridiculously because the name of a forensic supply company is emblazoned on the front. For example, folding carpenter's rulers cost just a few dollars compared to the $30–$40 versions sold through forensic supply houses (Figure 4.4). Although carpenter's rulers are not ideal for every occasion, they are excellent for photographing evidence on tall vertical surfaces. Including a carpenter's ruler in the photograph can indicate the height of a subject in the recorded image. Finding alternatives to the purchase of expensive forensic equipment applies to a myriad of other tools utilized by crime scene investigators, including packaging, lighting, and measuring implements.

In the end, different photographic efforts require a variety of different photographic scales. Regardless of the scale chosen, it must be correctly incorporated into the photograph. One key to an accurate image is to ensure that the scale is in the same focal plane as the subject. This is especially true when close focusing because the depth of field will be much shallower in macrophotographs. In order to obtain this alignment, a set of *helping hands* is often useful (Figure 4.5). Helping hands are a pair of alligator clips attached to a movable, but lockable, set of adjustable arms. The arms are then attached to a heavy, secure base. By clipping a scale to the alligator clips, the scale can be positioned into place alongside the subject so that when the photograph is recorded, all the

Figure 4.4 Collapsible carpenter's rulers are very advantageous to investigators because they fold up small but can be extended 6–8 ft in length in order to indicate the height of evidence such as a bullet strike, as depicted in this figure.

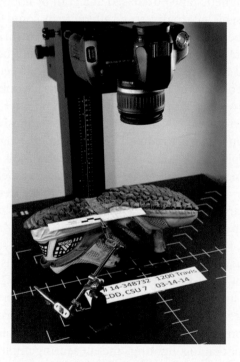

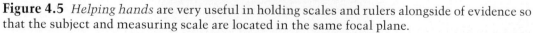

Figure 4.5 *Helping hands* are very useful in holding scales and rulers alongside of evidence so that the subject and measuring scale are located in the same focal plane.

important information and subject material will be aligned in the same focal plane. In general, reference scales are necessary tools for crime scene photography. In addition to the style of scale selected, the measuring device must be positioned next to the subject not only so that it is in the same focal plane but also so that it is properly exposed and does not create a shadow on the subject or become washed out because of the chosen light source.

Fingerprint Photography

The photographing of latent and visible fingerprints is always a good idea, especially when the physical recovery of such evidence may threaten the destruction of the print. Latent prints can be located on innumerable types of surfaces including flat countertops, rounded doorknobs, blue-steel revolvers, and backlit glass doors. Because of this broad range of environmental conditions and surfaces, depth of field and lighting difficulties will naturally present themselves. In order to solve such dilemmas, crime scene photographers must analyze the photographic composition and assess the subject in order to determine the best way to set up the camera and lighting. Lighting, contrast, and depth of field must be addressed individually when photographing fingerprints or any other evidentiary subject (Figure 4.6).

To begin with, a common misunderstanding is that fingerprint photographs must be recorded in a one-to-one relationship; they do not, especially when photographing in a 35 mm film format. Because 35 mm film or a full-frame digital camera measures 24 mm × 36 mm, the recording of a one-to-one fingerprint, much less a palm print, is physically impossible. It is too much information (fingerprint, scale, and photo identification tag) to fit into such a confined space as 24 mm × 36 mm. Medium- and large-format cameras are more capable of capturing a true one-to-one image, but their use in the field is very rare. The printing or developing of the images is made with a one-to-one relationship, but not the actual capture. Once again crime scene supply companies try to cash in on this misunderstanding by selling one-to-one lens adapters for 35 mm cameras. These lens adapters suffer greatly from vignetting (the softening or darkening of an image's corners) and are incapable of capturing larger subjects like palm prints. The use of diopters, extension tubes, or true macro lenses is a better alternative.

Lighting, contrast, and alignment are all key factors in capturing a valuable and accurate evidentiary photograph. The camera's lens must be positioned perpendicularly to the

Figure 4.6 Composing a fingerprint's image requires a scale, case information, proper contrast, and illumination. This figure includes each one of these aspects. In addition to a selected aperture of f/22 in order to extend the depth of field around the curved surface, illumination was provided by an electronic flash projected from the side at a 45° angle in order to obtain quality lighting of the subject.

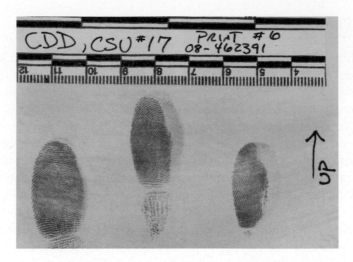

Figure 4.7 The inclusion of identifying information into one's photographs helps identify and verify the image without having to refer to a photo log.

subject, regardless of where the fingerprint is situated. The use of a tripod is strongly recommended. For those awkwardly positioned fingerprints, a Bogen–Manfrotto articulating arm support may prove invaluable. A stable camera platform will help eliminate camera shake from developing in the image. In addition, when using a tripod or other camera support, the photographer can more easily examine the camera-to-subject alignment and confirm that a perpendicular relationship has been achieved. Hand-holding the camera prevents this ability and is not appropriate.

If at all possible, some form of identifying documentation should be included in the photograph (Figure 4.7). Notations of the case number, photographer's initials, date, and location of print are typical. This seems like a great deal of information to squeeze into a close-focused subject, but it is not unreasonable. Case numbers and dates are merely numbers and take up very little space. Three initials will identify the photographer, and a *print identification number* that can be cross-referenced with the investigator's written report is all that is necessary. Placing a small identification number next to the print acts the same as placing numbered placards next to a series of fired cartridge cases. It identifies the evidence. The small, but legible, inclusion of such information makes identifying the print in a courtroom much less troublesome. Furthermore, by including the case information or subject identifiers into the photograph, it acts as an excellent substitute for a photo log. A photo log is used by some agencies to document the subject of each and every photograph. This can become quite a burden for those agencies that do not have the manpower to send more than one or two crime scene investigators to the scene of a major crime. A digital camera's *metadata* (a photograph's recording information/data) documents all of the camera's settings, while the composition's identification tag informs the viewer what the subject is. Consequently, there is no longer the need to maintain a formal photo log. Investigators must follow their agency's protocols, but digital imaging has definitely decreased the need to maintain photo logs.

The case information that is included as part of the actual photographic print helps ensure that the latent print identification is not misplaced, errantly misfiled, or mistakenly

(a) (b)

Figure 4.8 (a) The proper set up of an accurate, close-focused image requires the scale to be on the same plane as the subject and the scale to be aligned horizontally or vertically (not diagonally) within the viewfinder. (b) shows how a pair of helping hands and some modeling clay can help maintain a level alignment between the scale, identifiers, and the photograph's subject.

discarded. If the inclusion of such information is just not possible or not required by a particular agency, then a series of photographs should be recorded leading up to the fingerprint impression. The series of images can substitute for a single image with all necessary information included. In fact, every piece of evidence should be photographed as a series of images, regardless of whether or not an identification tag was used in the composition.

A suitable scale or ruler should also be included in the image and placed in the same focal plane as the print or piece of evidence (Figure 4.8). Maintaining the same plane of focus is important because it ensures that the subject and scale will both be accurately focused. There is another alignment issue that investigators should strive to maintain. Because the imaging chip used in digital cameras are primarily created by light-capturing diodes arranged into rows and columns, it is recommended that any scales included into a composition be aligned with the edges or sides of the viewfinder or image. Placing a scale across the diagonal of the imaging chip's mosaic of pixels could potentially create an error in any scale measurements made from the final recorded image.

Many investigators use preprinted adhesive stickers similar to address labels for their examination quality photographs. The use of stickers saves time, but an investigator can also handwrite the identification information on a small slip of paper and place it next to the subject. Although this amount of information and effort may seem excessive, the value of protecting the chain of custody is invaluable. Fully documenting the scene's evidence is vitally important and a series of photographs documenting a single piece of evidence may resemble something like the following hypothetical print found on a bedroom's doorknob.

The following set of photographs can be recorded in order to fully document the location of the fingerprint impression:

- Overall view—photograph showing the room and the door together.
- Midrange view—photograph showing just the door and the doorknob.
- Close-up view—photograph showing the doorknob and identifying information. If necessary, the information can be handwritten on a surface with an indelible marker.
- Examination quality view—photograph of just the fingerprint impression, with a properly oriented scale and identification tag.

Lighting a fingerprint impression or other minute piece of evidence can be difficult because of reflective surfaces, backlit subjects, or contrasting backgrounds. Fortunately, there are several solutions including different lighting and compositional techniques. Photographers need to examine difficult compositions, identify the challenges, and determine the best method to address those challenges. Crime scene photography is simply not a *point-and-shoot* endeavor. Recording quality crime scene photographs requires a little thought, planning, and execution. As an example, one should not simply point and shoot their important compositions, especially while using the camera's built-in flash. Pop-up flashes can be very useful in some circumstances, but not in all. Pop-up or built-in flashes are best utilized as a fill flash or as a supplemental light source. They are not designed to be the primary light source for all types of compositions. Specifically, when close focusing on subjects, the camera lens can cause a curved-shaped shadow to appear in the image. The light cast from the top of a camera and aimed just a few inches from a subject may be blocked by larger camera lenses. This is easily seen in the review screens of digital cameras, but there are no warning sirens on film cameras to alert the photographer about this particular danger. An additional benefit of having the camera supported upon a tripod is the ability to view the flash's coverage of the subject during the actual capture of the photograph. The photographer can observe and see if any shadows are cast because of an interfering piece of camera equipment or other obstruction.

As readers will find in Chapter 6, one advantage of flash photography is that it ensures a more accurate capture of colors. However, contrast between the fingerprint and its background is sometimes more important than an accurate color rendition in fingerprint photography. Black-and-white film or monochrome image capture mode on a digital camera is preferred since the known prints are going to be compared to black-and-white exemplars. Latent print examiners will be grateful if they can compare similarly captured black-and-white prints. Although flash photography is not necessary for accurate color rendition, it does provide a measurable and uniform illumination source. The flash should be connected to the camera with a sync chord so that the flash can be directed upon the subject at desired angles to avoid distracting reflections in the image. Additionally, the flash should be projected onto the subject from about an arm's length away. The 2–3 ft distance will ensure a more even lighting across the subject. When the flash is placed too close to a subject, an overexposure of the image can result, especially that part of the composition or subject closest to the light source. Manually calculated flash exposures, as well as other techniques, are discussed in Chapter 6. For now, flash exposures can be recorded with the flash set to an automatic exposure mode, using the camera's through-the-lens (TTL) metering. The photographer should still ensure that the light source is cast at an appropriate distance and angle to the subject in order to capture the best possible image.

An alternative to flash photography is to use the scene's natural or ambient lighting. If one can see the latent print clearly in the viewfinder, the image can generally be effectively recorded with just natural light. Frequently, ambient light offers a more even tone on the surface in which a fingerprint is located. Ambient lighting is often ignored as an option in photography because different light sources throw colored light upon a subject or the light is not intense enough to allow a photographer to hand hold the camera. Photographs of fingerprints should be recorded with the camera supported in some manner anyway, and therefore, capturing longer, ambient light exposures should not be an issue. The color of light should also not be an issue in fingerprint photography because images are primarily photographed in black and white. Therefore, consider using ambient lighting when photographing fingerprint evidence or any other evidence for that matter.

There may be times while composing a photograph that the camera itself and the lens cast a shadow on the surface containing the fingerprint. Electronic flash is one solution to this problem, but fear of an overexposure or reflective surfaces may create anxiety or doubt in a photographer. In those cases, a simple flashlight can be an excellent source of illumination. Flashlights can be specifically cast upon a subject to avoid shadows or harsh reflections (Figure 4.9). A major advantage of this technique of illumination is that the lighting can be immediately evaluated by looking through the camera's viewfinder. By peering through the viewfinder and finding just the right angle of light to cast upon the subject, a superior image can be captured. Metering this light is easily accomplished through the camera's light meter and the technique of painting with light on a macro scale is discussed later in this chapter.

Flashlights do have an inherent minor flaw. They can produce rings of light in the image. An easy way to eliminate these distracting rings is to place a piece of fingerprint tape across the flashlight's lens. This will soften and smooth out the light as it passes through

Figure 4.9 A flashlight of any size can be a very effective light source for illuminating small pieces of evidence, quite similar to painting entire crime scenes with light. The projected light can be visualized in the viewfinder and the angle adjusted for the best end result. In addition, the light can be painted across the subject to eliminate distracting rings that may be created by the flashlights lens. Stretching fingerprint tape across the flashlight's lens can also help eliminate those distracting rings cast by the light source.

the tape. As always, bracketing of exposures is recommended. If a crime scene photographer is more comfortable utilizing the electronic flash, a flashlight can still be of service. The flashlight can be used to find the best angle at which to direct illumination onto the subject and then the electronic flash can replace the flashlight's position as the exposure is recorded. In this manner, the photographer gets the best of both worlds. He or she can visualize the light's reaction with the subject and still utilize the camera's automatic metering systems.

Contrast is a key component of fingerprint photography. The ability to create a clear defining line between the foreground (visible fingerprint) and the background is the ultimate goal. Contrast can be accomplished through filtration, choice of lighting, and/or variances in exposure. Digital photography and the introduction of programs such as Adobe Photoshop® have greatly improved the ability of examiners to make fingerprint comparisons. However, as great as the technological advances have been in recent years, the actual image capture remains paramount. Digital enhancement programs can only do so much. The philosophy of garbage in–garbage out applies to these image enhancement programs and the capture of sharp-focused and properly exposed images will only make any post-capture editing that much better.

A light's color does not necessarily have a bad effect on a composition. Photographs of visible and latent fingerprints that are destined for comparison purposes can actually be improved by altering the color of light impacting the subject. The actual color of light can be changed or colored filters can be used to alter the light cast into the composition (Figure 4.10). Since latent print photography is best recorded in black and white, the color of the light will not negatively impact the final image by leaving a distracting hue. In fact, through the use of filters or colored light sources, investigators can dramatically increase contrast and consequently, ridge detail in their images. The contrast is between the fingerprint and the background, whether the print has been enhanced with black graphite powder or white cyanoacrylate fuming and/or colored dye stain. Creating separation between the subject and background is the goal, and an investigator has a few options in order to accomplish this task.

Contrast in an image is improved by darkening or lightening the background. This will cause the fingerprint to stand separate and apart from the surface on which it lays. Adding colored filtration to black-and-white images is the most inexpensive and least complicated way in which to increase an image's contrast. The primary colors of light are red, green, and blue, and photographers should have at least these three main filters in their photographic kits:

- Wratten #25 (red)
- Wratten #47 (blue)
- Wratten #58 (green)

There are a variety of filter densities available for purchase in addition to the primary filter choices listed earlier, but possessing the three principle filtration colors will assist photographers in creating more striking and valuable images. Most digital cameras come equipped with an internal red and green filter. However, an external blue filter will still need to be carried by digital photographers. Any colored object can be lightened in a black-and-white image by photographing through a similarly colored filter. For example, the effect of adding a red filter to the camera and taking a picture of a red apple would be to lighten the apple's appearance in a black-and-white image (Figure 4.11). If the desire is to darken the

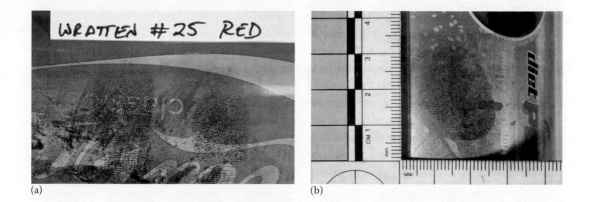

Figure 4.10 The latent fingerprints present in figures (a), (b), and (c) were enhanced with black graphite powder. In order to photograph the blackened ridge detail against the dark-colored background, colored filters were added to lighten the background of each image. (a) The red background of the Coca-Cola soda can was lightened with a Red #25 filter. (b) The blue background of the Diet Pepsi soda can was lightened with a Blue #47 filter. (c) The green background of the Sprite soda can was lightened with a Green #58 filter. (Photographed by Curtis Klingle, Retired Crime Scene Investigator, City of Bryan (TX) Police Department, Bryan, TX.)

appearance of the apple, then attaching a blue or green filter to the camera will accomplish that goal. In order to darken a particular color of an object, one needs to attach an opposite colored filter to the camera. Merely to emphasize the point, if an image is recorded on color film, adding a colored filter to the camera will only create a red, blue, or green staining to the overall image. Consequently, filtration and colored light sources are best utilized with black-and-white film or digital camera setting.

Filters work to block specific wavelengths of light, while allowing other wavelengths or a specific color of light to pass through. Using individual or distinct colored light sources to cast illumination upon a subject will create results very similar to filtration. Therefore, shining a red light onto a red apple will cause the apple to lighten in intensity as compared to the background. Colored light sources can be found at most lighting stores and even some department stores, but commercially (nonforensic) available lights may have too

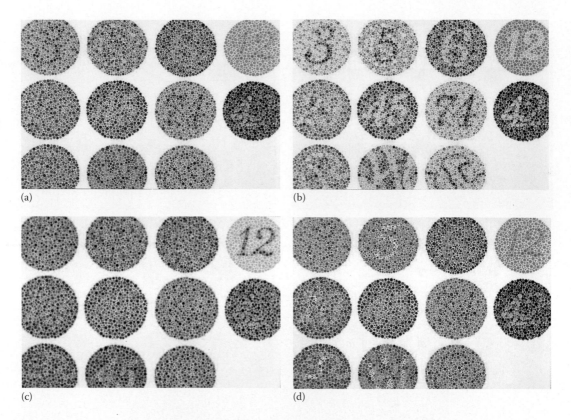

Figure 4.11 (a) was recorded without any filtration. (b) was recorded of the same image utilizing a red filter. (c) was recorded utilizing a blue filter. (d) was recorded utilizing a green filter.

broad of a wavelength range and the results may not be as desired. Light-emitting diode (LED) light sources with specific wavelength bulbs are an investigator's best bet for an inexpensive light source:

- Red (approximately 670 nm)
- Green (approximately 532 nm)
- Blue (approximately 470 nm)

Colored light sources must be used in a dark environment so that there is no other illumination impacting the subject. On the other hand, colored filters can be used in any environment. The choice is up to the individual photographer. Investigators should practice and experiment with their filters and light sources in order to learn if any exposure compensation is necessary and recognize those particular situations when one technique may have a better chance of success.

For those fortunate enough to have an ALS (alternate light source) at their disposal, the fine-tuning of the colors can be a much easier task (Figure 4.12). (An ALS, such as a SPEX CrimeScope® or ROFIN Polilight®, is capable of casting light at very specific wavelengths, i.e., colors.) Not every surface upon which a latent fingerprint is deposited will be the perfect shade of red, blue, or green that match standard colored filters. ALS units have an advantage because they can be adjusted to find the best wavelength or hue and, therefore, the best contrast. ALS and UV light sources can also be utilized with fluorescent

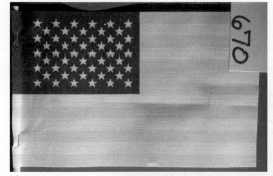

(a)

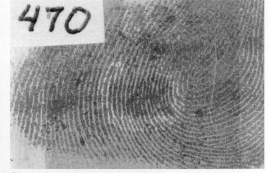

(b)

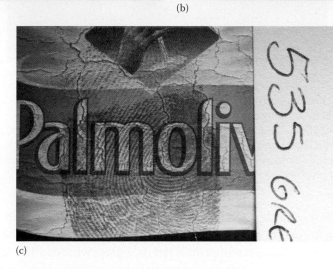

(c)

Figure 4.12 Instead of filtering white light, these figures were recorded with an ALS. (a) The red stripes on the American flag were removed by an ALS set at 670 nm. (b) The fingerprint visible in this figure rested on white lettering with a blue background. The blue background was removed with an ALS set at 470 nm. (c) The green background of the Palmolive® bottle was removed by adding green light (532 nm) to the green background. No filters were used in the capture of these images. Only the introduction of a colored light was used to lighten the matching colored background.

fingerprint powders. The use of fluorescent powders and UV light sources are covered in Chapter 10. At this point, the current goal is simply to increase the contrast between a latent print and different colored backgrounds.

A composition's contrast can also be affected by exposure, namely, by increasing or decreasing the intensity of light (exposure compensation). Investigators should strive to record a series of photographs by changing the exposure values. There are additional advantages to bracketing exposures when it comes to altering an image's contrast. Whether contrast is improved through the increase or decrease in exposure depends on the subject and the intensity of its color. Even though the extra, bracketed exposures require a little more work, latent print examiners will appreciate having a choice of images from which to select when making a comparison. In the end, how an image appears comes down to an individual's preference and having a choice of images is always a good thing.

Backlit subjects, such as fingerprints found on glass surfaces, can be another difficult photographic composition (Figure 4.13). Finding the right balance between a bright

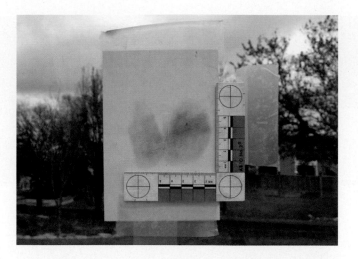

Figure 4.13 Metering backlit subjects and creating contrast can be difficult, but not impossible. This figure shows a palm print found on a backlit window. An artificial background for the fingerprint was created by taping a white index card to the exterior side of the window. It was recorded at ISO 100, f/9, for 1/200th of a second. A flash was added to the subject to create a balance between the shaded processed print and the sunlit background. A closer-focused image would be required for a comparison to be made, but this figure demonstrates the proper way to orchestrate such a photographic endeavor.

background and a dark or less-illuminated foreground is paramount to recording a useful image, but not an overly difficult task. Fingerprints can frequently be found in backlit environments, such as when a latent print is left on a glass window. The first challenge is to create contrast with the fingerprint. By taping one or two white index cards to the opposite side of the window, an investigator can create contrast for a black-powdered latent print. The index cards block out any distracting backgrounds that may be present in the image, as well as subdue the difference between the highlights and shadows causing the backlighting issue. If the sun or other light source is strong, light can pass through the card causing exposure difficulties. In that case, adding additional index cards or other less translucent material to the back of the window may help eliminate the backlighting. Remember that when capturing a subject with a predominantly white surface area, the camera will want to underexpose the image in order to turn the white subject into an 18% gray subject. To ensure obtaining a quality image, bracket the exposures and, more specifically, increase the subsequent exposures to capture a more color-accurate, white-balanced, and properly exposed composition.

Additional challenges that can face crime scene photographers are the variety of surfaces fingerprints can be found on. Fingerprints are not always found on smooth, flat surfaces. Latent prints can be deposited on curved and textured surfaces just as easily as on a clean, flat piece of window glass (Figure 4.14). Unfortunately, the documentation and recovery of such prints is more difficult. When a latent print is located on a flat surface, depth of field is not ordinarily an issue, because the fingerprint is completely present on a single focal plane. Although depth of field is not an issue in such circumstances, photographers might consider choosing an aperture of f/8 or f/11 because the resulting image's overall sharpness will be better. One word of warning for those photographers using the inexpensive 18–55 mm *kit* lenses: many of these lenses have a clearly visible barrel distortion

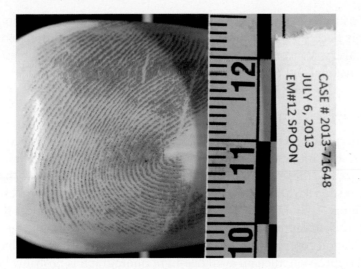

Figure 4.14 Latent prints are most frequently found on flat surfaces, which make the focusing and depth of field issues uncomplicated. However, on rounded, curved, or textured surfaces, the depth of field can become a major issue. Closing down the aperture to the smallest possible setting will help ensure the best zone of sharp focus throughout the photograph. This photo was captured at ISO 100, f/16, for 1 s. (Photographed by Andrew Taravella, Crime Scene Investigator, Houston Police Department, Houston, TX.)

at the 18 mm focal length and should be avoided at all costs when capturing examination quality photographs. This is mentioned because the 18–55 mm kit lens so popular with law enforcement agencies trying to save money.

Latent prints can also be found on a variety of shaped, curved, and/or textured surfaces. Smaller apertures are needed to increase a composition's depth of field so that the entire print will be sharply focused in the recorded image. The camera must be aligned close to the subject in order to capture the fine details of the fingerprint. As a result, depth of field will already be significantly reduced and the aperture must be minimized in order to compensate for the close-focusing nature of the image, as well as the curved or textured surface. Extremely small apertures, such as f/22 or f/32, may be outside the lens' sweet spot, but the improvement in the image's depth of field offsets any softening of the photograph's corners that may develop due to the smaller aperture.

Footwear and Tire Wear Impressions Photography

Footwear and tire wear impression evidence is frequently overlooked by investigators. Sometimes, the failure to notice and recover these types of impressions is because first responders have a tendency to destroy such items before the crime scene investigator arrives. Footwear and tire wear impression evidence is fleeting and requires a desire to search for and document these valuable items. One cannot just assume that such impression evidence is not present or holds little value. Suspects have learned to wear gloves and to wipe down surfaces they have touched during a criminal act, but until they learn to fly, footwear and tire wear impressions will continue to be of value to investigators. Some of these impressions may be lifted by tape or casting material, but most need to be photographed in order for comparisons to be made. Regardless, the photographic documentation of all impression evidence is necessary because of the risk of destroying the impressions through the process of recovery. Footwear and tire wear impression evidence comes in two general forms: 2-Dimensional and 3-Dimensional impressions.

2-Dimensional (2D) Impressions

Similar to fingerprints, 2D impressions can be further separated into visible and latent impressions. Visible impressions are the most easily photographed. Like any other comparison photography, the impression must be perpendicularly aligned with the camera, the subject must fill the viewfinder, and lighting should be orchestrated to best illuminate the impression (Figure 4.15). For a majority of visible impressions, the most difficult decision to make is whether to capture the image using a flash or ambient lighting. If the footprint or tireprint has good contrast with the surface upon which it lies and ambient light creates a well-defined impression, then an available-light photograph is probably best. Impression evidence is better recorded with the camera mounted to a tripod in order to ensure a perpendicular alignment and to prevent camera shake in the image. Even scenes with diminished ambient light can provide excellent quality photographs without the assistance of flash. These latter photographs may require longer exposures, but a few seconds of time should never be an issue or concern when photographing evidence.

Flash photography is an extremely useful tool for impression photography, but when used incorrectly, it can create problems with the scene's documentation. When light is insufficient or uneven across an impression, flash photography is necessary. The first and foremost rule of flash photography is to separate the flash head from the camera in order to cast a more even light across the subject and to avoid distracting and detail-eliminating reflections in the captured image. Typically, casting the electronic flash at an oblique angle across the subject provides the best results. If the photographer is not sure which angle will provide the best results, a flashlight can be used to find it. The photographer can peer through the camera's viewfinder while shining the flashlight at different angles and, when the best angle is observed, the electronic flash can be placed in

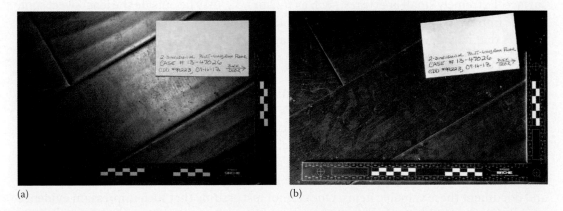

(a)   (b)

Figure 4.15 (a) is a 2D footwear impression recorded by illuminating the impression with the pop-up flash. In addition to the hot spot visible in (a), notice that the latent footwear impression is not visible in the slightest. Light must be cast from an oblique angle to bring out the details of an impression. (b) shows the same impression recorded with oblique lighting.

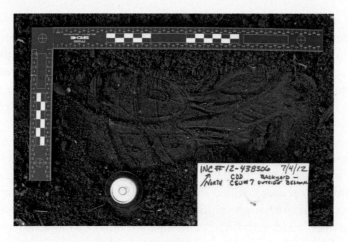

Figure 4.16 This photo was recorded at ISO 100, f/11, for 0.8 s with a flashlight illuminating the subject. The flashlight was swept quickly from one side of the impression to the other during the exposure.

the same position and the photograph recorded. As always, bracket a series of exposures to ensure a quality result.

Investigators can also consider the option of photographing the subject with illumination provided by a flashlight (Figure 4.16). If an impression appears well illuminated in the viewfinder when searching for a good angle, then serious consideration should be given to recording at least one image by using a flashlight in addition to the electronic flash-illuminated image. When using a flashlight, painting or moving the light across the subject during the exposure can help eliminate shadows and hot spots. Smaller apertures and lower ISO values will necessitate a longer exposure, thereby giving the photographer enough time to pass the light over the subject repeatedly. Do not forget to bracket one's exposures, adjusting the duration of the exposure, the angle at which the light is applied, and the distance between the light and subject.

Using a camera's pop-up or built-in flash is extremely useful in a number of situations, but not for illuminating impression evidence, especially evidence found on reflective surfaces. Pop-up flashes cause hot spots in an image and can eliminate important details from impression evidence. To avoid such circumstances, the flash needs to be separated from the camera. Synchronization cords or *sync cords* allow electronic flashes to be separated from the camera, while still maintaining communication so that automated features can be utilized. Sync cords come in a variety of lengths. A cord that can uncoil to 6 ft in length is preferable, but a 2 or 3 ft sync cord is much cheaper and is adequate for most assignments. For those with slightly deeper pockets, there are wireless transmitters for flash equipment and these can make challenging photographs a bit easier to capture.

Flash photography has one major drawback: light falloff (also known as the inverse square law). Basically, as light travels from its origination source, the amount of light lost over a distance is equal to the difference squared. This topic is discussed in detail in Chapter 6. Light falloff can affect impression evidence, especially if the impression's length extends away from the light source used to illuminate the subject. In 2D impression evidence, the loss of light means that the illumination falling on one side of an impression is much harsher or brighter than the side farther away from the light source. To combat this distracting attribute, the flash needs to be pulled further away from its subject so that distances between the near and far sides of a subject are not measurably so diverse. Essentially keeping the light source separated from the subject decreases the mathematical difference between one end of the subject and the other, as well as their relative distances from the light source. Since the distance ratio is not as drastic because the light source was pulled away from both ends of the subject, the lighting ratio is also decreased, thereby providing a more even lighting of the subject.

Once a footprint or other impression has been photographed, an attempt can be made to lift the impression from the surface. A number of variables can affect the type of lift attempted, but whether it is completed with an electrostatic dust lifter, tape, gel lifter, or other medium, it is recommended that an additional set of photographs of the lifted impression be recorded. Although prints enhanced with black graphite powder and transferred to a white index card with fingerprint tape are fairly durable and long lasting, other impressions lifted with electrostatic dust lifters or gel lifters may not be so durable. The chance that the impression could be compromised over time requires an immediate record of the impression before it is packaged for storage.

Preferably, the photography of recovered visible and latent prints should be completed in a controlled environment with a stable camera platform and controlled lighting. In fact, there will be times when it might be necessary to completely darken the environment and illuminate the impression with UV light or other ALS. Lighting will most likely be the most difficult aspect of the photographic process, because tape, gel lifters, and the black metallic film used with electrostatic dust lifters can cause unwanted reflections and lack the contrast necessary for a useful photograph. Therefore, the controlled environment of a photographic studio or laboratory is preferred when photographing already recovered pieces of impression evidence.

Sometimes, oblique lighting is not sufficient to create adequate contrast between a lifted footwear impression and the medium used to recover it. Suspected latent footwear impressions may be lifted and upon lifting them, the impressions seem to disappear. Before discarding the attempted lift, the tape or gel lifters can be examined using UV light. UV light may be able to excite very small particles of dust and fibers, thus allowing them to be more visible to the human eye (and the camera) (Figure 4.17). UV energy can excite the dust particles and bring them into the visible range of the electromagnetic spectrum, yet keep the background completely darkened. The added contrast between the impression and background creates a more useful image for examiners. Footwear examiners need to be informed that the resulting photograph was captured using UV light, because the photographed impression will be a reverse image of any known inked impression. The ridge detail created by an inked impression will be composed of black details against a white background. A fluorescing impression is composed of white details photographed against a black background. As with most areas of forensics, keeping the lines of communication open between the investigators and laboratory is invaluable.

3-Dimensional (3D) Impressions

Tire and footwear impressions are commonly found at outdoor crime scenes. Frequently, they are found in a soft substrate and create a 3D impression that can be cast using material such as Dentstone. However, prior to making any castings, impressions should be photographed. Photographing 3D impressions poses a number of potential problem areas including depth

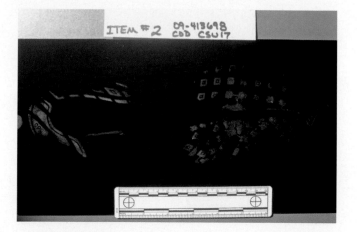

Figure 4.17 Footwear impressions can be lifted using a number of techniques, including the use of an electrostatic dust lifter and/or gel lifters. Photographing footwear impressions lifted at a crime scene will help preserve the very fragile nature of this evidence. Keeping the lifted impression flat, positioning the camera perpendicular to the subject, and directing the light obliquely across the subject help ensure a well-balanced and useful photograph that examiners will appreciate. This photograph is of a gel-lifted impression and was illuminated with an ALS. The UV light was needed to bring out the fine details of the 2D impression. The photograph was recorded at ISO 100, f/8, for 3.2 s.

of field, perspective, and lighting. Fortunately, careful preparation, composition, and light evaluation will result in a valuable image that can be utilized for comparison purposes.

Depth of field can be an issue depending on the depth of the impression and whether the impression is located on an inclined surface. Impressions found in very soft soil may be several inches deep and those several inches of depth can create a soft or unfocused image. In order to eliminate shallow zones of sharp focus, the camera's aperture setting should be closed down to a smaller aperture. Once again, photographing in a *Program* or automatic mode may result in the camera choosing a larger aperture than required. Therefore, recording images in a *Manual* mode and taking control of one's photography will improve an investigator's overall performance. Along with deep impressions, inclined surfaces can also cause perspective issues. It is possible to compensate for small inclinations with a small aperture, but to ensure a proper perspective from one end of the impression to the other, the camera needs to be mounted on a tripod at the same slope or angle as the ground. The solution to this dilemma is neither difficult nor expensive. Circular levels—small round levels with round circles imprinted in the middle of them—are used to visualize a 360° plane. Circular levels can be purchased for just a couple of dollars at most home improvement stores and investigators will need two bubble levels to effectively position a camera on an inclined surface. Place one level on the surface containing the impression and the other on the back of the camera. The back of the camera equates to the film or digital chip's alignment. Position the camera so that the circular level on the back of the camera matches the circular level lying next to the impression. The camera can best capture the impression from a perpendicular alignment when the two circular levels match (Figure 4.18).

A 3D impression needs shadows in order to define the details and minutia of the impression. Unlike other photographic efforts, ambient lighting is not always the best choice because the directionality of light cannot be controlled. Photographing indented

Figure 4.18 This figure shows what could be included in a 3D impression photograph that gives the examiner the most information, including a scale, an identification tag, and a thumbnail in order to show the angle of light cast across the impression.

impressions in low-light conditions is actually easier than capturing them in the daytime. An electronic flash is the best light source to capture 3D impressions. The flash should not be attached directly to the camera's hot shoe during image capture; it needs to be separated from the camera and connected by a synchronization cord or other wireless means. Similar to 2D images, a longer (6 ft) synchronization cord outperforms shorter (2 ft) cords because of light falloff (Figure 4.19). Creating a balanced flow of light across the entire impression will improve the value of the image.

With the flash projecting light from several feet away, the next step is to decide at what angle the light will be delivered. The light should be flashed at an oblique angle; somewhere between 15° and 45° typically results in an excellent image (Figure 4.20). The exact angle that the light should fall onto a subject will depend on the actual depth of the impression. A flashlight can substitute for an electronic flash and moved about the image until the best

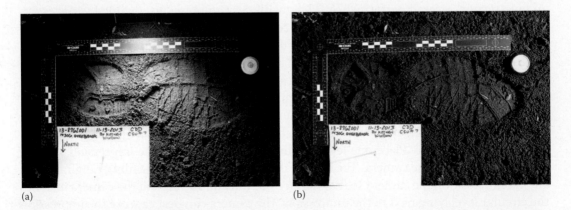

(a)   (b)

Figure 4.19 (a) was recorded with the head of the flash in close proximity to the top edge of the image. Observe how the placement of the light affected the overall quality of the image. (b) was captured with the camera and evidence positioned identically, but the flash was pulled further away from the subject. Observe the evenness of light falling across the entirety of the subject.

Figure 4.20 Light should be cast at an oblique angle across one's 3D impression. Casting the light somewhere between 15° and 45° is ideal.

angle is found. The flash can then replace the flashlight and a worthwhile image recorded. Investigators might consider making a visit to their local golfing supply store and picking up a *ball marker*. A ball marker is used by golfers to mark a ball's position on a putting green. A ball marker can be inverted and placed alongside an impression, giving viewers of the captured image an idea as to the light's direction of travel and the angle at which the light falls across the photograph (Figure 4.21). A flattop thumbtack may also be used, as long as it stands up straight.

Additionally, when 3D impressions are photographed with a light source projected from oblique angles, it is recommended that at least three photographs be taken. Additional defects (defects in the shoe's outsole, not defects in the image) and details may be made visible in an impression by projecting the light from different positions around

Figure 4.21 Placing a golf ball marker or thumbtack in the image will tell examiners the direction and angle the electronic flash was cast across the subject and assist them with making an identification. Three-dimensional impression evidence is best captured by creating shadows with electronic flash. The flash should be cast at low and oblique angles across the subject so that the impression's ridges create the necessary contrasting in the details of the impression.

(a)   (b)

Figure 4.22 These figures show two images of the same impression with the flash cast in two different directions. Compare image (a) to image (b) and observe how one image's minutiae appears raised and the other appears indented.

the subject (Figure 4.22). An investigator should imagine a 360° circle around the impression and move the light source in approximately 120° increments around the perimeter for each subsequent photograph. This series of photographs is easily envisioned. Lighting impression evidence from different angles is important because some indented impressions may appear as raised impressions. Having multiple photographs helps eliminate making a mistake in identifying the source of the impression. For those without a versatile tripod who are simply photographing downward between the extended legs, the direction of projected flashes is quite simple. A tripod has three legs and three sides. By projecting the electronic flash's light through each open side of the tripod's legs and across the impression, a photographer cannot help but capture a set of quality images that can serve as a link between a suspect and the crime scene. In addition, if the tripod legs are unavoidably visible in the image, the photographer should try to be sure the legs do not cause shadows to appear that conceal parts of the impression.

Maintaining a stable platform is important in order to record a stable image, as well as ensure a proper subject to camera alignment. Tripods are necessary for this photographic task and as stated previously, they come in a variety of sizes, features, and capabilities. However, the legs of a tripod can be troublesome to a photographer because they can often times be seen in the captured image or create shadows in an image. Tripods with a sidearm or a boom extension are preferred, because they take the legs of the tripod out of the picture (literally). Some tripods allow a photographer to invert the neck or center column of the tripod and allow the camera to be mounted upside down and underneath the tripod's extended legs. Mounting the camera upside down is an excellent alternative to the sidearm attachment and actually can provide an even more stable platform on which to mount the camera. Regardless of the style of tripod available, one should not be recording impression evidence while hand-holding their camera.

Just as many crimes occur during the day as they do at night. The daytime sunshine may make some photographic images easier to record and assist investigators in finding evidence, but the sun is not necessarily the photographer's best friend. The sun can cause deep shadows, backlighting difficulties, lens flair, exposure errors, and a host of other problems. In tire and footwear impression evidence, the sun can completely obliterate any visible details from appearing in an evidentiary photograph. Three-dimensional impressions are made visible through oblique lighting, and when a bright sun is present in the overhead sky, the important identifying details of an impression can be easily lost.

One needs to create a barrier between the sun and the impression in order to produce a shadow (Figure 4.23). At times, a blackout curtain can be extremely useful to photographers in blocking out unwanted ambient light. Not only is a blackout curtain useful in tire and footwear photography, it can also be useful when photographing with ALSs, when luminol is utilized, and/or other situations where extraneous light is detrimental to the final image. Blackout curtains do not have to be expensive or purchased from photography supply stores. Fabrics purchased from local fabric or craft stores can serve as excellent substitutes and save the photographer money. Merely look through the choices of solid-black-colored fabrics and purchase 4–5 yd² of a durable material. The cost should not be

(a)   (b)

Figure 4.23 (a) illustrates how to establish an artificial shadowed environment for impression evidence. (b) is the resulting image after blocking out the ambient sunlight and using an electronic flash to bring out the details of the indented impression. This technique can be used in a number of applications when ambient light needs to be removed from a subject in order to capture a better quality image. This figure was recorded at ISO 100, f/16, for 1/60th of a second.

more than a few dollars per square yard, which compares quite favorably to the price of commercially produced blackout curtains. These can run as high as $50 a piece, depending on the size. Whichever source the photographer chooses, the curtain or fabric can be used to create a dark shadow across the entire area holding the impression. With the tripod and camera positioned over the impression, the blackout curtain can be draped around the tripod forming a makeshift teepee. With the sunlight no longer shining onto the impression, the flash can now be projected across the subject at an oblique angle in order to bring out the ridge detail. When the ambient light surrounding the impression remains rather bright, the photographer should close down the camera's aperture. The combination of a small aperture and a flash-synchronized exposure of 1/60th or faster shutter speed setting, the ambient light should not adversely affect the flash's ability to form the shadow details needed to make a comparison. For those investigators who do not have a blackout curtain, anything opaque can serve as a substitute. For example, many investigators carry a variety of paper bags and boxes in their crime scene vehicles for packaging evidence. These bags and cardboard boxes can be held up between the impression and the sun in order to create a shadow. Basically, anything opaque can be used to create a shadow, even an investigator's own body. Investigators just need to be innovative and seek to solve photographic problems with the resources available.

Painting with Light on a Macro Scale

Many crime scene photographers are familiar with the nighttime photography technique of *painting with light*. This technique is a way in which photographers can add light to low-light compositions in order to record brilliantly illuminated photographs and is discussed in Chapter 7. This painting with light technique can be applied to very small subjects, such as insects, fired bullets, and other small pieces of evidence, as well as overall crime scenes. Recording sharp-focused, well-illuminated photographic images is a very important skill for the crime scene photographer. Evidentiary photographs have many purposes, but none more important than providing the jury with true and accurate representations of the crime scene and any recovered evidence. If those evidentiary photographs are not properly focused, illuminated, and composed, then the jury will likely have doubts as to the competency and capability of the investigator. Therefore, it is extremely important that photographers take the extra effort to record truly exceptional evidentiary photographs.

As with any macrophotograph, the depth of field and image composition is extremely important. In regard to composition, one should strive to have the subject fill the viewfinder. When composing small pieces of evidence in the camera's viewfinder, one can easily see the need for a close-focusing lens or set of extension tubes. It may be necessary for the lens to be just a centimeter away from the subject in order to fill the viewfinder. Being so close to the subject will cause two major difficulties. First, lighting the subject will be a challenge, which is the purpose of painting one's subject with light. Secondly, depth of field suffers tremendously by having such a short focusing distance. Depth of field is the zone of sharp focus and because it can be extremely shallow in close-focusing situations, the focus point must be carefully selected and a proper aperture chosen. A camera's autofocus feature will focus on the subject closest to the camera's lens and this will effectively reduce one's potential zone of sharp focus by half. In addition, the camera may not select a focus point that is of primary importance to the photographer. The actual point of focus should

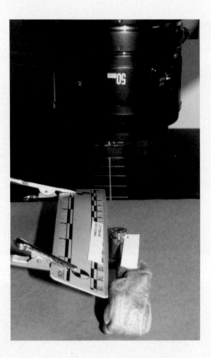

Figure 4.24 Close focusing on evidence will severely affect the depth of field and subject's focus. Photographers should strive to manually select their point of focus and choose a very small aperture in order to maximize the image's depth of field.

be placed on the most important aspect of the composition and in approximately the middle of the subject's range of sharp focus in order to maximize the overall image's depth of field. In addition, the photographer should select the smallest aperture available on the camera's lens. Smaller apertures will maximize the depth of field. Figure 4.24 illustrates how close the camera's lens can end up being from the subject. One can see how difficult adding flash illumination or ambient lighting to such a composition might be.

A major difficulty created by subjects composed so close to the camera's lens is the inability of light to reach into and around the subject. Many subjects will not be flat or on a single plane of focus. They will have curves, crevices, and areas of shadow that must be addressed in the composition. As a result, flash photography or ambient light photography may not be able to produce a quality photograph. Compare the photographs depicted in Figure 4.25. Figure 4.25a was created with a flash. Figure 4.25b was created with ambient light from the copy stand's light sources. Figure 4.25c was recorded by painting the subject with light, which will be discussed and explained later.

Painting with light is a process of adding light to a composition in order to increase the details found in the areas of shadow. This procedure is most commonly done in outdoor crime scenes photographed at night but can be adapted for use in macro and/or close-up photographic endeavors. The basic principle of painting with light is that *light is additive*. Light does not have to be added to a composition all in an instant. It can be added to a subject over time, so that the cumulative amount of light applied to a subject creates a powerful and well-illuminated photograph.

Where to begin the recording of a difficult composition is usually the most challenging part of the entire photographic process. Everyone's approach to photography is slightly

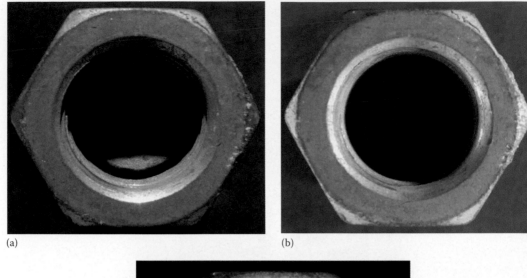

(a)   (b)

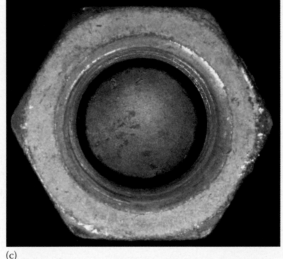

(c)

Figure 4.25 All three figures are of the same composition. (a) was recorded with flash illumination. (b) was recorded with ambient light. (c) was recorded with a combination of the ambient light and flash.

different, but hopefully, the goal is the same: capturing an accurate representation of the subject. The first step should be to stabilize the camera on a copy stand or similar device and attach the remote or shutter release cable. Set the camera for *Manual* focus and *Manual* exposure. Unless the photographer has a particular preference, one should consider an ISO value of 100, because the recorded images are generally sharper and have better color saturation than higher ISO values. The aperture should be set to the smallest available setting, especially when the subject has any depth to it. The final exposure variable is the length of the exposure (shutter speed) and that will be determined a little later.

The next task is to compose the actual subject. The subject should fill the viewfinder and the camera placed parallel to the subject (lens perpendicular to the subject). This may not be necessary for a round or spherical shaped subject, but any and all scales should be parallel to the film plane (or imaging chip). If at all possible, consider raising or elevating

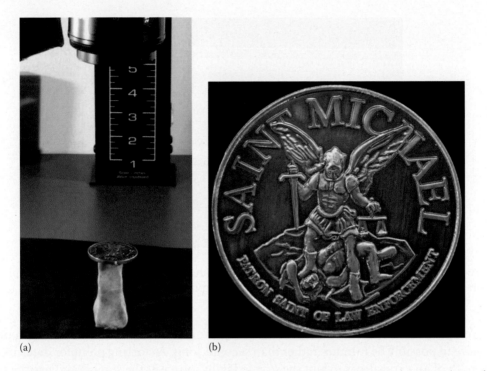

(a)   (b)

Figure 4.26 (a) illustrates the manner in which (b) was mounted during the recording of the image. The exposure values for figure (b) were ISO 100, f/22, for 2 min.

the subject above the level of the copy stand's base, as is demonstrated in Figure 4.26. By elevating the subject, the background will be blurred or not even visible in the image and therefore, not competing with the subject for the viewer's attention. Raising the subject away from or above the background will move the background out of the zone of sharp focus. Furthermore, the *inverse square law* will be applicable during the application of light to the subject, thereby limiting the light striking the background and allowing the subject to be isolated or separated from the object's background. Consider having a black, light-absorbing, background to the composition. The black background will help absorb stray light during the painting with light procedure. A solid white background could also be considered, if the subject would create a nice contrast. Proper composition is much more than a point-and-shoot endeavor. Compose the image to show the best side or facets of the subject and have a purpose for the composition; do not simply capture a haphazard or random image. Finally, manually focus the subject so that the depth of field is maximized and as much of the subject is in the zone of sharp focus. Remember that in extremely close-focusing compositions, the zone of sharp focus extends approximately one-half forward and one-half rearward of the point of actual focus, instead of one-third to the front and two-thirds to the rear.

Now that the basics are taken care of, it is time to determine the shutter speed or length of the exposure. The length of the exposure will depend on the particular light source used by the photographer. Although some ambient light can be incorporated into an image, for now, turn off all the lights in the work area and only illuminate the subject with the selected light source. Once again, remember that it is the accumulation of light during the entire painting process that will create the final image. With the ambient light restricted or

Figure 4.27 Metering one's light source placed stationary on the subject will provide photographers with a starting point for the length of one's exposure.

not even present, low ISO values, and smaller apertures, be prepared for the length of the exposure to possibly be minutes rather than seconds long. A starting point for determining the length of an exposure is to aim the selected light source at the subject and use the camera's light meter to determine the length of the exposure (Figure 4.27). The length of the exposure can be adjusted slightly by physically moving the light closer (thereby shortening the exposure) or further away (thereby lengthening the exposure) from the subject. The final exposure's length may not be exactly what was determined in this evaluation process, but it should be within a couple of stops and give the photographer a good starting point for the exposure.

Because the subjects are small pieces of evidence and not expansive crime scenes, the light source selected to paint one's subject should be equally small. Single-bulb LED and small penlight-style flashlights are preferable for use in these small compositions. One could use stronger, more powerful light sources, but the risk of overexposing the image or creating hot spots in the image will increase. In addition, by using less powerful light sources, one has the ability to apply the light more evenly and into and across the small crevices and undulating surfaces that might be found on the subject. Flash exposures and more powerful light sources will speed up the process of photography. However, by using less powerful light sources, the creativity, the depth, and the brilliance of the composition can improve markedly. Practice with one's favorite flashlight in these types of photographs will make the exposure evaluation much easier in subsequent endeavors, because the length of the exposures will remain relatively constant as long as the choice of apertures and ISO values remain the same.

The main purpose of painting small pieces of evidence with light is to ensure that the subject is illuminated on all its surfaces and limit the amount of distracting shadows that may develop on items with undulating surfaces. The casting of light onto the evidence is similar to painting an outdoor crime scene. Add light evenly across all the subject's surfaces, circling around the subject during the entire length of the exposure. It is advisable to wave the light back and forth as it encircles the subject. What this painting effect

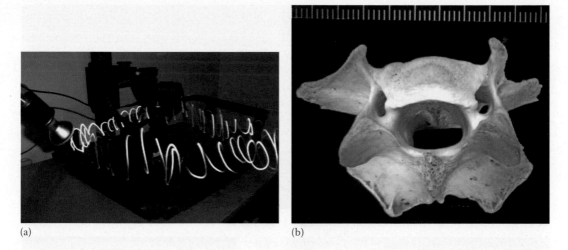

(a)   (b)

Figure 4.28 (a) demonstrates the casting of light across the subject from all sides to provide equal illumination across the entire subject. (b) is the resulting image from (a). The light source was a single-bulb LED flashlight (ISO 100, f/36, for 30 s).

might look like is seen in Figure 4.28. There will be times when the casting of light will be unintentionally passed over or off the subject, but that is expected and is easily overcome by adding a little more time to the exposure. Practicing this technique will provide the photographer more confidence in their ability to produce brilliant and compelling pieces of photographic evidence. As examples of odd-shaped subjects with a multitude of different surfaces, painting with light on a macro scale is an excellent tool to photograph entomological evidence (Figure 4.29a and b), ballistic evidence (Figure 4.29c), and jewelry or other small (Figure 4.29d), colorful items that might find their way into one's investigation.

A single-bulb LED light with a flexible head and a fiber-optic flashlight attachment for small penlight flashlights (available at tool supply stores) are outstanding devices to complete a specific type of evidentiary photograph that can provide a great deal of information to viewers. Pistols and other firearms are frequently used during criminal acts, and when recovered, the examination and photography of the barrel's interior can provide valuable information on whether or not the weapon had been fired or if blood and/or tissue had been drawn back into the weapon's barrel. Compose the image with the gun's barrel aimed up toward the camera's lens and slide a small flashlight into the weapon's breach or the back end of the barrel. The light will be shined up through the barrel and provide illumination inside the barrel, while ambient light or painted light can be cast around the exterior of the weapon (Figure 4.30).

The difference between forensic photography and the casual photographer is the ability to take control of one's photography. Stepping out of one's comfort zone and setting the camera to *Manual* focus and *Manual* exposure determinations will allow the photographer to create better, more accurate evidentiary images. The next step to improving one's photography is to examine and analyze a composition and determine how and where light needs to be applied in order to record the best possible image. Slowing down the photography process, turning out the lights, and utilizing small flashlights to illuminate the evidence will allow the photographer to be more creative and apply light to specific areas

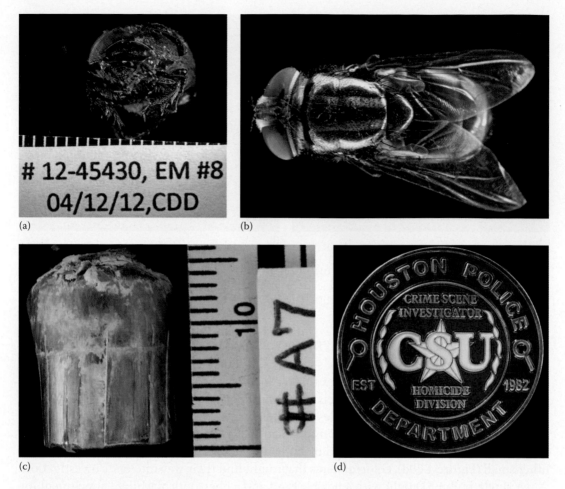

Figure 4.29 (a and b) are examples of entomological evidence. (a) was recorded at ISO 400, f/22, for 30 s and (b) was recorded at ISO 400, f/25, for 100 s. (c) is a photograph of ballistic evidence and recorded at ISO 100, f/22, for 5 s. (d) is an image of a challenge coin (jewelry) and was recorded at ISO 100, f/16, for 20 s.

of the composition that will provide the investigation with better evidentiary photographs that can be utilized in court. In conclusion, painting with light techniques can be applied to both large and small compositions. Painting with light techniques simply allows photographers the ability take control of their photography, whether the subject is an expansive crime scene or an individual green bottle blowfly.

Conclusion

Photographing evidence meant for examination by others means that images will face an increased level of scrutiny. Although every image has the potential to be meaningful at trial, photographs destined for comparison to tangible pieces of evidence must be captured with a precise attention to detail. Composing and photographing these images should not be rushed. The camera should be stabilized on a tripod or copy stand, apertures selected

Figure 4.30 An interior of a pistol's barrel was illuminated in this figure by a single-bulb LED flashlight. The exposure values were ISO 100, f/22, for 22 s.

for a reason, and the capture of an image planned rather than haphazardly taken. Although photographs can be captured by hand-holding the camera, the photographer risks a blurry image with poor perspective. Lighting should be selected carefully, even orchestrated to ensure even illumination across the entire subject. Depth of field remains important and must be specifically addressed to ensure the sharpest possible image. Additionally, getting in close is critical to providing examiners with enough resolution and detail to make comparisons and analysis of subjects. Quality photographs do not just happen, they are created.

End of Chapter Questions

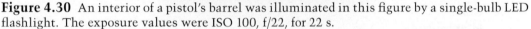

1. Which of the following can influence the quality of a close-focused image?
    a. Lighting
    b. Depth of field
    c. Perspective
    d. All of the above

2. Which of the following is important about *perspective* in regard to examination quality photographs?
    a. Image is recorded from *eye view*
    b. Image is recorded from a *normal view*
    c. Image is recorded with the camera lens perpendicular to the subject
    d. Image is recorded with the camera on the same focal plane as the subject

3. What can substitute for a formal *photo log* in an examination quality photograph?
   a. Scale
   b. Subject identification tag
   c. Date and time stamp
   d. All of the above

4. What statement is most true when photographing scales?
   a. Scales should be aligned with the viewfinder's borders or frame
   b. Scales should be included in all photographs
   c. Scales should only be black or white in color
   d. Scales are not necessary in evidentiary photographs

5. What is the SWG that provides guidance to crime scene photographers?
   a. SWGPHOTO
   b. SWGDAM
   c. SWGIT
   d. FISWG

6. Latent print photography should generally be photographed in _____.
   a. Black and white (monochrome)
   b. Color
   c. Film capture
   d. Using an electronic flash

7. Digital recordings of latent fingerprints should be recorded _____.
   a. Only as a film image
   b. At 1-to-1 size (in relation to recording media)
   c. As a *raw* image
   d. As a JPG image

8. Digital recordings of latent fingerprints should be recorded _____.
   a. With 500 ppi of capture
   b. With 1000 ppi of capture
   c. With 10-megapixel or greater size cameras
   d. With 10 pixels per millimeter of capture

9. Which file is an example of *lossless* compression?
   a. JPEG
   b. TIFF
   c. *raw*
   d. All of the above

10. What is the result of adding a blue-colored filter to the camera's lens when photograph-ing in black and white (monochrome)?
    a. Nothing changes because the image is photographed in black and white.
    b. Blue subjects become darker than they would naturally appear
    c. Red subjects become lighter than they would naturally appear
    d. Blue subjects become lighter than they would naturally appear

11. JPEG images are acceptable for _____.
    a. Photographs of a time, place, and event
    b. All crime scene photographs
    c. Comparison and analysis photographs
    d. Photographs of persons or individuals

12. JPEG images are an example of
    a. Fractal compression
    b. 1-to-1 compression
    c. Lossy compression
    d. None of the above

13. Which of the following is an important key to photographing 3D impression evidence?
    a. Oblique lighting
    b. Perpendicular lighting
    c. White lighting
    d. Alternate lighting

14. If a digital camera had an imaging chip that measured 3000 pixels × 2000 pixels, what would be the capture area required for a fingerprint photograph?
    a. 150 mm × 100 mm
    b. 30″ × 20″
    c. 75 mm × 50 mm
    d. 6″ × 4″

15. Tire wear or footwear impressions should be recorded at _____ ppi.
    a. 250
    b. 500
    c. 750
    d. 1000

16. What is a guiding principle of *painting with light*?
    a. Light is objective
    b. Oblique application of light
    c. Guide number = aperture × distance
    d. Light is additive

17. One key to an accurate image is to ensure that the scale is in the same focal plane as the subject.
    a. True
    b. False

Photography Assignments

Required Tools: Copy stand or tripod, cable release, various light sources, scale (ruler)

Photography Subjects: Small photographic subjects, such as fingerprints, footprints (2D and 3D), bullets, cartridge cases, insects, colorful subjects, and supplies to create a personal template for fingerprint photography

I. Determine the size of your camera's imaging chip and create a template for finger-print photography (1000 ppi).

II. Determine the size of your camera's imaging chip and create a template for footwear photography (500 ppi).

III. Take a photograph of a millimeter scale as close as possible with your available equipment. (This will give the photographer an idea of how close they can expect their macrophotographs to be.)

IV. Record an image in *raw* and convert the image to a *TIFF* file using the software that came with the camera. Observe the size of the TIFF file once created and compare it to the size of the *raw* file.

V. Demonstrate your ability to properly photograph the following subjects:
   A. A processed fingerprint (remember format, resolution, orientation, scale, and identification)
   B. An unprocessed fingerprint
   C. A fingerprint placed on a round clear glass surface (drinking glass or bottle)
   D. A 3D footprint
   E. A 2D footprint

VI. Demonstrate your ability to properly photograph a small subject using the painting with light technique:
   A. Insect
   B. Fired projectile
   C. Fingerprint or serial number on a curved surface

VII. Demonstrate your ability to separate the primary colors of light using filtration (photograph various colored subjects, such as fruit, graffiti, or multicolored magazine covers):
   A. Red filter
   B. Green filter
   C. Blue filter

Additional Readings

Bevel, T. and Gardner, R.M. (2008). *Bloodstain Pattern Analysis with an Introduction to Crime Scene Reconstruction*. 3rd ed. Boca Raton, FL: CRC Press.

Bodziak, W.J. (2000). *Footwear Impression Evidence: Detection, Recovery, and Examination*. 2nd ed. Boca Raton, FL: CRC Press.

Brooks, D. (1986). *How to Control and Use Photographic Lighting*. Tucson, AZ: HPBooks.

Burnie, D. (2000). *Light*. New York: Dorling Kindersley Publishing, Inc.

Byrd, J.H. and Castner, J.L. (2001). *Forensic Entomology: The Utility of Arthropods in Legal Investigations*. Boca Raton, FL: CRC Press.

Coppock, C.A. (2007). *Contrast: An Investigator's Basic Reference Guide to Fingerprint Identification Concepts*. 2nd ed. Springfield, IL: Charles C. Thomas Publisher, Ltd.

Davis, P. (1995). *Photography*. 7th ed. Boston, MA: McGraw Hill.

Duncan, C.D. (2011). Painting with light. *Chesapeake Examiner* (Fall), 49(2):4–10.

Eastman Kodak Company. (1990). *How to Take Good Pictures: A Photo Guide by Kodak*. New York: Ballantine Books.

Fisher, B. (2005). *Techniques of Crime Scene Investigation*. 7th ed. Boca Raton, FL: CRC Press.

Gardner, R.M. (2005). *Practical Crime Scene Processing and Investigation*. Boca Raton, FL: CRC Press.

Geberth, V.J. (1996). *Practical Homicide Investigation: Tactics, Procedures, and Forensic Techniques.* 3rd ed. Boca Raton, FL: CRC Press.

Grimm, T. and Grimm, M. (1997). *The Basic Book of Photography: The Classic Guide.* New York: Penguin Books.

James, H.J. and Nordby, J.J. (2005). *Forensic Science: An Introduction to Scientific and Investigative Techniques.* 2nd ed. Boca Raton, FL: CRC Press.

Miller, L.S. (1998). *Police Photography.* Cincinnati, OH: Anderson Publishing Company.

Robinson, E. (2007). *Police Photography.* Burlington, MA: Academic Press.

Scientific Working Group in Imaging Technologies. (2014). Retrieved August 22, 2014 from http://www.theiai.org/guidelines/swgit/index.php.

Nighttime and Low-Light Photography 5

Documenting nighttime crime scenes should not cause stress to any investigator because the recording of still images in low light can actually be easier than capturing similar photographs during the day. In nighttime conditions, lighting is frequently more evenly spread across a crime scene, and although shadows will be present, the contrast between the shadows and highlights is not always as intense as it can be in the daytime. Consequently, the differences between the lighter and darker sections of a composition can be dealt with more easily in low-light conditions than in daytime compositions. Furthermore, photographs recorded during the nighttime are frequently more pleasing to the eye than daytime compositions.

As a review, exposures are the result of the total amount of light allowed to enter the camera, and the amount of light is the product of intensity and time. Of course, the amount of light needed to record an image is also based on the sensitivity of the recording media or the ISO value. Intensity is determined by the size of the lens' diaphragm (aperture), and the time is determined by the duration the shutter (shutter speed) is allowed to remain open. Any image recorded in daylight can also be recorded in low-light conditions because these exposure principles do not change whether it is daytime or nighttime. Low-light photography merely requires patience because recording quality images in low light necessitates longer exposures.

In general, low-light photography requires longer timed exposures. As a result, photographers should not rush their compositions. In addition to patience, a sturdy tripod is paramount. Too many investigators, especially the inexperienced, prefer to take handheld photographs and depend on an electronic flash to illuminate a subject. Although using an electronic flash in low-light conditions may be time efficient, the end results are not always rewarding. Another handicap crime scene photographers commonly create for themselves is their reliance on *Program* mode photography (Figure 5.1). Although camera metering systems are adaptive to many different environments, too many factors can affect the final result. In the end, human beings are better than a computer chip at deciphering and assessing the lighting conditions surrounding a photographic subject. Certainly *Program* mode photography can be used to capture quality low-light images. However, as with all photography, taking control of the camera and selecting settings with a purpose or for a reason will more likely result in better photographs.

When the sun goes down, lighting does not cease to exist. Sunlight is usually replaced by manmade illumination, but even the night skies can provide enough light to record a quality photograph. Obviously, nighttime-ambient lighting is more intense in urban environments. However, even in rural jurisdictions, there is enough natural light to record an image. Clearly nighttime photographs taken in ambient light will require longer exposure times, but it is actually possible to allow enough light from the scene to make the image appear as if it had been captured during the daytime. This may not be the truest and most accurate photograph to present to a jury, but it will provide the jury with an excellent

(a)   (b)

Figure 5.1 (a) was recorded in *Program* mode using electronic flash illumination and was recorded at ISO 400, f/4.0, for 1/60th of a second. Observe the amount of background information lost due to a lack of light. The flash did exactly what it was designed to do—find its first subject, calculate the appropriate amount of light, and turn itself off. (b) was recorded in *Program* mode without a flash and used only ambient light at ISO 400, f/4.0, but required 8 s to complete. A few extra seconds of time recorded a much better overall composition.

representation of a crime scene's physical attributes. In the end, light is available in a multitude of forms and it is merely a matter of locating, metering, and properly exposing for that light to capture truly outstanding images at night.

Attributes of Light

There are several attributes or characteristics of light, all of which can affect nighttime and low-light photography (Figure 5.2). The three primary attributes of lighting affecting crime scene photographers include

Figure 5.2 This illustrates the variety of lighting conditions, colors, and intensities that are present during the nighttime. Observe the green tint of the mercury vapor light striking the exterior of the building and the two different intensities of the incandescent lights shining inside the two doorways. (Photographed by Jeffrey Cruser, Police Sergeant, Houston Police Department, Houston, TX.)

- Intensity of light
- Color of light
- Directionality of light

Unlike the daytime when the sun is typically the sole light source and possesses only one directionality, one level of intensity, and one *white* light, nighttime lighting possesses many more variables. And these variables actually help make nighttime photographs more engaging and interesting for the viewer. Nighttime lighting originates from a variety of sources—everything from streetlights and security lamps to the moon. The multitude of individual light sources cast a variety of intensities and colors across the landscape, which potentially can make nighttime photography more attractive than simple daytime exposures. Similar to daytime lighting, the overall intensity of nighttime lighting varies depending on the environment, weather, and other factors. Recognizing and identifying these attributes and either compensating or using them to create better photographs is a desirable skill to possess.

Intensity is by far the easiest attribute of light for the photographer to control. Recording an image has always been about measuring the intensity of light and determining the relationship between shutter speed, aperture, and ISO value that creates the best possible exposure. The ISO value, aperture, and shutter speed combine in a reciprocal relationship in order to form a properly illuminated image. Simply increasing the ISO value, enlarging the aperture, or lengthening the exposure time will increase an image's overall exposure and vice versa. Therefore, adjusting the intensity of light is easily accomplished through any one of these three values.

If cameras are allowed to make all the exposure decisions (*Program* mode) in low-light conditions, they will likely open up the aperture to the largest aperture. Increasing the size of one's aperture to increase the amount of light allowed into the camera may not always be the most effective choice in low-light situations. Apertures not only allow more or less light into the camera, they also control an image's depth of field. Depth of field is extremely important in crime scene photography and is often necessary to maximize in order to show relationships between key pieces of evidence, evidence and the physical scene, or essential identification information. One of the major drawbacks of working in an automatic or *Program* mode in nocturnal situations is the camera's tendency to open the lens to its largest aperture, thereby shrinking the photograph's depth of field (Figure 5.3). Although the exposure may be excellent and the entire scene well illuminated, the information or evidence present in the photograph may not actually be in focus. Therefore, despite the fact that a larger aperture permits shorter exposure times, depth of field should not be sacrificed for the quick and easy capture of an image. One can also choose higher ISO values to record light more easily in low-light conditions. However, higher ISO values may cause grain to develop in film images and noise to develop in digital images. The degradation of the image by choosing higher ISO values is not always the best choice. Consequently, the only variable left to adjust is time (shutter speed). Longer time exposures are extremely beneficial in low-light conditions.

The time value or shutter speed value is the best choice of the three exposure settings to sacrifice in low-light photography. Apertures need to remain small in order to maintain the depth of field. ISO values should remain low so that sharp, colorful images are recorded. However, shutter speeds can extend over several seconds to even minutes in length, yet still produce excellent overall photographs. Therefore, the photographer should choose his or her aperture and ISO settings for a purpose, and the shutter speed can frequently be

(a)   (b)   (c)

Figure 5.3 (a) was recorded in full *Program* mode, with the flash used the record the image, (a) was recorded at ISO 100, f/4.0, for 1/60th of a second (b) was recorded in *Program* mode, but the flash was not used and the image was recorded at ISO 100, f/4.5, for 5 s. Although (a) has good lighting, the depth of field is too shallow. Just because an investigator works in low-light or nighttime conditions, he or she should not give up on capturing images with deeper depths of field. (c) was recorded at ISO 400, f/22, for 30 s. Sharp-focused backgrounds are absolutely possible in low-light conditions and should not be sacrificed merely to save time.

determined by the camera's light meter. Bracketing images (reducing and increasing exposure) is always advantageous and helps to ensure the best composition. Exposure bracketing should be managed through the adjustment of exposure times.

The only real difference between recording photographs in daytime versus nighttime is the amount of time needed to capture a particular image. Most cameras utilized by crime scene investigators meter light up to and including 30 s in length. However, at times the shutter speed value will exceed 30 s, but the photographer will still need to figure out an exposure evaluation. Remember that a stop of light is equal to one-half or twice the amount of light from the next full stop of light. Therefore, a typical shutter speed dial will be broken down into full stops of 1–2–4–8–15–30 s. Depending on the camera's manufacturer, most photographers have the advantage of having one-half- or one-third-stop increments between the full-stop settings. These incremental stops are extremely beneficial because they allow for the fine-tuning of a photograph's exposure. The fine-tuning of a photograph's exposure is especially important in digital photography, because of the lack of exposure latitude as compared with film photography.

Once a photograph requires an exposure greater than 30 s, the photographer must use a bulb (B) or time (T) exposure. In the bulb mode, the lens will remain open as long as the shutter-release button remains depressed. Bulb exposures will require a cable or remote release. Otherwise, the photographer must hold the shutter button down manually during a lengthy exposure, while trying not to shake the camera. Bulb exposures are frequently necessary in low light when minimizing the size of the aperture in order to create a better depth of field. One problem or challenge that faces a photographer recording bulb exposures is that cameras are unable to evaluate light in the bulb mode. The solution to this challenge is simple: reciprocity. Breaking down light into stop values allows photographers to compare apples to oranges or apertures to shutter speeds to ISO values. As a result, the photographer simply needs to switch the shutter speed value over to 30 s and adjust the ISO and/or aperture values until the camera finds a proper exposure value with the light meter. Reciprocity can then be used to adjust the ISO and aperture values back to the originally desired settings and make the reciprocal or equal adjustments to the shutter speed in order maintain the proper exposure.

For example, say an investigator is photographing a drive-by shooting scene with cartridge cases strewn along an extended roadway. Clearly, depth of field is important because all evidence placards must be both visible and identifiable in the image. As a result, an aperture of f/22 is recommended. Unfortunately, the ambient lighting conditions prevent the camera from finding 18% gray with the smaller aperture choice, and the photographer rolls past 30 s on the shutter speed dial while trying to find a proper exposure. As the camera clicks over to the bulb setting, the camera stops the evaluation process because it does not know the length of the exposure in the bulb mode. In order to determine the proper exposure for such low-light conditions, the photographer should set the camera to the *Manual* capture mode and place the shutter speed value back to 30 s. The next step is to slowly adjust the aperture dial gradually toward larger openings until the camera finds the proper exposure. Now the photographer has a total exposure value and merely has to make equal and opposite adjustments to each value (ISO value, aperture, and shutter speed) in order to return the camera back to the f/22 aperture. For example, adjusting an aperture from f/5.6 to f/8.0 is a decrease of light by one stop, and an equal and opposite adjustment in the length of the exposure is a doubling of the time, that is, 4–8 s. In the end, the amount of light entering the camera is halved by the change in the aperture size, and the amount of time the light is allowed to enter the camera is doubled. Therefore, the total amount of light exposure is the same, but the increase in depth of field is improved. Returning to our poorly illuminated drive-by shooting hypothetical, follow the logical progression of determining an exposure in the following detailed example (Figure 5.4):

- Photographer desires an ISO value of 100 for a sharper, more colorful image and an aperture of f/22 for a better depth of field.
- Poorly illuminated scene causes underexposure warning in the camera at ISO 100 and f/22.
- In *Manual* mode, the camera desires an f/8 aperture at 30 s (ISO 100).
- Three stops of light separate f/8 from f/22 (f/11–f/16–f/22).
- In order to match the loss of light through the aperture, the photographer must double the amount of time by three stops.
- Final exposure equals f/22 at 4 min (30 s doubled to 60 s doubled to 120 s doubled to 240 s or 4 min of exposure).
- An exposure of ISO 200, f/8 at 30 s is exactly the same as an exposure of ISO 100, f/22 at 4 min in regards to light.
- With film, reciprocity failure may require a slightly longer exposure, but it does give the photographer a general idea as to the exposure's length.
- The photographer may bracket the exposure lengths to ensure a quality photograph.

Although most nighttime environments have sufficient ambient light to make reasonable exposures, the investigator may not be able to achieve an exposure reading even when

Figure 5.4 This poorly illuminated scene was metered by the camera and a proper exposure was found at ISO 3200, f/4.0, for 30 s. The camera could meter light up to 30 s, the aperture was opened up, and the ISO value increased until a balanced exposure could be found. The exposure values were adjusted to record a better photograph and, eventually recorded at ISO 400, f/8, for 15 min, an exact reciprocal change in exposure values so that the composition would develop as expected.

opening the aperture to its widest diameter. On those occasions, the photographer can adjust the film speed setting. ISO values may be evaluated in the same manner as the relationship between aperture sizes to shutter speeds. ISO values can be increased so that the camera has more light-gathering ability, thereby giving the camera the ability to meter light in very dim conditions. Once the camera is able to achieve a balanced-light exposure, the photographer can make the reciprocal change between the ISO value and shutter speed in order to capture the best possible image. If the photographer does not have a broad range of ISO values, he or she always has the ability to change both the aperture and the ISO value in order to find a properly metered exposure. The decision as how best to meter light in low-light environments comes down to the photographer's skill level and which settings are more easily adjusted on their particular camera.

On a digital camera, the ISO setting can easily be changed to a higher value until the light can be evaluated. The film speed settings of film cameras may also be temporarily adjusted manually to a higher speed, regardless of what the film canister's DX coding automatically selects. By overriding the DX coding, a film photographer is able to determine an accurate exposure. However, film photographers must be sure to remember and return the ISO setting to the value matching the film loaded into the camera, making the reciprocal changes with the shutter speed. Digital photographers have an advantage as they can choose to remain at a higher ISO value and record an image with one of the camera's preset time values (30 s or less).

As another example to emphasize this reciprocity technique, imagine an investigator is called to investigate a death in a rural, wooded environment. There is little ambient lighting and although a flash would be of value, the investigator wants to capture the available lighting conditions without supplemental light sources. Depth of field is not the issue, only the recording of the true and accurate lighting conditions. The photographer has selected an ISO value of 400 and receives an underexposure warning at f/2.8 (lens' largest aperture) and 30 s. In this hypothetical example, the crime scene investigator can determine a proper exposure through the following steps:

- Underexposure reading at ISO 400, f/2.8, and 30 s.
- Manually adjust ISO value to ISO 3200, where a proper exposure is found at f/2.8 and 30 s.
- Determine the difference between the true and desired ISO speeds (three stops: 400–800–1600–3200).
- Return ISO setting to 400 and double the length of exposure three times to match the change in the ISO value.
- Exposure time for ISO 400 at f/2.8 = 4 min (30–60–120–240 s or 4 min of exposure).

Although the exposure of a truly low-light environment may seem impossible, the photographer can meter light in almost any environment by adjusting camera settings and making reciprocal adjustments. The investigator may ask why not simply photograph low-light crime scenes with high-speed film all the time. The answer is that doing so sacrifices the rich color and sharper images offered by lower ISO values. Patience is a virtue and longer exposures provide the photographer the ability to capture truly outstanding photographic images. In addition, as will be discussed in Chapter 7, the longer exposure times provide photographers greater versatility to add supplemental light into a composition.

As has been discussed, cameras are quite capable of metering light in many low-light conditions. However, there is one necessity and that is light. The camera does not need a lot of light, but clearly needs some illumination so that the camera's light meter is capable of obtaining a proper exposure. Figure 5.5a was recorded in an extremely dark warehouse during the nighttime. The figure shows a properly exposed picture of an overhead crane. The exposure was recorded at ISO 400, f/4.0, for 8 min, which was a seven-stop *overexposure* from what the camera wanted as a proper exposure. The lesson learned from this example is that cameras are fallible and cannot always be trusted. Experience is certainly an advantage. However, any amount of experience should inform photographers

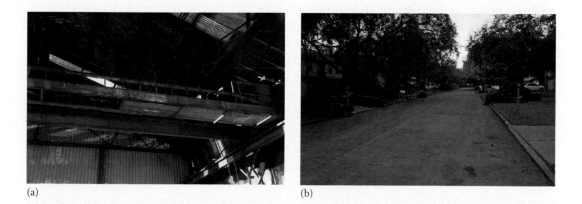

(a)   (b)

Figure 5.5 When there is a significant lack of light shining within a composition, cameras are generally unable to evaluate a proper exposure. (a) is just such a composition and is technically a seven-stop overexposure according to the camera's light meter. The exposure was recorded at ISO 400 and f/4.0 and recorded for 8 min. Generally, allowing the exposure to extend for several minutes is necessary for extremely dark compositions. (b) was recorded during a power failure and once again, the camera was unable to make an accurate light evaluation. The exposure was allowed to continue for 4.5 min (ISO 400 and f/5.6). The length of the exposure was determined after a 2 min exposure came up just a little underexposed and the photographic was a bracketed exposure by basically doubling the amount of light from the underexposed first image.

that an exposure of ISO 400, f/4.0, for 4 s will never be able to record an image in such a dark environment in which the overhead crane was found. So, what is an investigator to do when recording images in extremely dark conditions? The answer is simple: add more time to the exposure. Figure 5.5b was recorded during a power failure at night, and once again, the camera was unable to accurately meter the scene. This image was recorded at ISO 400, f/5.6, for 4.5 min. One does have the option of speeding up the exposures by increasing the ISO value, but as described earlier, photography is a *give-and-take* endeavor, and the trade-off with higher ISO values is a less-sharp and less-colorful image. As a result, there is no immediate need to jump the ISO value up to a much higher setting or even open up the aperture, sacrificing the composition's depth of field, in order to record an image. Sacrificing the image's depth of field or color and sharpness is not necessary. Simply extend the length of the exposure and bracket one's exposures until a quality image is recorded. Not every dimly illuminated composition will be an exact seven-stop difference between the camera's metering of a really dark crime scene and a quality photographic image, as with Figure 5.5a, but experience and the ability to immediately review one's efforts should make the recording of a quality image easily obtained after just two or three attempts. Digital photographers are fortunate that they are able to review their images immediately after recording them. Film photographers will have to bracket their compositions in order to ensure an accurately recorded photograph. Every composition is different and *flexibility* in evaluating crime scenes for light is the key to recording images in low-light conditions.

The direction light travels and impacts a surface is another attribute of light that affects crime scene photographers. As discussed in Chapters 4 and 6, the direction from which light is applied to a piece of evidence can make the difference between being able to visualize the subject and having it disappear completely from view. Any light originating from a source will have directionality. Light can filter down onto crime scenes from a number of directions, and it is this aspect of ambient or available light photography that makes nighttime photography so beautiful (Figure 5.6). Daytime lighting originates from a single source, the sun. Electronic flash illumination also originates from a single source, unless multiple flashes are utilized in a painting with light undertaking. In contrast, using a nighttime crime scene's natural lighting offers the potential of multiple sources of light impacting a composition from multiple angles.

An investigator does not step outside into a black void when working crime scenes after the sun goes down. Regardless of what defense attorneys may want a jury to believe, there is typically enough light to identify people, vehicles, and transpiring events in nighttime, low-light conditions. Crime scene photographers must be able to accurately capture images in the lighting conditions found after dark. Nighttime illumination comes in a myriad of forms and intensities ranging from the moon to streetlights that filter down onto a scene. The multidirectional aspect of these light sources is the advantage of ambient light photography over flash photography. The light traveling across the scene from different angles provides a 3D quality to the photograph versus the 1D or 2D perspective present in daytime or flash photography.

This 3D aspect of ambient light photography brings out details in images that may be missed by the investigator who always relies on an electronic flash to photograph at night. Details can be lost in the shadows created by a fired electronic flash, whereas light falling from multiple sources can help fill in shadowed areas. Shadows are still present in

(a)   (b)

Figure 5.6 (a) and (b) illustrate how nighttime lighting conditions can actually create a more interesting and eye-pleasing photograph because the illumination impacting the scene comes from various sources and directions, giving a 3D appearance to the image. (a) is a daytime recorded image, while (b) is a time exposure capturing the different light sources illuminating the landscape and was recorded at ISO 400, f/16, for 10 s.

the nighttime and that particular dilemma can be overcome by adding electronic flash or other light sources to the composition. Painting with light and shining light onto areas of shadows is discussed in Chapter 7. For the time being, simply allowing ambient light to filter over a scene and be recorded through the use of a timed exposure will help the investigator create more illuminating photographs, both literally and figuratively. Furthermore, it can actually be more *true and accurate* than a photograph recorded with flash.

In addition to providing a 3D appearance to images, controlling the direction of lighting has other advantages to the crime scene photographer. Oblique, side-, and backlighting are important to forensic work. Certainly, backlit subjects can cause problems for the photographer and the camera. However, a subject can be deliberately backlit to reveal hidden details. For example, watermarks and other antiforgery imprints found on documents and currency can be photographed by using backlighting. There are many ways to illuminate different types of evidence, and crime scene investigators should use these nondestructive processes before utilizing more destructive ones. Backlighting evidence is not limited to questioned documents. Any semitransparent subject can be photographed through backlighting, items from fingerprints to fauna and flora (Figure 5.7).

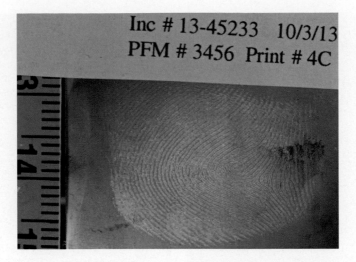

Figure 5.7 Backlighting evidence can be used to bring out or enhance hidden details found in thin pieces of evidence, such as depicted in this photo. The background light was created by a small flashlight placed underneath the tape, thereby illuminating the fingerprint found on the sticky side of the tape.

Creating backlighting is not difficult. The necessary tools for the job are reasonably affordable and may already be in a photographer's arsenal. Using an old photographic slide viewing table is one option. By placing the slide viewing table underneath a securely mounted camera, the evidence can be placed on top of the illuminated board, thus allowing light to pass through the evidence and be photographed. If a crime scene investigator does not have an already constructed light board, one is easily built using a piece of translucent material that can support the minimal weight of thin pieces of evidence. Slender pieces of plastic, preferably semitransparent white for accurate color balance, can be purchased at the neighborhood hardware or hobby store. A supporting structure, such as a wooden box, can be built to support the sheet of plastic, and a small fluorescent or incandescent light can be mounted underneath the plastic. When the need arises, having the hardware on hand to backlight evidence will save a lot of time and frustration.

Color is another attribute of light that has a significant impact on a composition's quality. Those who remember high school physics will recall that as light passes through a glass prism, the waves of light are separated into individual colors. Humans typically see light as white, but white light actually consists of all the colors of the rainbow, from red to violet. Visible light waves are found on the electromagnetic spectrum between 400 and 700 nm. Light waves below 400 nm are referred to as ultraviolet (UV), and wavelengths longer than 700 nm are known as infrared (IR). Photography is possible in the UV and IR spectrums, and those topics are covered in Chapter 10. The human eye naturally interprets most visible light as white; however, cameras record the more accurate and individual colors of light cast by the numerous light sources found in nighttime conditions.

As stated earlier, nighttime illumination impacts a scene or photographic subjects from multiple directions and from multiple sources. This is fortunate because all the colors and directionalities of nighttime lighting help create vivid and artistic quality images. Different colored light sources commonly encountered at crime scenes include

- Incandescent (typical house lights)
  - Color: deep yellow to orange
- Fluorescent (common home and business lighting)
  - Color: green (discontinuous light source)
- High-pressure sodium (streetlights)
  - Color: yellow
- Low-pressure sodium (streetlighting—not very common)
  - Color: deep orange
- Mercury vapor (street and security lighting)
  - Color: blue to green
- Metal halide (car dealerships and sports arenas—best white balance)
  - Color: white

The color of light actually produced by any one source can vary between individual lights because of its age and any screening device or glass encasements that might surround the actual bulb. As will be discussed, the color of light can add value to an image, and photographers should not necessarily be bothered by the unique or variable light colors found in nighttime environments.

One light source that may pose a particular issue to photographers is a fluorescent light. Fluorescent lighting is a discontinuous light source. The light pulsates, creating alternating brightness and dimness. The human eye does not see the light pulsating, but a camera can. In order to ensure that an ambient light photograph recorded under fluorescent illumination receives an adequate exposure, the photographer must keep the shutter speed below 1/60 of a second. When there are numerous fluorescent tubes present in the composition, the risk of an underexposure is not as great because all the pulsating lights average out. However, just to be safe, exposures slower than 1/60th of a second are recommended when utilizing fluorescent lighting as the primary light source.

Colored lighting offers several benefits for crime scene investigators. The first is simply the quality of a well-photographed time exposure that accurately records a scene's illumination. Photographs taken during the daytime or solely with flash illumination frequently have a monotone appearance. Nighttime photographs are greatly improved over other images because of the variety, brilliance, and color present in a nighttime lighting. The colored light sources give photographs a strong, dramatic look that can impress the viewer. An additional advantage of having the different colors visible in the recorded image is that during testimony, the crime scene investigator can accurately identify the type of light source present at the location based on its color and appearance (Figure 5.8).

Because of the advantage of being able to identify light sources by their colors in front of a jury, using filters or a digital camera's color or white balance to color correct an image is not always advantageous. Investigators utilizing digital cameras need to know how to manipulate the various camera functions so that the recorded image ends up as intended, specifically in regard to color. Digital cameras can be set to *daylight* (white-balance setting) during the nighttime so that the colors of individual light sources are reproduced more accurately. Photographers may wish to bracket their exposures by resetting their white balance to *auto* or to the prevalent light source present on the scene, thereby recording images with and without color balancing (color compensation). Once again, bracketing exposures is the one sure way to guarantee the best end result. Film photographers can also bracket their exposures by photographing with and without color-compensating filters.

Figure 5.8 This illustrates the variety of colors that can be found at any given crime scene. The colored light sources include high-pressure sodium lamps along the roadway (yellow), fluorescent lights inside the bank (green), mercury vapor lamps mounted in front of the building (blue-green), and white-balanced metal halide lamps illuminating the flags in front of the bank. The streaks of light passing through the image were caused by passing vehicles.

The color of light can be measured through the Kelvin scale. In 1848, Lord Kelvin, or William Thomson (1824–1907), who wrote *On an Absolute Thermometric Scale*, established the *absolute zero* temperature as being equivalent to approximately 273° below 0°C. He further defined zero temperature as having no thermal (heat) energy. Increases in heat cause increases in temperature. As this principle applies to visible light and photography, increases in the Kelvin temperature of light change the visible color of that light. Black is described as a lack of color. In physics, a *blackbody* or *blackbody radiator* is an object that absorbs all light and allows no light to pass through or reflect off it. Heating this blackbody causes it to change color, and those colors can be compared to the colors given off by various lamps. As the Kelvin temperature increases to approximately 3000°, a blackbody radiator begins to glow orange. Incandescent and tungsten lights are typically found around the 3000°–3400° range. Orange and red colors are actually considered warm temperatures, which seems in conflict with an increasing of temperatures along the Kelvin scale. As the heat increases, the blackbody begins moving from the red region into the blue region. At around 4000 K, one will typically begin to find fluorescent lights, which have a green cast. Nearing the 5500° plateau, a blackbody radiator will begin to turn a shade of blue, comparable to daylight illumination. Blue is often referred to as a *cool* color. Of course, daylight temperatures can vary depending on the cloud cover, time of year, and time of day. Electronic flashes typically operate somewhere around 6500 K but give off the best white-balanced light for photography.

All in all, the color of light is less important to crime scene photography than the intensity. For the photographer concerned with the color of light, knowing the Kelvin temperatures of light sources will make choosing a compensating filter or digital camera setting much easier. For photographers who must have all the gizmos and gadgets, color meters are available that will evaluate different light sources and determine the exact Kelvin temperature of an ambient light source. Color meters can be rather expensive, and although they are useful in crime scene photography on rare occasions, the cost–benefit analysis makes them largely an unnecessary luxury. Fortunately, digital cameras typically possess a custom calibration or evaluation of light for color (custom white balance). Along with the typical white-balance settings such as auto, daylight, fluorescent, and incandescent, digital cameras are now capable of customizing colored light in 100° increments. The photographer merely places a sheet of clean white paper or in some cases an 18% gray card, underneath the light source. Filling the viewfinder with the white sheet of paper or gray card allows the camera to calculate the light's color temperature based on the known white or gray value of the photographed paper. The exact way in which this evaluation is achieved can vary between cameras and manufacturers. Therefore, one must refer to their camera's instruction manual. To evaluate the light, the photographer may either need to actually photograph the paper or simply position the camera over the known subject. In either case, once the custom white-balance setting is entered into the camera, subsequent photographs can be exposed without any unwanted hues or shadings in the final recorded image.

Filtration may be necessary when photographing without electronic flash in nighttime environments, as well as indoor environments. Flash is excellent for providing a color-balanced image, but flash photography does have a couple of drawbacks. Flashes might cause the finer details of some subjects to become washed out. For example, photographing small bloodstains or capturing a victim's injuries might be better recorded under ambient light conditions versus the utilization of a flash unit. In order to record the accurate color of a piece of evidence or injury in ambient light, filtration may be necessary. Investigators cannot possibly anticipate every light source, much less every light source's age and any filtering that the light may pass through prior to striking a subject. However, possessing standard compensating filters for fluorescent and incandescent lighting is an advantage for film photographers. Equally, digital photographers should be familiar with their camera's white-balance features and be familiar with compensating for the unwanted hue of the various light sources commonly encountered at crime scenes.

Two of the most common filters used by crime scene photographers are the 80 series and fluorescent-to-daylight (FL-D) filters. Incandescent lighting casts a yellow to orange tone on film that can be compensated for by an 80A or 80B filter. These blue filters ensure that the recorded image is balanced for white. Because the age of a light can impact the depth or intensity of the tonal range of the light's color, having both an 80A filter and an 80B filter ensures a more accurate white tone. The 80A filter is slightly more dense and will remove a little more orange to yellow hue than an 80B. The 80B filter, being slightly less dense, is also capable of balancing the less intense yellow tone of high-pressure sodium lamps. The green color of fluorescent lighting is compensated for by using an FL-D filter, which has a pink tone and converts the green hues of fluorescent lighting to white. The FL-D filter can also be used to help remove the blue-green tones of mercury vapor lamps. Digital cameras have built-in color compensation settings for both incandescent and fluorescent lightings.

Another way to adjust for colored light is by intentionally overexposing the image. Underexposed photographs typically have richer, more vivid colors. On the other hand, overexposed images will cause the colors to fade and gravitate more toward a whiter tone. By *overexposing* a composition by one, maybe two, stop of light, color values can become more balanced for white, while the overall image's exposure is not detrimentally altered (Figure 5.9). It bears repeating that bracketing exposures ensures recording an image that is acceptable in both color tones and intensity. In addition, everyone has different perceptions of light and color. By having two or three photographic images of a nighttime crime scene's composition, witnesses can choose the image that most closely resembles the

(a)   (b)

Figure 5.9 These series of images were recorded with the color balance set to *daylight*, thereby accurately recording the true color of the scene's lighting. (a) was recorded as metered by the camera (ISO 100, f/11, for 8 s). (b) was recorded by increasing the exposure by two stops (ISO 100, f/11, for 30 s). Notice how the image's tone became more balanced for white, without a drastic effect occurring to the image's overall exposure value.

lighting conditions they recall at the time of the incident under investigation. Therefore, recording an image that may be slightly overexposed to the eye of the photographer may still have value to another individual.

Reciprocity Failure: Film versus Digital

The ability to accurately adjust an exposure's shutter speed, aperture, and/or ISO value is predicated on the concept of *reciprocity*. Reciprocity is a rule in photography that states an image's exposure remains constant as long as the product of shutter speed, aperture, and film speed remains constant. Basically, reciprocity allows a photographer to compare apples to oranges or, in other words, make equally valued changes in one's camera settings in order to maintain or obtain a properly exposed photograph. During low-light or nighttime endeavors, this reciprocal relationship starts to fail with film recordings and is known as *reciprocity failure*. Reciprocity failure occurs because of a decrease in sensitivity to light in the film's emulsion (light-gathering ability of the film's chemical compounds). Essentially, after a few seconds of exposure time, the reciprocal or equivalent relationships between apertures and shutter speeds stop working in a truly reciprocal manner. Thus, film ceases to be influenced by additional light during long exposures as one would expect during typical daytime exposures. This reciprocity failure offers a great benefit for crime scene investigators utilizing film by providing a great deal of exposure latitude and making it rather difficult to overexpose a nighttime composition. However, with the switch to digital imaging, the question that many have is: "Does reciprocity failure still occur when recording low-light images with a digital camera?"

The short and simple answer is that reciprocity failure does *not* apply to digital imaging. Because a digital imaging chip does not possess a silver-halide chemical emulsion, the imaging chip will continue to record light after the first few seconds in the same manner it does while photographing much shorter exposures. The photographs depicted in Figure 5.10a and b were recorded on film and with a digital camera set at ISO 400,

Figure 5.10 (a) was recorded with a digital camera. (b) was recorded with a film camera. Both images (a and b) were recorded with camera settings of ISO 400, f/4.5, for 2 s. (c) was recorded with a digital camera. (d) was recorded with a film camera. Both images (c and d) were recorded at ISO 400, f/2.8, for 30 s, which is a 5⅓-stop overexposure. Observe how the film image was far more tolerant (*reciprocity failure*) of the *extra light* added to the image.

f/4.5, for 2 s. The overall appearances of both the film and digital recordings of the two images are nearly identical. However, the intentional overexposure of the composition by five and a third stops of light ended up drastically different. Remember that a one-stop change in light is equal to one-half or twice the value of light as compared to the next full stop. Figure 5.10c and d is recorded at ISO 400, f/2.8, for 30 s. Reciprocity failure (the decrease in sensitivity of the recording film to light) clearly occurs in the film image (Figure 5.10d), but light continued to have a large impact on the digitally recorded image (Figure 5.10c) throughout the exposure. Although there is a slight overexposure in Figure 5.10d, the overall composition was not completely destroyed by a fivefold increase in light. In contrast, the digital image (Figure 5.10c) was completely washed out by the additional light. Figure 5.10c is similar to what one would expect during a daytime composition that was overexposed by five stops.

It is important for crime scene photographers to recognize that reciprocity failure does not carry over when switching from a film-based system to digital imaging. Although one is sacrificing the latitude or room for error when capturing low-light images with a digital camera, the trade-off is that one can more accurately predict or calculate a nighttime composition. With film, one could estimate their time exposures and bracket their compositions in the hope that enough light was recorded. However, digital-exposure calculations

(a)   (b)

Figure 5.11 (a) was recorded at ISO 3200, f/1.8, for 1 s. (b) was recorded with a seven-stop change in exposure values and was recorded at ISO 100, f/32, for 8 min. The exposure difference was necessary in order to make the foreground and background become more focused.

are very straightforward and are the same in the daytime as they are in low-light compositions. Figure 5.11a was recorded in extremely low light, requiring an ISO of 3200 and an aperture of f/8, and was exposed for 1 s. Figure 5.11b was recorded at ISO 100 and f/32 and was exposed over the span of eight full minutes. The change in ISO value from 3200 to 100 was a loss of five stops of light. The change in aperture value from f/8 to f/32 was a loss of an additional four stops of light, for a total loss of nine stops of light between Figure 5.11a and b. In order to balance the exposure in a reciprocal fashion, a total of nine stops of light were added to Figure 5.11b by increasing the length of the exposure from 1 s to 8 min: 1–2–4–8–15–30–60–120–240–480 s. Notice how the light values of the two images are similar and how the depth of field improved in Figure 5.11b. Such an adjustment could be quite advantageous to a crime scene photographer. Oftentimes, investigators give up on depth of field in low-light conditions because their cameras will not meter exposures with extremely small apertures. However, a digital photographer requiring an extensive zone of sharp focus can predict with certainty the length of an exposure outside of 30 s. The first step is to open up the camera's aperture and increase the ISO value to the point where the camera can obtain a proper exposure. Next, meter the ambient light and determine a balanced exposure for the wide-open aperture and higher ISO value settings. Finally, make reciprocal adjustments in the settings so that the large aperture can be decreased to a more desirable opening. This process is demonstrated in Figure 5.11a and b. Figure 5.11a was metered with the ambient light, and then the reciprocal changes were made to achieve an equally illuminated image in Figure 5.11b.

There are a number of trade-offs when choosing between digital and film imaging. As far as low-light and long time exposures are concerned, the main trade-off is the choice between the predictability of digital imaging and the exposure leeway offered by film imaging. Fortunately, with a little deliberate and creative composition, a digital photographer can have the best of both worlds. As long as one arranges their composition in a way that keeps harsh light sources out of the image, then unintentional overexposures with digital media are not going to be as damaging as what might occur during a daytime exposure. Digital photographers have the added bonus of reviewing their images immediately after capture. They can review their images and make corrections for exposure errors prior to leaving the crime scene.

As another potential photographic challenge, when an investigator needs to paint their scene with light or reconstruct the scene of a shooting with lasers, the exact length of the ultimate composition may not be known until the painting process or laser reconstruction is completed. Certainly, one can bracket the photograph's capture, but by keeping harsh light sources out of the image, an accidental overexposure will not unduly harm a photograph. Of course, one must still be mindful of underexposing an image. Compare Figure 5.12a and b (both images were digitally recorded). Figure 5.12a's exposure evaluation was determined by the camera and was recorded at ISO 400, f/8, for 15 s. Figure 5.12b was intentionally overexposed by three stops and was recorded at ISO 400, f/4.0, for 30 s. Although Figure 5.12b is brighter, the overall composition did not degrade as much as one might expect from a daytime image overexposed by three stops, especially in the darker foreground. One of the great benefits of digital imaging is the ability of the average person to adjust exposures with ease during postcapture editing. Figure 5.12c was an intentional overexposure of the same composition by five stops of light and was recorded at ISO 1600, f/4.0, for 30 s. However, with a *small* amount of exposure correction with Adobe Photoshop®, an acceptable image was easily obtained. It should be noted that if a photographer anticipates exposure difficulties or is dealing with drastic contrasts in their composition, then it would be advantageous to record the digital image in a RAW (uncompressed and unprocessed) format. RAW images typically have greater bit depth over JPG images

(a)

(b)

(c)

Figure 5.12 (a) was recorded as metered by the camera. (b) was intentionally overexposed by three stops of light. There was no postcapture editing for figure (b). (c) was intentionally overexposed by five stops of light, but the image was processed with Photoshop® in order to help improve the image.

and, consequently, record a greater amount of information that can be extremely valuable for adjusting exposure levels in postcapture editing programs.

A vast majority of agencies have now completed the conversion from film to digital imaging, and individual photographers are typically dependent upon what their agency dictates as the method of capture. However, digital photographers may not want to toss their old film cameras into the trash just yet. Digital cameras typically suffer from *noise* during long exposures, especially with cropped-sensor cameras. Noise refers to the unwanted artifacts or random pieces of information added to photographs during long exposures. Noise can also be found in images recorded at high ISO values (ISO 1600 and higher). Most frequently, noise occurs in the form of unwanted red, blue, and green pixels added to a digital photograph. Some digital cameras have built-in noise-reduction filters, but these noise-reduction filters can only do so much, and they do not come close to the sharpness and clarity that film is able to offer. In addition to the noise-reduction filters found on the camera, postcapture editing programs such as Adobe Photoshop have noise-reduction features that can be used to create even better images. Figure 5.13a was recorded at ISO 3200, f/22, for 20 min and was captured without any noise-reduction filters applied. Figure 5.13b was recorded at the exact same settings, but high-speed and long-exposure

(a)   (b)

(c)

Figure 5.13 (a) was recorded with a cropped-sensor Canon 40D camera without any noise-reduction filters applied. (b) was recorded with a cropped-sensor Canon 40D camera with the high-ISO and long-exposure noise-reduction filters turned on. (c) was recorded with a full-frame sensor Canon 6D camera without any noise-reduction filters applied. All three exposures were recorded at ISO 3200, f/22, for 20 min.

noise-reduction settings were selected on the camera. The details visible in Figure 5.13b are far superior to those found in Figure 5.13a. As a comparison, Figure 5.13c was recorded of the same composition and the same exposure values of ISO 3200, f/22, for 20 min, but the image was recorded with a full-frame sensor camera. There was no postcapture editing or noise reduction utilized in Figure 5.13c. The benefits of a full-frame digital camera are quite apparent.

Crime scene investigators should utilize all the tools available to them in order to accurately document their crime scenes, as well as capture the sharpest possible images. Digital cameras can certainly capture crystal clear images, even in the nighttime. Furthermore, low-light exposures can be accurately calculated even in the poorly illuminated environments. Digital image files can also be easily processed in order to improve the overall quality of the image. However, there are still times when extended time exposures are necessary, and the fact that reciprocity failure can be quite beneficial to a photographer and to the final recorded image, a film camera should be available to all crime scene investigators. Film's failure of reciprocity helps prevent overexposures. Film also offers the advantage of not adding extraneous noise to long exposures. Consequently, investigators should consider keeping a film camera or two in their arsenal for those times when exposures lasting tens of minutes or longer become necessary. Whichever photographic format is used to capture low-light images, photographers can improve their images through careful composition, deliberate exposure calculations, and an understanding of reciprocity and reciprocity failure.

Working Low-Light and Nighttime Crime Scenes

One of the first steps in processing any crime scene is to thoroughly examine and search the location for evidence. When working nighttime crime scenes and preparing for their photographic documentation, this examination of the scene must also include an evaluation of the ambient lighting conditions. There will always be some light present, no matter how dim it may appear to be. Light does not simply disappear into some black hole when the sun goes down. Before embarking on a nighttime photography assignment, the photographer must also have the necessary tools. Point-and-shoot cameras are notoriously ineffective in low-light conditions. A single-lens reflex (SLR) camera offers the versatility needed by today's investigators and is one of the two primary tools photographers must possess. The other of course is a tripod.

With exposures lasting tens of seconds instead of tenths of a second in low-light environments, an SLR camera with a *bulb* or *time* exposure setting is often required. To utilize the bulb feature, an investigator will need a remote-shutter release. These come in a variety of styles, but the electronic remote release is preferred. The remote release is physically attached to the camera, either through an electrical-contact link or threaded into the shutter release button. There are IR remotes available to photographers, but be aware of the IR remote's range. If the IR remote is moved out of range from the camera, it may trigger the camera to stop the exposure.

Unless the investigator is using an older, mechanical-shutter 35 mm camera such as the Pentax K1000, an ample supply of batteries is essential, especially when the photographer is going to perform a large number of time exposures. Extra batteries are also vitally important when using a digital camera because they tend to drain a battery much faster than film cameras. In addition to metering the light and holding the shutter open during the exposure, the digital camera must also write the image to the storage media when the shutter closes.

Tripods, often a forgotten implement in a crime scene investigator's arsenal, are also essential. A surefire way to destroy one's ability to accurately document a low-light crime scene is to leave the tripod at the office or, worse yet, have it available to the investigator but fail to use it. Correctly utilizing the tripod will greatly enhance the final recorded images. Tripods are meant to stabilize a camera, but if extended improperly, they can act more like a swaying pendulum than an anchor. The upper portion of a tripod's legs should be extended first, then the lower segments, and finally the neck. The neck should be used to fine-tune the position of a tripod's head, but it should not be used as the primary means of extension. If the tripod is lightweight, an extended neck can move or vibrate during long exposures. Draping a weighted bean bag or some other flexible weight across the tripod's legs or center column may help stabilize a camera mounted on a lightweight tripod.

When actually photographing a nighttime crime scene, consider switching to the *Manual* exposure mode. *Program* mode is very limiting. In addition to giving the photographer more control over the aperture and shutter speed settings, the *Manual* mode makes the bracketing of exposures much easier (Figure 5.14). Digital images cannot always be properly evaluated by reviewing them through the small LCD screen on the back of the camera. Bracketing the images for different exposure levels, composition, and subject matter is vital. As previously mentioned, recording low-light images is not that much

(a)   (b)

Figure 5.14 Evaluating a nighttime crime scene begins by determining where light is shining and its intensity. In compositions possessing a high contrast between the shadows and highlights, the photographer measures the most intense light found on the scene, and an appropriate combination of ISO value, aperture, and shutter speed is chosen. Photographers should locate the brightest area within the camera's field of view and determine an exposure for that small area. In (a), the brightest area of the scene is underneath the light just out of view on the left side of the image. With the ISO set at 100 and the aperture set for f/8, the camera decided a 4 s exposure was needed to properly expose the small grass area underneath the light. This gives photographers a starting point. Now the bracketing of exposures can occur by increasing the length of the exposure for two or three additional photographs. (b) is a three-stop increase in light (from 4 to 30 s), and although the small illuminated area of the composition is slightly overexposed, the overall image was greatly improved.

different than photographing in the daytime. The basic steps to nighttime photography will be discussed in the following pages and include the following:

- Securely mount camera to tripod.
- Choose aperture and ISO value as desired.
- Compose the image in the viewfinder.
- Meter the composition and determine the exposure's length.
  - For evenly illuminated scenes, metering the overall composition should be adequate.
  - For scenes with a lot of contrast, meter the brightest part of the scene and bracket the photographs toward longer exposures, recording a series of increasingly illuminated images.
- In the coming chapters, the addition of supplemental light into the composition will be discussed.
  - Adding supplemental light in order to create a balance between the shadows and highlights oftentimes results in the very best image.

After switching to the *Manual* mode on the tripod-mounted camera, the next step is to compose the image in the viewfinder. Remember, the photographer is responsible for what is included in the image. The camera cannot determine the scene's composition. Next, the investigator needs to select a film speed or ISO setting. The values of sharper, more colorful photographs that result from ISO 100 or 200 settings are well worth the extra effort and time that will be required. Faster film speeds allow for shorter exposures. However, since the camera will be mounted on a tripod anyway, the advantage of shorter exposure should not be an issue. Now that the photographer is properly equipped and the light-gathering ability (ISO setting) of the camera is set, it is time to choose an aperture.

Typically, when photographing the scene-establishing or overall scene photographs, the camera lens' focal point is more likely going to be near or at the *infinity* mark. Since overall photographs are taken from a distance, the focus point is typically at the end of the focus ring (infinity). The infinity mark is designated by ∞ symbol. Depth of field is not a serious concern since typically everything beyond 20–30 ft should be in sharp focus when the camera is focused at infinity. The choice of an aperture is up to the photographer, but selecting an aperture somewhere in the middle of the lens' aperture range is usually best. When in doubt, start with an aperture of f/8 or f/11, which is typically found in the middle of the lens' range of apertures. Of course, when depth of field is an issue and needs to be extended, smaller apertures (f/16 or f/22) should be selected. Now the photographer has two of the three exposure variables chosen, and only the length of the exposure is left to determine.

Up to this point, the photographer has composed his or her image and has chosen two of the three exposure variables (ISO value and aperture). The next step is to evaluate the scene for lighting and determine the length of the exposure. Also as a reminder: investigators should not be in a rush to complete the scene's photography. Before photographing a low-light crime scene, remember to survey and examine the scene thoroughly and photograph with a purpose or with a goal in mind. One should never rush through a scene's photographic documentation solely because it's *easier* or less work.

The photographer should now evaluate the scene for light intensity in order to find a proper shutter speed. Photographers should identify the areas of shadows, the areas of highlights, and any specific harsh or hard light sources projecting light directly onto the scene or into the camera lens. Areas of harsh lighting cause photographers the greatest difficulties, and those scenes may need additional help in getting the image into balance. Creating balance in compositions that contain areas of strong contrast (light) is easily accomplished with the adding of supplemental light and is covered more fully in Chapter 7. For now, the focus of this discussion will be on the evaluation of light, the actual composition of images, and the recording of images solely with ambient light.

In composing a photograph, investigators should seek to limit the impact of harsh light sources. Harsh light sources that project directly into the camera frequently cause the camera to underexpose the image. In addition, a halo or starburst effect around the light source may appear, and this can create unwanted distractions in the photograph. For these reasons, an investigator should limit the light source's visibility in the camera's viewfinder. One only needs to remove the actual area where the light is being emitted, that is, the actual light bulb or light source. The area where the light is falling onto the scene can still be incorporated into the scene's image.

Limiting these point light sources in the viewfinder and ultimately in the final recorded image is often a simple matter of composition. For example, streetlamps that line a roadway can be kept out of the final recorded image by simply tilting the camera slightly downward so that the lamps' bulbs are just outside the picture's frame. The photographer will still be able to see where the light falls and where the shadows are located and even identify the light by its color, but the distractions caused by the starbursts and halos of light will be limited. Not only will the limiting of harsh light sources assist in the quality of the final recorded image but it also helps the camera meter the scene's lighting more accurately.

Tilting the camera to remove streetlights from an image is especially beneficial for those lamps closer to the tripod-mounted camera. However, more distant lamps may still have a negative effect. For these lamps, try positioning the camera so that harsh light sources are fully or partially blocked by a natural barrier present in the foreground. For instance, strategically positioning a stop sign, a telephone pole, or a tree between the camera and the light source can block the harsh light but will still leave the majority of the scene visible and the ambient light conditions clearly discernible (Figure 5.15).

Strong television camera lights and strobe lights on police cars can also be quite troublesome to crime scene photographers because they can alter the natural lighting conditions and cause exposure metering difficulties. Safety is a concern for investigators and police officers alike, and strobe lights protect the crime scene from intoxicated drivers and curious onlookers. However, if a photographer has strobe lights flashing into a camera's lens and/or viewfinder, the camera's light meter can actually be seen fluctuating in synchronization with the on and off strobe effects of the police lights. One solution is to turn off these lights or any other light sources not naturally a part of the crime scene's location during the recorded exposures. A police vehicle's strobe lights, for example, are typically designed with front and rear flashers. Both sides of the light bar do not have to be turned off, only the ones that point into the crime scene. The other strobes directed away from the scene for safety and security can remain illuminated. The decision to turn lights on or off belongs to the investigator, but the scene's natural lighting should not be altered if possible, since it might result in an inaccurate portrayal of the scene's natural illumination.

If changes in lighting are made, a series of photographs should be taken that show the actual lighting conditions present at the time of the incident as well as the changes made to improve the photograph's composition or exposure. Bracketing of exposures in order to

Figure 5.15 Strategically placing impediments between harsh light sources and the camera can help create better photographs by eliminating glare, halos, and unintended streaks of light from developing in the image. As seen in this photograph, the harshness of the porch light has been eliminated, but the area impacted by the light source is still discernible.

capture the most *true and accurate* exposure of any crime scene's composition is definitely a recommended practice. The cost of film or digital storage space should never outweigh the value of completeness. Therefore, taking a few extra photographs here and there should not be an area of concern.

After composing the image, the next challenge to be addressed is where to begin the metering process in order to determine the third exposure variable (shutter speed). Because cameras are different in their light metering capabilities, photographers must be familiar with and understand how their personal equipment functions. Photographers are not always able to simply frame the image and let the camera decide what is the best exposure. The camera may misinterpret a portion of the scene's lighting because of a nearby light source that impacts the camera's metering, but that same light may not necessarily affect the entire composition. In addition, light may enter the eye piece or eye cup of some cameras, which can also affect the camera's light metering. Knowing whether or not one's personal camera allows this to occur is extremely important. Simply covering the eye piece with a cloth or some other cover (one's eye as he or she looks through the viewfinder) during the metering of light will prevent any light leakage from affecting the light metering of the composition.

As for actually metering a scene's lighting, it is not always a difficult task. In fact, the majority of scenes one encounters will likely be easily evaluated for light by the camera. If the scene's light is evenly distributed, whether bright or dim, light meters can generally determine an 18% gray value and find a shutter speed to match the chosen ISO and aperture values that will do justice to the exposure. However, for those scenes with a noticeable difference between the shadows and highlights, the photographer should locate the brightest area of the crime scene and determine the exposure value for that specific area. Most likely, this will be an area beneath a light source, such as a business's security lamp or a streetlight. The area of highlights will frequently become the starting point for the photographer working in low-light situations (Figure 5.16).

The most accurate way to meter a small area of a larger picture is to walk over to the brightest spot and meter the light using a gray card. Fill the camera's viewfinder with the

Figure 5.16 When examining a nighttime crime scene for light, especially when there are extremes in the highlights and shadows, photographers should begin their exposure by metering the lights in the brightest portion of the scene (ISO 400, f/8, for 20 s). If necessary, light can be added to the areas of shadow or the overall exposure increased in subsequent exposures.

gray card, making sure the card reflects the full intensity of the light source and that no shadows are cast across the card. Since the ISO and aperture values have already been chosen, manually set the shutter speed so that the light meter is balanced to zero in the viewfinder. Remember the aperture should be selected to meet any depth of field concerns and the shutter speed can be adjusted last in order to find the proper light exposure. If a gray card is unavailable, meter on a surface close in reflectivity to 18% gray, such as a grass lawn or gray-colored vehicle. The camera should be in *Manual* mode because if the camera is in the *Program* mode, once the camera is returned to the tripod for the actual exposure, then the exposure values just determined will be changed to match the new orientation. Recording the image in the *Manual* mode will ensure that any aperture and shutter speed settings selected while metering the area of highlights will remain set when the camera is moved away and the actual image is recomposed. In the *Manual* mode and with the camera returned to the actual composition (not just the area of highlight), the camera's light meter will likely display an underexposure warning. And while this may be true for the entire image, the brightest section of the crime scene will be properly evaluated and recorded. Do not worry if the overall exposure is underexposed. This deficit in lighting will be addressed shortly.

A second way to meter a small section of a crime scene is to use the camera's spot meter. The spot meter will meter only the light in the very center of the viewfinder. Using the spot meter, the camera can be aimed toward the brightest portion of the scene from the spot where the photograph will be recorded from. The photographer will still need to lock in the aperture and shutter speed values so that when the camera is reoriented, the exposure values do not change. In addition, when using the spot meter, it is best not to focus on a large black vehicle, solid white wall, or similar subject, because the extremes of black and white can cause inaccurate light evaluations. Whichever technique chosen to meter light, the photographer should now record an image with these metered exposure values.

Now that the first exposure has been captured, the next step is to record a series of bracketed exposures. The general rule of thumb for bracketing exposures with film photography is to increase each subsequent exposure by one to two full stops of light, because print film generally has two stops of exposure latitude. However, when using digital media, the exposure latitudes are, at best, half of what film is capable of tolerating. Consequently, when bracketing exposures with a digital camera, it is recommended to record a series of bracketed exposures in half-stop to one-full-stop increments. The total range of exposures may still incorporate two or maybe even three stops of total light, but they are recorded in half-stop intervals. It is commonly believed that exposure errors can be corrected through photo editing programs, such as Adobe Photoshop. Crime scene photography, however, is about image capture, not image manipulation. It is better to capture a quality image at the crime scene, rather than to hope an image can be salvaged in postcapture editing. Photo editing software has made the editing of photographs available to anyone with a computer, and unfortunately the photographic skills of the crime scene investigator have taken a back seat to the flashier abilities of those with computer skills. This textbook, however, is about image capture and is designed to help investigators working in the field where the lighting is anything but perfect and the evidence must be photographed as it lies. And even for those photographers blessed with postcapture editing skills, having a better image to start with will only help improve the end result.

Because this set of bracketed photographs were started by metering the brightest portion of the composition, the bracketed series of exposures is commonly accomplished by simply increasing the overall lighting in each subsequent image. However, merely allowing the camera lens to remain open for longer times may not always do justice to the image. The best images have a balance between highlights and shadows. During the daytime, photographers use fill flash to lighten shadows and create a balanced exposure. Nighttime exposures are recorded in a similar manner, and flash can be added to the less-illuminated portions of a crime scene in order to create better photographs. Because nighttime photographs benefit from longer exposures, the photographer is afforded plenty of time to add light where needed. The addition of light can be as simple as adding a single flash to an individual piece of evidence or extensively painting a crime scene with light. Flash photography and painting with light are the next advances in low-light photography and are discussed in Chapters 6 and 7.

By themselves, timed exposures allow ambient light to burn into the photograph and can make visible all the critical details of a composition. Furthermore, timed exposures greatly improve crime scene documentation, much better than utilizing flash-synchronized exposures. *Program* mode photography can be extremely limiting. Thus far, this discussion has mostly concerned itself with the overall or scene-establishing photographs in the crime scene photographic process. However, timed exposures can also greatly improve midrange and closeup photographs. For example, in midrange or relationship photographs, the goal is to relate pieces of evidence to each other or to specific parts of the scene. A few shell casings lying next to each other on the ground are easy to capture in a single photographic frame. Depth of field may not even be an issue, because all the casings are in the same plane of focus. However, the image may not be all that interesting to the jury, but by adding a little artistic flair, a touch of compositional creativity, and low-light photography skills, the final result can become much more intriguing and effective. Placing the cartridge cases in context with the scene's environment and allowing the background environment to burn into the camera over time can definitely enhance the composition and the impact of the image.

When a photograph is composed with evidence in the foreground and the crime scene trailing away into the background, maximizing the image's depth of field is very

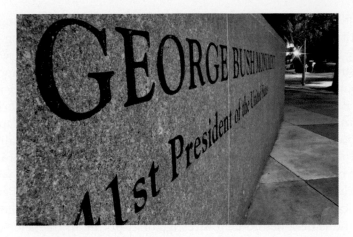

Figure 5.17 This image was recorded at ISO 100, f/22, for 30 s. The f/22 aperture created a deep depth of field, while the limited ambient light was allowed to burn into the image. Focus was set on the "G" in *George* and observe how the entire president's name is legible because of the f/22 aperture.

important. If the background is blurred and out of focus, the image's potential value is lost (Figure 5.17). During daytime exposures, quality depth of field images are more easily captured because the brighter conditions are more conducive to closing down the aperture. Unfortunately, many photographers believe that such depth of field magic cannot be attained at night. They are mistaken. Recording such images simply requires a little patience, longer exposures, and a tripod. The key to taking meaningful photographs with purposeful composition and quality depth of field is taking the camera off *Program* mode and selecting apertures and shutter speeds for a specific, deliberate purpose. In low-light situations, automated cameras have a bias toward large aperture openings in order to gather in all possible light. This bias occurs whether or not a flash is utilized in the photograph. However, the trade-off for the light-gathering ability of larger apertures is the sacrifice in depth of field. Long blood trails, a series of fired cartridge cases, and even evidence found at the opposite ends of a staircase may be improperly photographed because the *Program* mode setting on the camera chose the largest aperture available to it. To record outstanding images, the photographer must make the effort, work with the appropriate aperture, and let the light filter into the camera over time instead of choosing the quickest solution.

Ambient light photography is not limited to outdoor environments (Figure 5.18). Many indoor crime scenes require time exposures to accurately document the environment. Parking garages, warehouses, and the showrooms of large stores are just a few examples of indoor environments that also may call for ambient light photography. Documentation of these structures can be improved through longer exposures that allow all parts of the scene to burn into the recorded image. Using a flash diffuser or bouncing the flash in order to allow the light to trickle into the background is another technique to improve an image's appearance. However, oftentimes, the best alternative is to merely allow the shutter to remain open so that the ambient light can illuminate the entire field of view, just as one would do in an outdoor environment. As another advantage, ambient light is frequently more even and balanced than the harsh light produced by a flash unit.

Figure 5.18 This figure illustrates how indoor scenes can be enhanced by photographing them with ambient lighting instead of electronic flash. Warehouses, stores, and other large structures are quite similar to outdoor environments in that the flash is unable to reach the back recesses of a composition. This photo was recorded at ISO 200, f/8, for 1.6 s in order to let the entire environment burn into the photograph. (Photographed by Curtis Klingle, Retired Crime Scene Investigator, Bryan (TX) Police Department, Bryan, TX.)

Time exposures in low-light situations allow the scene's background to burn into the image and can provide additional information to the viewers. Yet while using flash in the *Program* mode can be limiting, there are situations when adding flash adds value to the image. Each technique (flash and ambient light photography) has its advantages; however, combining the two techniques can create more powerful pieces of photographic evidence. Putting these two forms of photography together is not difficult, but once again requires a little planning, a little patience, and most definitely a desire to capture meaningful images. Combining timed exposures and flash into a single image is not a difficult task. Simply meter the ambient light falling across the subject's area, and add flash to highlight something of value, such as a piece of evidence somewhere in the composition. Adding flash into a composition is best done over short distances; therefore, do not try to illuminate a subject too distant into the background. Metering and exposing for ambient light while adding flash to a particular subject is sometimes referred to as *dragging the shutter* or *slow synching* (Figure 5.19).

Both ambient light photography and *dragging the shutter* are useful in preventing the dark backgrounds and edges around the composition's perimeter that commonly occur with *Program* mode flash (synch speed) photography. Automatic or *Program* modes are great for the casual photographer, but not for the professional crime scene photographer. The automatic mode frees the typical user from having to think about shutter speeds and apertures and lets the photographer focus on the subject's composition. However, crime scene investigators must concern themselves with all aspects of photography, including composition and exposure.

Photographing crime scenes is very different from working in a controlled setting, such as a photographic studio. Portrait photographers do not have to deal with motor vehicles, obstructions, poor or contrasting lighting, and other obstructions casting distracting shadows across their subjects. In addition, crime scene investigators are not allowed to move evidence or other parts of the crime scene in order to orchestrate a better photograph

Figure 5.19 The background in this photo was metered and recorded at ISO 400, f/11, for 30 s. The evidence markers were concealed by the shadowed foreground, but a balance between the foreground and the background was completed by adding light to the foreground with an electronic flash.

in every situation. Investigators must work with the environment they are in and still capture quality photographs, and using a scene's natural lighting is an important tool for capturing those quality photographs.

Conclusion

Photographing in low light requires diligence to create true and accurate representations of crime scenes. Hand-holding the camera and relying on *Program* mode flash photography is a waste of time and effort. Investigators are trying to tell a very important story with their photographs, and those photographs must be in focus, be composed to provide the most information for the viewer, and be properly exposed to shed light on all areas of a composition. In low-light conditions, time exposures captured with the camera mounted on a tripod are one of the best options available to the crime scene photographer. Whether the crime scene is indoor or outdoor, better photographs can be recorded by working with longer exposures and avoiding handheld, *Program* mode photography.

The next logical progression in low-light photography is incorporating more advanced lighting techniques into one's images. Adding flash illumination to a low-light composition is an important ability for crime scene investigators to become proficient at. Flash photography is discussed in the next chapter (Chapter 6).

End of Chapter Questions

1. Which is NOT an attribute of light?
   a. Color
   b. Direction
   c. Duration
   d. Intensity

2. Which attribute of light is the *easiest* to control by the photographer?
    a. Color
    b. Direction
    c. Duration
    d. Intensity

3. What is the drawback when higher ISO values are chosen?
    a. Tripods are necessary.
    b. Grain or noise develops in the image.
    c. Depth of field is reduced.
    d. Low-light images are near impossible to record.

4. What is the drawback to larger apertures?
    a. Depth of field is reduced.
    b. Timed exposures are necessary.
    c. Reciprocity fails.
    d. Flash photography is required.

5. What occurs in the bulb exposure mode?
    a. Shutter speed increases to 30 s.
    b. Timed exposures are prevented.
    c. Depth of field is maximized.
    d. Lens remains open as long as shutter button is depressed.

6. A photographer is working a nighttime crime scene and has recorded a properly exposed image at ISO 400, f/8, for 4 s but requires a deeper depth of field. What would be the proper reciprocal exposure values?
    a. ISO 400, f/4, at 1 s
    b. ISO 100, f/8, at 15 s
    c. ISO 400, f/16, at 15 s
    d. ISO 400, f/22, at 1 min

7. A photographer is working a nighttime crime scene and has recorded a properly exposed image at ISO 400, f/8, for 4 s but wishes to have a much longer exposure in order to have time to add some electronic flash into the background. What would be the proper reciprocal exposure values?
    a. ISO 100, f/22, at 2 min
    b. ISO 100, f16, at 30 s
    c. ISO 400, f/8, at Bulb
    d. ISO 800, f/16, 1 min

8. Which of the following exposure values is *equal* to ISO 100, f/2.8, at 1 s?
    a. ISO 200, f/8, at 8 s
    b. ISO 400, f/5.6, at 2 s
    c. ISO 800, f/16, at ¼ of a second
    d. ISO 1600, f/22, at 4 s

9. A photographer is working a nighttime crime scene and has recorded a properly exposed image at ISO 400, f/8, for 4 s but wishes to have a greater depth of field as well as a sharper and more colorful image. What would be the proper reciprocal exposure values?
   a. ISO 800, f/2.8, for 1/8 of a second
   b. ISO 100, f/32, for 4 min
   c. ISO 800, f/32, for 15 min
   d. ISO 100, f/2.8, for 2 s

10. Which statement is most true?
    a. Alternate light sources refer to external flash units.
    b. Cameras can meter light in the bulb exposure mode.
    c. Time exposures are frequently better than flash-sync exposures in low light.
    d. Digital cameras have difficulty working in low light.

11. Which type of lighting has application to crime scene photography?
    a. Oblique lighting
    b. Sidelighting
    c. Backlighting
    d. All of the above

12. What color of light do high-pressure sodium lamps produce without any color-balancing actions?
    a. Yellow
    b. Red
    c. Green
    d. Blue

13. What color of light do mercury vapor lamps produce without any color-balancing actions?
    a. Red to orange
    b. Yellow to orange
    c. Blue to green
    d. Blue to violet

14. What shutter speed would be best when photographing in fluorescent light?
    a. 1/30 of a second
    b. 1/90 of a second
    c. 1/250 of a second
    d. Fastest flash-sync speed

15. What is measured by the Kelvin scale?
    a. Size of aperture
    b. Color temperature of light
    c. Ambient temperature
    d. Total exposure value

16. Which statement is most true about color compensation?
    a. Digital cameras can only compensate for color when RAW capture is selected.
    b. Digital photographers cannot utilize external filters for color compensation.
    c. Film photographers must select a film type to match the dominate color of light.
    d. Digital cameras can utilize both external filters and internal filters in adjusting the white balance for an image.

17. Which statement is most true about reciprocity failure?
    a. Reciprocity failure is applicable to film photography.
    b. Reciprocity failure is not applicable to digital photography.
    c. Reciprocity failure makes overexposure of nighttime images less likely.
    d. All three statements are accurate.

18. Besides a camera, what tool is most important for nighttime photography?
    a. Electronic flash
    b. Depth of field
    c. Tripod
    d. Fast (large aperture) lens

19. Which tactic is best when dealing with streetlights that are visible in the composition?
    a. Ensure bulbs remain in the image to document their existence.
    b. Crop bulbs just out of composition or conceal bulbs from the viewfinder's view.
    c. Always balance the ambient lighting for white.
    d. Turn off the light's power, but photograph their locations.

20. Which personal trait would benefit a photographer more at nighttime crime scenes?
    a. Patience
    b. Speed or quickness
    c. Irreverence
    d. All of the above

21. Every composition is different and _____ in evaluating crime scenes for light is the key to recording images in low-light conditions.
    a. Preciseness
    b. Durability
    c. Flexibility
    d. Precision

22. What is one of the major drawbacks of using automatic or *Program* modes in low-light conditions?
    a. Erroneous exposure due to darkness.
    b. Improperly focused images.
    c. It is more time consuming.
    d. The camera's tendency to use wide-open apertures resulting in less depth of field.

23. The color of light is commonly measured through the
    a. Kermit scale
    b. Kleinmann scale
    c. Kelvin scale
    d. Klopnik scale

Photography Assignments

Required Tools: Tripod and a cable release

Photography Subjects: Safe outdoor (nighttime) environments, indoor environments

   I. Take a series of photographs demonstrating the difference between *Program* mode ambient light and *Program* mode flash photography:
      A. Record a nighttime image in *Program* mode using a flash (internal and/or external flash).
      B. Of the same composition, take an image in *Program* mode, but without flash illumination.
      C. Of the same composition, record an image at ISO 100 with a small aperture (f/22), and record lengthy timed exposure (if necessary, think *reciprocity* for exposure calculations).
  II. Demonstrate the ability to maximize the depth of field in nighttime conditions by photographing a series of subjects set out at different distances from the camera:
      A. Record an image in *Program* mode.
      B. Of the same composition, record an image with a smaller aperture to improve the depth of field.
 III. Demonstrate the ability to record ambient nighttime images:
      A. Record low-light images where streetlights are a part of the compositions.
         1. Make note of any exposure compensation required.
      B. Record low-light images where exposures last longer than 30, 60, and/or 120 s.
  IV. Demonstrate the ability to take a closeup photograph at night, and ensure the background of scene is visible (adding flash is acceptable to highlight foreground's subject).
   V. Compose a low-light composition possessing street or other common light sources, but keep the actual bright light sources (bulbs) out of the composition. Record a series of images, intentionally overexposing each subsequent image:
      A. Record a first image at what the camera believes is accurately exposed.
      B. Record subsequent images, +1, +2, +3, +4, and +5 stops of light.
      C. Make note of findings and the camera's limits to overexpose images in low-light conditions.
  VI. Record a series of photographs under various types of lighting (if recording in a digital format, set the white balance to daylight in order to observer the colors produced):
      A. Record an image under fluorescent lighting.
      B. Record an image under incandescent lighting.

    C. Record an image under mercury vapor lighting.

    D. Record an image under high-pressure sodium lighting.

    E. Record images under unique lighting available to the photographer.

VII. Record a series of low-light photographs indoors:

    A. Find a long hallway and photograph the entire length:

      1. Take one with a flash set to flash-sync speed.

      2. Take one using ambient lighting.

      3. Take note of the quality of lighting and depth of field.

    B. Find an expansive indoor environment, such as a warehouse or gym, and photograph the indoor composition (turn out the majority of lights, if not all the lights):

      1. Take one flash-synch speed.

      2. Take one using ambient lighting.

      3. Take note of the lighting differences.

VIII. Record a low-light photograph with motion visible in the image:

    A. Running water

    B. Cars traveling along the roadway

    C. Trees blowing in the wind

Additional Readings

Birnbaum, H.C. (1996). *Existing Light Photography*. 3rd ed. Rochester, NY: Eastman Kodak Company.

Davis, P. (1995). *Photography*. 7th ed. Boston, MA: McGraw Hill.

Duncan, C.D. (2009). Reciprocity failure: Film vs. digital. *Chesapeake Examiner* (Fall), 47(2):10–15.

Fisher, B. (2005). *Techniques of Crime Scene Investigation*. 7th ed. Boca Raton, FL: CRC Press.

Frost, L. (1999). *The Complete Guide to Night and Low-Light Photography*. New York: Amphoto Books.

Gardner, R.M. (2005). *Practical Crime Scene Processing and Investigation*. Boca Raton, FL: CRC Press.

Miller, L.S. (1998). *Police Photography*. Cincinnati, OH: Anderson Publishing Company.

Robinson, E. (2007). *Police Photography*. Burlington, MA: Academic Press.

Flash Photography

6

Although the quality and amount of training varies between departments and agencies, new investigators are thrust into a world rife with low-light photographic opportunities, mainly because they are likely to start their careers on the least desirable shifts—evenings and nights. Low-light conditions should be viewed as opportunities, not as frustrating to near impossible obstructions. Actually, low-light conditions provide investigators with the chance to choose from a variety of light sources, techniques, and methods to inventively illuminate subjects in a way that creates the most impressive and artistic images not always available to photographers working daytime crime scenes (Figure 6.1). Contradictory to what one might expect, one of the more harmful pieces of equipment given to new investigators is a *superduper* powerful flash, especially when they are told that it can illuminate anything and everything. Electronic flashes are superior pieces of equipment, but they can be extremely detrimental to low-light photography and the processing of nighttime crime scenes. As long as there is any amount of ambient light, images can be accurately and reliably captured with and without the addition of electronic flash. To record a true and accurate low-light photographic image, the photographer merely needs to take the time to analyze the subject and determine if the addition of electronic flash is necessary and, if so, where and how to add the supplemental light into the composition. Flash photography is certainly an advantageous tool for investigators, as long as its limitations are understood and compensated for.

Guide Numbers

To start a discussion on flash photography, the investigator must first understand the concept of guide numbers. A guide number is a value offered by manufacturers that indicates the amount of power or light output a particular flash unit possesses. Guide number values are typically offered in relation to ISO 100 speed film or a digital camera's ISO setting. The value of a guide number is not arbitrary. A guide number is the product of the f/number (size of an aperture) and the distance between the flash and subject. The formula can be adjusted so that if two of the variables are known the third variable can be calculated. The three formulas for guide numbers and their variables are as follows:

- Guide Number = Aperture × Subject Distance
- Aperture = Guide Number/Subject Distance
- Subject Distance = Guide Number/Aperture

Manufacturers may occasionally provide additional values and information based on alternative ISO values and subject-to-flash distances based on the metric system. Furthermore, guide number values can change (have different values) for the same flash unit based on the flash head's *zoom* setting. A flash's zoom is designed to adjust the produced light's field

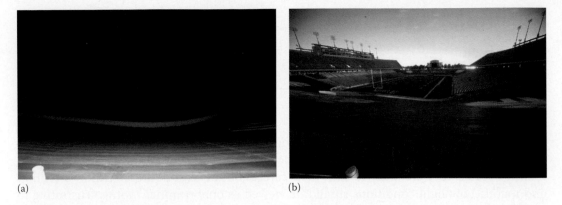

(a)   (b)

Figure 6.1 (a) was recorded in a completely darkened football stadium with a full-power flash (160 guide number) and in *Program* mode at ISO 100, f/3.5, for 1/125th of a second. (b) was recorded in the *Manual* mode without a flash at ISO 100, f/4.5, for 30 s.

of view or coverage to match the focal length of the lens mounted to the camera. Wider-angle lenses will tell the flash to allow the light to be more dispersed, while longer focal length lenses will communicate to the flash that the produced light should be focused more tightly. Typically, the longer focal lengths or zoom settings will provide higher guide number values.

Photographers must be sure that their flash calculations are accurate and that they use the correct set of values when manually determining exposures. As an example, assume an investigator's flash has a guide number of 120 for an ISO 100 rating and for distances in feet. Knowing that a flash has a certain value, the investigator merely needs to find the right combination of aperture size to match the distance between the flash and the subject in order to properly expose a composition. Please note that the subject distance value is the distance between the flash and the subject, *not* the distance between the camera and subject. This distinction is extremely important when it comes to time to paint crime scenes with light.

As with any mathematical calculation, the photographer needs to solve for a single unknown. However, the basic guide number formula (GN = Aperture × Subject Distance) leaves two unknown values, assuming the photographer is armed with an accurate guide number value. As a result, the photographer must decide which of the two unknown values is most important to control. Aperture controls depth of field; therefore, if a deep zone of sharp focus is important to the image's composition, an aperture of f/16 might be chosen. Using the previous fictive guide number of 120 and an aperture of f/16, the flash must be 7.5 ft away from the subject needing illumination (120 [GN] divided by f/16 [aperture] equals 7.5 ft). In another example, assume the physical crime scene dictates the distance at which a flash can be projected toward a subject. As an illustration, the same flash with a guide number of 120 is directed toward a subject by a flash set 30 ft away. The proper aperture for such an exposure would be f/4.0, because 120 (GN) divided by distance (30) equals an aperture of f/4.0. Most modern flashes have a *through-the-lens* (TTL) automatic mode that can be selected and eliminate the need to calculate flash exposures. However, like the automatic mode on the camera, there are limitations, and knowing how to operate a flash in the *Manual* mode will help photographers take more control over their photography and capture more accurate and compelling images.

There will be times when a flash's output is too powerful for the image being composed. In those situations, most off-the-camera flashes have a variable power setting. The power settings are often printed on the flash or LCD screen as fractions, full, ½, ¼, ⅛, and 1/16, and may go down as far as 1/128th power. These variable power settings can be extremely useful in close-focusing and painting with light situations. One will notice that the fractional settings are broken down by half (½) of the previous setting, which is equivalent to a single stop of light. Some flashes can be further fine-tuned by breaking down the amount of light into halves or thirds of a stop.

On the flash itself, the variable power settings are typically broken down into full stops, with each lower power setting one-half the value of the previous value. Calculating a flash's light output using one of the variable power settings is not extremely complicated, but it does require thought. Remembering that a stop of light is one-half or twice the amount of light of the next full value, the photographer will realize that a half-power reduction in flash power is equal to a one-stop change in light. Unlike the ease of calculating shutter speed adjustments, one cannot simply divide a flash's guide number by the fractions found on the variable power control, but must think of the changes in power levels as changes by f/stops. For example, using a flash unit with a 120 guide number, the resulting changes in power settings would approximately equate to the following:

Output of Light (120 Guide Number)	Change in Stops of Light	Aperture and Distance	Effective or New Guide Number
1/1—full power	0	f/16 at 7.5 ft	120
½	One stop	f/11 at 7.5 ft	82.5
¼	Two stops	f/8 at 7.5 ft	60
1/8	Three stops	f/5.6 at 7.5 ft	42
1/16	Four stops	f/4.0 at 7.5 ft	30

Everything involved in the calculation of photographic exposures revolve around the concept of stops. Stop values allow the photographer to compare and adjust the different camera settings in equivalent values, including apertures, shutter speeds, ISO values, and the power of the flash's output.

It is rather straightforward to make corresponding changes between apertures and flash output. However, if the photographer desires to keep an aperture at a constant value and still reduce the amount of flash output, the distance between the flash and subject must be reduced. To determine the distance between the subject and the flash when reducing the power of the flash, the photographer should take the following steps:

- Identify the flash's full power guide number (i.e., 120 GN).
- Select a desirable aperture size (i.e., f/8).
- Select the preferred reduction in flash power (i.e., 1/8 or −3 stops).
- Conceptually calculate an equivalent reduction in aperture (i.e., f/8 − 3f/ stops = f/22).
- Divide the hypothetical aperture into the full power GN (i.e., 120/22 = 5.45 ft).
- Resulting distance will provide a proper exposure for a reduced-power flash at the desired aperture and shortened distance between flash and subject (i.e., 1/8 power of 120 GN flash at f/8.0 should be exposed at 5.45 ft).

Granted, manual-flash calculations are not the easiest concept to grasp. As another illustration to assist readers in understanding the manual calculation of flash exposures, observe the changes in distance in the following power reductions:

Output of Light (120 GN)	Hypothetical Calculations	Distance at f/8 (ft)
1/1 (Full power)	$120/8 = 15$	15
1/2 (−1 f/stop)	$120/11 = 10.9$	10.9
1/4 (−2 f/stops)	$120/16 = 7.5$	7.5
1/8 (−3 f/stops)	$120/22 = 5.45$	5.45
1/16 (−4 f/stops)	$120/32 = 3.75$	3.75

Manually calculating flash exposures is not often grasped quickly or easily. Practice and experience are required. Although these manual calculations may seem perplexing at first, when the concepts are understood, they help create extremely powerful images in low-light conditions. Painting crime scenes with light often requires calculations such as these, because reducing the amount of flash can improve the composition in a number of different situations. Full-power flashes, especially those with higher guide numbers, tend to cause foregrounds to overexpose, thus compromising the overall value of the image. Painting with light requires that individual subjects within a composed image be illuminated independently (Figure 6.2). Therefore, reduction in the power of flashes and the shrinking of distances between the flash and the camera are absolutely essential to create nighttime photographs with balanced illumination.

Unfortunately, these math calculations are not necessarily reliable because they are dependent upon the accuracy of the guide numbers provided by the manufacturers and the guide numbers quoted by manufacturers are sometimes exaggerated. Although companies may not out-and-out lie about their products, the numbers can be misleading. The guide numbers come closest to accuracy in environments with highly reflective (white) surfaces, 8 ft ceilings, and close-together walls such as those found in hallways. In these conditions, the photographer may rely upon the quoted guide number. However, the percentage of crime scenes found in narrow hallways with glossy-white painted walls and low ceilings is probably quite low. In addition, as flashes age over time, their maximum output of light can subside. As a result, investigators must test and practice with their equipment to know exactly how it will respond at an actual crime scene. Furthermore, equipment should be tested in different environments, specifically in both outdoor and indoor environments. By testing the flash in different environments, the photographer will have a better idea on how the equipment will perform in a variety of crime scenes.

A series of test photographs can be exposed to determine the flash's true and accurate guide number. First, attach the flash to the camera and set the camera on a tripod. Set the camera to the manual exposure mode. Select an ISO value of 100 in order to compare the results with the flash's quoted power levels. Photographers that routinely use higher ISO values can complete subsequent test photographs at those values. The shutter speed should be set at or just slower than the flash-synchronization speed. Typically, 1/60–1/90 of a second will provide excellent results. The shutter speed must be close to the synchronization speed so that only the light produced by the flash is used to record the image and not any ambient light present. The series of test photographs do not have to be recorded in complete darkness, but will be more accurately recorded in dimmer environments.

Figure 6.2 Dumping intense light across an entire image from a single location causes overexposed foregrounds and underexposed backgrounds. However, by illuminating subjects individually, decreasing the distance between flash and subject, and cutting the power of the flash, one can create well-balanced images that will provide greater information and create a positive impression on the viewer. This dark landscape was recorded at ISO 400, f/16, for 83 s. Multiple flashes of a flash reduced to 1/16th power were cast across the evidence placards in order to create a more balanced photograph.

Anything slower than 1/60 of a second may allow too much ambient light to be included in the image and invalidate the test. The shutter speed must be fast enough to limit the amount of ambient light recorded so that the amount of light visible in the recorded image is primarily provided by the flash.

Next, use a tape measure and extend it 10 ft away from the camera. Any distance could be measured out and used, but the number 10 is easier to calculate exposures and guide numbers with. Have a dry erase board or a tablet of paper placed 10 ft away from the camera. On the target or board, the photographer will write in clear, large print the different aperture values available, that is, 4.0–5.6–8.0–11–16–22. Finally, take a series of flash photographs of the board or tablet, changing the apertures and corresponding lettering on the dry erase board or tablet. The flash being tested must be set to *Manual* and *full* or "1/1" power setting. Using the TTL mode will invalidate the test, because the camera will be determining and adjusting the light output of the flash. Cycle through the range of apertures within two to three f/stops of the expected result based upon the manufacturer's quoted guide number. Using the previous example of a flash rated with a 120 guide number, the expected result for a proper exposure at full power and from 10 ft away would be with an aperture around f/12. An aperture f/11 would be the closest full stop. Therefore, recording a series of bracketed exposures between apertures f/5.6 and f/22 should provide a photographer with an accurate guide number. If the camera's capabilities allow, breaking down the exposures into third or half stops will provide even more accurate information.

For those still using film, it is recommended to record these test images on slide film because the exposure latitude is much less than with print film and the differences between individual exposures are more clearly seen. If the images are recorded on print film, be sure to advise the developer not to make any corrections or compensations to any printed photographs. Preventing corrections during printing will help the investigator evaluate the flash's effective guide number more accurately.

For digital photographers, recording the images in *raw* and viewing them without any enhancements or adjustments is recommended. Because digital cameras have small exposure latitudes similar to slide film, test photographs taken with a digital camera are just as accurate. From the series of recorded images, select the image with the best lighting on the subject 10 ft away from the camera and flash. Evaluate the light striking the labeled target or board, not something seen in the foreground or background. Flashes are designed to properly illuminate subjects at specific distances and the goal of this exercise is to determine the flash's most-accurate guide number for a *full-power* flash exposure.

While reviewing the recorded photographs, determine which image looks best, identify the aperture used during its capture, and multiply the aperture value by ten, and the result will equal the effective guide number for a full-power flash output on the electronic flash being tested. The photographer is now armed with an accurate guide number value and this value will become indispensable when it comes time for manual-flash exposures and painting with light endeavors. The most effective guide number will probably vary depending on whether the image was recorded in an indoor or an outdoor environment. In addition, photographers utilizing flashes possessing a zoom feature may wish to record one series of images with the flash set to a wide angle (24–28 mm) and another set to a telephoto range (>100 mm).

To understand how an electronic flash operates in a variety of environments, the photographer needs to test the equipment and critically examine the results in both indoor and outdoor environments (Figure 6.3). The resulting guide numbers for outdoor environments provide investigators the right combination of flash power, aperture, and distance for future painting with light exercises. In the indoor test photographs illuminated in Figure 6.3 (a-c), the effective guide number for the flash tested resulted in 110 (f/11 × 10). The quoted guide number by the manufacturer was 120 and the difference between the two values is nothing to be concerned about. If the difference was greater than a full stop of light, then one may want to double-check the camera's settings and/or equipment. Now armed with an accurate guide number, manually calculated flash exposures can be completed more accurately. For example, a ½-powered flash exposure would allow a 10 ft subject-to-flash exposure at an f/8 aperture. As a review, this was determined by having a full-powered exposure equal 10 ft at f/11. Reducing the power of the flash to ½ equals a loss of one stop of light. A change in aperture size would move the camera's lens from an aperture of f/11 to an f/8 and the one-stop increase in light offsets the one-stop decrease in the flash's power setting. Getting comfortable with the relationships between stops and guide numbers will better serve photographers in nighttime and low-light compositions. In contrast to the indoor test photograph, the outdoor test photographs seen in Figure 6.3 (d-g) using the same flash unit show that an aperture of f/8 (effective guide number of 80) was most accurate.

Although guide numbers are typically quoted in relationship with an ISO value of 100, higher ISO speeds have more light sensitivity and therefore can record electronic flash over greater distances or with smaller apertures. Some instruction manuals provide users with greater information concerning the abilities of their equipment when used to capture flash exposures at alternate ISO values. In addition, exposure information with various ISO values is frequently found right on the flash, either accessed through some sort of sliding display or on the LCD screen. However, if the photographer chooses to use the guide numbers discovered during the testing of the equipment, there is a simple formula that can be used to determine the appropriate guide numbers for different ISO ratings: guide number for ISO 100 film multiplied by the sensitivity factor is equal to adjusted guide number for film other than ISO 100. The sensitivity factors for the different film speeds are listed as follows:

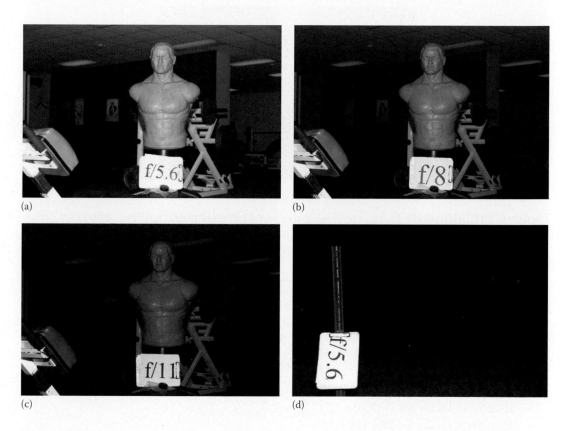

(a)

(b)

(c)

(d)

Figure 6.3 Electronic flashes are rated by their guide numbers but react differently in diverse environments. As a result, photographers need to test their flashes in order to know how they will operate at an actual crime scene. As shown here, a flash with a guide number of 120 was used in an indoor and an outdoor setting to create (a) through (g). Each image was recorded with the flash set to full power and positioned 10 ft from the subject. The ISO was set to 100 and a shutter speed of 1/125th of a second was selected. The aperture was set as noted in each individual picture: (a) f/5.6, (b) f/8, (c) f/11, (d) f/5.6, (e) f/8, (f) f/11, (g) f/8. Observe how the target of each flash was relatively similar in regard to illumination, but how the surrounding surfaces in the outdoor compositions were unable to record any of the flash's light. (g) was recorded by metering the ambient light using the ISO 100 and f/8 values determined in the test photographs and an exposure time of 30 s was chosen by the camera and used to record (g).

(Continued)

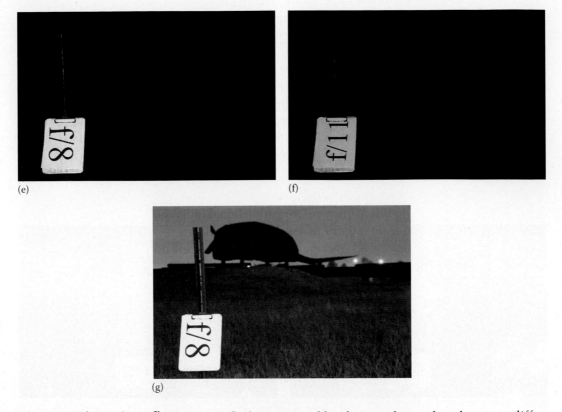

(e)   (f)

(g)

Figure 6.3 (*Continued*) Electronic flashes are rated by their guide numbers but react differently in diverse environments. As a result, photographers need to test their flashes in order to know how they will operate at an actual crime scene. As shown here, a flash with a guide number of 120 was used in an indoor and an outdoor setting to create (a) through (g). Each image was recorded with the flash set to full power and positioned 10 ft from the subject. The ISO was set to 100 and a shutter speed of 1/125th of a second was selected. The aperture was set as noted in each individual picture: (a) f/5.6, (b) f/8, (c) f/11, (d) f/5.6, (e) f/8, (f) f/11, (g) f/8. Observe how the target of each flash was relatively similar in regard to illumination, but how the surrounding surfaces in the outdoor compositions were unable to record any of the flash's light. (g) was recorded by metering the ambient light using the ISO 100 and f/8 values determined in the test photographs and an exposure time of 30 s was chosen by the camera and used to record (g).

- Sensitivity factor for ISO 50 = 0.71
- Sensitivity factor for ISO 100 = 1.0
- Sensitivity factor for ISO 200 = 1.4
- Sensitivity factor for ISO 400 = 2.0
- Sensitivity factor for ISO 800 = 2.8
- Sensitivity factor for ISO 1600 = 4.0

Notice how the sensitivity factors equate or match what may be seen on an aperture ring. Once again, everything is broken down into stops of light so that different functions can be compared. As an example, imagine a photographer possessing a flash unit with a 120 guide number for ISO 100 and wishing to take a flash exposure with their ISO value set to 800. Here would be the mathematical computations:

- Guide number = 120 at ISO 100
- Desires to set camera to ISO 800, which has a sensitivity factor of 2.8
- 120 (guide number) × 2.8 = 336 (new guide number for ISO 800)

Now armed with the 336 guide number, the photographer wishes to record an exposure with an aperture of f/22. The question of how far away must a full-powered (1/1) flash be positioned from the subject requires more math:

- Subject distance = guide number/aperture
- Subject distance = 336 (guide number)/22 (aperture)
- 336/22 = 15 (subject distance from flash)

Understandably, math is not everyone's most favorite subject, but basic math skills will help investigators in their photographic compositions. Fortunately, today's cameras come with many automated features to assist in these sometimes tedious mathematical computations.

Flash Operation

Flash exposure calculations and adjustments for different ISO ratings are not necessary for all flash photography, only when the flash is completely disconnected from the camera during painting with light projects or possibly for specially composed, close-focusing endeavors. Today's flashes are all manufactured for a particular manufacturer's camera and operate quite efficiently in *TTL* metering mode. Crime scene investigators may also see a setting on their camera or flash for *E-TTL* (electronic TTL), A-TTL (advanced or automatic TTL), or simply an "A" for automatic metering mode. TTL metering allows the camera to determine the amount of flash output to record a properly illuminated subject. However, a camera capable of TTL metering does not necessarily guarantee that the overall composition will be properly illuminated, only that the *first* subject impacted and targeted by the flash's light is properly illuminated.

Electronic flashes that are operated in an automatic or TTL mode are capable of capturing exceptionally illuminated photographs. However, automatic modes can just as easily damage or be detrimental to a photograph. An electronic flash operated in a fully automatic mode will fire the flash at the time of the exposure. The light will travel out and seek its first subject, and when the reflected light reaches the TTL sensor and reaches 18% gray, the flash turns itself off and the supplemental illumination is stopped. If the first object reflecting the flash's light is not the intended subject, and the intended subject is further or deeper into the scene, there is a chance it will not receive adequate illumination. There are a number of techniques used to offset this problem and they will be discussed later in this chapter. The total amount of light produced by the flash is actually a product of time or length of burn for the flash. The flash will cast its light between approximately 1/1,000th and 1/40,000th of a second. The longer the burn or the longer the light is emitted from the flash, the greater the amount of light is cast onto the subject. As a result, reducing a flash's power effectively reduces the flash's *length of burn*. This makes more sense and helps explain the painting-with-light theory discussed in Chapter 7.

In addition to reading the flash's instruction manual, the crime scene photographer also needs to practice with their equipment in order to understand how it will react in different situations and conditions. Critically evaluating one's own crime scene photographs on a routine basis will serve as a good learning tool and help investigators continually improve their work product. Examining one's own work for failures as well as successes will help guide investigators in future photographic assignments. In regard to the actual photographic equipment, someone familiar with the operation of one camera system can be slightly befuddled by the functions of another. For example, two different camera systems may operate in completely different manners when the flash is set to an automatic or TTL mode and the camera is set to the *Aperture Priority* mode. One system may fire the flash in this mode but meter and set the exposure for the ambient light. This can cause problems if the photographer is not paying attention because the shutter speed may slow to the point where a tripod is needed to ensure a sharp-focused image. On the other hand, a different system working in *Aperture Priority* may make the assumption that the camera is hand held and that the corresponding shutter speed will be set to match the rule of thumb that the shutter speed needs to be equal to or faster than one over the focal length of the lens. Although the image can be recorded without a tripod, the background of the photograph may be lost if the photographer does not compose the image correctly. Therefore, investigators need to practice and become familiar with their specific equipment in order to predict and control the outcome of their crime scene photographs. Practice, experience, and critical evaluation of one's work are all important tools for improvement.

Built-In or Pop-Up Flashes

A camera's built-in flash, also known as a pop-up flash, is not appropriate for the majority of crime scene photography tasks. These flashes lack the power and versatility of an off-the-camera electronic flash. Built-in flashes are designed to add fill light to an image, not to illuminate an entire scene, especially a scene with any depth. These flashes typically have guide numbers (power ratings) between 40 and 60, which means the flash has an effective range of approximately 10 ft with an aperture of f/4 to f/5.6 at ISO 100. Granted, this distance can be increased with higher ISO settings, but this merely creates a different set of problems (lack of rich color and added grain or noise). Increasing the ISO value in order to use a pop-up flash may cause a lack of color saturation in the image and is likely to overexpose the foreground of an image so that the background can be reached by the underpowered flash. Furthermore, because a built-in flash is mounted just above the lens of the camera, in close-focusing situations, the lens can actually cast a shadow across the image by blocking the light projected from the flash. On the other hand, a built-in flash is extremely convenient and effective for some photographic endeavors that require fill flash and highlighting of subjects between 4 and 10 ft away from the camera. All built-in flashes are not equal and the photographer must test a new camera to understand the limitations and capabilities of a pop-up flash.

A pop-up flash can also be useful in tight quarters, where the physical placement of the camera, photographer, and an off-the-camera flash is impossible. Photographing the interior of cars, in between walls, and other close confines can sometimes be much easier if the subjects are illuminated with just the pop-up flash. The key to photographing with the built-in flash is to use it within its capabilities and not ask it to do too much. For example, photographing a fired cartridge case lying on a sidewalk from a perpendicular and standing orientation is perfect because the single focal plane in which the entire image is located can be accurately captured. However, it would not be appropriate to photograph an elongated row of fired cartridge cases spread out across an entire roadway with the pop-up flash. A built-in flash cannot properly illuminate both sides of a wide roadway and still provide a quality photographic image.

Overexposures caused by the built-in flash being aligned too close to a subject are not uncommon with point-and-shoot cameras. Many SLR cameras can automatically adjust a pop-up flash's power for less illumination and do not always have difficulty with overexposing an image. Investigators must test their equipment, because some photographic equipment may be better able to capture close-up images without overexposing the compositions. Cameras with fewer exposure compensating features are frequently unable to adjust for different lighting conditions. By manually controlling the exposure values, one can compensate for inadequate automated features. This is effective with both pop-up and off-the-camera flashes. One of the more effective ways to prevent washing out of the subject is to place a little distance between the flash and the subject. Since a pop-up flash cannot be moved away from the camera, one can create separation with the subject by using a longer focal length. For example, when one has a desire to close focus on a small piece of evidence and a zoom or telephoto lens is available, the lens should be rotated to a longer focal length in order to bring the subject close and the photographer is able to take a step back from the subject in order to create additional distance between the flash and subject. Similar to off-the-camera flashes, pulling the flash away from the subject will broaden the light so that it is more evenly applied to the overall subject, while the longer focal length lens brings the subject closer or larger into the viewfinder. The separation may also help prevent harsh reflections. Hot spots and unwanted reflections are commonly caused when a built-in flash is used, because of the close position of the flash to the lens and the fact or rule that the *angle of incidence equals the angle of reflection* (Figure 6.4). Consequently, built-in flashes frequently cause unwanted hot spots or reflections, especially when photographing reflective or close-focused subjects.

Figure 6.4 As the laser beam's reflection off the mirror shows, the angle at which light impacts a surface is equal to the angle in which it reflects off that surface. A camera's flash acts similarly to the laser's beam of light.

One of the most irritating consequences of using a pop-up flash is *red-eye*, which occurs when the flash reflects off the back of a person's retinas and causes bright red pupils to appear in the captured image. To avoid this condition, it is necessary to separate the light source from the camera. Since this is impossible with the built-in flash, photographing in ambient light is one sure way to combat the distracting nature of red-eye. Off-the-camera flash units can be used to prevent red-eye, but even these external flashes that are attached directly to the camera can cause red-eye. The light must be moved so that it does not project along the same line of sight as the camera's lens, once again because the angle of incidence equals the angle of reflection. Some cameras have a red-eye reduction feature, but these may not work very well. The feature operates by firing a pre-flash burst of light that theoretically shrinks the subject's pupils prior to actually firing the flash used to capture the image. In addition to being ineffective, the pre-flash can cause subjects to move during the actual exposure because they mistakenly believe the first flash was the moment of capture. Use of the pop-up flash should be limited when photographing people due to the common appearance of red-eye. It is not hard to imagine what a defense attorney might say about his client's photograph being shown to witnesses when the defendant's eyes are a burning, incriminating, sinister shade of red.

Investigators do not always get to choose their equipment. Photography gear is often dispensed by those unfamiliar with the job and without a complete understanding of crime scene documentation requirements. Therefore, those investigators with less versatile equipment, and especially for those using non-SLR cameras, must pay special attention to the composition of their subjects and the orientation between the camera and subject. Instruction manuals should offer guides to minimum focus distances for the lens and the preferred ranges for the use of the built-in flash. However, running a test roll through a newly purchased or assigned camera is always a good idea. Additional testing of equipment may be necessary for different variables, such as ISO settings.

As far as ISO values go, cameras operating with a pop-up flash should be loaded with or set to at least an ISO value of 400. The light produced from the small flash attached to the camera is more easily recorded at higher ISO speeds. Additionally, ambient light is recorded more efficiently with higher ISO values, and together the two light sources help balance the overall composition.

With the move toward digital imaging, a clear and underutilized benefit of digital photography is the ability to change the ISO settings on the fly. For example, an investigator can set the camera to ISO 100 and record a set of nighttime ambient-light photographs documenting the exterior of a crime scene, switch to ISO 400 to record a set of flash exposures of a building's interior, and then switch back to ISO 100 to capture close-up flash exposures. This versatility in working with ISO values and flash capabilities gives the digital camera a clear advantage that should be frequently utilized by crime scene photographers. Using the ISO value to assist in the recording of pop-up flash exposures is also a useful skill to master.

Off-the-Camera Electronic Flash Photography

The crime scene photographer should not assume that an electronic flash is similar to the *plug-n-play* ability of computer accessories. Electronic flashes come in many different forms, with unique features, power ratings, and compatibility aspects. Even how a flash cooperates with a camera varies between models. As a result, the most important element of flash photography is a complete comprehension of the flash's instruction manual. Just like a camera's manual, the guide must be read and reread so that the photographer will have a clear understanding of how a flash will respond in different environments and how to adjust the different settings. Because police officers have a tendency to be hardheaded, it bears repeating that crime scene investigators should practice with their equipment before attempting to document an actual crime scene. Their photography will improve tremendously when they are able to accurately predict a flash's effect upon an image. This ability comes with experience and the investigator's willingness to critically examine his or her photographs.

Flash photography is an awesome tool for crime scene investigators to better document a crime scene. It offers a number of beneficial applications and can be an absolute necessity at times. However, crime scene investigators should never rely on the flash to illuminate an entire crime scene. Electronic flash is not a panacea for all the poorly illuminated compositions and scenes. It should be used for a specific purpose and not merely as a shortcut to photographing dimly lit crime scenes. When a flash is operated correctly and within its abilities, the results can be spectacular. Flash photography can add highlights, depth, and detail to one's photograph. The application of light must always be done thoughtfully. Photographers should have an understanding of their abilities and limitations, as well as their equipment's abilities and limitations. This is true, especially when it comes time for flash photography. Fortunately, many times, even small amounts of ambient light are enough to record outstanding low-light images. However, frequently, the ability to add one or more flash bursts to a composition will only serve to improve an already good photograph.

Benefits of Flash Photography

One of the most beneficial aspects of electronic flash is that it is white balanced, which means that the light cast into a composition will show the accurate colors of the subject being photographed. For example, photographing a white motor vehicle parked beneath a high-pressure sodium streetlight at night will cause the vehicle to appear more yellow than white. However, adding flash to the exposure can counteract the effects of the sodium light and record the color of the vehicle more accurately (Figure 6.5). This can be very important in photographing subjects where color is important, such as bruising. The color of a person's bruises may help tell investigators the approximate age of such injuries. However, if the wounds are photographed in the wrong colored light, the results can be confusing and/or misleading. The value of an accurate white-balanced image provided by flash photography should not be underestimated.

Flash photography is not just for low-light conditions. It can be quite useful during the daytime as well, because the electronic flash can add light to the shadowed areas of a composition (Figure 6.6). Shadows can occur in both daytime and nighttime conditions, but during the daytime, a bright sun means greater contrast and darker shadows. The flash can fill in those dark shadows and bring them into an acceptable balance with the daytime's ambient lighting. Furthermore, in the daylight, even taking a simple photograph of a suspect can be difficult if the individual is wearing a baseball cap or has protruding brow ridges. This is when a camera's built-in flash is ideal. The small pop-up flash typically cannot overpower the intensity of sunlight, but it can be used to fill in small areas of shadow. For larger shadows, a more powerful flash may be needed.

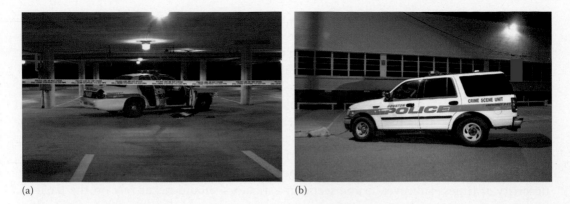

(a)   (b)

Figure 6.5 Photographing in ambient light has a number of benefits. However, a subject's recorded color may not be completely accurate due to the ambient-light source shining on the subject. Adding electronic flash to the image can provide a more accurate color rendition. (a) shows a white police car parked under high pressure sodium lamps. (Photographed by Alton Holmes, Crime Scene Investigator, Houston Police Department, Houston, TX.) (b) has another vehicle parked under high pressure sodium lamps, but an electronic flash was added to capture the accurate color of the crime scene vehicle. (Photographed by Jeffrey Cruser, Crime Scene Investigator, Houston Police Department, Houston, TX.)

(a)   (b)

Figure 6.6 Trees, vehicles, houses, and even evidence markers can cast shadows across a day-time crime scene and individual pieces of evidence. (a) illustrates how the shadows caused by the vehicle conceals the three evidence markers from view. Fill flash was added to (b) in order to cast light onto the markers hidden underneath and inside the vehicle.

Electronic flashes can also be used to cast light on already illuminated subjects, with the additional light creating greater depth and highlights, thereby creating a more infor-mative or eye-pleasing photograph. Furthermore, light provided by a flash can be passed over already illuminated subjects at an oblique angle in order to bring out hidden details and features. Supplemental light can be added obliquely or at any angle in order to help specific subjects stand out and apart from the rest of the image (Figure 6.7). Once again, putting a little thought and flair into one's crime scene photography will help impress a jury with one's skill and dedication toward their responsibilities and duties. Adding *fill flash* to enhance the existing light can improve a photograph by helping eliminate small areas of shadow that may conceal portions of the subject. Today's external flashes with

Figure 6.7 In this daytime exposure, flash was added to the composition and obliquely cast across the surface of the vehicle identification number (VIN) plate in order to bring out the necessary detail. Oblique lighting is especially needed when the VIN does not possess any contrasting color.

their variable power settings and TTL metering have made flash photography much easier than when all flash exposures had to be calculated manually.

Another benefit of off-the-camera flashes is that the light can be more precisely aimed to highlight specific subjects, such as a particular piece of evidence. Not only can an external flash unit be aimed, it can also be bounced, diffused, and softened in order to create a more natural-appearing illumination of the subject. Photographers should strive to not only understand how much light the flash is producing, but where its placement will best serve the recorded image. Many external flashes have built-in rotating or swiveling heads, as well as built-in diffusers. Once again, the selection of the correct flash for crime scene work is a personal decision and is up to the individual photographer, but such features do help create better images.

Since a number of different features are available on today's external flashes, the photographer should perform a cost–benefit analysis to determine which particular flash to purchase by comparing the flash's features and power rating against the price tag. For those crime scene photographers who are issued equipment and have no say in the type of flash equipment they will be using, aftermarket products are available that can make scene documentation a little bit easier, such as diffusers and reflectors. These products were introduced in Chapter 2 and their use will be utilized throughout this chapter.

Externally mounted flash units, even those mounted directly to a camera's hot shoe, can provide just enough distance between the flash and lens to help eliminate red-eyes in a subject. Grip flashes or external flashes mounted to a bracket, such as a Stroboframe®, can assist in separating the flash from the camera lens, thereby reducing red-eye and unwanted reflections. However, the path of light traveling from side-mounted flashes must be carefully monitored in close-focusing situations. The light may skirt right past the intended subject, which will then not be properly illuminated. Additionally, an external flash mounted directly to the camera's hot shoe can cause the shadows to be cast onto a subject by passing over the camera's lens on its way to the subject (Figure 6.8). Some flashes not only rotate the flash's head upward in order to bounce light off a ceiling; they are also able to rotate downward to a very small degree so that the flash can illuminate close-focused subjects. It is also possible that the light produced by an externally mounted flash can pass over the top of a subject unusually close to the camera. To avoid this, choose a flash capable of directing its light at a downward angle or, better yet, connected to the camera by a sync cord.

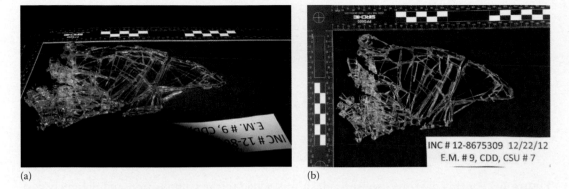

(a)   (b)

INC # 12-8675309 12/22/12
E.M. # 9, CDD, CSU # 7

Figure 6.8 (a) illustrates how a camera's lens can create a shadow on a subject that is too close to the lens. The lens can create a circular shadow along the bottom of the image, especially when close-focused images are recorded with the pop-up flash. (b) was recorded with the flash separated from the camera, connected by a synchronization cord, and directed upon the subject a short distance away from the camera's lens.

Sync cords are extremely valuable to crime scene photographers, because they effectively permit the photographer to direct the path of light more accurately onto the subject. Ring flashes are another alternative for close-focused subjects, but they can be rather expensive for the average public servant. Even if a photographer is limited by their equipment or lack thereof, with a little thought and planning, a good investigator can work around any equipment limitations. The quality of a photographer's work is less about the quality or amount of equipment used to record the image and more about the photographer's ability to get the most out of their equipment.

A major advantage of electronic flash is that it is predictable and measureable. Whether used in full *Manual* or automatic mode, the results (amount of light produced) can be calculated and predicted. Photographers utilizing either the full automatic or a priority mode can be confident in the quality of the final image they capture—once they understand how a flash operates and the relationship between shutter speed, aperture size, guide number, and the camera's TTL metering system. Today, with the increasing use of digital cameras, a photographer's confidence is increased by reviewing their recorded photograph on the camera's LCD screen. However, eliminating the need to review every flash exposure will serve to increase the crime scene investigator's efficiency at a crime scene. In addition, understanding what is wrong with a reviewed image and knowing how to correct the observed deficiencies will be improved with the understanding of the relationships between subject distance, aperture, guide numbers, and electronic flash functions.

Detriments of Flash Photography

As demonstrated in the text, flash photography can be extremely advantageous in the photographic documentation of crime scenes and recovered evidence. Much of photography is about give-and-take or trading one value for another. For example, photographers can have better depths of field through smaller apertures, if they are willing to extend exposure times. Flash photography is similar. Electronic flash can add much to a composition, but it can create problems as well. The shortcomings of flash photography can be overcome,

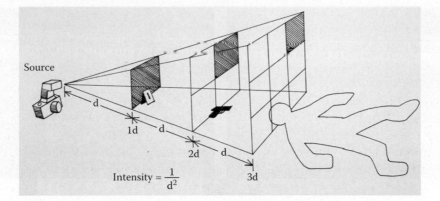

Figure 6.9 This figure illustrates how light fall-off or the inverse square law can be detrimental to crime scene photographers. As the distance between two subjects increases from a single light source, the amount of light lost is a squared total, which may result in poorly exposed flash images. (Sketch drawn by Daniel Nunez, Sergeant, Houston Police Department, Houston, TX.)

but their presence must be recognized and the photographer must be ready and able to compensate for them.

One of the more detrimental aspects of the electronic flash is that it suffers from the effects of light fall-off, also known as the *Inverse Square Law*. As light leaves its source, whether it is a flashlight, streetlight, or electronic flash, its intensity quickly diminishes. Specifically, the amount of light lost is a squared amount (Figure 6.9). As the distance between subjects illuminated by a single light source increases, the amount of light lost is equal to the reciprocal of the squared difference. For example, if one subject is 3 ft from a flash and another subject is 9 ft away from the flash, the amount of light needed to illuminate the far subject is nine times ($3 \times 3 = 9$) greater than the amount of light needed to illuminate the near subject. As it relates to a photographic image, either the foreground subject will be severely overexposed because it received nine times the amount of light necessary or the background subject will be severely underexposed by at least a factor of 9. A single burst of light from a flash unit can properly expose for only one distance, not an entire crime scene.

Electronic flash (Figure 6.10) suffers tremendously from light fall-off because of the fact that it is such a small and harsh light source. The sun is also a harsh light source but is extremely far away, and as a result, it provides a more balanced and even intensity to all subjects that fall under its rays. Even a tall light pole found along a freeway can provide more even lighting because the proportional distance between different subjects and the streetlight is less drastic than a flash held in proximity to a subject.

For smaller, individual subjects, illumination by electronic flash can produce excellent results. However, the light from a single flash unit can also create 1-dimensional images. This is because when the light travels from a single source to illuminate a subject, the final image can appear flat. The term *flat* refers to the lack of contrast and depth in this context. Basically, the result can be dull and uninspiring. Ambient-light sources often come from a number of directions, such as the moon, streetlights, and house lights. Illumination originating from different sources and at different angles in relation to the subject creates a more 3D image, thereby adding depth. Consequently, it is sometimes beneficial to

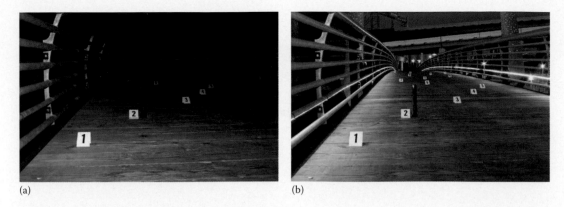

(a)   (b)

Figure 6.10 (a) demonstrates how photographs can suffer from light fall-off. The flash exposure was manually calculated to impact evidence placard #2 and the flashlight. Observe how the light falls away as the evidence placards get further and further away from the camera. The background information beyond the evidence markers is completely lost. However, (b) illustrates a better way in which to capture poorly illuminated crime scenes. The same amount of flash was added to the composition, but the length of the exposure was determined by the ambient light. Instead of a flash-synch exposure of 1/60 of a second, (b) was recorded over 30 s.

take advantage of ambient-light sources instead of solely relying on one's flash equipment. Combining the two forms of light often produces the best and most dramatic results.

Electronic flash does record color accurately. However, the colors provided by the different ambient-light sources can create vivid and multihued images, which is not as likely with flash exposures. As discussed in Chapter 5, ambient light comes from a number of different sources and these diverse light sources possess a diverse number of colors that are visible in the recorded photographs. The different colors of light from various light sources provide additional information to the viewer, as well as being much more aesthetically pleasing. In certain situations, a scene's ambient lighting might just be a better alternative than relying solely on flash illumination, but combining the two can be advantageous.

Battery power is always an issue for crime scene photographers and flash units especially can drain batteries quite rapidly. Fortunately, thyristor circuitry allows a flash to recycle the unused power for less than full-power flash exposures and channel it back into subsequent exposures. Older flashes used to dump unused power and drain a flash's power source even more quickly. Although maintaining a reserve stock of batteries or battery packs for the flash may cost extra money, the benefits of having the ability to use an off-the-camera flash are well worth the expense. As an alternative, rechargeable batteries may be more expensive initially, but over time they can alleviate the expense of buying regular batteries in bulk.

An annoying and possibly damaging aspect of flash photography can result when aftermarket or older flashes are attached to more modern digital cameras. These flashes have been known to have slightly different voltage levels than digital cameras and, as a result, have been known to fry or destroy a digital camera's electronic circuitry, including the imaging chip. Be aware that such potential damage may be caused by an aftermarket flash unit. It is recommended that photographers ensure that their chosen flash equipment is compatible with their camera. While photographers tend to be creatures of habit and fiercely loyal to specific manufacturers of cameras and flash equipment, the rules have changed because of the electronic circuit boards that are now integral parts of modern cameras. Fortunately, for the photographers who desire to use an aftermarket or alternate manufacturer's flash with their cameras, there are voltage-protected synchronization cords such as the Wein *safe-sync module* or *safe-sync high-sync voltage regulator* that can help protect their equipment.

Using Electronic Flash in a Variety of Low-Light Conditions

Investigators are seldom blessed with picture-perfect lighting conditions, portrait studio environments, or a team of assistants willing to organize subjects in a consummately orchestrated arrangement in order to ensure perfect lighting, impeccable depth of field, and flawless contrast. Consequently, crime scene photographers must supplement the ambient light with flash illumination in order to record a quality image. Electronic flash is the most common source of supplemental lighting and flash photography is not merely a nighttime requirement. Even in the daytime, photographers will need the flash to help balance out an exposure and remove shadows from an image. Many of a crime scene investigator's duties take him or her into dark alleys, poorly illuminated fields, and abandoned properties without electrical power. In these situations, flash photography is oftentimes desired, if not completely necessary. Deciding when a flash is necessary and knowing how to apply the light to a subject will improve a crime scene photographer's work product.

Most of the time, a flash is first reached for by photographers in low-light or nighttime conditions. Although flash photography can be beneficial in these poorly illuminated scenes, the photographer must first decide whether it is even necessary. Crime scene documentation procedures should never be dictated by speed or how long it takes to complete the photographic documentation of a location. Therefore, a flash should not be used solely because it is an expedient way to photograph a crime scene quickly. Flash photography should be used because it is needed for a specific purpose, such as adding highlights, emphasizing a particular subject (evidence), or filling in shadowed areas of a crime scene. Accordingly, the photographer must first decide whether to use flash or mount the camera on a tripod and record a time exposure.

When photographing a limited number of subjects or pieces of evidence, utilizing a flash to record the image is oftentimes acceptable. As long as the evidence is roughly the same distance from the flash and the background is not especially deep, flash photography is a quick and effective tool. However, when photographing overall or wide-angle views of a crime scene, a better solution may be to take a time exposure. A crime scene illuminated by a couple of streetlights and/or other ambient light may not need a flash at all. Utilizing a flash is about understanding the relationship between aperture and the distance the subject is from the flash (i.e., guide number). The best flash exposures are recorded with the flash set to illuminate only a specific range of subjects. Therefore, if a crime scene photographer is faced with a scene having significant depth to it, then ambient-light photography should always be considered before trying to do too much with an electronic flash.

Although a particular scene may not be illuminated by the sun, it may still possess balanced-light intensity across the location. Consequently, a flash is not necessarily required when the ambient lighting is sufficient. In order to reemphasize the point, the fact that a flash exposure can capture an image in 1/60 of a second and a time exposure may take as much as 30 s does not mean the more expedient way is the best way. By taking the extra time, foregoing the flash exposure, and capturing a time-exposed image, the crime scene investigator will be rewarded in the courtroom.

A photographer must learn to look not only at the evidence needing documentation but also the location and intensity of lighting present at a location. Seeing where shadows are and how the ambient light, as well as any supplemental light, will affect the final recorded image is an extremely important aspect of photography. Once again, crime scene photography is not a point-and-shoot endeavor. Photographers are encouraged to evaluate their scenes, identify the lighting challenges, and determine the best way to accurately record the environment or subject.

Light is everything to an image. Without illumination, no image can be recorded. On the other hand, if too much illumination is cast, the subject will be washed out and still nothing will be recorded. Therefore, crime scene investigators must avoid tunnel vision and a harried approach to crime scene photography. Important compositions must be examined for lighting and evaluated for deficiencies and a decision must be made on how best to record the image using only ambient lighting, only electronic flash, or a combination of the two.

Combining flash photography with timed exposures maximizes the best of flash and ambient-light photography. Combining the two forms of light into one image is commonly referred to as *slow-synching* or *dragging the shutter*. Basically, the exposure is recorded with the flash illumination, but the shutter speed is slowed down to allow the less-intense ambient light to burn into the photograph over time. Allowing the entire scene to be recorded through the natural lighting and then supplementing that light with flash illumination will provide definitive results and greatly improve an investigator's body of work. As a reminder, always have a tripod available regardless of the nature of the photographs being recorded (Figure 6.11). It is not acceptable to risk a blurry image from being recorded because of laziness or the false belief that one can hand hold a camera stable enough during longer-timed exposures.

Before embarking on more difficult crime scene compositions, photographers must be comfortable with and be able to operate their equipment in less complicated situations. Since an investigator works a crime scene by recording images from general to specific, the recording of overall or establishing photographs is the perfect place to start a flash photography tutorial. Wide-angle views of scenes with any depth to them cannot be easily and accurately photographed at night in an automatic or *Program* mode. In the fully automatic mode, most cameras open their apertures to the largest possible size and fire the flash at a synchronization speed. As a result, the image's background will be void of information because of both the shallow depth of field and light fall-off. Furthermore, the flash will fire and seek out its nearest subject to meter the reflected light. The meter will immediately tell the flash to shut down because an 18% gray value has been reached. An 18% gray value may have been reached for the foreground, but the light most likely did not illuminate the background adequately. Photographers should also be aware that the TTL-metered flashes seek the first object in view of the camera and that may not be the photographer's actual subject or point of focus. One may be photographing a bullet strike to a vehicle's window, but the flash may register the light of the front edge of the car and cause the bullet strike in the background to be underexposed. Therefore, when utilizing flash, the photographer must be aware of the flash's ability to reach and meter the actual subject of the photograph. In the end, be aware of what the camera is seeing and doing.

(a)   (b)

(c)

Figure 6.11 A handheld flash exposure of a nighttime crime scene can be more detrimental than beneficial in the photographic documentation of a crime scene. (a) shows an exposure at flash-synch speed (*Program* mode, ISO 400, f/3.5, for 1/125th of a second); (b) is an image of the same composition but recorded without a flash (ISO 400, f/11, for 20 s). The camera properly exposed for the fountain in the background, but the foreground was still underexposed. (c) was recorded with a combination of flash and the same exposure values as (b).

Think like a camera, compose an image with purpose, and the resulting photographs can only improve.

As for the actual operation of the flash unit, the flash and camera each have *Manual* and automatic modes. Manual operation of the flash will be discussed later, but for now, it is easier to simply set the flash mode to the automatic or TTL mode. Although the flash is set to an automatic mode, the camera can still be operated in any of the automatic, priority, or *Manual* modes. The automatic flash mode is simply operating the flash's ability to achieve an 18% gray value from the first subject the camera identifies. And just to reemphasize the point, the flash-metered subject does not have to be the subject chosen by the photographer as the point of focus. Of course, setting a camera's capture mode to full automatic will force the camera to choose both the aperture and shutter speed. However, there are occasions when using one of the priority or *Manual* modes would be more beneficial. For example, if the photographer desires a slower shutter speed to allow background light to burn into the image, then the *Shutter Priority* or *Manual* mode may be more applicable. On the other hand, in close-focusing situations where depth of field is paramount, the photographer could utilize the *Aperture Priority*, select a small aperture, and still have the flash determine the proper amount of light output. Additionally, even though the camera's operator switches to *Manual* and selects both the aperture and shutter speed, the flash can still be used to calculate the amount of flash in an automatic TTL flash mode. As long as the flash is set to TTL, the camera will attempt to provide the proper flash illumination even though the camera is set to *Manual*. Remember, metering ambient light, calculating flash exposures, and focusing are all completely different tasks. Although the camera can do all three tasks at once, photographers who take control of one or more of these tasks will be rewarded with better photographic images.

The metering of ambient light and the evaluation of the light produced by an electronic flash are two completely different functions. As a result, photographers can operate their equipment in different or in similar modes (camera set to *Manual* and flash set to automatic or vice versa). Those still using film and who are therefore unable to review the captured image should remember to take a quick peek on the back of the flash and see if the flash exposure check lamp is illuminated. When the check lamp comes on after an exposure, the TTL meter has recorded a proper flash exposure (according to the camera). It is important to remember that the TTL meter can be fooled by reflective surfaces, and although the exposure check light illuminates, the final recorded image may still be underexposed. Of course, digital cameras have the advantage of having their images available for review right after the moment of capture. However, realize that the image seen on the small preview screen may not appear the same as a full-size image. Consequently, recording a series of bracketed images is always recommended. With all that said, the photographer's first decision is to decide what capture mode the camera (*Program, Aperture Priority, Shutter Priority, Manual*) will be set in and what mode (*Manual* or TTL) the flash will be set to. Most investigators will forego the manual-flash calculations and choose the TTL flash mode. That decision is more than acceptable, just be aware of how the flash works and what it is seeking to illuminate.

Directionality of Light from Electronic Flashes

After determining how the image will be recorded, the next step is determining how the flash will be applied to the composition. The direction at which light is applied to a subject is an enormously important aspect of flash photography. The directionality of light can affect shadows, reflections, and the harshness or softness of the light recorded. Light produced by a flash can be bounced off surfaces, such as a wall or ceiling, in order to change the directionality of light and thus have a tremendous effect on the final appearance of a photograph. There are also a number of different styles of diffusers that can change the directionality and appearance of light falling onto a subject. Consequently, when crime scene investigators are processing a crime scene and determining the value of evidence, they also must determine the best manner of illuminating that evidence or subject.

Direct lighting of subjects is easy and suitable in a number of applications. An external flash mounted directly to the camera's hot shoe is a perfect example of how direct lighting is created. Even a camera's built-in flash is capable of throwing light directly onto a subject. However, there are a couple of problems with direct lighting. The illumination provided by a flash mounted directly on the camera may cast shadows behind objects sitting in the path of the traveling light. This is true for any light source traveling across the field of view. However, when the primary light source illuminating the subject is coming from one main source, the shadows can be quite distracting. Shadows can be beneficial in some circumstances, such as when trying to photograph ridge detail on footwear or tire wear impressions. The photographer must anticipate and recognize the potential results when light is cast across the composition and what information may be lost because of any shadows that are formed.

One of the more common environments where unintentional mistakes are made by crime scene photographers is while working indoors. For example, doorways can pose a number of difficulties to crime scene photographers. To begin with, the camera's TTL metering typically identifies the door frame as the composition's subject and causes the flash to put out just enough light to properly illuminate the doorframe and not what may be of value behind it. Consequently, be cautious of doorways or large pieces of furniture inside a home and be ready to compensate for such impediments (Figure 6.12). In addition, most interior walls of a home come in some shade of white and the camera's meter attempts to turn the white wall 18% gray. As a result, the image could be underexposed from the start, and the background information could be completely lost. Most of the time, there are a variety of reflective surfaces that photographers can use to bounce light off of in order to achieve a more even illumination across the scene. For example, bouncing the flash off the ceiling can create a more balanced illumination and remove distracting shadows or reflections from developing in the image.

(a)   (b)

Figure 6.12 (a) illustrates how intermediate objects such as furniture and doorway frames can cause the camera's TTL metering to shut down the flash before it can reach the background. Additionally, foreground objects can cast shadows over important pieces of evidence present in the background. (b) provides a better balance between the highlights and shadows by *dragging the shutter*, allowing the background light to burn into the image and provide illumination to the entire scene. (a) was recorded at flash-synch speed of 1/60th of a second, while (b) was recorded at a slower 1/15th of a second, allowing ambient light to create a balanced exposure.

Figure 6.13 This image was recorded using a tripod-mounted camera and metering the sunlight impacting just the window. The room's illumination was provided by electronic flash to create a balance between the early morning sun-illuminated window and the flash-illuminated interior. The photograph was recorded at ISO 400, f/16, for 3 s.

A basic concept in capturing quality flash photographs is to strike a balance between the highlights and shadows. This practice extends to much of photography and should be quickly grasped by crime scene investigators in order to capture those images most telling and informative to the viewers. This balance is best achieved by allowing enough time in the exposure to either permit some background light to burn into the image or let the flash's illumination to filter into the composition through diffused or bounced lighting (Figure 6.13). Bouncing the light or using a diffuser allows light to filter into the background and still allows the photographer to capture images with a handheld camera. Slow-synching an exposure might create a shutter speed that is too slow to hand hold the camera, but it will allow a composition's background to become more visible in the recorded image. Crime scene photography can be a frustrating challenge at times, but practice and experience will help bring all a photographer's skills to the attention of a jury or others viewing one's body of work.

Using grip-style external flashes and mounting external flashes to a flash bracket, such as a Stroboframe, are effective ways to change the direction of lighting and can assist with helping eliminate reflections, red-eye, and unwanted shadows. However, it is easy to forget that the flash is mounted to the side when deeply involved in the documentation of an expansive or detailed crime scene. It is not uncommon for an investigator to move from one room to the next to photograph an establishing or overall image from just behind a doorway only to have the flash fire and strike one edge of the doorway's frame, thus completely failing to illuminate the interior of a room. The crime scene photographer should remember to step into doorways before commencing the recording of an image. However, if the doorway provides an important link between one room and the next, then the photographer may need to be more creative in composition. The camera can be positioned outside the doorway and the flash placed inside the room for discharge. If the flash can be remotely fired, then this setup is workable and not difficult. If the photographer does not possess a remote flash, then he or she will have to illuminate a room's interior using full *Manual* settings and basically paint the interior of a scene with light (Chapter 7). The proposition is not difficult, but requires an investigator to recognize the lighting problem, plan a solution, and then execute the photographic endeavor. In regard to doorways, be sure to orient the camera to the doorway's orientation. Too much wasted space results in a composition when vertical doorways are captured by a camera held in a horizontal orientation.

As far as directionality of a flash's illumination is concerned, the photographer utilizing a grip-style flash must be cognizant of what the flash is capable of illuminating and what it cannot physically reach. Side-mounted flashes are great for longer-range exposures but can be detrimental to photographic results in a close-focusing situation. The photographer must always be cognizant of where the flash is aimed, especially side- or grip-mounted flashes. For example, if the photographer is imaging a fired cartridge case on the ground and has the placard or tent marker placed between the evidence and the flash, a large shadow created by the tent marker may conceal the subject and investigators will be left without a useful evidentiary photograph. It is very likely that the flash's confirmation light for a proper exposure will illuminate in this situation, giving the photographer a false sense of security.

In regard to unwanted shadows, if the photographer is worried and not sure whether a distracting shadow will be created in a picture, he or she merely has to keep one eye on the subject during the flash exposure. It is the little things like improperly exposed photographs that can cause major problems in court. Suffice it to say that the photographer must be aware of the flash's direction of travel so that errors do not occur or are compensated for. The flash should be aimed with purpose and with specific intent so that the light reaches the intended subject. Grip-mounted flashes or any flash set apart from the camera might not be able to place light on a subject near the camera's lens in a close-focusing situation. It is best to separate the flash from the camera and specifically aim the flash onto the subject in order to ensure proper illumination (Figure 6.14). For extremely close-focusing situations, review Chapter 4 on painting with light on a macroscale.

Figure 6.14 Focusing on important subjects and illuminating them with electronic flash is best done by separating the flash from the camera and aiming the light onto specific areas of shadow that require illumination. In this photo, the row of presidential statues was illuminated by a nearby streetlight, but the streetlight caused harsh shadows under the eyes, under the necks, and to the right sides of the monuments. The ambient light was metered (ISO 100, f/8, for 15 s), and the flash was separated from the camera and cast into the areas of shadow in order to create a balance between the highlights and shadows.

Figure 6.15 Mirrors are the ultimate reflective surface. This photo illustrates how directing a flash's illumination at an angle across the subject removes any harsh reflections that would have been caused by the flash mounted directly to the camera. It was recorded at ISO 100, f/4.5, for 4 s. The flash was manually calculated and fired from the side of the composition.

Another detrimental aspect of photographing with direct flash illumination is the creation of unwanted reflections in the image. Light travels in a very predictable way. The angle at which a light is projected is equal to the angle at which it reflects (or the angle of incidence equals the angle of reflection). Unfortunately, the severity of the light returning to the camera often overwhelms the actual subject. Especially detrimental to flash photography are shiny surfaces like glossy-painted surfaces, tile floors, and marble countertops (Figure 6.15). These surfaces reflect the light produced by the flash and may conceal subjects lying upon them. Although the flash confirmation light will illuminate indicating a proper exposure on the back of a flash unit, the end result can be anything but pleasing. One solution is to hold the flash at an angle to the subject and away from the camera so that the harshness of the light reflects away from the camera, while the subject is illuminated in the camera's field of view. Separating the flash from the camera is very often a recommended practice.

Clearly, the direction a flash is projected across the subject is important for an accurate and well-illuminated image. No one has declared crime scene photography to be easy, and even though an investigator can put everything on *Program* mode and just snap photograph after photograph, this does not mean the end result will have any value. Fortunately, even if photographers are comfortable with their camera's *Program* mode capabilities, results always improve when the photographer gives a little forethought to the orientation of the flash to the subject. Consequently, in addition to all the other responsibilities, a crime scene investigator must be cognizant of the camera's flash, the impediments present in the

(a)   (b)

Figure 6.16 (a) and (b) are photographs of an unilluminated hallway. (a) was recorded at ISO 100, f/4.5, for 1/60th of a second and the flash was mounted to the camera; (b) was recorded at ISO 100, f/14, for 70 s and the flash was cast in three locations throughout the length of the hallway in order to create a more evenly illuminated hallway. Manually selecting the camera's settings allowed the photographer to control the depth of field and the ambient light, which was a challenge in this composition.

light's travel, where shadows may hide important pieces of evidence, and when reflective surfaces may cause harsh highlights to appear.

It is common for photographers to be constrained by their environments. For example, hallways, especially long hallways, can be quite problematic. Hallways present a number of challenges including camera orientation, depth of field, and illumination (Figure 6.16). To begin with, the camera should be placed in a vertical orientation to match the alignment or shape of the hallway. Secondly, because the hallway will likely be running away from the camera, the depth of field must be extended and compensation must be made through smaller aperture choices. Illuminating a hallway utilizing only a flash should be avoided, especially for longer hallways. Because of the hallway's length, the need for smaller apertures, and light fall-off, a flash is just not the most appropriate choice. The camera should be tripod mounted and an ambient-light exposure recorded. Electronic flash can still be added to the composition to highlight a specific section of the hallway or a specific piece of evidence. Painting hallways with light is also a possibility, especially if the crime scene investigator is working in a low-light environment, such as scenes without electrical power or abandoned properties. Photographers must not assume that all indoor photographs can be effectively recorded with flash exposures. Think about what the camera is viewing and how light is recorded in order to capture the most valuable and accurate images.

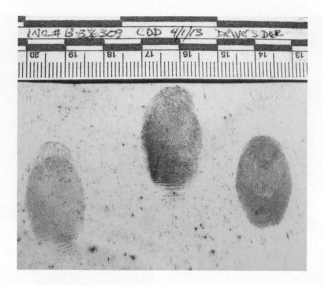

Figure 6.17 Reflective and painted surfaces, such as the white vehicle seen in this figure, can cause difficulties for photographers. Casting the flash obliquely across the surface will assist in eliminating unwanted glare and reflections. The electronic flash was held approximately 3 ft above the set of fingerprints present on the highly reflective paint on this car.

Another frequently encountered environment that complicates flash photography occurs when investigators process motor vehicles. Cars and vehicles offer a number of challenges to photographers because of the numerous reflective surfaces, the numerous nooks and crannies found inside the vehicle, and the numerous ways in which evidence can land or imbed themselves inside a vehicle. The shiny paint jobs, chrome trim, and glass surfaces found on cars, trucks, and other vehicles can be quite a challenge to crime scene photographers. Like any light-reflective surface, a camera's light meter can be fooled into an underexposure or a reflected hot-spot may develop in an image. When dealing with reflective surfaces, the photographer should seek to add light obliquely to the subject if possible. Casting light across the subject and from a different angle as the camera will help capture a more light-accurate photograph, as well as help eliminate distracting reflections (Figure 6.17). Photographers should also be aware of their own positions in the composition and avoid recording a reflected image of themselves in the photograph.

Because of the small confines of the passenger area of cars, getting light onto small objects like fired cartridge cases, fired bullets, and droplets of blood can be difficult. Shadows are formed by gear shifts, steering wheels, and headrests. Additionally, fired bullets pose a particularly aggravating challenge because their flight paths take them into some unbelievable locations. Once a bullet deflects off an intervening object and tumbles, it is not uncommon for investigators to find bullets tucked into the most hard-to-reach locations. Capturing and recording these small pieces of evidence is still possible, even in the narrow confines of an automobile (Figure 6.18).

Often, the use of a large off-the-camera flash can be detrimental to the capture of a quality photograph, because the flash just cannot fit into the car's small confines. In these circumstances, the light produced by the flash can be blocked from reaching the subject or, because of the close confines, it may not even be possible to aim the light at the subject. There are a few options available to investigators who find themselves in this predicament.

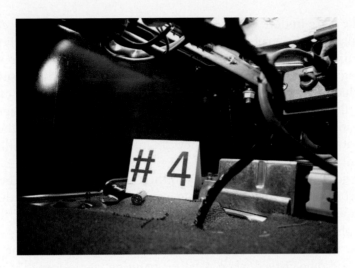

Figure 6.18 A picture of the fired casing found lying underneath the driver's side car seat was recorded with the flash attached to a sync cord and a Sto-Fen diffuser attached to the flash's head.

First, they may be able to use their pop-up flashes. Investigators still must be aware of reflective surfaces and avoid being too close to the subject, but photographing a subject from an effective distance away with a built-in flash could record a quality image. An *effective distance* is close enough to fill the viewfinder with the subject but far enough away that the pop-up flash can reach over the camera's lens and illuminate the whole subject. A second alternative is simply to use only ambient lighting to record an image. If the ambient light is evenly spread across the subject matter, even if it is somewhat caliginous, an available-light photograph may be the best solution. If the light is somewhat diminished, then stabilize the camera with a small tripod or beanbag support. Although this may require more time and effort, the final results will reward the extra exertion. Finally, it may be necessary to be a bit creative when illuminating the smaller nooks and crannies that are commonly associated with the interiors of motor vehicles. Placing a flash's head beneath a seat or into a door panel may provide the proper illumination. The flash should have a soft box or diffuser attached so that the light does not end up being too harsh, causing an unintentional overexposure. Using a flashlight to illuminate small nooks and crannies is another possible solution. The light provided by the flashlight can be previewed through the camera's viewfinder and the flashlight can then be adjusted to the best possible position. The composition can be metered for light by the camera and the photograph recorded. Just as with a flash, the light from the flashlight may need to be diffused. Fingerprint tape, a thin sheet of notebook paper, or other translucent filter can be placed over the flashlight's lens to soften the light. In conclusion, just because a photograph is a challenge does not justify failing to attempt a recording. On the contrary, these opportunities are the ones in which the photographer can shine and demonstrate their professionalism and dedication to the job.

Conclusion

Flash photography is probably the most difficult of all aspects of photography, basically because electronic flash illumination can be so limiting. Crimes do not occur in a photo studio; they take place in dark alleys, abandoned homes, and every conceivable environment. As a result, crime scene photographers are not blessed with perfectly arranged lighting or even quality ambient lighting. Consequently, they are required to supplement the available lighting with flash illumination. Unfortunately, electronic flash suffers from a few drawbacks, including its 1D appearance, light fall-off, and its ability to create unwanted shadows and reflections. Fortunately, photographers have options to improve an overall image's composition. They can introduce multiple flashes into the image, they can combine ambient light with flash illumination, or they can merely forego the flash illumination and use only ambient lighting.

Flashes are graded by guide numbers and these guide numbers can be used to determine the correct amount of light placed onto a subject. Guide number values are equal to the f/number (aperture) multiplied by the distance between the flash and the subject. This formula allows photographers to predict the exact output of a flash when working low-light crime scenes, as well as to calculate flash exposure settings based on the guide number. Guide numbers become critical when used for painting crime scenes at night. Working low-light crime scenes is not especially difficult and the use of electronic flashes can add tremendous value to a scene's overall illumination. The next chapter will expand upon the basic flash operation to improve a photographer's ability to accurately, fairly, and truthfully document a nighttime crime scene.

End of Chapter Questions

1. What is the formula for calculating a flash's guide number?
    a. Guide Number = Aperture × Shutter Speed
    b. Guide Number = Aperture × Subject Distance
    c. Guide Number = Shutter Speed × ISO Value
    d. Guide Number = Aperture × 10 (ft)

2. A photographer possesses a flash having a guide number of 120. The photographer wishes to have an aperture of f/8. How far must the flash be positioned from the subject?
    a. 9 ft
    b. 12 ft
    c. 15 ft
    d. 18 ft

3. A photographer has a flash having a guide number of 160. The photographer wishes to properly expose a single subject that rests 10 ft from the camera (and flash). Depth of field is not important. What should the aperture be set for a full-power (1/1) flash exposure?
    a. f/4
    b. f/8
    c. f/11
    d. f/16

4. A photographer tests his brand new flash to see what the power or effective guide number for his equipment. Using a subject 10 ft away from the flash, a proper exposure was obtained with an aperture of f/11. What is the effective guide number value?
    a. 56
    b. 110
    c. 220
    d. Depends on length of exposure

5. A photographer sets up a composition, where the subject is 5 ft away from the flash unit. The flash's guide number at full power is 160. The photographer desires to minimize the depth of field and desires an aperture of f/4. What is the proper reduction in the flash's power setting?
    a. 1/32
    b. 1/64
    c. 1/128
    d. Not enough information to calculate flash exposure

6. A photographer has set up a properly exposed composition with an aperture of f/22 and a full-power (1/1) flash. The flash's power is reset to 1/8th power. With everything else being equal, what is the new aperture to match the adjustment in flash power?
    a. f/2.8
    b. f/4
    c. f/5.6
    d. f/8

7. A photographer has a composition setup where he wants to manually fire a flash toward a specific target in the scene. The flash's guide number is 110, but the photographer is photographing the scene at ISO 400. The subject will be 10 ft away from the flash when fired and the chosen aperture is f/11. What would be a proper power setting for the flash unit?
    a. 1/1
    b. 1/2
    c. 1/4
    d. 1/8

8. A photographer possesses a flash with a guide number of 120 at ISO 100. He wishes to record an image on ISO 50 speed film. What would be the equivalent guide number value?
    a. GN = 35
    b. GN = 85
    c. GN = 120
    d. GN = 168

9. A photographer possesses a flash with a guide number of 160 at ISO 100. He wishes to record an image at an ISO setting of 800. What would be the equivalent guide number value?
    a. GN = 113
    b. GN = 320
    c. GN = 448
    d. GN = 532

10. A photographer possesses a flash with a guide number of 110 at ISO 100. He wishes to photograph an image at an ISO setting of 400 and at aperture of f/11. The flash will be manually fired at full power (1/1). How far should the intended subject be from the flash at the new ISO 400 setting?
    a. 20 ft
    b. 25 ft
    c. 30 ft
    d. Not enough information to determine distance

11. A flash's mode (automatic or *Manual*) does not have to match the camera's exposure mode (automatic or *Manual*).
    a. True
    b. False

12. The flash is connected to the camera's focus and will always attempt to make a proper flash exposure to the point of focus.
    a. True
    b. False

13. In regard to light, the angle of incidence equals the angle of _____.
    a. Refraction
    b. Reflection
    c. Absorption
    d. Impact

14. Which ISO setting is the best choice for flash photography?
    a. ISO 100
    b. ISO 400
    c. ISO 800
    d. Depends on equipment, subject's distance, and environment

15. Which is a beneficial aspect of electronic flash photography?
    a. Reciprocity
    b. Reciprocity failure
    c. Light is white balanced
    d. Can be operated in *Manual* mode

16. Flash photography is not necessary in outdoor, daytime exposures.
    a. True
    b. False

17. What type of flash is designed for close-focused subjects?
    a. Ring flash
    b. Built-in flash
    c. TTL flash
    d. Fill flash

18. What detrimental aspect of flash photography should the photographer be constantly aware of?
    a. Bounced flash
    b. Reflective metering
    c. Inverse square law
    d. Guide number formula

19. In nighttime environments, one may hand hold a camera effectively for up to 1 s.
    a. True
    b. False

20. What is the TTL flash metering trying to determine?
    a. 18% gray
    b. Daylight balance
    c. Proper ambient-light balance
    d. All of the above

21. When can a flash that is attached directly to the camera's hot shoe be problematic?
    a. Portrait photography
    b. Photographing reflective surfaces
    c. Macro photography
    d. All of the above

22. What is an effective alternative to direct flash lighting?
    a. Diffused lighting
    b. Ambient lighting
    c. Bounced lighting
    d. All of the above

Photography Assignments

Required Tools: External flash unit (preferred), with extra batteries

Photography Subjects: Safe outdoor (nighttime) environment and a larger indoor environment, such as a gym, mirrors or reflective surfaces, and indented footwear or tire wear impressions

   I. Complete a test of your electronic flash(es):
      A. Set camera and flash 10 ft away from subject. It would be a good idea to place a placard in each photograph matching the camera's aperture.

    B. Set flash to *Manual* flash and at full power (1/1). Set the camera to ISO 100 and at sync speed (1/60th or higher). The ISO value can be adjusted to individual photographer's needs if necessary.

    C. Record a series of images changing the aperture through an adequate range of stops. Make note of flash's *zoom* setting and maintain its consistency.

    D. Review the images and choose the best exposed photograph.

    E. Guide number will be equal to the aperture used in the best photograph multiplied by 10 (for the 10 ft distance).

    F. Complete a series of photographs for each electronic flash (built-in and external flashes).

    G. Complete a series of photographs for different *zoom* values if your flash has the ability to adjust the focus of the flash's light.

    H. Complete a series of photographs for indoor and outdoor environments.

II. With the flash set to *Manual*, calculate a proper (*Manual*) flash exposure for the following:

    A. A nighttime subject such as a mailbox or other similar-sized subject
1. Take a series of photographs of the same composition but at different ISO values: 100, 200, 400.
2. Manually calculate a flash exposure of a reflective surface, separating the flash from the camera and casting the light obliquely onto surface.

    B. Photograph a room's interior, manually calculating the flash exposure:
1. Use direct lighting.
2. Use bounced lighting (be sure to calculate the full distance traveled by the light).

    C. Manually calculate a macrophoto that is close focused from a distance of just 1 to 2 ft.

III. Demonstrate *slow-synch* or *dragging the shutter* exposures:

    A. Meter a nighttime, outdoor exposure and use the flash to illuminate a subject in the foreground.

    B. Record the same image in the full-auto mode and compare results.

    C. Meter a low-light, indoor exposure and use flash to illuminate a subject in the foreground.

    D. Record the same image in the full-auto mode and compare results.

IV. In a low-light, indoor setting, record a series of photographs that demonstrate your ability to use bounce or otherwise diffused lighting techniques (TTL—automatic flash exposures are acceptable):

    A. Record an image with the flash fired straight off the hot shoe.

    B. Record an image with the flash bounced off the ceiling or appropriate wall.

    C. Record an image using a flash diffuser.

    D. Review images and observe the differences in lighting.

V. Photograph a car's interior in the nighttime by standing outside the car and shooting through the window.

VI. Record a flash photograph of the following (TTL—automatic flash exposures are acceptable):

    A. A street sign in the nighttime

    B. A motor vehicle in the nighttime

    C. A small/macro subject

    D. A reflective subject, such as a mirror or chrome object

    E. An indented impression (footprint or tire print)

Additional Readings

Davis, P. (1995). *Photography*. 7th ed. Boston, MA: McGraw Hill.

Grimm, T. and Grimm, M. (1997). *The Basic Book of Photography: The Classic Guide*. New York: Penguin Books.

McKern, C. (April 25, 2009). Flash photography made simple. Retrieved April 25, 2009, from http://www.vividlight.com/articles/611.htm.

Painting with Light 7

Painting with light is the application of light onto a subject or into an entire composition and can be compared to painting a fence with a brush or roller. Instead of using a paintbrush, the photographer simply uses a light source. The types of lighting available for use are innumerable. Illumination can be added to a composition with electronic flashes, flashlights, alternate light sources (ALS or polylight), or anything that emits visible radiation. The photographer simply must select a light source and imagine the scene as an artist's canvas and determine the best way in which to cover that canvas with paint (selected light source). Similar to painting a fence, two coats of paint are typically better than one. The greatest aspect of painting with light is its broad application to crime scene photography. A photographer can use painting with light techniques for the overall composition of a crime scene or for just a small, individual piece of evidence.

Painting with light is necessary when reduced lighting creates a need for added illumination and a single flash is not sufficient to illuminate the subject or subjects. Painting-with-light utilizes the theory that light is additive. Light can be continuously poured onto and over a subject until a proper exposure is obtained. The final recorded image is obtained after the application of all the wanted or needed light is added to the composition. Consequently, the final product is the total accumulation of light. Photographers should not think of the streaks or individual brush strokes of light, but rather of the finished product. Like painting a fence, one does not worry about the individual brush strokes, one only cares that the fence appears uniform in color at the end. In painting with light, photographers are looking for a uniform light exposure.

Some investigators may fear that all this light being dumped into a composition may cause an overexposure. Fortunately, it is rather difficult to overexpose images in low-light conditions. The techniques discussed in this chapter are easily duplicated without a great fear of overexposing the subject matter. Reciprocity failure occurs with film images and revolves around the concept that exposure reciprocity fails during long exposures. Fortunately, the failing of reciprocal exposure relationships allows film photographers a great deal of latitude in low-light conditions. This is not to say that overexposing an image is impossible, but nighttime photography can be much more forgiving to mistakes than working in the daylight. Although reciprocity failure applies to film-captured images, digital photographers will be surprised by the amount of light that can be added to a nighttime composition without the risk of severely overexposing an image. As far as the additional light is concerned, investigators have the added benefit of choosing the particular light source which best fits the situation. For example, a photographer can utilize a variable-powered electronic flash, a portable spotlight, or even a small penlight flashlight. On the other hand, daytime exposures are typically dictated by the sun and the limitations associated with such a strong light source. Consequently, nighttime environments offer a greater versatility and creative opportunities for the crime scene photographer (Figure 7.1).

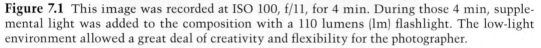

Figure 7.1 This image was recorded at ISO 100, f/11, for 4 min. During those 4 min, supplemental light was added to the composition with a 110 lumens (lm) flashlight. The low-light environment allowed a great deal of creativity and flexibility for the photographer.

Adding light to an image is about filling in shadows and shedding light into the darkness. In the previous chapter (Chapter 6), the limitations of flash were discussed. Frequently, when a flash exposure is deemed necessary, simply taking an ambient or available light photograph suffices in capturing a quality image. Even under nighttime conditions, leaving the lens open for an extended period of time will provide enough light to filter down and illuminate much of a crime scene. However, shadows are still frequently found in low-light and nighttime conditions, just as they are during daylight hours. The key to a good photograph is finding a balance between the highlights and shadows of a composition. Granted, there are computer programs capable of repairing exposure errors and the drastic contrasts between bright highlights and dark shadows. However, a crime scene investigator's job is to capture quality photographic images and not rely on the computer to save a poorly recorded image. The old saying, garbage in–garbage out has real meaning, and investigators must strive to provide the best possible image for any subsequent enhancements that may be necessary.

Types of Lighting

The first decision an investigator needs to make in adding light into a photographic composition is to decide which type of light should be utilized. Literally, the number and types of lighting implements are limitless and every investigator will have his or her own personal preference. Typical light sources include but are not limited to, the following:

- Electronic flashes
- Portable spotlights
- Police style flashlights (Four D-cell equivalent)
- Smaller flashlights (penlight, LED lights, etc.)
- Ultraviolet flashlights or fluorescent tube black-lights
- Alternate light sources

Most of these lights, except for the alternate light sources, are typically carried by a crime scene investigator in one form or another. Therefore, having to purchase additional equipment should not be necessary. High-powered flashlights and spotlights are excellent for illuminating the larger expanses of an overall photographic composition. The smaller, less intense, lights can be used to illuminate smaller areas or just a single piece of evidence. Electronic flashes can be used for either activity because their output of light (power setting) can be adjusted for different tasks.

Painting with Light Using Electronic Flashes

Painting a crime scene with an electronic strobe flash generally requires disconnecting the flash from the camera; therefore, an investigator must be comfortable with the guide number (GN) value of their equipment and how to calculate flash exposures. The guide number reflects the flash's power and is vitally important for any photographer who is manually calculating their flash exposures. There are some ingenious gadgets available to photographers that allow flashes to be wirelessly connected to the camera so that they can be operated in an automatic/TTL (Through-The Lens metering) mode. Keeping with the *less is more* philosophy, there is simply no reason to purchase these expensive toys for the sake of convenience. However, if mathematical computations are not a photographer's strong suit and the photographer has more disposable income than the average police investigator, then a wirelessly connected flash could be helpful. However, wireless flashes are synchronized to the tripping of the shutter and subsequent flashes added to the composition still must be done in a *Manual* mode unless the investigator possesses a series of slave flashes. Slave flashes are synchronized to fire with the camera's primary flash. One drawback of slave-flash photography is the added expense of the additional equipment. As will be shown, there is no need to purchase a multitude of flashes. One quality flash will suffice. Therefore, it is best if photographers get a comfortable grasp on guide number calculations and their own personal equipment. Instead of acquiring multiple pieces of expensive equipment, photographers simply need to remember the formula: guide number equals the subject distance multiplied by the aperture. The formula has three variables and it can be mathematically structured to solve whatever variable is unknown to the photographer. These formulas were first presented in Chapter 6, but bears repeating:

- Guide Number = Aperture × Subject Distance
- Aperture = Guide Number/Subject Distance
- Subject Distance = Guide Number/Aperture

Please note that *subject distance* refers to the distance between the flash and subject, not the distance between the camera and subject. Of course, if the flash is attached to the camera, then the subject distance is the same value.

The main drawback with flash is light fall-off or how the Inverse Square Law affects the evenness of light traveling across a crime scene. Light fall-off can occur with small subjects such as footwear impressions, as well as over larger expanses such as an overall crime scene. Correcting for light fall-off in close-focusing situations is fairly easy because of the small confines of composition. Photographing an overall scene's composition in low-light conditions will frequently incorporate several hundred square feet and contain multiple shadow-causing impediments such as vehicles, trees, and other physical structures.

A single flash casting over such a large area will not be able to reach into every shadowed recess, and the distracting nature of overexposed foregrounds and underexposed backgrounds caused by light fall-off is more than a possibility. The solution to this dilemma is to cast multiple flashes from multiple firing positions in and around the crime scene so that the entire location is evenly illuminated.

Dragging the shutter, which allows available light to burn into the image, and adding flash illumination to the composition are the most basic forms of painting with light. Allowing the shutter to remain open and placing flash illumination onto a subject or subjects in order to add highlights is just the beginning. The resulting photographs will be head and shoulders above any *Program* mode flash capture. Adding flash illumination to the areas of shadow in a composition will only improve the end product. Due to light fall-off, casting a single burst of light from an electronic flash over an extensive distance may not provide the light balance desired. Even if the flash strikes a distant subject with the proper illumination, the foreground will likely be overexposed, especially if the distance between the subject and flash is great. In order to prevent the effects of light fall-off and causing overexposed foregrounds, one needs to work in close proximity to the areas needing illumination.

Crime scene investigators can begin the process of painting a crime scene by examining the scene, especially evaluating nighttime crime scenes for highlights and shadows. The shadows are the target areas where light will be added by the investigator. These shadowed areas may be located under vehicles, behind houses, beneath tree canopies, or any structure that stands between a light source and a surrounding surface. The illumination of these shadowed areas is the goal. In addition to areas of shadow, light can also be directed onto specific targets, such as signs, license plates, or specific pieces of evidence, in order to bring the viewer's attention to a specific subject within a composition.

The first step in recording an impressive photograph is to determine the best combination of ISO value, aperture, and shutter speed for the ambient light conditions. Selecting an ISO value (or film value) of 100 will give photographers extra time to add the needed flash illumination and paint their scenes. Although it is quite common to choose ISO 400 as a setting when capturing images with the assistance of electronic flash, the advantages of sharpness and color saturation provided by slower speed films are worth the extra effort. Another advantage of choosing an ISO value of 100 is that guide numbers are typically quoted at ISO 100 and the calculations of apertures and subject distances are so much easier when ISO 100 is selected. As should be known, the choice of aperture can affect an image's depth of field, but smaller apertures do require greater power from the investigator's flash. As an added benefit, photographers might find that small apertures will give them more time to paint the crime scene with light. Investigators should not rush through a crime scene's photographic documentation. The extra time required by the smaller apertures and an ISO Value of 100 are beneficial in that they will give the photographer additional time to walk into and around the crime scene, adding supplemental light where needed.

Determining exposure settings in low-light is pretty much the same as photographing with ambient light in any other environment. The only difference is the desire to have longer exposures, if possible, to give the photographer the time needed to add any necessary supplemental light. Selecting small apertures and an ISO value of 100 will help ensure longer exposures, even in well-illuminated nighttime crime scenes. Once the variables of aperture and ISO are chosen, the camera's light meter can be used to determine the approximate shutter speed. For those scenes completely without ambient light and where the entire landscape needs supplemental illumination, the shutter speed is inconsequential. The length of the exposure ends up being however long it takes the investigator to finish adding the illumination to the scene. Nighttime crime scenes are remarkably flexible.

ISO values and apertures are chosen for specific purposes by the photographer. The one variable or corner of the exposure triangle remaining is the length of the capture (shutter speed). Fortunately, shutter speeds possess inherent range and versatility, which provides photographers a great deal of latitude in their compositions and exposure evaluations. For the most part, photographers can trust their cameras to meter the ambient light and correctly determine a proper exposure. Investigators should simply be aware of harsh light sources, like spot lights, strobe lights, or bright security lamps that may trick the camera's light meter and cause an underexposure. Metering ambient light was discussed in Chapter 6. It is a critical component and starting point for painting crime scenes with light.

The next component in painting with light is the application of supplemental light. Investigators have many choices of light sources, but electronic flash units are extremely valuable because they are balanced for white light and their output is measurable and predictable. Photographers should be familiar with the guide number values of their flash equipment. Remember that the quoted guide numbers of a flash are for indoor and more reflective environments, rather than outdoor locations. Therefore, photographers must test their equipment and possess a more accurate guide number before progressing any further. Once a photographer has a working guide number in mind, then the process of painting the scene can begin. It is easiest to work with simple numbers, so if the distance between the subject and flash remains constant at approximately 10 ft, the camera's proper aperture can be easily determined by dividing the flash's guide number by 10. For example, if a flash's guide number equals 110, then selecting an aperture of f/11 would be best (f/11 × 10 = 110 GN). A 10 ft distance may not be possible in every situation, but it gives the photographer a starting point from which to work. Basically, 10 is a very easy number to use when mentally performing mathematical computations. In addition, light fall off is less damaging at such close distances. Casting light with only 10 ft separating the target and the flash unit helps provide a more even and natural lighting appearance.

The process of painting with light is a methodical, planned undertaking. The scene is evaluated for light, the exposure settings are selected, and the physical process of adding light to a crime scene begins. There are some basic tips or hints that will help create better images when adding light to one's scene. By keeping distracting bursts or unwanted fragments of light out of the final recorded image, a photographer's painted photograph will be far more valuable. To begin with, investigators must ensure that any cellular telephones or police radios with visible power lights are concealed or turned off. Remember, light is additive and these lights may unintentionally streak through the image if they are visible to the camera. In addition, most flashes have ready lights and flash exposure confirmation lights on the back of the flash units and those too must be kept hidden from the camera's view. Simply keeping one's thumb over the flash's power light will suffice.

If at all possible, when the flash is within the field of view of the camera, photographers should hide themselves behind some physical structure in the scene, such as a tree, car, mailbox, or anything that can conceal the investigator's body when the casting of light is actually performed. Hiding the photographer's entire body from the camera's view has a couple of important benefits. First, the red or green light on the back of the flash unit is less likely to streak through or appear in the image. The impediment will help hide the unwanted light, but a finger should be kept over the small red or green bulb in order to keep it hidden from the camera's view. A second benefit created by hiding the photographer's body is that it helps prevent silhouettes from developing in the image. If the photographer stands between the flash and the camera, a silhouette may be formed in the photograph because the light reflecting off the subject will be blocked by the investigator's body. Therefore, hiding behind some impediment not only ensures that extraneous light is not accidentally recorded, but that no unintentional silhouettes are formed in the final recorded image.

Beyond the streaks of light and silhouettes that can form on an image, the physical direction in which the flash's head is pointed can cause problems within a photograph. Clearly a flash directed back toward the camera will cause a large burst of light to become visible in the image. Even flashes only slightly angled away from the camera can cause distractions within the photograph. To ensure that the camera does not record bursts of hot light in the image, the flash head needs to be completely concealed from the camera's view either by hiding behind some sort of physical structure or ensuring that the flash is pointed completely away from the camera's view. Be aware that with the flash directed away from the camera, the back of the flash will be directed toward the camera and consequently, the flash's ready lights may be visible to the camera. These ready lights are not intense enough to burn into an image by being visible for just a fraction of a second, but they should not remain in view of the camera for any extended period of time. Ultimately, it is a fine line between the advantages gained by physically stepping into the camera's view in order to get within 10 ft of a subject and not leaving distracting streaks or bursts of light in the recorded image. With a little practice and forethought, the idea of painting with light while in the camera's view is not all that difficult.

If there is no object or obstruction behind which the photographer can conceal themselves, the photographer still has a couple of options to avoid leaving a silhouette or other unwanted visual defects in the final recorded image. The photographer can attempt to eliminate a silhouette by casting additional light (additional flashes) over their previous position in the image. Basically, the photographer can eliminate the presence of silhouettes by treating them like shadowed areas in need of further illumination (Figure 7.2). Firing multiple flashes, covering one's *tracks* through the composition will help eliminate unwanted silhouettes. Photographers should work back to the camera, in this manner an investigator can cover his or her tracks and remove the silhouettes from the image. To accomplish this, an investigator should walk to the furthest part of the scene observed in the camera's viewfinder and add the first burst of flash to the scene, then work back toward the camera, adding additional flashes approximately every 10 ft and aiming the light toward the area where the investigator previously stood. By painting or layering light over the photographer's footprints, any silhouettes should be removed. In addition, photographers should add light to other areas of shadow needing supplemental illumination, in addition to covering one's own tracks, while they are working themselves back to the camera. It may appear silly, but when there is nothing to hide behind and the flash must be cast in clear view of the camera, a photographer should hold the flash away from his body in order to diminish the chance of creating a silhouette (Figure 7.3). Remember to cover any lights on the back of the flash with a finger or some other obstruction in order to prevent any unwanted streaks of light in the final image.

Another way to prevent distracting manifestations from appearing in one's photographs is to work from the perimeter of an image. Staying outside the view of the camera makes it easier to avoid these manifestations of light and silhouettes from developing, but there is a trade-off. The distance the flash's light must travel may cause hot spots or

Figure 7.2 This figure illustrates common errors possible when painting with light, including what happens when the lights on the back of the flash are visible while the photographer is walking through the composition. The photographer must also remember to conceal any lights emitted by radios and cellular telephones. Silhouettes are highly distracting and are created by casting the flash's light while the photographer stands between the flash and the camera. Other common errors are caused by poor positioning of the flash, either by projecting it too close to the subject or pointing it back toward the camera and illuminating the investigator working through the scene during the painting process.

Figure 7.3 The statue in this figure was illuminated by an electronic flash that was manually fired and completely separated from the camera. In addition, the flash was fired with the photographer standing in between the camera and sculpture. Note that there was no place where the photographer could hide while casting the light onto the subject. Potential silhouettes of the photographer were removed by firing additional electronic flashes toward the areas where the photographer previously stood as he walked back toward the camera. As a result, any potential silhouettes were removed from the image.

unnatural areas of highlights to appear in the image. Depending on the composition of the image, this effect can be minimized. For example, the camera can be placed in a vertical orientation, thus making the width of the composition less and thereby reducing the distance a flash must reach into the scene from its perimeter. This may require recording a few extra images in order to document the entire crime scene, but as long as the entire scene is photographed, it should not matter how many images are required to fulfill that task. Divergent ambient lighting and shadowing conditions, plus distinctive subjects and features of a particular location make every scene unique. Consequently, investigators must decide what combination of ambient light, supplemental light, and compositional orientation works best for any given scene. The ability to make these decisions quickly will come with experience, and experience can be gained by crime scene photographers who practice and experiment with their equipment. When there is downtime at work, investigators should travel about their jurisdiction, take pictures under different lighting conditions, and discover which techniques works best for them.

One of the disadvantages of flash photography is the unidirectional aspect of the light source. This aspect of flash photography can cancel out the benefits offered by flash photography, such as color correctness and its ability to create highlights. In addition, the firing of a single flash onto a subject can cause shadows to form on the opposite side of the object being illuminated. This deficiency can be overcome by firing multiple flashes upon a single subject from different angles. Not only will firing multiple flashes help eliminate shadows, the added illumination will assist in providing depth to the subject. The inexperienced photographer may fear overexposing an image, but nighttime photography is very forgiving. Even with eliminating the reciprocity failure from the equation, film has an approximate two-stop exposure latitude that benefits photographers (digital photographers have approximately one-stop of exposure latitude). As an example, assume that one burst of light from a photographer's flash unit properly exposes the subject, two stops of light would allow the photographer to cast four additional flashes ($1 \times 2 \times 2 = 4$) onto the subject and still obtain a useful image. Because a stop of light is twice the amount of light from the next stop of light, the photographer can double and redouble the amount of light (number of flashes) applied to a subject and still record a quality photographic image. The latitude of film and the flexibility of low-light conditions allow photographers to double and redouble a single burst of light from their flash towards a subject without having to be overly concerned with an overexposure, especially if the angle at which the light is applied to the subject is changed. However, when in doubt, remember to bracket the exposures. By changing the angle the light is applied to a composition, even digital photographers can double and re-double the amount of flash illumination added to a composition without the fear of overexposing an image to the point of damaging the final result.

Remember, a *stop* of light equals one-half or twice the amount of light, therefore doubling the amount of flash from one to two flashes, and then two flashes to four will keep the exposure within the two stops of latitude for film. Digital cameras do not have as much exposure latitude as film, but adding just two additional flashes to an exposure is still well within the latitude of a digital camera. Recording in the *raw* (uncompressed and unprocessed) format will increase the latitude and react more like film as far as latitude is concerned. *Raw* images typically record images with greater bit depth, thereby processing more information and exposure latitude than images recorded as JPG photographs. Additionally, the light should not be cast onto the subject from the same exact firing position each time. By casting light at different angles into the scene, the light is technically illuminating different surfaces, thereby giving the photographer even more flexibility in the exposure. In the end, it is difficult, although not impossible, to overexpose a nighttime image without truly blasting the composition with an extreme amount of light. The photographer cannot necessarily stand 3 ft away from a subject and fire off a full-powered flash 12 times, but only has to keep the flash's guide number, aperture size, and distance from

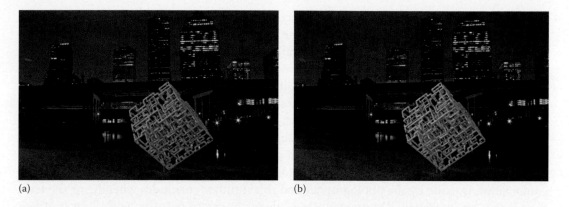

(a) (b)

Figure 7.4 (a) was recorded by metering the ambient light and adding a single, calculated flash exposure to the white PVC cube. A little ambient light fell on the subject and the composition required illumination to make the subject more visible and balanced in the image. (b) was captured with the exact same camera and flash settings (ISO 100, f/16, for 30 s). However, the flash was fired across the subject not just once, but four times from different angles. The presence of shadows between the pipes was reduced by the extra illumination, but the overall illumination of the subject was not damaged by the extra bursts of light from the flash.

subject in mind while adding varying angles of light cast onto a subject. Understanding the mathematics involved in flash exposure calculations will certainly result in much better low-light compositions.

Imparting a single flash on to an individual piece of evidence is quickly accomplished and can be achieved with the flash set to the full-automatic mode. However, painting-with-light is about firing a multitude of flashes onto a myriad of subjects from an assortment of directions (Figure 7.4). Adding such illumination is not difficult because low-light environments offer a tremendous amount of latitude and flexibility. It is best to work at shorter distances (10 ft) and to apply light specifically at the different targets or subjects. Working in this way, the danger of overexposing other areas of the composition is greatly reduced. To work in close, the photographer must frequently reduce the flash's power. Remember that the reduction of power is accomplished through stops of light. For example, a 1/16th reduction in the flash is equal to four stops of light (1–½–¼–⅛–1/16). Calculating power reductions was discussed in Chapter 6 and photographers are now going to reduce the power of their flashes in order to provide a more even lighting to their subjects and record better illuminated images. Depending on the guide number of the flash used, the photographer may also wish to reduce power in order to prevent overexposing specific subjects within the scene. In painting with light techniques, the power reductions are used so that more than one burst of light can be applied to a single subject. Once a photographer has found the correct relationship between the aperture size and the flash's power output, the flash can be reduced two to three additional stops. In order to compensate for the loss of light caused by the power reduction, the number of flashes added to each target will be equal to the power reduction value on the flash. For example:

- Minus one stop—2 bursts of light from the flash added to the subject (1/2 power)
- Minus two stops—4 bursts of light from the flash added to the subject (1/4 power)
- Minus three stops—8 bursts of light from the flash added to the subject (1/8 power)
- Minus four stops—16 bursts of light from the flash added to the subject (1/16 power)

The total amount of light produced by the increased number of reduced-power flashes will equal approximately one full-power flash. The flash must remain relatively stationary in its application of light to result in an equal totality of light output. However, when painting with light, moving the light source around and across the subject is highly recommended. Painting with light is meant to improve a subject's illumination. The flash illuminations should be swept across the subject from different angles and positions. Simply adding the appropriate number of reduced flashes from the same position will result in about the same total amount of light placed onto a subject as a full-powered flash. As a result, the total number of flashes should be increased past the number mathematically calculated based on the reduction of power. The decision on the total number of flashes added to a composition is made by the photographer and this number concludes when he or she feels the scene is appropriately illuminated. One rule of thumb in painting with light is *When in doubt, add more light*. Experience will help investigators get a feeling for when a subject has been illuminated properly. The reason a two-stop reduction in a flash's power, but cast four times, mathematically equals one full-power flash is because a flash's output is determined by the time (length of burn) the flash's light is expelled from the unit. With the total amount of time the light is cast from the flash unit being equal, the total amount of light placed into the composition is equal.

When painting a large subject or space, a safe starting point is simply to double the amount of light mathematically determined. Because the light source will be moved about the composition and cast at various angles, the risk of overexposing a composition is lessened. The doubling of supplemental light is not meant to double the amount of ambient light, only the supplemental light. Photographers should have already determined the proper ambient light calculation and are now ready to consider how to add light into the areas of shadow or at specific subjects. The next step is to determine a full-power flash calculation for the subject and it is this value that all painting with light efforts will be based upon. Increasing the amount of supplemental light by doubling or even re-doubling should not negatively affect the outcome, because the flash will be projected from different locations and onto slightly different surfaces. The chance of overexposing the image is limited because of the constant repositioning of the flash unit. However, investigators must be cognizant of the length of the exposure so that the ambient light does not cause an overexposure (Figure 7.5).

By now, it should be clear that painting with light is not just a *hope and pray* method of illuminating a crime scene. It is a planned opportunity to execute the skills of the investigator. Observe the following hypothetical photographic endeavor and flash-exposure calculations:

- Investigator is working a poorly illuminated scene that needs painting
- Photographer possesses a 160 GN flash unit
- Camera's aperture set to f/16 and the flash should be fired approximately 10 ft away from target surfaces (f/16 × 10 = 160 GN)
- Camera meters ambient light in the background to be properly exposed at ISO 100 and f/16 (matching flash calculations) for a 30 s exposure
- Photographer chooses to reduce flash power by two stops or to ¼ power
- In order to compensate for the reduction of power, the photographer will fire 16 bursts of light from the flash unit at the target (a 2-stop reduction in the flash requires 4 bursts of light from the flash unit and a twice-doubling of that value equals 16 total flashes)

Painting with Light

(a)   (b)

Figure 7.5 Both figures were recorded at ISO 100, f/16, for 30 s. A 160 guide number flash was cast at full power from 10 ft away in (a). In (b), the flash's light was reduced to 1/8th power and cast eight times from the same firing position. Observe how both images are largely equal in their appearance.

- The 16 flashes are cast across the subject from different angles in order to ensure the elimination of shadows and a complete coverage of the subject with light are made
- Figure 7.6 is the resulting image

Sixteen bursts from the flash unit onto a subject may sound like far too many, but the reduction in the power of the flash in combination with the small aperture helps protect

(a)   (b)

Figure 7.6 (a) was recorded with one full-power (GN 160) flash exposure which properly exposed the back tires of the bicycles set 10 ft from the flash unit. (b) was captured with 16 bursts of light from a 160 guide number flash. The flash was set to ¼ power, was positioned approximately 10 ft from the subject, and the same exposure settings of ISO 100, f/16, for 30 s were used. Technically, the amount of flash illumination cast onto the subject was two-stops overexposed, but because the light was cast from different angles across the subject, the overall exposure was not unduly harmed by the extra light.

the image from overexposure. In addition, changing the firing position of the flash during the painting effort helps reduce the intensity of the total amount of light impacting any one surface. Consequently, overexposing the subject is less likely. When in doubt, add more light and bracket the exposures by changing the amount of light projected onto a subject or scene. Do not alter more than one exposure variable at a time when bracketing exposures, simply take additional photographs by varying the amount of flash added to the composition or the power of the flash's settings. Digital imaging certainly offers a major advantage to photographers in that they can evaluate their recordings immediately.

Some higher-end flash attachments have the ability to create a strobe effect (Figure 7.7), which is used by photographers to stop motion and show the various positions or stages as a subject moves through a photograph. This feature has advantages to crime scene photography because it can automatically project a softer, more even total light appearance onto a painted subject or scene. Instead of firing a single flash calculated to properly illuminate a subject, the photographer can reduce the amount of light (power) produced by the flash, and then using the strobe feature, fire a pulsating stream of small, individual bursts of light across the subject. The flash unit should be moved to direct the pulsating light across the subject from different angles, much like manually adding individual

Figure 7.7 Using a flash's strobe effect allows the light impacting a subject to be feathered and spread across a subject in a more seamless manner. The amount of light output by the flash can be reduced, but the number of flashes increased so that the total amount of light is ultimately the same. It is a poorly illuminated photograph of a statue of baseball player Craig Biggio. The amount of light needed to properly illuminate the subject was reduced by a factor of 1/8th, but the flash was fired 32 times from varying positions around the subject. The image was recorded at ISO 100, f/10, for 49 s. The increase in light did not cause an overexposure because the light was added from all around the statue's perimeter. In addition, the overall illumination was more even and nearly all shadows were removed by casting the light from multiple locations.

flashes of light. By using less power but many more flashes, the light is feathered across the composition in a more continuous and even manner. This technique can be utilized without a strobe feature as long as the flash has a manual/variable power setting. The photographer simply has to repeatedly fire the flash unit manually. The strobe effect feature simply makes the process easier because the photographer does not have to manually depress the flash's firing button in smooth, consistent intervals.

The total number of flash or light bursts imparted onto a subject should be *at least* equal to the amount of reduction in power from the calculated flash exposure. For example, if a flash attachment's exposure was reduced from full power to 1/16 power in order to utilize the strobe effect and painting technique, then at least 16 flashes at that power setting should be directed onto the subject. In this example, 16 firings of the flash is a minimum number, because light fired in this manner does not quite add up to the same power as firing a single full-power flash since the light is being moved around the composition during the exposure. Therefore, when in doubt, add more light. If 16 flashes of light at 1/16 power are thought to be needed for a proper exposure, then adding 1 stop of total light by casting 32 more bursts of light should not have a detrimental effect on the photograph. Low-light photography is very forgiving. These painting with light techniques are best geared towards illuminating specific targets, large or small. Illuminating large expanses of space might be better accomplished with flashlights.

As a review, the steps to illuminate a subject hidden in the shadows or to highlight evidence within a crime scene include the following:

- Position the tripod-mounted camera and compose the image in the viewfinder
- Evaluate the scene and identify areas needing supplemental illumination
- Meter the ambient light and determine the time needed to match the chosen aperture and ISO value
- Using the aperture value and a distance of 10 ft (easiest number for calculations) from flash to subject, determine the flash's proper power or output value
- Reduce the flash's power setting and increase the planned number of flash firings the appropriate amount (equal to or greater than the number of the flash's power reduction)
- Select a spot(s) from which to illuminate the subject and plan the illumination process, deciding where to fire the flashes from and at what angle to apply the light onto or across the subject
- Start the exposure, cast the flash's light, and if possible, review the results
- Bracket exposures to ensure quality image capture

Light is additive and as long as the ambient light conditions allow for the exposure time to continue, the painting process can continue until the photographer is confident enough light has been added. Remember, low-light conditions offer the photographers more flexibility in regards to potential over exposures than does daytime compositions.

Electronic flashes are best utilized when the distances between the subject and flash are kept short. That is not to say that an overall or orientation range photograph cannot be enhanced by electronic flash. Due to the problem of light fall-off, overexposing the foreground is an all too-common occurrence. There are times when an overall photograph of an entire landscape or a crime scene needs help bringing out the small details. If the lighting is relatively even across the entire image, merely taking a timed exposure may suffice in recording a useful photograph. However, when one section of the crime scene has more light than another, the key is to create a balance between the bright and not-so-bright portions of the composition. It is all about balance. Using the flash to illuminate specific sections of a crime scene, while extremely effective, may not be the best solution for overall or wide-angle views of the scene. There is a surprisingly simple answer to this dilemma: substitute a flashlight for the electronic flash.

Painting with Light Using Flashlights

Those inexperienced with painting techniques may be surprised to learn that adding light to crime scenes with a flashlight can be much easier than with a camera's flash. One reason is that using a flashlight does not require mathematical computations. Just as valuable, the light emanating from a flashlight is visible to the photographer and can be specifically directed onto a subject a lot easier than a flash unit. Furthermore, the light can be layered or featured into the image for a much more balanced exposure much easier than with an electronic flash. Flashlights also have versatility because of the variety of lights available for use. Similar to the variable power settings of electronic flashes, flashlights come in a variety of sizes and strengths; crime scene investigators will benefit by having several different flashlights available because of the wide variety of subjects they encounter. Painting with flashlights still requires practice, but can be easier to work with, especially for those not blessed with the gift for computing mathematical equations.

The typical flashlight used by police officers and police investigators is some form of a four D-cell size flashlight, which is more than adequate for painting crime scenes. Investigators who routinely encounter especially dark environments, such as those who work in largely rural jurisdictions, may wish to invest in a rechargeable spotlight that has a bit more power. Spotlights come in a variety of strengths, ranging anywhere from 1 to 15 million candle watts in power. The 15 million candle watt power light sources are capable of painting extensive crime scenes, but they may be too strong for painting smaller or less far-reaching locations (Figure 7.8). A secondary benefit of possessing a very powerful

Figure 7.8 This poorly illuminated scene was painted with a 15 million candle watt flashlight. The exposure values were ISO 100, f/22, for 8 min. The shutter speed value was simply the amount of time it took to layer multiple layers of paint (light) across the composition.

spotlight is its ability to assist investigators in the search of outdoor crime scenes. Therefore, investigators should consider carrying a typical police officer's flashlight and a spotlight for nighttime crime scenes. Investigators will also find small penlight flashlights or similarly less-intense flashlights useful. These flashlights are used to paint smaller subjects, such as individual pieces of evidence.

Flashlights do have drawbacks. In addition to the fact that sometimes they can be a little too intense for more delicate photographic endeavors, they frequently cast a yellow stain onto film. Standard flashlight bulbs cast a colored light onto film that is consistent with high-pressure sodium street lights or incandescent bulbs. Digital cameras can have their white balance positioned to the incandescent light setting and the light recorded will have a closer value to white. Photographers using film can add an 80A or 80B filter to their lens to compensate for the color shift. The choice of filters is personal and will depend on the individual light source and even the age of the flashlight's bulb. The current trend in tactical style flashlights is to incorporate LED lights into the flashlight's housing. The major benefit of an LED flashlight is that these lights are more color correct and cast a color closer to true white. Some LED lights may have a slightly bluish tint, but are not typically as distracting as the yellow tint caused by older style flashlight bulbs. LED flashlights also come in different wavelengths, producing various colors of light. These lights can shine more specific wavelengths of light from ultraviolet to infrared. This can be quite beneficial in searching for trace evidence as well as photographing evidence such as semen and blood. The specific uses for these lights are discussed in Chapter 10.

The process of painting with flashlights begins much the same as painting with electronic flash. The ambient light falling across the location must be evaluated and metered for the proper combination of aperture, shutter speed, and ISO value. When evaluating a crime scene for lighting, a photographer must determine where light should be added. Sometimes added illumination may only be needed to highlight a small area of shadows or a single piece of evidence. At other crime scenes, the entire landscape will need additional light. After evaluating a composition for the lighting conditions and identifying the areas of shadow, the photographer must select an ISO setting. Many crime scene photographers prefer an ISO of 400 for nighttime photography. And for hand held flash photography, ISO 400 is probably best. However, ISO 100 offers advantages in color, sharpness, and the additional time necessary to complete an exposure can be valuable for painting purposes. Slower film speeds and lower ISO settings are more valuable to crime scene investigators, because they offer more time to work towards creating a better quality image. And since the camera will already be mounted upon a tripod for a time exposure, there is not any reason to rush. Is there really a difference between spending 5 s taking a photograph versus waiting 20–30 s for an image to be recorded?

Once the lighting has been evaluated for the location of shadows and areas needing supplemental light, the photographer needs to estimate how much time will be required to completely cover the necessary areas with the extra light. At this point, the photographer has chosen an ISO value and a shutter speed (time estimation). The camera can now meter the ambient light and an appropriate aperture can be selected. If a specific aperture is required for the composition, then the time value can be adjusted through reciprocity. If a balanced exposure by the camera is found, then the process can proceed. Adjustments made through reciprocal changes in the exposure may have to be made in order to reach a set of values that work for the photographer. The estimation of time and light evaluations will improve with experience and practice, but one only needs to find a ballpark figure.

If a photographer comes up a little over- or underexposed, the camera's settings can be adjusted and a second photograph can be recorded.

It is a good idea to capture an ambient-light only photograph with the determined settings before adding any artificial light by means of a flashlight or electronic flash. An issue could be raised in court about a scene's ambient lighting and although the photograph would be a true and accurate portrayal of the crime scene and the placement of evidence, a photograph enhanced with artificial lighting may not be a true and accurate portrayal of a crime scene's actual lighting conditions. In addition, recording an ambient light only photograph with a digital camera allows the photographer to evaluate the recorded image and fine tune the composition prior to adding additional light to the photograph. Never fail to take enough photographs; it is better to have a series of photographs from which to choose from rather than be forced to depend on just one image to provide all the necessary information.

The evaluation or metering of ambient light for any composition will be different in nearly every circumstance. For investigators who work in urban environments, the ambient lighting will likely be quite plentiful. For investigators working in more rural jurisdictions, the ambient light may be somewhat lacking. Furthermore, cloud cover and the brilliance and size of the moon can impact a camera's metering of light. A low-cloud ceiling in an urban environment can actually create much more ambient light because city and street lights will reflect off the clouds and onto the scene. On the other hand, a moonless, cloudless sky can create a much darker photographic environment. In those times when the ambient light is so dark that the calculation of an exposure time exceeds several minutes, one may not be able to accurately meter a crime scene for light. This challenge is not difficult to overcome. A photographer simply paints his composition with light and ends the painting process when all the surfaces have been illuminated by the light source (Figure 7.9). There is no need to leave the lens open any longer because the photograph is no longer being recorded due to the lack of ambient light. A crime scene photographer must be able to adapt to changing environments and constantly keep in mind the fact that although a set of camera/exposure settings worked before, they may not work exactly

Figure 7.9 This was recorded in the interior of a warehouse and completely lacked any ambient light. The environment was made visible by painting the interior with light. This photograph was recorded at ISO 400, f/11, for 50 s. (Photographed by Alton Holmes, Crime Scene Investigator, Houston Police Department, Houston, TX.)

the same each and every time. Flexibility and the ability to adjust to an individual scene's ambient lighting are critical if the photographer is going to create images that have value and quality.

The actual process of adding light to a scene with a flashlight or spotlight is quite straightforward and easy. One advantage of using a flashlight instead of an electronic flash is that the physical light can be seen falling onto the subject. The light can be applied deliberately and specifically to those areas where illumination is most needed. In addition, the light can be turned on and off between the areas needing light and those that already have enough ambient light. Furthermore, a flashlight's illumination can be projected onto an area from different angles simply by moving the light around the periphery of the composition during the painting process. Moving around the periphery of the composition will result in more evenly illuminated photographs and the overall image will possess a more three-dimensional appearance. In fact, the idea of moving in an arc around the perimeter of the camera's view has other benefits. The light will appear much more natural if it is not projected from a single point. Furthermore, shining a stationary flashlight onto a single subject from a single position can cause the same detrimental effect as casting an electronic flash onto a distant subject. It may cause an overexposed foreground due to the Inverse Square Law and light fall-off. By moving in an arc from behind the camera, the foreground's illumination will be spread out and dissipated, thereby giving a more balanced overall exposure.

Another advantage to using a flashlight instead of an electronic flash is that a great majority of the time, the investigator does not have to walk into the scene in order to cast light across a subject (Figure 7.10). Because of light fall-off and the Inverse Square Law, electronic flashes are best when cast over short distances and for specific pieces of evidence or areas needing illumination. As a result, investigators are frequently required to physically place themselves in view of the camera to illuminate a subject. This is not always necessary when using a flashlight to illuminate a crime scene. Flashlights have very

Figure 7.10 Flashlights and spotlights do not create as much harshness in the foreground of an image as electronic flashes. Flashlights have a *hot* center, but because they are painted across a scene like a paintbrush across a canvas, the light is feathered or layered into a photograph. As a result, the light is more evenly distributed and its appearance is more natural. This photograph was recorded in a poorly-illuminated location and was painted with a 15 million candle watt spotlight. The camera settings were ISO 100, f/8, and the exposure lasted 1 min.

definable, intense centers and these centers can be directed to the specific areas of a composition that require additional illumination. Although light fall-off does affect light cast from a flashlight, the effect is diminished because the flashlight is kept moving throughout the length of the composition, similar to painting a fence with a brush. One cannot paint an entire fence simply by pressing the brush against a single picket and painting with light follows a similar principle.

As a warning, hotspots can occur if the light is left on a single spot for too long. Therefore, it is imperative to keep the light moving across the image. Keeping the light moving not only applies to the beam's target, but also to its source. The overall image will be improved if the investigator physically walks around the composition's perimeter while waving the light back and forth across the scene. All this movement ensures that the light falling onto a subject will be layered like paint on a picket fence. The end result will be a more natural, even, and balanced photograph. Applying two coats of light to a composition is also a recommendation. Waving the light source in a vertical pattern for the first coat and a horizontal pattern for the second coat will only serve to eliminate any unwanted shadows (Figure 7.11).

Even in urban jurisdictions, crime scene photographers will find themselves needing to paint large environments with light. Just as with any other timed exposure, where harsh or bright light sources are present, the photograph's composition must be aligned in a way to eliminate these sources of distracting illumination. Sometimes these light sources cannot be completely eliminated, but their effect upon an image can be diminished by the way the camera is positioned or by placing an intervening object between the camera and the distracting light. Once the composition or orientation of the image is set and the camera is securely positioned atop the tripod, the exposure settings can be selected. A photograph

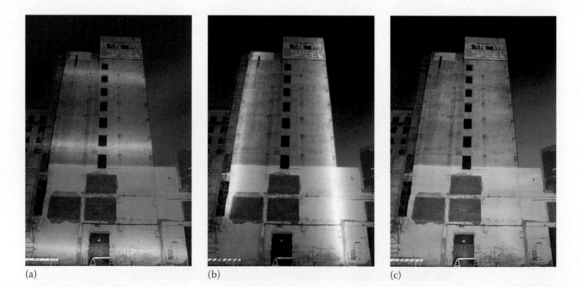

(a) (b) (c)

Figure 7.11 (a) illustrates the painting of an abandoned high-rise building with vertical brush strokes of light. (b) illustrates the painting of the building with horizontal brush strokes of light. (c) puts the two coats of light together for a single balanced photograph. (c) was recorded at ISO 100, f/8, for 30 s. The length of the exposure was determined by how long it took to paint the landscape. The ambient light was negligible and therefore the photograph was completed when the second coat of light was applied.

with an expansive area of shadows may require more time to complete. Fortunately, photographers once again benefit from and the fact that it is difficult to overexpose images at night. An investigator should have plenty of time to add supplementary light in a nighttime composition. As a reminder, a photographer should possess a cable release in which to hold the shutter open for the extended exposures (bulb setting). Without a cable release, most cameras are limited to 30 s for their longest exposure.

To reiterate the process, during the exposure, light will be added to the composition very much like one would paint with a brush. The brush is simply replaced with a flashlight. The actual length of the exposure is determined by an evaluation of the ambient light using the camera's light meter. Do not worry if the light is so sparse that the camera cannot obtain a light evaluation. In those cases, the exposure will simply be the length of time needed to completely cover the scene with supplemental light. With the camera positioned and the shutter held open, the photographer can apply the first coat of light. Light does not have to be directly applied to the foreground, because it will be filled in with the fringes of the flashlight's beam. Remember to walk around in a semi-circle outside the camera's view, changing the perspective of the flashlight's beam (Figure 7.12). Direct the most intense portion of the flashlight's beam or the center of the beam, onto the furthest point from the camera needing enlightenment. The light should be moved across the composition horizontally from one end to the other in a smooth, consistent pace. A second application of light can be applied by shining the light up and down (vertically) across the entire composition. In this way the light is applied with two coats, one with vertical strokes and one with horizontal strokes. This ensures that all the dark recesses are illuminated. The camera's shutter can then be closed and the photograph completed. The pace of the light's movement across the scene should not be so fast that gaps of darkness are left. Neither should it be so slow that areas of overexposure are created. The key is to keep a smooth, even pace throughout the painting process. Photographers should stay focused and be careful not to leave any unwanted areas of shadow.

The length of the exposure should more or less correspond to the chosen aperture and the metering of the available or ambient light. If the exposure takes more time to complete than originally anticipated, the photographer should not worry. However, if the time needed to paint is less than expected or estimated, the photographer should choose to leave the shutter open in order to complete the photograph. For example, imagine a scene's ambient light dictates a 20 s exposure, but the only target needing supplemental light is a car and

Figure 7.12 Moving around the scene in a semi-circle and out of view of the camera's lens, the photographer can better add light to the composition in order to help eliminate shadows and cast a more even lighting across the entire composition.

this only requires approximately 5 s of painting. The exposure should be allowed to continue for the full 20 s so that the proper amount of ambient light can be recorded. As with any other important crime scene photograph, bracketing the exposures is recommended.

Do not change multiple variables at one time when bracketing photographs. For example, in subsequent exposures leave the aperture settings the same, but double the length of time for the composition. Doubling the length of the exposure is equal to the addition of one stop of light. Another alternative is to maintain the original exposure's length, but open and/or close the aperture by one or two stops. Changing more than one variable at a time may cause too extreme a change in the overall composition's lighting. Crime scene photographers need to practice with their own equipment (flashlights and spotlights) to master painting with light techniques. They must know the relative strength of their light sources and have a basic idea of how much time will be needed relative to preferred aperture sizes. Practice makes perfect, or in the very least, helps significantly.

Some crime scenes will have layers to them, meaning that there is a depth of different distances between the camera and photographic subjects. In those cases, photographers must be sure that they do not unintentionally overexpose the foreground while illuminating the background. Although it is *difficult* to overexpose a nighttime photograph, it is *possible*. When there are different levels of distance between the camera and the area contained within the viewfinder, the photographer should seek to illuminate the farthest part of the scene with the brightest portion of the light and allow the less intense portion of the flashlight's beam to filter across the foreground and middle-ground of the composition to help illuminate those portions of the photograph (Figure 7.13).

If there are areas in the foreground that are concealed or hidden by natural features of the scene, the photographer can purposely apply light to those areas by maneuvering the light and the beam in a way that will illuminate all the recesses of a particular object or structure. Every composition will be different in its need for light, and crime scene

Figure 7.13 Even difficulties caused by a variety of depths in a particular composition can be overcome by concentrating the strongest portion of the light's beam onto the farthest points in the composed image, while allowing the beam's periphery to filter across and sufficiently illuminate the foreground. This photo was recorded at ISO 400, f/16, for 25 s. The flashlight's bright center was concentrated on the tractors in the background, which allowed the light's periphery to filter across the evidence markers in the foreground, thus avoiding an overexposure of the foreground.

investigators must get used to looking at a scene not only for the placement of evidence, but also to recognize where light falls and where it does not. There will be times when only a small portion of the scene, maybe just a street sign, needs a little additional illumination. At other times, a large amount of illumination may need to be added, for example, when a body is discovered on a completely dark golf course. Experience and practice in painting crime scenes with flashlights and spotlights will improve an investigator's ability to accurately document a crime scene. As an example of a flashlight illuminated crime scene, follow the ensuing evaluation, planning, and execution of a painting with light endeavor:

- A poorly illuminated crime scene and overall scene photograph needs supplemental light
- A tripod-mounted camera evaluates light at ISO 800, f/4, for 30 s
- Photographer desires ISO 100 setting at f/8 and time is not an issue
- Reducing ISO 800–100 is a three-stop reduction of light and an f/4–f/8 is another two-stop reduction in light.
- Increasing length of exposure five stops changes a 30 s exposure to approximately 16 min (30–60–120–240 or 16 min). This is basic exposure reciprocity.
- Since light will be painted across the crime scene, the photograph is completed when the photographer decides there has been enough light added to the composition. The evaluation of ambient light is made inconsequential because the composition was painted.
- Using a 15 million candle watt spotlight, the crime scene was painted for 4:30 and the image's recording was stopped (Figure 7.14).

Painting with Light Using Alternate Light Sources

A number of crime scene searching and fingerprint processing techniques utilize alternate light sources. Alternate light sources are necessary because they assist investigators and photographers by making visible what is not seen by the human eye in natural light. At least for now, camera flash units do not come with the ability to adjust the light's nanometer wavelengths. Consequently, illuminating the subject with an alternate light source is

Figure 7.14 Dark composition was painted with a 15 million candle watt spotlight and an LED flashlight. The exposure settings were ISO 100, f/16, for 4.30 min.

Figure 7.15 As seen in this photograph, bones and skeletal material can fluoresce when illuminated with ultraviolet light. The surrounding ground cover absorbs the UV light, thereby creating a natural contrast. The UV light was painted across the scene throughout the exposure. The camera settings were ISO 400, f/8, for 30 s.

required. These sources frequently permit the intensity of the light to be adjusted. Adjusting the power of an ALS is advantageous to painting with light. Lower power settings allow the light to be added to the composition through painting with light techniques. The quality of the image is improved when the light source is moved over and around the subject during the exposure (Figure 7.15). Intense light sources have hot centers and less-brilliant edges so important details may be lost through both the over- and underexposing of portions in the image. Painting the subject with light will help even out the overall lighting and appearance of the composition. Cameras are capable of metering the excitation of electrons by ultraviolet and near-ultraviolet light sources. Therefore, the metering and photographing of such evidence is largely the same as illuminating a subject with a flashlight, similar to the way discussed in Chapter 4. There is likely to be some exposure differences, but the camera's light meter will allow the photographer to be close to a properly exposed image. Moving the alternate light source across and around an image will remove hotspots and make the edges of the image sharper and more balanced. Remember to bracket the exposures in order to ensure the best possible image is available.

Crime scene investigators likely have their personal preferences as to the lights they prefer to use when searching crime scenes. Small and portable are two common features of alternate light sources used in the field. These two features often cause investigators to mistakenly believe they cannot photograph evidence still in place at a crime scene. Even these small, hand held flashlights that are engineered to pass specific wavelengths (*blue* lights), are commonly found in an investigator's arsenal of tools for searching crime scenes. These lights can and should be used to photograph areas under investigation (Figure 7.16).

Whether painting with an ALS or white flashlight, the same mantra applies to both small subjects and large subjects: Light is additive! Pull out the tripod, stabilize the camera, and prepare for recording a quality image. Naturally, the ambient light will be quite low

Figure 7.16 Alternate light sources, even small hand-held or battery operated lights, can be utilized to highlight trace evidence found at crime scenes. This photo is a view of an entire room, including a small stain pattern found on the chair's seat cushion. The ambient light was diminished by turning off the room lights and allowing a time exposure to record. During the exposure, an ultraviolet fluorescent black light was directed across the stain in order to enhance its appearance in the image. This image was recorded at ISO 100, f/11, for 30 s and the black light was painted across the subject throughout the entire exposure.

in order to be using an ALS. A small amount of ambient light should not hurt the overall appearance of the image. In fact, it may actually improve the composition. Most frequently, ambient light will need to be reduced for these exposures, either by turning off the location's lighting, closing doors, or lowering window blinds.

The next step is to determine if the camera is capable of achieving an ISO value, aperture, and shutter speed combination with the ALS and ambient light present. Be sure to cast the ALS into the composition during the metering process, so its light is included in the evaluation process. This should get a photographer to a starting point. Then it is merely a matter of bracketing a set of exposures to obtain a positive result. Similar to painting an outdoor crime scene, sweep across the entire composition with the ALS so that a smooth and even result is achieved. If painting the scene is finished prior to the end of the exposure, the photographer should allow the photograph to continue recording, as long as he or she believes an adequate amount of alternate light was applied. Light can be specifically applied to just a small area of a composition or the entire composition. It is up to the photographer and the requirements of the particular crime scene. In addition, it is always a good idea to mark evidence with a numbered placard or pointer arrow so that viewers are aware of the image's subject. Photographing with alternate light is covered more thoroughly in Chapter 10.

Conclusion

Film and digital photographs recorded at night or in low-light conditions are very forgiving to the photographer. Reciprocity failure sounds like a negative term, but is quite beneficial to film photographers. Between the low-light environments and reciprocity failure, overexposing images can be quite difficult. Even though digital imaging does not benefit from reciprocity failure, it too possesses a great deal of exposure latitude during the nighttime. In regards to applying light to a crime scene, one should remember that *light is additive*. Furthermore, investigators must think in terms of the end result and not the individual steps required to achieve a final image. Painting with light typically requires longer exposures in order to allow enough time for the painting process. ISO settings of 100 and smaller apertures are beneficial toward that end. All painting with light endeavors begin by metering the ambient light and then applying the chosen light source smoothly, evenly, and repeatedly across the composition.

The choice of light source is varied. Electronic flashes are best over shorter distances and when color-accurate exposures are demanded. Flashlights work well over more expansive scenes or distant subjects. Flashlights should be cast over the subject in at least two layers in order to ensure a full coverage of the scene. Powerful flashlights and spotlights are better over even longer or greater distances, and finally, small flashlights and ALS units can be used to paint smaller subjects and individual pieces of evidence.

Low-light photographs offer a tremendous amount of flexibility to the photographer. It is rewarding to capture photographs that appear to have been taken in the daytime, but were actually captured in dark, dismal-light environments. Those who are unfamiliar with painting with light techniques will not understand why the photographer is waving his flashlight around like a wild-man, but the end results will speak for themselves. As for court, remember that photographs enhanced (even greatly enhanced) with painting techniques are designed to make the environment visible and show the placement of evidence. However, before any painting with light photograph is recorded, a series of bracketed exposures recording only ambient light conditions should also be captured. Ambient light photographs will be a true and accurate representation of the scene's lighting condition, while the painted photographs accurately document the scene's physical elements. Take plenty of photographs and record all aspects of the crime scene. The value of completeness is never outweighed by the cost of film (or digital media).

End of Chapter Questions

1. Which light source is used in *Painting with Light* photographic compositions?
   a. Electronic Flash
   b. Flash Lights
   c. Alternate Light Sources
   d. All of the above

2. When is painting with light required:
   a. In fill-flash situations
   b. In low-light situations where a single flash is insufficient
   c. On small, single subjects
   d. In all low-light situations

3. What is a guiding principle in painting with light compositions?
   a. Guide Number formula
   b. Inverse Square Law
   c. Light is Additive
   d. None of the above

4. What is a major drawback of painting with electronic flash?
    a. Inverse Square Law
    b. Guide Number value
    c. Inability to predict outcome
    d. Limited ISO range

5. If one subject is 5 ft away from the camera and a second subject is 25 ft away, how much less light strikes the second subject if the first subject is properly exposed with a flash?
    a. 5 times less light
    b. 10 times less light
    c. 25 times less light
    d. None of the above

6. If a photographer's electronic flash has a guide number of 160 at ISO 100 and chooses an aperture of f/22, how close does the flash have to be to the subject?
    a. 3 ft
    b. 5 ft
    c. 7 ft
    d. 9 ft

7. When a photographer initially evaluates a nighttime crime scene, what should the investigator be looking for?
    a. Looking for areas of highlights and areas of shadows
    b. Seeking place or places to position one's self to add light to the scene
    c. Starting exposure values for the ambient light
    d. All of the above

8. When choosing an ISO value, which value will give the photographer more time to paint with light (with all else being equal)?
    a. ISO 100
    b. ISO 400
    c. ISO 1600
    d. None of the above

9. When choosing an aperture value, which value will give the photographer more time to paint with light (with all else being equal)?
    a. f/4.0
    b. f/8.0
    c. f/16.0
    d. None of the above

10. When adding electronic flash to a composition, what *general* rule will help photographers record better painted with light photographs?
    a. Use 1/8th power on one's flash unit
    b. Use full-power flash whenever possible
    c. Work in close, within 10 ft or so when adding light
    d. When in doubt, add less light to composition and let ambient light filter in

11. When adding electronic flash to a composition, how should one add light into the composition?
   a. Work from the background back to the camera
   b. Work from the foreground to the background
   c. Ensure light is added obliquely to the composition
   d. Ensure light is added perpendicularly to the composition

12. A photographer has manually calculated a full-power flash exposure. If the variable-power setting is reduced to 1/16th power, how many flashes from the same distance and position would give approximately the same exposure?
   a. 8 bursts of flash
   b. 16 bursts of flash
   c. 32 bursts of flash
   d. Does not matter, since TTL will adjust for a proper exposure

13. A photographer has manually calculated a full-power flash exposure. If the variable-power setting is reduced to ¼th power and the photographer continuously moves the flash around the periphery of the subject, how many flashes would likely result in the best exposure?
   a. Two bursts of flash
   b. Four bursts of flash
   c. Eight bursts of flash
   d. Does not matter, since TTL will adjust for a proper exposure

14. What is one benefit of using flashlights instead of electronic flashes?
   a. Light from a flashlight is easily metered by the camera
   b. Light from a flashlight is easily balanced for white
   c. Light from a flashlight is easily used with the camera set to *Program* mode
   d. Light from a flashlight is easily applied from outside the camera's view

15. What statement is most true?
   a. The final recorded image is the result of the most intense light source visible
   b. The final recorded image is the result of all light added to the composition
   c. Ambient light is more important than supplemental light
   d. Any exposure errors can be corrected in post-capture editing

Photography Assignments

Required Tools: External flash unit, flashlights (both large and small), tripod, cable release, and extra batteries.

Photography Subjects: Safe outdoor (nighttime) environment. Small and large photographic subjects, such as bullets and cars

   I. Electronic Flash Painting:
      A. In a nighttime environment, manually calculate and record a full-power flash exposure of a single subject (target of flash)

B. Reduce power of flash and record same exposure with appropriate number of flashes
   1. Reduce power to ¼th and fire flash 4 times from static position
      a. Increase number of firings to 8 and 16 times, but fire from multiple positions around composition
   2. Reduce power to ⅛th and fire flash 8 times
      a. Increase number of firings to 16 and 32 times, but fire from multiple positions around composition
   3. Reduce power to 1/16th and fire flash 16 times
      a. Increase number of firings to 32 and 64 times, but fire from multiple positions around composition
C. Photograph a parked vehicle in as dark of an environment as possible and paint it with electronic flash
D. Paint an open field or parking lot type of environment with light, walking through the composition adding light to the composition
E. Paint the front yard to a home, adding light from behind points of cover, filling in all the shadows of the composition

II. Flashlight Painting:
A. Photograph a parked vehicle in as dark of an environment as possible, painting it with a flashlight
B. Paint an open field or parking lot with a flashlight
C. Paint a more cluttered outdoor composition, such as the front yard to a home, filling in all the shadows of the composition

III. Painting specific (smaller subjects) with light
A. In an overall, nighttime composition, highlight a specific item with a light source to make it *pop* or stand out in the photograph

IV. If available, record an alternate light photograph using painting with light techniques
A. A possible subject could simply be a drawing on paper using fluorescent markers (high-lighters)

Additional Readings

Fisher, B. (2005). *Techniques of Crime Scene Investigation*. 7th ed. Boca Raton, FL: CRC Press.

Kramer, R. (April 25, 2009). Painting-with-light. Retrieved April 25, 2009, from http://www.officer.com/print/law-enfocement-technology/painting-with-light/1$25177.

McManigal, P. (April 25, 2009). How to utilize night photography at a crime scene. Retrieved April 25, 2009, from http://www.helium.com/items/212310-how-to-utilize-night-photography-at-a-crime-scene.

Bloodstain Photography

8

The photographic documentation of bloodstain evidence can be problematic for both the photographer and the examiner trying to interpret patterns from a scene he or she may not have visited. The documentation and analysis of bloodstains and bloodstain patterns is critical for any reconstruction efforts. Unfortunately, the photographic documentation process is typically hindered by incomplete scene photography, an assortment of lighting problems, and photographers who underestimate the importance of perspective in the documentation of bloodstains. By understanding some of the pitfalls in accurately portraying a bloodstained crime scene and proper documentation procedures, investigators can better present bloodstain evidence in court and assist investigators who may be called upon to interpret stains found at a crime scene.

Complete Scene Documentation

Lack of thoroughness may be the number one complaint bloodstain examiners have when reviewing a case (Figure 8.1). Failure by the scene investigator to completely and accurately photograph a bloodletting event can hinder any criminal investigation. Each and every stain pattern must be individually photographed in a manner by which the stain can be oriented within the crime scene and angles of impact or other important properties of the stain and/or pattern can be determined. Remember, one of the most important rules in crime scene photography is that the value of completeness always overrides the cost of film. Since most law enforcement agencies have converted to digital imaging, there is absolutely no excuse for incomplete scene documentation. Also as a reminder, crime scene investigators must avoid tunnel vision. Bloodstain and bloodstain patterns only have meaning and value if they can be placed into context with the scene. Therefore, photographers must strive to completely document the whole scene and not just the most interesting bloodstain patterns.

Much like documenting bloodstains found at a crime scene, investigators need to examine the clothing of those persons involved in a violent crime or other blood-shedding event. Stains found on these individuals should be photographed as found (Figure 8.2). In other words, the stained clothing should be photographed as it was worn by the individual and again after the clothing was recovered as evidence. Specific techniques of photographing bloodstain evidence will be discussed throughout this chapter, but for now, reminding investigators to document the clothing as it is found on a person is the goal.

Every stain that is worth documenting at a close-up level also needs to be oriented to and within the entire crime scene. Therefore, photographers should not focus in on individual stains and individual patterns without first putting them into context or showing their relationship with other pieces of evidence. Photographers must consider the *big picture* and take a *holistic* approach to documenting a bloodstained scene. Individual stains and stain patterns photographed for detail must also be photographed to show their relationship to other stains present in the scene and to the overall scene itself.

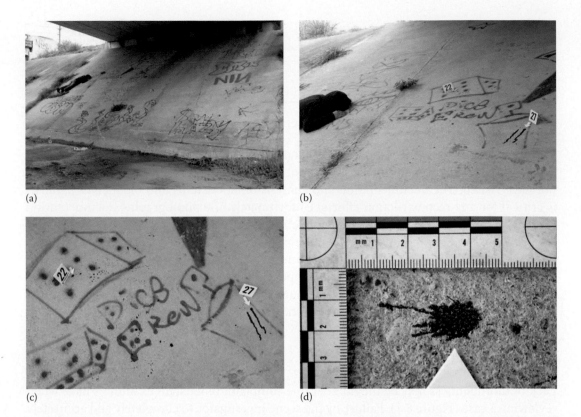

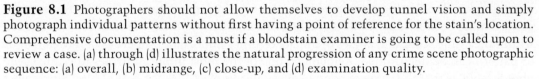

Figure 8.1 Photographers should not allow themselves to develop tunnel vision and simply photograph individual patterns without first having a point of reference for the stain's location. Comprehensive documentation is a must if a bloodstain examiner is going to be called upon to review a case. (a) through (d) illustrates the natural progression of any crime scene photographic sequence: (a) overall, (b) midrange, (c) close-up, and (d) examination quality.

There is not much difference between the documentation of a bloodletting event and the documentation of any other criminal act. Unfortunately, it is quite common and quite easy to get tunnel vision while documenting bloodstained crime scenes. Investigators simply must be aware of the possibility of looking at a scene without taking into account that a full and proper documentation of the bloodstained evidence can help refute or corroborate witness statements. True and accurate bloodstain photography requires an honest commitment to both recording a sufficient number of images in order to ensure that the scene is fully documented and a commitment to creating images of excellent quality so that an examiner who was not present at the crime scene can perform a viable reconstruction.

Photography Tools and Aids Used in Bloodstain Photography

Investigators should be equipped with the proper tools in order to properly document a bloodletting event. Crime scene supply companies sell a large assortment of documentation tools, including

- Assorted scales
- Adhesive identifiers/labels (letters and numbers)

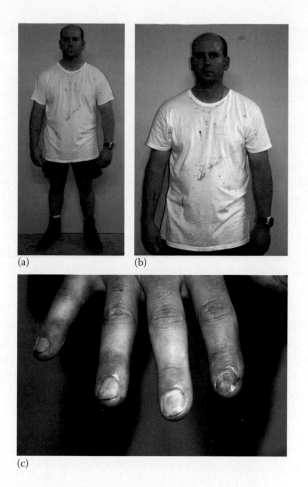

(a)   (b)

(c)

Figure 8.2 It is important to document bloodstains and injuries found on people in the same manner as stain patterns found on surfaces within the crime scene. Once again, orientation of the stains for the examiner is essential. Therefore, (a) overall, (b) midrange, and (c) close-up photographs of an individual are essential to the establishment of a stain's location on the individual. The value of showing jurors where and upon whom important stains were found can be critical. (Photo courtesy of Christine Ramirez, Texas Engineering Extension Service, College Station, TX.)

- Large print rulers (*spatter sticks*)
- Carpenter's rulers
- Lasers and carpenter levels
- Assorted pointers and arrows

Obviously, scales are important in many aspects of crime scene photography and their usefulness does not have to be reiterated here. Scales come in a number of different styles and colors. Having a selection of different scales will allow the investigator the versatility to match the scale to the surface, for color contrast and attachment (i.e., magnetic or adhesive scales). Some one-time use scales (adhesive scale tape) allow investigators to individualize the scale to the scene. These adhesive tape scales have the added advantage of allowing investigators to handwrite stain identifiers or specific case information onto the adhesive tape. This can be quite advantageous. In general, adhesive identifiers and scale tape that are marketed by forensic supply companies are extremely beneficial to investigators and are quite professional looking in the recorded images. However, these identifiers can also be found in many craft stores for half the price. An assortment of permanent-ink markers (Sharpie® markers) can also be used to create identification tags right on the scene. Permanent markers allow the investigator to personalize the identifiers to the particular scene and are used extensively in the *quadrant mapping* of bloodstains, which is discussed later in this chapter. Therefore, investigators should have several permanent-ink markers and different colors of markers when working bloodstained crime scenes.

As for the large print rulers, these are of great assistance in showing the overall dimensions of a stain pattern or group of stain patterns (Figure 8.3). These rulers are typically 4 ft in length, with large numbers imprinted on the bright-colored scale. Such rulers are sometimes marketed by forensic supply companies as *spatter sticks* and are easily visible in crime scene photographs. Although these scales are worth the extra cost, adequate substitutes can be found at home improvement stores. Metal yard sticks and carpenter rulers are a fraction of the cost and although not as bright and visible as spatter sticks, they are still effective. The metal yard sticks are also useful when building a quadrant map at a scene. Therefore, having one of those to go along with a set of spatter sticks is helpful.

A couple of different types of levels are also handy in documenting bloodletting events. Laser levels that project a visible red line onto a surface can be used for photography and to project a plumb line onto a vertical surface. The plumb line is a perfectly vertical line that can be projected onto a surface next to a bloodstain of interest. When accurately photographed, viewers of the image are able to calculate precise angles of impact from the recorded image. Just as a reminder, for the accurate determination of bloodstain angles

Figure 8.3 *Spatter sticks* are an easily legible set of scales that can be used to show the overall dimensions of a bloodstain pattern or group of patterns. Carpenter rulers are an inexpensive alternative, but not nearly as visible.

of impact, the camera's body must be parallel (lens is perpendicular) to the target surface. The laser level can also be used to assist in building quadrant maps. Carpenter levels or bubble levels are used in conjunction with permanent markers to build quadrant maps and drawing plumb lines onto bloodstained surfaces. The laser levels simply prevent having to draw through bloodstained surfaces, but both tools are valuable to the crime scene investigator.

An assortment of evidence pointers, arrows, and other identifying markers enhance images by showing position, measure, and proportion of bloodstain evidence. Once again, forensic supply companies sell a broad range of evidence markers and pointers. And once again, investigators can make their own markers and pointers. Small pointers or arrows are a common type of evidence marker. An investigator can create his or her own in a number of ways. A durable and inexpensive solution is to take empty liquid detergent bottles and cut small arrows out of the plastic (Figure 8.4). The hard plastic is easily cleaned in bleach after a particularly bloody event and easily replaceable if the recovery of such arrows is undesirable. Smaller forms of plastic arrows can be made from plastic coffee stirrers. Coffee stirrers found at fast-food restaurants or purchased from the supermarket are thin plastic wands with a rectangular paddle-shaped end for stirring coffee. The rectangular-shaped end can be trimmed to a point with scissors (Figure 8.5).

Arrows can also be created from laminated paper or address labels (Figure 8.6). Arrows or pointers can be cut from colored construction paper, placed over a contrasting colored paper, and then laminated. The lamination allows the markers to be cleaned and reused. In addition, they can be written upon with a dry erase marker in order to add more information to the image. Laminated arrows and evidence pointers are lightweight and can be affixed to walls or other vertical surfaces by using a tack, thumbnail, plumber's putty, or other tacky material. Any number of shaped arrows can be printed onto address labels using a computer and word processing software. Address labels have the added benefit of already having an adhesive back side. The types of pointer printed onto the address labels are nearly infinite, but can include a scale, sequential numbering, or even

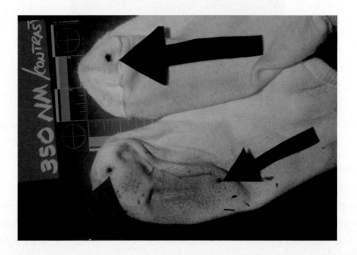

Figure 8.4 An option for pointing out bloodstain evidence or any other type of evidence is to create arrows from different colored liquid detergent bottles. The arrows can help identify small, but important, pieces of evidence within a composition. Not only are these pointer arrows free, they are easily cleaned with bleach and can be reused.

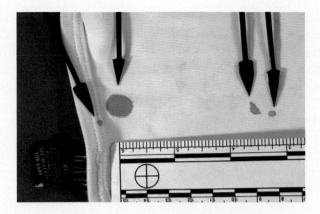

Figure 8.5 This shows fast-food restaurant coffee stirrers used as evidence pointers. By cutting the one end to a point, excellent evidence pointers were created. These small pointers are excellent for directing a viewer's attention to exceptionally small bloodstains.

Figure 8.6 Adhesive address labels or adhesive arrows used to point out important items on documents can be purchased at an office supply store. These inexpensive pointers can be used on a number of surfaces, but are especially useful on vertical surfaces where gravity prevents the use of other types of evidence markers.

the crime scene photographer's name. Blank space can also be left on the label to allow the investigator to write in incident-specific case information. Personally constructed arrows such as these are also inexpensive enough to be disposable. A little creative thinking by the photographer in creating evidence markers and pointers can have immeasurable value to an image's viewer.

Regardless of the tools and implements used by the crime scene photographer, jury members and those attempting to interpret a crime scene's bloodstain evidence must be able to link bloodstain photographs together. Incorporating orientation and evidence markers within each image will help clarify an often difficult subject. In addition, viewers of bloodstain photographs must be given as much information as possible regarding the position, direction, and orientation of bloodstains within the scene. A scene's thorough photographic documentation does not just happen.

Laser Levels and Bloodstain Documentation

Laser levels can be useful in the documentation of bloodstain evidence, in addition to helping build quadrant maps. Unlike the lasers utilized in shooting reconstructions, laser levels used in bloodstain pattern documentation produce a straight line instead of a dot or point of light. Laser levels come in a variety of styles and with different options. Some simply project a single straight line and cost less than $10. Other lasers are capable of projecting crosshairs onto a surface and even others that have self-leveling capabilities that are able to project accurate plumb lines on their own. Although these more sophisticated levels may cost 10 times as much, they certainly can make the documentation of bloodstain patterns much easier.

Lasers can be used in a couple of different ways by bloodstain examiners. Because scenes of bloodshed are contaminated with biohazardous material, investigators may not wish to drag their pens, levels, and rulers through blood-soaked surfaces (Figure 8.7). The laser's line of light is a substitute for having to physically draw a plumb line through the bloodstained surface and having to later dispose of or repeatedly disinfect the investigator's equipment. Typically, the plumb lines provided by lasers are projected onto vertical

(a) (b)

Figure 8.7 A laser level that draws a visible laser line across a bloodstained subject can be a useful tool to prevent investigators from having to bloody or soil their equipment by dragging them through a bloodstained surface. (a) Illustrates the use of such a laser level. The laser level can be photographed next to a stain (b) in order to calculate angles of impact from the photograph.

surfaces and photographed for reconstruction purposes. The laser's line creates a reference point from which subsequent angles of impact can be determined. The projected line can be placed alongside or through a particular impact stain pattern and photographed. The resulting photograph can then be examined and the angle of impact determined by measuring the intersecting line of the laser and the long axis of the bloodstain under examination.

Photographing a laser line is easily accomplished and does not require special filters or other equipment. Crime scene investigators should mount their laser levels to a tripod and project a plumb line onto the surface being examined. A second tripod is likely going to be necessary because the best photographs are recorded using a timed exposure (ambient light) versus a flash exposure. A flash might wash out the intensity of the laser's light. Therefore, recording the image by adding time to the exposure will produce better results. Photographing laser lines in sunlit-outdoor environments may be problematic for a similar reason. Creating a shadow over the area being photographed may help in brighter conditions. Using a tripod-mounted camera offers another benefit by making it easier for the photographer to ensure that a perpendicular alignment is obtained between the camera and subject. A perpendicular alignment is crucial for any subsequent reconstruction efforts. With the laser and camera properly aligned, an ambient light photograph can be recorded. The laser's light is typically not intense enough to cause exposure problems. Simply meter the ambient light and capture the photograph as with any other crime scene image. In brighter environments, try and eliminate the light source or attempt to create a shadow over the subject in order to help the laser's light to become more visible in the photograph.

Quadrant mapping will be discussed next and these laser levels, especially those able to project a set of crosshairs, can help create quadrant mapping grids on a surface. The laser's lines can then be traced with a permanent marker and photographed. Self-leveling lasers are very effective when creating quadrant mapping grids and will save the investigator a great deal of time in the construction of their frameworks. Although laser levels are not a necessity in documenting bloodstain evidence, their use can make documentation easier.

Quadrant Mapping of Bloodstain Evidence

The complete and accurate documentation of bloodstained surfaces is an important aspect of any crime scene where blood was shed and the analysis of such bloodletting events would prove useful in the determination of transpired events. The photographic and written documentation of such bloodstained evidence is not the easiest task for a crime scene investigator, especially those new to the endeavor. Quadrant mapping is a bloodstain documentation technique that can be used by both experienced and inexperienced investigators alike. Although the technique can be time consuming, the results are well worth the effort.

Many investigators are familiar with the documentation technique that focuses on documenting bloodstains and bloodstain patterns developed by criminalist Toby Wolson of the Miami-Dade Police Department in Miami, FL. The technique is known as *roadmapping*. Due to the nature of the steps employed in this technique, the roadmapping of bloodstain evidence is the last form of documentation conducted by investigators prior to leaving a crime scene. When done properly, roadmapping allows the viewer to plainly see selected bloodstains and bloodstain patterns by means of the identifiers, which are considered the *signs* of the roadmap. The identifiers should be included in photographs along with their patterns to help prevent the viewer from getting *lost* in the blood evidence due to a lack of perspective or a lack of orientation. Roadmapping is a widely used method of bloodstain documentation. Nonetheless, it is easy for the viewer of the photographic documentation to get lost in the blood evidence. If the photographer does not retain discipline in maintaining proper perspective and orientation during image capture, the potential for confusion among different bloodstains is quite possible. As an alternative to roadmapping, another documentation technique is offered and has been coined *quadrant mapping*.

Roadmapping is an excellent system of identifying and documenting bloodstain patterns found in crime scenes. However, it relies upon the investigator's ability to recognize and identify the different bloodstain patterns found at the crime scene. For those less-experienced crime scene technicians, this can be an overwhelming task. Quadrant mapping can be accomplished by any investigator, regardless of their experience or inexperience in bloodstain pattern analysis. Quadrant mapping provides accurate and the to-scale documentation of bloodstained surfaces. Typically, this technique is best applied to flat surfaces, such as walls, floors, and ceilings. Odd-shaped and movable surfaces such as clothing would still benefit from documentation through roadmapping.

Necessity is the mother of invention. Quadrant mapping grew out of a need to reproduce crime scenes in the courtroom and allow for the independent analysis of bloodstain patterns. Before the days of digital projectors and Microsoft PowerPoint, crime scene photographs were routinely adhered to bulletin boards in some sort of logical order in order for the jury to visualize the entire crime scene at once. A photographer's *orientation* or *overall* photographic views of a general crime scene were routinely placed side by side upon the bulletin board in order to give the appearance of a panoramic view of the crime scene. Quadrant mapping simply goes a step or two further, by creating a specific framework or matrix of rows and columns that are independently photographed and can be reassembled for further analysis or courtroom presentation. Quadrant mapping is a thorough, comprehensive method for documenting bloodstain evidence and allows for the visual reproducibility of the scene. This reproducibility is critical when an analyst is unable to examine the scene in person and must rely on the work product of others for the basis of examination and opinion.

Necessary Tools

- *Sharpie®* or other permanent markers
  - Stick-on labels and/or tags
- Scales
- Leveling device(s)
  - 1 to 4 ft bubble level
  - Laser level
  - 3 ft straight edge
- Camera equipment
  - Single-lens reflex (SLR) camera
  - Off-the-camera flash
  - Flash-synchronization cord
  - Tripod
    - Full-size tripod
    - Minitripod or beanbag camera support

Although the accurate documentation of bloodstain evidence is an important aspect of crime scene investigation, one should not develop tunnel vision and forget about the value of properly documenting the overall crime scene prior to any quadrant mapping efforts. Without orientating the stained surfaces to the overall crime scene, investigators may be left wanting for information. Therefore, investigators should not forget to completely document the crime scene via videotape, measurements, sketching, and photographs prior to tackling specific bloodstained surfaces. In addition, quadrant mapping is an extremely invasive technique and therefore should be the last stage of documentation in the scene's investigation. Quadrant mapping is typically utilized on those crime scenes involving more complicated and numerous bloodstain patterns. It would be unnecessary to use quadrant mapping on a simple blood trail or for just a couple of transfer stain patterns. However, it is extremely valuable when multiple events are occurring at one's crime scene, and the need to separate and analyze the sequence of events is a challenge. Quadrant mapping is best utilized on flat surfaces, such as vertical walls, horizontal ceilings, and floors. When encountering such surfaces, quadrant mapping allows the reproducibility of the surface under analysis for peer review, independent analysis, and courtroom presentation.

Quadrant mapping is similar to building a grid over skeletal remains. Instead of building a grid out of string over the scattered remains of an individual, an investigator will be drawing a grid onto a bloodstained surface with permanent markers. Grid squares are typically going to be smaller than those of a skeletal recovery, with each square typically being 1 ft^2. However, the size of the grid squares can vary depending on the size of the area upon which the grid will be created. Thus, very large walls or floors could have grids measuring 2 ft × 2 ft or 3 ft × 3 ft. The squares will be aligned along the wall or floor surfaces in rows and columns. Each row and column in the grid is identified with a letter and number. For example, each row would be labeled with a number and each column with a letter. As a result, each individual grid square created by the intersecting columns and rows can be cross-referenced by their location's unique identification by combining the column's letter and row's number, that is, A4, B6, and C2. It truly does not matter if the letter or number identification is applied to either the row or column. However, by identifying rows with numbers, investigators will have a quick reference as to the approximate height of a stain or stain pattern based simply on the square in which it was found. When the grid square of each row is 1 ft in height, the number assigned to each square will represent the approximate height up from the floor. Figure 8.8 is a graphic representation of what such a grid should look like. This constructed grid would cover the bloodstained surface being examined, and each individual square will eventually be photographed and notations about the stains and stain patterns recorded. Once the photographs are printed, the quadrant map can then be pieced back together like a puzzle and examined or analyzed away from the actual crime scene. Figure 8.9 is a crime scene in which quadrant mapping was utilized. One will also notice that several of the bloodstain patterns have been circled and identified. Once the grid is placed onto the surface and each square is photographed and documented, individual patterns that were found extending across several grids or squares can be identified and rephotographed as a whole. These larger stain patterns can be identified and rephotographed individually, apart from the individual quadrants. Having different colored permanent markers will be a benefit. Drawing the grid itself in one color and using a different colored ink pen for the grid or square identifiers and the stain or pattern identifiers will help eliminate confusion when viewing the photographed images.

Building the quadrant map or grid is a painstaking process and will require precision and patience. A few tools will make the process easier, but one must still have an eye for

	A	B	C	D	E	F	G	H
6	A6	B6	C6	D6	E6	F6	G6	H6
5	A5	B5	C5	D5	51	F5	G5	H5
4	A4	B4	C4	D4	E4	F4	G4	H4
3	A3	B3	C3	D3	E3	F3	G3	H3
2	A2	B2	C2	D2	E2	F2	G2	H2
1	A1	B1	C1	D1	E1	F1	G1	H1

Figure 8.8 Each side of each square or block measures 1 ft in length. Each column and row has a unique identifier, which in turn provides a unique identifier for each individual square.

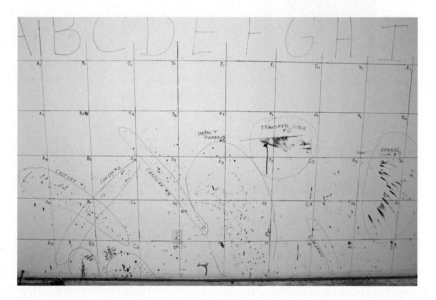

Figure 8.9 Bloodstained wall where quadrant mapping was used to help document the stains and stain patterns found at the crime scene.

detail. Bubble and/or laser levels will offer great assistance to the constructor of a quadrant map. At the very least, one must have a bubble level—straight edge—similar to the one seen in Figure 8.10. Such levels are easily found in any home improvement store and come in a variety of sizes. Obviously, a 3 or 4 ft long level would have an advantage, but even a 1 ft level can be used. Using a shorter level simply requires resetting the level on to the bloodstained surface more often. However, a shorter level is easier to manipulate by an individual investigator working alone at a crime scene. A laser level is also a helpful piece of equipment that can help insure the accuracy of the drawn grid. A laser level projects a horizontal or vertical laser line onto the surface being mapped. The laser lines can be used to verify one's work with a standard level as seen in Figure 8.10 or be used in combination with a plain

Figure 8.10 The key to creating a successful quadrant grid is to maintain 90° angled corners. A laser level can act as a check for one's work with a standard level.

Figure 8.11 A laser level can also be used along with a plain straight edge in order to build the quadrant grid.

straight edge to draw the grid as seen in Figure 8.11. As an imperative reminder, the key to a successful quadrant map is drawing straight and level lines (borders) and having perfect 90° or right-angle (square) corners.

Once the vertical and horizontal lines are drawn in place, which is the most difficult and time-consuming task of this process, the investigator should next label the columns and rows. Utilizing the column and row identifiers, each square should then be marked to clearly identify each square from any other square in the grid. Figure 8.12 is an example of an individual quadrant or square in the overall grid. Once the entire quadrant grid is drawn and labeled, it should be photographed. Photographing bloodstained surfaces is demonstrated in Figures 8.12 through 8.18. Investigators should ensure that their quadrant lines are bold and their quadrant identifications are legible in order to eliminate any possible confusion or disorientation when reconstructing the quadrant map (Figure 8.13). Photography and note taking is a constant endeavor during the quadrant mapping process. Investigators should photograph each step of the process, including:

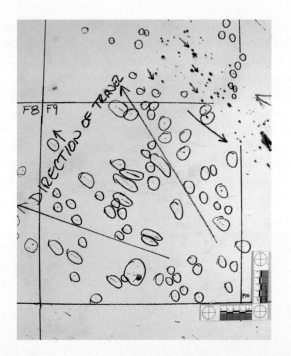

Figure 8.12 Each drawn box should be identified by their column and row identification. Having each drawn square identified in the recorded photographs will help ensure that each stain pattern is properly positioned during any future reconstruction and/or analysis.

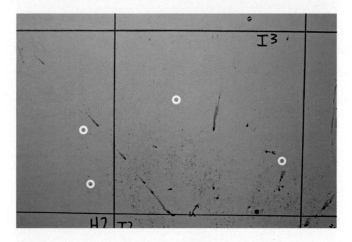

Figure 8.13 Investigators should ensure bold lines and legible identifiers in order to create useful photographic images. One alternative to circling stains of interest with a permanent marker is to use notebook paper hole reinforcements.

- In situ condition of the crime scene
- Initial laying out of the quadrant map
  - Overall framework
  - Individual squares
- Individual stains and stain patterns of interest

The key to any successful documentation of a crime scene is to capture a complete and full photographic record of the scene and all its evidence, including a full range of orientation, evidence-establishing, and close-up photographs. In addition to recording images at each level of documentation, an investigator must also record a full set of images at each stage or step of intrusion into the scene. For example, a full set of photographs should be recorded of the bloodstained surface as it was found, another set after the quadrant grid is drawn into place, and additional sets of photographs for any and all stain and stain pattern identifiers added into the quadrant map. One should not be shy in the number of photographs recorded. It is far better to have too many photographs than not enough. Figures 8.14 through 8.17 show a series of photographs that locate and position Quadrant #E12 within

Figure 8.14 Included in a photographer's orientation photographs should be the bloodstained surface prior to any quadrant mapping efforts.

Figure 8.15 An orientation photograph of the same wall seen in Figure 8.14; however, at this stage in the process, the quadrant map has been drawn onto the bloodstained wall.

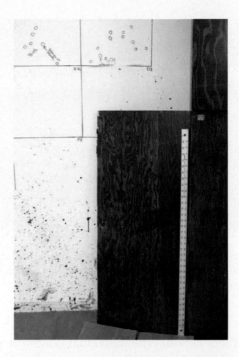

Figure 8.16 An evidence-establishing photograph of the small area of bloodstained evidence found near Quadrant E12.

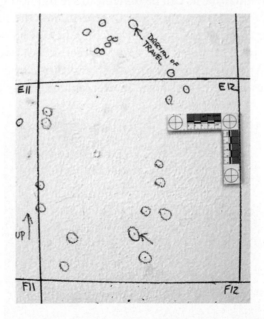

Figure 8.17 A close-up photograph of Quadrant E12, including an ABFO #2 scale for reference.

the crime scene. Each individual quadrant should be photographed, regardless of whether or not it has bloodstains in the particular quadrant.

Stains and, in particular, stain patterns will not always reside within a single quadrant. As a result, after photographing each individual quadrant, regardless of whether or not the area contained any bloodstains, the investigator should also identify stain patterns of

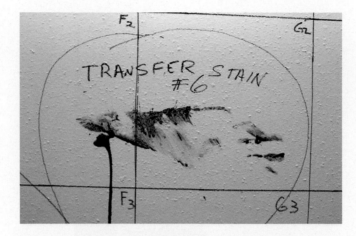

Figure 8.18 Stain patterns are likely to extend beyond the boundaries of an individual quadrant. As a result, additional photographs should be recorded of the stain patterns as a whole. The location of this transfer stain is easily identified by the F2–G2–F3–G3 quadrant identifiers found in the image.

interest and photograph them as well. The individual quadrant identifiers placed in each square while building the quadrant map will serve as an easy reference as to the exact location of each stain pattern. Figure 8.18 is an example of a transfer pattern that spans across several quadrants. Individual stains can be difficult to see in photographs, especially when the stains are extremely small. Investigators can return after the first round of photography and bring attention to individual stains by circling them with permanent markers and indicating direction of travel for particular stains of interest. An example of such notations is seen in Figure 8.19. As a substitute for drawing a multitude of circles across the blood-stained surface, an investigator can use hole reinforcement circles to highlight individual

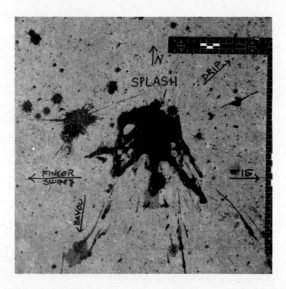

Figure 8.19 The more information that can be included into a particular image is invaluable when it comes time to conducting any reconstruction efforts based on the photographic evidence.

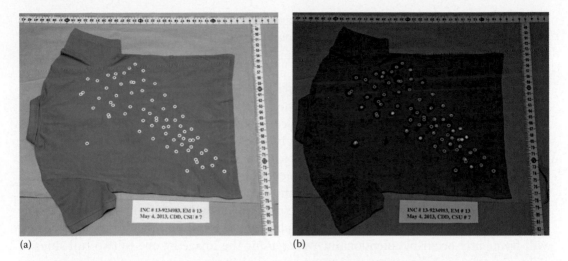

(a)   (b)

Figure 8.20 (a) Using notebook paper hole reinforcements can be used to bring attention to particular stains of interest, especially those that are so small as to not be visible in over-all photographs. (b) A photograph of the same shirt, but was recorded after the application of Bluestar, a blood reagent. (b) Recorded at ISO 400, f/8, for 8 min.

stains of interest. Hole reinforcements will highlight stains exceptionally well when photo-graphing with electronic flash, as seen in Figure 8.20.

In regard to photographing bloodstained walls and floors, a few photographic tips may be helpful in recording accurate and useful images. Photographing bloodstained crime scenes is not a point-and-shoot enterprise and investigators should not rush the process. A few techniques can aid investigators in recording quality bloodstain photographs, including

- Maintaining perpendicular alignment between the camera lens and subject
- Using a tripod or beanbag support
- Choosing ambient light over flash illumination when appropriate
- Diffusing, bouncing, or otherwise widening any flash added to the scene
- Intentionally overexposing primarily white-colored surfaces
- Recording a sufficient number of photographs

First, maintaining a perpendicular alignment between the camera lens and the bloodstained surface is extremely important. Without perpendicular alignment, angle calculations and/ or other determinations made from the resulting photographs will be inaccurate, thereby affecting the analysis and resulting opinion. The American Board of Forensic Odontology (ABFO) #2 type scales have leveling circles printed on them, and these can be used to con-firm that the camera is properly aligned. Moreover, using a tripod to record the photo-graphic images will be quite beneficial in helping to ensure proper alignment. Handholding a camera in the photographic process introduces too much potential for an alignment error. An added benefit to using the tripod is the ability to utilize ambient lighting in recording the images. If one is fortunate enough to have an evenly illuminated surface, not necessarily a well-illuminated surface, but a surface that has balanced lighting, the better choice may be to utilize ambient light to photograph the composition instead of flash photography.

However, that is not to say that flash photography cannot be employed to create outstanding photographs. Quite the contrary, flash frequently assists in creating powerful photographic images, but one will find that diffused or bounced flash, which eliminates the harshness of the supplemental light, will more often than not help in the photographic task. At the very least, when using electronic flash, pull the flash away from the subject and place it at an angle to the surface, if at all possible. By casting a wide path of light across the subject, the potential problems caused by unwanted reflections and hot spots will be diminished. Be aware that not only surfaces can be reflective, but blood can also be reflective, and therefore, angling the light toward the surface will help eliminate the unwanted reflections.

Regardless of whether one is using ambient light or flash illumination, white surfaces will cause exposure metering problems for the camera. Light meters will want to turn the white surfaces 18% gray and thereby underexpose the image. As a result, depending on the amount of white surface visible in the composition, one will find that a proper exposure will frequently occur by intentionally *overexposing* the image by one to two full stops of light. Simply adjust the exposure compensation dial on the camera or adjust the exposure in the *Manual* exposure mode. When lacking experience in recording difficult-to-meter photographs, bracketing is one's best solution for ensuring that a properly exposed image is recorded. One should never ask, "Should a photograph be recorded?" but rather, "Were enough photographs taken?" in order to guarantee that a true and accurate documentation of the crime scene was completed.

In conclusion, quadrant mapping is an effective method for documenting bloodstains and bloodstain patterns at a crime scene. It provides a methodical way in which to specifically orient the stains and stain patterns to the crime scene and efficiently reproduce the documentation efforts for analysis purposes and to a courtroom audience. Although the presentation of the results may be efficient, the act of constructing and recording the quadrant map itself is quite demanding. The investigator must be patient, deliberate, and dedicated to producing a level and square map, as well as photographing the results completely and professionally. With a little practice, all investigators, regardless of bloodstain pattern analysis experience, can reproduce blood evidence found at a crime scene in a logical manner that can tell a story, be peer reviewed, and functionally analyzed as part of any reconstruction effort.

Photographing Bloodstains on Difficult Surfaces

A number of challenges can present themselves when documenting bloodstained crime scenes. One frequently encountered problem in photography occurs when trying to capture bloodstains, especially small stains, on difficult surfaces such as white or reflective walls and floors. Cameras do not see color; they can only evaluate the intensity of light on a scale from black to white. Exposure determinations are based on an 18% gray value. As a result, underexposed images occur frequently because the camera is *seeing* a mass of white in its viewfinder and desires to lower the needed exposure in order to turn the white surface an 18% gray color. Underexposures could cause difficulties upon reviewing scene photographs in a bloodstain pattern case. An examiner may find it difficult to correctly judge a pattern's size, shape, and distribution, because of the poor exposure evaluation.

There are several solutions to this quandary presented by underexposed images. The most accurate way to evaluate ambient light falling onto a subject is with an incident light meter. However, a much less-expensive method is to use an 18% gray card and the camera's reflective light meter. Once the camera is set into position for the image's capture, the photographer can slide a gray card into the camera's view just a hair above the subject's surface and set the ISO value, aperture, and shutter speed for a proper exposure. The camera's metering value should be balanced in the middle or at *zero*, without any sort of compensation. The gray card should fill the viewfinder so that the evaluation of the light's intensity is accurate. If one's subject is too expansive for the gray card to fill the viewfinder, then the camera's *spot metering* or *partial metering* mode can be selected so that extraneous surfaces will not affect the evaluation process.

Photographers can use a gray card to meter exposures before every shot, which could become quite time consuming, or they can simply bracket their exposures by taking a second or even a third photograph of the same subject. Increasing the exposure by one full stop with each subsequent exposure should provide the photographer with an accurate image somewhere within the series of bracketed exposures. Bracketing exposures is a very effective way to ensure an image's accurate capture. In regards to the specific task of photographing red bloodstains on a largely white background, there should be no need to intentionally underexpose the images. In fact, if the composition of the substrate and bloodstain is primarily white, the photographer will more likely need to intentionally overexpose the image by as much as two full stops of light. The number of photographs taken at a crime scene should never be limited because quality documentation of the bloodletting event is of paramount importance. Even taking three photographs of a single subject at different settings is better than only taking two and hoping the composition was accurately captured. Believing that images are *good enough* because photo editing software such as Adobe Photoshop® can fix any errors is completely unsatisfactory. Once again, crime scene photography is about image capture, not about image processing and enhancement. Just remember that reflective and/or light-colored substrates tend to cause underexposures.

Increasing the exposure of light-colored subjects can be accomplished in a number of ways. Most cameras, even older more manually operated cameras, have exposure compensation buttons or dials that can increase or decrease a subject's exposure for one or more photographs. The exposure compensation buttons typically have a "+/−" icon or logo on the button. This ability to adjust a camera's exposure assists photographers in compensating for backlit and highly contrasting subjects. More advanced cameras may also have flash exposure compensating abilities. Flash exposure compensation can increase or decrease the amount of light placed onto a subject from the electronic flash. Another way to increase exposure and capture difficult bloodstains is to use both flash and available light to record a quality image. A flash can be used to enhance and highlight a photograph's subject. The first step is to evaluate the ambient light and select a proper aperture and shutter speed combination in order to balance the light meter. The photographer can then add a flash to provide a little extra light to the subject and record a more accurate photograph. The electronic flash should be obliquely angled onto the subject and not projected with the flash aligned with the lens. Bloodstains are quite reflective and the end result of a direct flash may cause the bloodstain to disappear from view. Finally, when in doubt, take multiple photographs at different settings (bracketing) and apply different amounts of light onto the subject. Blood is often found on predominantly white surfaces, such as clothing, walls, and tile floors. Therefore, be aware of the camera's tendency to underexpose photographs in these types of environments and be ready to make the appropriate compensations.

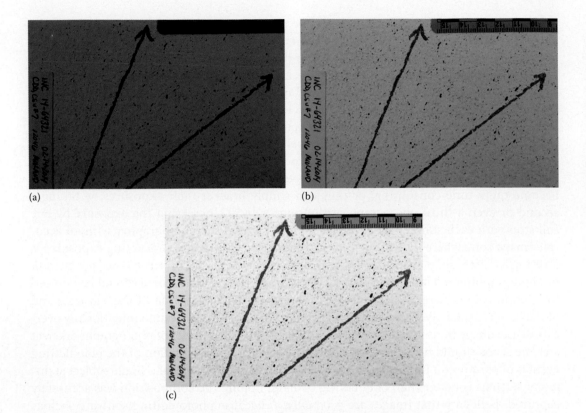

Figure 8.21 (a) was captured in *Program* mode and without any compensation for the exposure evaluation of the camera. The photograph resulted in an underexposure because the camera acted as it was designed, namely, to determine an 18% gray value. (b) added one stop of light and now the white substrate is a little closer to a true white color. (c) added an additional stop of light for a total of two stops added to what the camera deemed as a proper exposure. The more *white* included in a composition, the more compensation will be required. Since the exact amount of compensation will be different with each photographic endeavor, one should take multiple photographs in order to ensure a quality outcome.

Every camera has its own personality and idiosyncrasies. Cameras all work off the same basic principles, but meter light in slightly different ways (Figure 8.21). Investigators may find they only need to bump exposures half a stop or maybe as many as two stops for a similar composition recorded with two different cameras. Photographers need to become familiar with their personal equipment so that they know when something does not feel or sound right during the photographic process. One should also be aware that what is viewed on the camera's preview screen and what the final output looks like may be vastly different. A digital camera's preview screen can be adjusted for brightness, just like an image on a computer screen. However, it is the final printed image that most concerns investigators. Investigators must become familiar with their equipment and know the differences that may be common between what is viewed on the preview screen and how the end product appears on paper. The jury must have quality images to scrutinize, because if they believe the images have no value, that belief will transfer to the rest of the investigator's work and testimony. Impress the jury with the scene's photography and an investigator's remaining testimony will go much more smoothly. In conclusion, just because a photographer has the latest and greatest camera with all the bells and whistles, that does not translate to mean one does not have to bracket exposures, compensate for poor lighting, or take control of the photographic process.

Electronic Flash and Bloodstain Evidence

Using electronic flash to enhance the scene's lighting and assist in the recording of bloodstains is very common and effective. Flash is beneficial in accurately capturing the colors of stains or stain patterns, illuminating dark areas, and helping balance a scene's overall lighting. However, flash photography also comes with some disadvantages. For example, the metering of flash can be somewhat problematic, especially with reflective surfaces (Figure 8.22). Flash can cast unwanted shadows, as well as obliterate the actual subject (bloodstain evidence) from an image. Although electronic flash can be quite advantageous when working in low-light situations, flash exposures can create difficulty for investigators, especially if they are relied upon too much. A pop-up flash or an external flash mounted directly to the camera's hot shoe can easily create unacceptable images, by creating unwanted hot spots and/or reflections. Because the angle of incidence equals the angle of reflection in regard to light travel, electronic flashes are notorious for causing hot spots or streaks of light on reflective surfaces. This concept is very similar to *red eye* sometimes present in portrait photographs when the person's pupils glow bright red. To eliminate the red

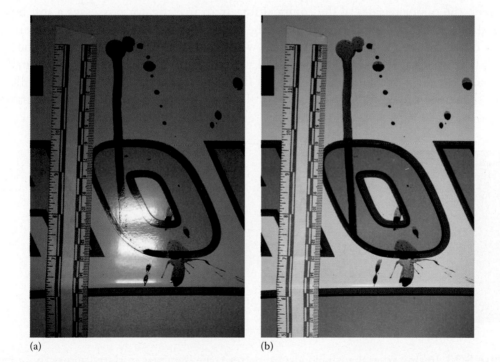

(a)   (b)

Figure 8.22 Reflective surfaces, such as high-gloss automobile paint, can create difficulties for bloodstain examiners. When photographing reflective surfaces, remember that the angle of incidence equals the angle of reflection and the flash needs to be pulled away from the camera and placed at an oblique angle to the subject. (a) Shows how a distracting reflection of light has been caused by a pop-up flash. By angling the flash onto the subject in (b), the bloodstains are much clearer and the distracting burst of light is now gone.

eye, the photographer must change the angle of the flash so that the light does not reflect off the back of a person's eyeballs. Bloodstain photography is no different. When photographing stains found on reflective surfaces, the flash should be held at an oblique angle from the subject. In this way, the harsh light originating from the flash will reflect away from the subject's surface at the same angle at which it was directed onto it. As a result, the only reflection recorded by the camera will be the subject and not the light applied to that subject.

When using oblique lighting to illuminate a more extensive (broader) bloodstain pattern, a photographer should remember the inverse square law. This rule dictates that the further light travels away from its source, the loss of intensity is a squared amount. As this applies to bloodstain photography, when the flash is too close to the subject, the end result may be that one side of the image is well illuminated, but the opposite side of the image gradually loses its brightness and causes a poor overall image. There are a few options to prevent a poorly exposed image (Figure 8.23). One option is to raise the angle of the flash so that the light impacts both sides of the composition from approximately the same distance, but this could cause hot spots or streaks of light to reappear. Another option is to pull the flash head farther away from the subject, but still keep it at an oblique angle. Pulling the flash farther away decreases the ratio of distance between the opposite edges of the composition from the flash. The decrease in ratio might be enough to offset the potential of the edge closest to the light source from being overexposed and/or the opposite edge being underexposed. Another option is to position the flash along the long side or axis of the stain pattern. Once again this will help decrease the difference in distance between the opposite sides of the composition. If an investigator possesses a soft box or flash diffuser, this too may help eliminate the severe contrast from one edge of the image to the other. Bouncing the light off a nearby white wall or ceiling can also diffuse the light being used to create the image. The overall photograph will possess better illumination and balance across the entire photograph if the light impacting the stain pattern illuminates the entire subject from a relatively similar distance. As one can see, a photographer

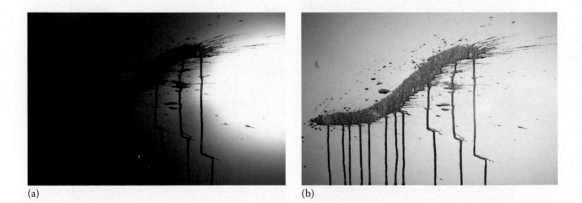

(a)   (b)

Figure 8.23 In this arterial gush bloodstain pattern, the light was initiated across the subject from right to left. In (a), the flash was placed close to the right-hand edge of the image, causing light falloff on the left side of the photograph, epitomizing the inverse square law. In (b), the image was created by raising the flash away from the stain, decreasing the proportional distance between the right and left sides of the stain pattern and creating a better light-balanced image. (Photo courtesy of Christine Ramirez, Texas Engineering Extension Service, College Station, TX.)

has many choices in how difficult images are recorded, but the end result is the same: a true and accurate representation of the crime scene and evidence.

Glass and Blood

For some reason, burglars and other criminals always find a way to cut themselves on glass or some other surface, thereby leaving behind valuable blood evidence for investigators. Many times, this blood is found on glass at the point of entry, which frequently causes issues because one side of the glass is extremely bright (exterior side) and one side is dark (interior side). Documentation of this bloodstain evidence is as important as its actual recovery. A common problem arises when the photographer attempts to photograph the transparent glass from the inside and the daylight from the outside affects the camera's metering. The subject is the bloodstain on the window, not the exterior part of the crime scene. When focusing and metering from the interior of a building toward the exterior, the camera will want to evaluate or meter the outdoor lighting and this will, of course, cause an underexposure of the bloodstain in daytime exposures. The photographer could simply meter the interior lighting to capture the image, but this would most likely result in the severe overexposure of the image where the exterior portions of the scene are visible. The secret lies in finding a balance between the exterior and interior lighting (Figure 8.24). The photographer should seek to balance the outdoor light intensity with the indoor light intensity and this is best done with flash. Electronic flash and through-the-lens (TTL) flash metering systems make this process easy, even in a *Program* or automatic mode. Simply evaluate the background light and determine an appropriate exposure for the brightest part of the composition (the outdoors). Be sure the shutter speed is not faster than the camera's flash-synchronization speed or the final image may not come out. Next, add in the flash to highlight the bloodstains. The flash should be offset from the camera to ensure that there are no distracting bursts of light visible on the glass.

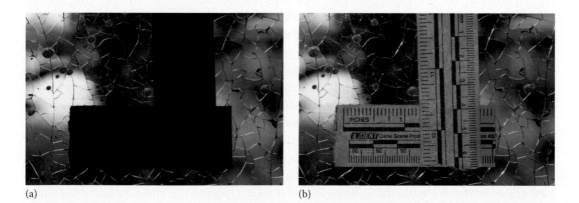

(a)   (b)

Figure 8.24 (a) A *Program* mode photograph of a strongly backlit subject. The evidence and scale present in the foreground are hidden from view. (b) Illustrates the importance of balancing the foreground and background illumination by adding flash to the composition. Also observe that a large aperture was chosen in order to blur the background so that it would not distract the viewer from the bloodstain evidence. (Photo courtesy of Mike Perez, Crime Scene Investigator, Houston Police Department, Houston, TX.)

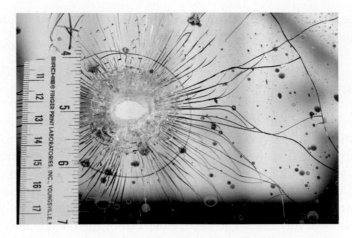

Figure 8.25 When photographing bloodstains on glass or windows, consider opening up the aperture to decrease the depth of field. This will blur the background, causing the bloodstain in the foreground to attract the attention of the viewer. In addition, consider using a contrasting background. This, too, will help create an image that will be visible, have sharper contrast, and be more identifiable. Figure 8.25 was recorded at ISO 100, f/3.5, for 1/25 of a second.

In addition to dealing with backlit situations, the photographer must also decide whether the background needs to be recognizable. The choice of aperture can be used to limit the depth of field and blur the background, or the depth of field can be extended to increase the focus throughout the composition. When photographing bloodstains, fingerprints, or bullet strikes that impact a glass surface, the background can be distracting to the viewer. In contrast to much of crime scene photography, in these instances, it may be more desirable to cause the image's depth of field to be as shallow as possible. By decreasing the depth of field, the background present behind the glass will be blurred to the point of being unrecognizable (Figure 8.25). In addition, the viewer's eyes will naturally be brought to the point of focus, which should be the subject of the photograph.

Decreasing the composition's depth of field is most easily done by selecting a large aperture. Different lenses have their own ranges of available apertures from which to choose. Typically, the popular zoom lenses will not have as large an aperture setting as a fixed focal length lens. Although space in an investigator's camera bag may be at a premium, a relatively inexpensive 50 mm lens with an f/1.8 or f/1.4 aperture should easily soften the focus of any background. The apertures of the less-expensive zoom lenses typically are in the neighborhood of f/3.5–f/4.0. Either of these options is preferable to point-and-shoot cameras that may only have a maximum aperture setting of f/8.0. In addition to increasing the size of the aperture, the photographer should consider getting closer to the subject by either increasing the zoom or physically moving nearer the bloodstain. An additional benefit to getting closer is that it is advantageous to fill the camera's viewfinder with the subject in order to maximize the information contained in the image.

Contrast should also be a consideration. Contrast may naturally occur by blurring the background through decreasing the depth of field, but it may also be artificially created by placing a contrasting piece of colored or white paper behind the subject. This can often be accomplished by taping a white piece of paper or index card to the opposite side of the glass, thereby creating a more visible contrast and recognizable subject.

Magically Disappearing Bloodstain

Bloodstains that are clearly visible at a crime scene have a tendency to disappear when photographed incorrectly. The surfaces upon which bloodstains impact, the lighting conditions, and the blood itself can cause difficulties in capturing a viable image. When utilizing flash photography techniques, the light emanating from the flash may bounce off the stain or pattern and create a glossy appearance, and that glossy manifestation can actually prevent the stain from being seen in the recorded image (Figure 8.26). This often occurs when the flash is mounted to the camera's hot shoe or when the built-in flash is utilized. It will be necessary to use a flash-synchronization cord and separate the flash from the camera in order to ensure that the bloodstain is recorded accurately. The angle of the flash does not have to be positioned at a severe angle, but it should not be perpendicular to the subject. As with other reflective surfaces, by angling the light onto the subject, the harsh reflection bounces away from the lens, but the subject's color reflects into the camera and is recorded. Once again, the use of a camera's pop-up flash is extremely limited in these types of situations.

An alternative to capturing bloodstain evidence with flash photography is to simply use the ambient lighting present at the crime scene. Ambient lighting has several advantages; the main benefit is that the light is typically more uniform and consistent. Ambient light is usually softer than the harshness of flash illumination. In addition, the light and subject are visible within the viewfinder and, if the photographer can see an image, he or she can photograph it. Even in low-light situations or at nighttime crime scenes, ambient lighting can be used to document bloodstain patterns found in difficult-to-photograph locations.

A crime scene photographer who decides to utilize available light merely has to set up the photographic project so that shadows are limited and then decide if any compensation is necessary for the various types of light sources encountered at the crime scene (Figure 8.27). Tripods are necessary for most low-light photography, and tripods can frequently leave shadows across a subject, just as a photographer's head or body can if the photographer stands between a light source and the subject. The position of a tripod can be adjusted so that neither the camera nor the tripod itself casts a shadow upon the subject. Tripods come in all types of styles and features. One particularly useful tripod has an

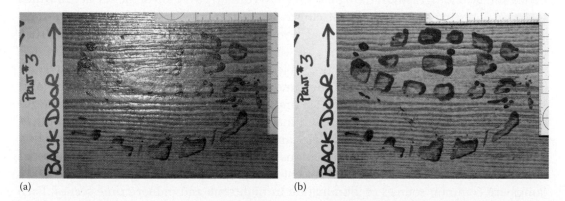

(a)   (b)

Figure 8.26 The bloody footprint in (a) was photographed with the flash mounted directly to the camera. The print is nearly obliterated because of the bright reflection created by the flash. The footprint found in (b) is the exact same transfer pattern not seen in (a), but the flash was held at an oblique angle and the stain is much more discernible.

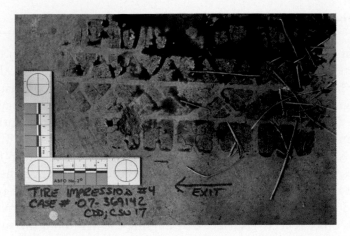

Figure 8.27 Although oblique-flash lighting often produces acceptable results, investigators forget about the option of using available light. These tire impressions made in blood were recorded in a well-illuminated nighttime environment and ambient light was used to illuminate the stain pattern. When recording in ambient light, photographers should be aware of shadows that may creep into the composition.

extension, boom, or sidearm that can hold the camera away from the support legs. The Bogen–Manfrotto articulating arm camera support, known as the Magic Arm, is also an extremely useful tool, especially for placing the camera in hard-to-reach areas. Not only can it help limit the shadows in an image, but it can also help keep the subject in perpendicular orientation with the camera. Even without an extension arm, a photographer must try to keep the legs of the tripod and their shadows out of any photographic images.

As for the photographers themselves, they must also keep themselves from leaving shadows in the crime scene photographs. They may even find it necessary to contort themselves to avoid leaving a shadow, but an easier solution might be to use the camera's self-timer, a cable release, or, if available, an infrared remote shutter release. The remote release allows the investigator to step away from the composition when the actual recording is made. Eliminating shadows is critical because of the precise nature of the bloodstain evidence and its photography. If the light source rests directly over top of the surface in which the stain is resting and the camera itself leaves a distracting shadow, then the solution is to remove the light source from the image. Some light sources cannot be turned off, such as streetlights or the sun. If that is the case, the investigator can use something to create a shadow large enough to cover the entire subject, such as a flattened cardboard box. These situations can occur either during the daytime or at night, and although adding additional shadows in low light seems detrimental at first, ambient light should still filter in from the sides of the image to provide enough illumination for a quality photograph. The length of the exposure will be longer, but the image can still be captured.

Nighttime and indoor lighting conditions may also cause difficulties for photographers and investigators. Fluorescent, incandescent, mercury vapor, and high-pressure sodium lamps are common sources of illumination in nighttime and indoor crime scenes. Each source may require some color compensation or adjusting of the digital camera's white balance, which was discussed in Chapter 5. Digital cameras can be set to the specific type of light source illuminating the subject and the final result will be a more color-accurate photograph. Most digital SLR cameras can even be fine-tuned for specific Kelvin scale temperatures. Therefore, digital photographers should have no excuse for recording an oddly colored image. When photographing with black-and-white (B&W) film or in monochrome, the color of the light source makes no difference to the final image because the camera is capturing only the intensity of light, not the color. However, in color photography and with nighttime or ambient lighting, it is important to use a filter to capture a color-accurate, white-balanced photograph.

Close Focusing

To create photographs with imagination and impact, photographers need to get up close and personal with their subjects. Although no one enjoys crawling around in blood, it is necessary in order to capture quality images for investigators and for courtroom testimony. Getting close to bloodstain evidence is necessary, regardless of its location, including bloodstains found along a home's baseboards or otherwise close to the ground (Figure 8.28). So that the photographic documentation of bloodstains is beneficial to the person who must attempt to analyze the recorded stains, photographers should strive to record images with the following recommendations in mind:

- Fill the viewfinder.
- Use a scale and have it on the same focal plane as the stain.
- Maintain a stable camera.
- Lens should be oriented perpendicular to the stain.
- Choose lighting carefully:
  - Direction of light cast
  - Choice between flash or ambient light
- Bracket exposures as necessary.

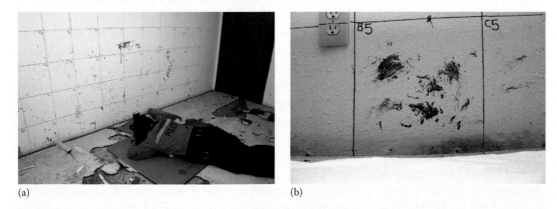

(a)   (b)

Figure 8.28 By placing flattened cardboard boxes, butcher paper, or similar materials as a barrier to the bloody surface, an investigator can get up close and personal with the subject. (a) Illustrates how a barrier can be placed between the photographer and biohazardous blood. Regardless of a stain pattern's location, perpendicularly oriented photographs are required to properly document many stain patterns, such as the stain pattern found in (b) that was located along the bottom edge of a crime scene's wall.

Photographs should strive to fill the viewfinder with the subject. The scale must be on the same focal plane as the evidence so that both items are in sharp focus and that any measurements and/or angle calculations made from the photographs are accurate. Far too often, photographers fail to change their perspective or position and record images from a standing or squatting position instead of ensuring a perpendicular orientation to the stain. This can be particularly problematic for bloodstain pattern analysts. When investigating particularly bloody crime scenes and after fully documenting the overall scene, investigators can lay down butcher paper or flattened cardboard boxes to create a protective barrier between themselves and the blood. Protective barriers are extremely useful and will shield photographers from biohazards as they get closer to the blood-stained evidence.

Perspective is a major issue in the determination of directionality of bloodstains from photographs. Evidence can be compromised by how and where the photographer captured the image. Investigators must be willing to maintain a proper lens to subject alignment, even if this requires the photographer to reach down and photograph those stains lining the baseboards of a home's wall or accurately capture those stains found on a ceiling. Tripods are helpful in these situations, in that they can ensure that a sharp image is captured by eliminating camera movement. However, some tripods may not allow the photographer to capture evidence that is in awkward or tight environments. An inexpensive *minitripod* or a large tube sock filled with rice can be used to secure a camera at ground level for those photographs that must be taken along baseboards or similar compositions. For stains higher on a wall or on the ceiling, a full-size tripod can guarantee both a perpendicular relationship and a stable platform from which to photograph the stain pattern. For stains in hard-to-reach areas where a tripod's legs will not fit, an articulating arm camera support, such as the Bogen–Manfrotto Magic Arm, will work wonders. How an image is captured is not as important as the image itself. Photographers must strive for a well-focused, stable, and perpendicularly oriented photograph.

Photographers can make a strong statement with their photographs by getting close to their subjects, and jury members want to be impressed with the work of crime scene investigators. For better or for worse, they will compare the photographer's actual efforts with the fictional characters seen on television. Therefore, crime scene investigators must strive to impress the jury with their photographic abilities. To achieve a full-framed, close-focused image, photographers have a choice between the use of diopters (magnification filters), extension tubes, or macrolenses. Leaving the close-focusing equipment in the camera bag is a terrible mistake. Therefore, photographers are encouraged to use all their skills and equipment in bloodstain photography, because it is so much more than a simple point-and-shoot, half-hearted task.

The same concepts that govern close-focus or macrophotography apply to the documentation of bloodstains. One last key concept to remember in regard to bloodstain photography involves depth of field. Bloodstains are not always found on smooth, flat surfaces. When bloodstains are found on curved or undulating surfaces, it is important to maintain a deep depth of field by selecting smaller apertures. Because macrophotography reduces the subject-to-camera distance, depth of field is at a premium. Photographers should seek to maximize depth of field through the use of smaller apertures. The aperture is the preferable choice to control depth of field in bloodstain photography because the choice of lens and the subject-to-camera distances are typically predetermined by the photographer's equipment. The goal is to fill the viewfinder with the subject. Of course, the smaller apertures will require longer exposure times and a tripod or copy stand may be necessary, but taking the extra effort will result in more powerful images.

Luminol, Bluestar®, and Other Chemiluminescent Blood Reagents

Luminol and *Bluestar* are chemicals that are applied to surfaces that are thought to possess latent bloodstains. These chemicals react with the iron found in blood and the reaction causes fluorescence. The fluorescence is not typically bright enough to be visible in anything except low-light environments. Consequently, the photography of these chemical reactions has always been a challenge to crime scene investigators. However, the photography of Luminol and Bluestar is not a complicated endeavor and merely requires a little patience on the part of the photographer.

There have been a number of methods suggested over the years on how best to photograph these chemical reactions. Everything from recording multiple images to advanced postcapture editing manipulations have been offered. However, there really is no need for any top-secret technique, advanced high-definition resolution (HDR) photography, or the use of an image enhancement program in order to document the latent bloodstain patterns found at a crime scene (Figure 8.29). The basic principles of exposure and light are all that is needed to record outstanding quality photographs, even in near-blackout conditions.

Figure 8.29 Settings: ISO 400, f/8, for 2 min. Image was recorded in complete darkness, which allowed the Luminol's fluorescence to burn into the image. Supplemental light was added with a flashlight bounced off the ceiling of the vehicle for several seconds.

Necessary Equipment

- Luminol or Bluestar
- SLR camera
- Tripod
- Cable release
- Flashlight or external electronic flash

Crime scene investigators will have their own personal preferences as to whether they prefer to work with Luminol or Bluestar. Luminol's sensitivity to blood is typically greater than Bluestar, being able to detect blood in as little as 1 part for every 300,000. Bluestar is sensitive to 1 in 10,000 parts and consequently requires a greater amount of blood to remain on a surface in order for it to be detected. The upside to using Bluestar is that the reaction is naturally brighter and easier to detect in environments that are not completely dark. Luminol reactions require that the location be as dark as possible. The choice between Luminol and Bluestar is up to the individual investigator, but the photography of either chemical's reaction is largely the same. As a result, when the author refers to a *Luminol reaction*, the reader should be aware that the concept under discussion applies to both Luminol and Bluestar.

Photographers can record the chemiluminescent image with any camera capable of *bulb* exposures, but the versatility provided by the SLR camera makes it a better choice for the recording of these chemical reactions. Certainly, if one only possesses a *point-and-shoot* style of camera, adjustments can be made to the exposure values in order to record a Luminol reaction. However, the image quality may suffer and the clarity of the image may not give the viewer exactly what had been detected in the crime scene. The photographer should also possess a cable release or remote capture device for the camera. Timed exposures that may last 30 s to 4 min or longer are possible and a cable release will be necessary to complete such photographs. Furthermore, in order to record such long exposures, the camera will need to be stabilized upon a tripod. The final tool necessary for recording a Luminol reaction will be for some sort of secondary light source. An external flash or even a flashlight is ideal.

Once again, understanding the exposure triangle will make the photographing of chemical reactions a much easier proposition. Once again, the three variables for any exposure evaluation are ISO value (film speed), aperture, and shutter speed. Pretty much everything in photography is a give and take process. Therefore, a photographer needs to evaluate the various exposure choices and decide what is acceptable for each photograph. To begin with, the ISO value controls how sensitive the camera (imaging chip or film) is to light. An ISO value of 100 requires more light than an ISO value of 1600. However, the color and sharpness of an ISO 100 image will generally be better than one recorded at ISO 1600. Many photographers find that an ISO value of 400 is a good compromise when recording Luminol reactions. However, nothing is written in stone as far as an ISO value, and as digital cameras continue to improve, one may find that the quality of images recorded at higher ISO values is perfectly acceptable. This is especially true with full-frame imaging sensors.

The next exposure variable needing consideration is the aperture or f/number. Larger apertures (small f/numbers) allow more light into the camera, but can create a shallow depth of field. Smaller apertures (larger f/numbers) reduce the amount of light coming into the camera, but increase an image's depth of field. The photographer's choice in apertures is another subjective selection. However, if the photographer does not have a specific reason for one aperture choice over another, an aperture selection of f/8 is a good compromise. An f/8 aperture typically falls in the middle of most lenses' range of apertures and is a good compromise between the light-gathering ability of the lens and the composition's depth of field. Furthermore, an aperture of f/8 is likely to be close to the camera lens' *sweet spot*, which simply is the aperture that provides the best corner to corner sharpness for any recorded image. In the end, the photographer should choose an aperture for a particular reason and not let the camera dictate what the aperture should be.

The final exposure variable is the shutter speed. The shutter speed is the most versatile of all the exposure values and the one that should be used to make the majority of any exposure adjustments in a Luminol composition. The ISO value and aperture value should be chosen for a specific reason or purpose. The time value or shutter speed can be altered or changed to balance the exposure for the chosen ISO and aperture selections. Of course there is a trade-off. A shorter exposure is more time efficient and is less likely to result in the development of *noise* in a digital image. Longer exposures require a little more patience and may result in the addition of *noise* to a composition. Many cameras have built-in noise-reduction filters that can be switched on to improve the captured image. Full-frame digital sensors are well known for creating very low noise images, even with images lasting several minutes in length. Although good Luminol compositions can be recorded over a few seconds, outstanding images can be recorded by allowing the image to be created over a few minutes.

To begin with, documenting crime scenes and/or recovered evidence is not simply a matter of photographing the subjects. Therefore, just because a quality image can be or is obtained does not alleviate the investigator from taking notes, measurements, and documenting his or her efforts in a thorough report. Furthermore, in order to ensure that the task of fully documenting the crime scene or evidence prior to being processed with chemicals, a full set of photographs of the subject or area should be recorded. Once the *in situ* and establishing photographs have been captured, the photographer can begin the chemical processing of the scene (or evidence).

The crime scene investigator should gather up all their equipment, including the camera gear and chemicals. The investigator should have some idea where they are searching for latent bloodstains. Ideally, it would be nice to photograph the suspected bloodstained area on the first application of chemicals. However, some scenes might be more extensive and require a little bit of a search using the chemicals first, and then the area of reaction can be photographed while adding a second application of chemicals to the surfaces. Either way, the task of photographing the reaction is largely the same.

To begin the photographic process, the photographer should firmly secure the camera to the tripod and compose the image within the viewfinder. A natural light photograph can be focused and recorded simply for the sake of thoroughness. At this point, the autofocus feature on the camera should be turned off. Once the lights are turned off (if not already), the camera will not attempt to refocus itself in the dark with the autofocus feature switched off. The next step in the process is to set the first two exposure variables: ISO value and aperture. Unless the photographer has a specific reason for anything else, an ISO value of 400 and an aperture of f/8 is an excellent compromise for the quality of image, light-gathering ability, and depth of field. The final exposure variable is the length of time that the exposure will last.

Figure 8.30 Settings: ISO 400, f/8, for 3 min. The image was recorded in complete darkness and supplemental light was added with an electronic flash bounced off the ceiling and set to a one-stop underexposure.

The length of the exposure will depend on the ambient lighting conditions. Assuming the Luminol or Bluestar is mixed and ready to go, the investigator should turn off the lights, whether working inside a home, a vehicle examination bay, or in the laboratory. The darker the environment, the easier it will be to observe the reaction and, believe it or not, record the image. If one is working in the daytime and lighting cannot be controlled, then the photographer may simply have to wait until the sun goes down. If the crime scene is an interior scene, then the investigator can always tape black trash bags or cardboard over the windows in order to prevent light from entering the room and ultimately, the composition. Whether the investigator is using Luminol or Bluestar, the darker the area can be made, the easier the composition will be to record (Figure 8.30). With the light removed as much as possible from the composition, then the length of the exposure becomes less important, because there is no risk of overexposing the composition. Furthermore, the amount of light added to the composition in order to put the chemical reaction into context is completely decided by the photographer. If ambient light is still visible in the crime scene, the photographer may be limited in the exposure's length so that the image is not overexposed.

With the introduction of digital imaging, Luminol photography has been made so much easier. Before applying chemicals to the scene, the photographer can fine-tune his or her exposure and record test shots to see how much supplemental light will be necessary to record a valuable image. To begin with, the photographer may not want a *properly* exposed image, because fully illuminating the composition is likely going to eliminate the visibility of any chemical reaction, especially if the reaction is weak. Therefore, slightly

Figure 8.31 Settings: ISO 400, f/8, for 13 s. Image was captured with a fairly well-illuminated environment. The ambient light was metered and set for one stop below a properly balanced exposure.

underexposing the image is going to provide a good balance between recording the reaction and the environment in which it is found. If the reaction is weak, a two-stop underexposure is a good starting point. If the reaction is stronger, a one-stop underexposure of the scene should result in a good quality image (Figure 8.31).

If the photographer was unable to eliminate all the ambient light, then he or she will need to meter the ambient light. Using the camera's light meter, the amount of time needed to record a proper image can be determined by setting the already chosen ISO value (ISO 400) and aperture (f/8) and then letting the camera tell the photographer how long the exposure must be. However, remember that the exposure may need to be underexposed a little. The photographer can record the *underexposed* image prior to the chemical processing of the scene and evaluate the exposure for possible adjustments. If the investigator was able to eliminate all the ambient light, then the exposure is much easier. The image can simply continue as long as desired and the supplemental light can be added with an electronic flash or flashlight. The flash's exposure compensation setting should be set to underexpose the composition by one to two stops of light, and the flash should be bounced off a nearby surface, because aiming the flash (or flashlight) directly onto the surface containing the latent bloodstains could unintentionally washout the chemical reaction (Figure 8.32). Another way to add supplemental light to the scene is with a flashlight. Casting a typical police-style flashlight (approximately 100 lumens [lm]) off a nearby surface (ceiling or wall) for 2–3 s will likely result in a quality and slightly underexposed image. The flashlight can be painted or moved across the ceiling or wall in order to provide a more even coating of light to the scene. How long to shine the flashlight across the subject is based on the intensity of the light, the distance the light has to travel, and the depth of the crime scene or subject matter. Once again, taking a practice exposure prior to the addition of chemicals to one's scene is a good recommendation. The image can be reviewed and the exposure fine-tuned for the actual Luminol recording.

If there is ambient light impacting the scene, then the length of the exposure will be limited so that the chemical reaction will not be washed out. However, if the investigator

Figure 8.32 Settings: ISO 400, f/8, for 4.5 min. Image was recorded in a darkened room for just over 4½ min, which allowed the faint Bluestar reaction to burn into the image. Supplemental light was added with a flash bounced off the ceiling and set to a one-stop underexposure.

is able to remove all or at least the vast majority of ambient light from the composition, then the photographer can simply let the chemical reaction continue to burn into the image for several minutes and not be worried about overexposing the overall image. In regard to photographic imaging, *light is additive*. As the Luminol or Bluestar chemicals react with the latent bloodstains, the reaction, even a weak one, can be allowed to continue for several minutes, and then the supplemental light provided by a flash or flashlight can be added to complete the image. It does not matter whether the supplemental light is added at the beginning, middle, or end of the exposure. How long to allow the chemical reaction to occur and to photograph depends on the intensity of the reaction. A Bluestar reaction may only take 1–2 min, while a faint Luminol reaction may take 3–4 min. Certainly, one can increase the ISO value and/or open up the aperture to take much quicker exposures. However, just because the exposure is captured in a shorter amount of time does not mean the image has better quality. Consequently, a little patience goes a long way and photographers that allow for longer exposures, smaller apertures, and lower ISO values will be rewarded with sharp-focused and more vibrant images (Figure 8.33). Once again, digital imaging has a tremendous advantage over film photography, in that the recorded image can be reviewed and the length of the exposure or amount of supplemental light can be adjusted to create a better final product. It should not take more than two to three attempts at obtaining a quality photographic image.

In conclusion, digital photography has certainly made the photography of Luminol and Bluestar reactions much easier by eliminating the amount of bracketing that was necessary in order to guarantee a result. Regardless of whether the image is recorded in film

Figure 8.33 Settings: ISO 400, f/8, for 2 min. The photograph was captured using a small amount of ambient light filtering into the room. The exposure is actually an *overexposure*. The camera's light meter showed that 30 s should have provided a balanced exposure. This image's capture shows the value of digital imaging and being able to adjust the composition's capture after reviewing a first *test shot* and making changes to improve the final image, which included the introduction of the chemical.

or by digital imaging, the techniques are primarily the same. After fully documenting the location with notes, photographs, measurements, etc., the photographer simply needs to follow a few simple steps in order to record a quality photograph:

- Compose image with camera firmly affixed to a tripod.
- Focus and turn off the autofocus feature on the camera.
- Set the ISO to 400 and the aperture to f/8 (unless other values are desired).
- If the room has ambient lighting, use camera to meter the light and set the exposure for a slight (up to two stops) underexposure.
- If the room is fairly dark, then the exposure can run for 2–4 min depending on the intensity of the chemical reaction observed during the exposure:
  - Remember to add in supplemental light with a flash or flashlight.
- Evaluate the composition for lighting and intensity of the chemical reaction.
- Rephotograph if necessary and make adjustments to the exposure.

Photographing Luminol or Bluestar is not a difficult proposition and should not be feared. The exposure is not likely recorded with the camera set to *Program* and with a little basic photographic skill, excellent recordings can be made.

Every crime scene photographer should practice these techniques prior to working an actual crime scene. Inexpensive substitutes to practice these techniques can be found at the neighborhood dollar store. Glow sticks and other phosphorescent toys make an excellent substitute for Luminol. A photographer can find a dark room, throw a glow stick onto the floor, and attempt to photograph it using the techniques described earlier. Photographers can then decide which technique works best for them. It is advisable to make written notes of the photographic exercises in order to remember how exactly the best image was recorded.

Bloodstains and Colored Substratum

Bloodstains will not always impact a nice white surface. They frequently come to rest on colored or dark (noncontrasting) surfaces. Oftentimes, bloodstains are found on clothing, carpeting, furniture, or almost anything covered by colored fabrics (Figure 8.34). These fabrics will come in a variety of hues and shades. Fortunately, freshly deposited blood comes in only one primary color, albeit blood can have a number of different shades. Color contrast filters using the primary colors of red, green, and blue can make the visualization of bloodstains easier for those examining the photographs.

The basic concepts for using colored filters are covered in Chapter 4 and can easily be applied to bloodstain photography. Colored filters are utilized with B&W film or with the monochrome setting on a digital camera. The primary color filters of red, green, and blue will lighten that particular color and darken the opposite color in the final recorded image. On occasion, an infrared filter can also be of value to bloodstain photographers (see Figure 8.35). As it relates to blood evidence, the use of a red filter will lighten the color of blood against its background and a blue filter will darken the appearance of blood against its background. A green filter may be used when the background is actually green in color, but the blue filter has a stronger effect on the intensity of blood and will likely give the photographer a better result (Figure 8.36). Digital cameras have built-in filters for red and green. These filters can be found in the camera's monochrome (B&W) settings within the menu system. Camera manufacturers have not yet routinely added internal blue filters in digital cameras. Cameras do have a blue tinting feature, but that is

Figure 8.34 This is an image of blue jeans recorded through a Wratten #47 (blue) filter in order to lighten the color of the blue jeans and darken the red staining. Creating contrast by darkening bloodstains and lightening the background (or vice versa) will result in better photographic compositions. (Photo courtesy of Curtis Klingle, Former Crime Scene Investigator, Bryan (Texas) Police Department, Bryan, TX.)

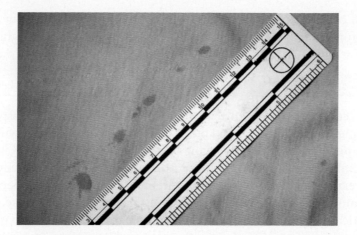

Figure 8.35 Photographing bloodstains found upon colored substrates can be made easier by using colored filters. The primary filter colors of red (#25), blue (#47), and green (#58) will lighten the same color and darken the opposite color. Of course, blood is red, and on rare occasions, red filters can be used to lighten the color of the blood and darken the similarly red-toned background. However, greater contrast can sometimes be created with an infrared filter, such as seen in this photograph. A Hoya 72R filter created the best contrast between the red sweatshirt and the blood. Investigators who attempt to create contrast with a red filter may wish to try an infrared filter as well.

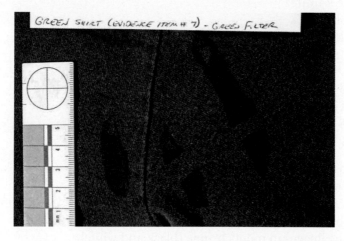

Figure 8.36 This image was recorded through a Wratten #58 green filter and allows investigators to see the bloodstain pattern impression found on the green shirt. Adding a filter matching the color of the substratum (green) and opposite the blood's color (red) will create the needed contrast by lightening the shirt's color and darkening the color of the blood.

not the same as a blue filter. As a result, photographers should purchase a Wratten #47A (blue) filter for bloodstain photography.

Investigators always have the option of using colored light instead of colored filters. Expensive ALS units are efficient and can be fine-tuned as to the wavelength of colored light that is produced. However, there are less-expensive alternatives, such as LED flashlights that project a specific colored beam of light. Standard wavelengths and colors include 470 nm (blue), 532 nm (green), and 650 nm (red). The choice of whether to use colored light or a colored filter is ultimately the photographer's decision. The selection is based on what creates the best contrast in the captured image. And, after all, improving a photograph's contrast is the fundamental reason behind using colored filters and/or light sources.

Conclusion

There are no excuses for taking shortcuts in crime scene photography, especially when it comes to documenting bloodstains and bloodstain patterns. When reviewing a case with a bloodstain examiner or a prosecutor, trying to explain why a picture did not come out or why and what information is missing from a particular image is an unenviable position. By bracketing exposures, choosing lighting carefully, and considering perspective issues, officers can demonstrate their competency to investigators and jurors alike. Photographers should also critically review their own work from time to time and seek to improve areas of deficiency. Individual effort will pay off with quality investigations, improved documentation, and successful prosecutions.

End of Chapter Questions

1. Who created the technique of *roadmapping* for bloodstain pattern documentation?
   a. Tom Bevel
   b. Christine Ramirez
   c. Toby Wolson
   d. Paul Kirk

2. What is one key to building an accurate quadrant map?
   a. 90° corners
   b. Building a quadrant map on all surfaces
   c. Ensuring every square is $12'' \times 12''$
   d. Creating the quadrant map early in the crime scene's processing

3. When photographing the individual quadrant squares, what is one key to accurately record each square?
   a. Ensure a flash is used to record the image.
   b. Ensure the camera's lens is perpendicular to the target surface.
   c. Record the images in monochrome (black and white).
   d. All of the above.

4. When recording surfaces such as white-painted walls, what does the camera tend to do?
   a. Fails to accurately focus
   b. Develops camera shake
   c. Overexposes the image
   d. Underexposes the image

5. The built-in or pop-up flash on the camera is a better choice of light source when photographing bloodstains, because of the close-focus nature of those images.
   a. True
   b. False

6. When a bloodstain is found on a pair of blue jeans and the photographer wishes to increase the contrast of the image by making the red bloodstains darker in the photograph, which colored filter would be the best choice?
   a. Red
   b. Blue
   c. Green
   d. Yellow

7. When a bloodstain is found on a section of green carpet and the photographer wishes to increase the contrast of the image by making the green carpet lighter in the photograph, which colored filter would be the best choice?
   a. Red
   b. Blue
   c. Green
   d. Orange

8. Which aperture would be the best choice to shrink the depth of field in order to bring the focus of the image's viewer to one particular bloodstain?
   a. f/2.8
   b. f/8
   c. f/16
   d. f/22

9. If a photographer is struggling in recording a quality image with the use of a flash, what is a good alternative?
   a. Keep trying to use the flash from different angles.
   b. Use postcapture editing program to improve the image.
   c. Document the subject in written form.
   d. Use ambient light.

10. In order to record Luminol reactions, one must remove all ambient light from the area being photographed.
    a. True
    b. False

11. What can be used to add a little fill light to a Luminol composition in order to provide context to the composition?
    a. Ambient light
    b. Flashlight
    c. Electronic flash
    d. Any of the above

12. Because *light is additive*, Luminol reactions are generally improved through longer exposures.
    a. True
    b. False

Photography Assignments

Required tools: Colored filters (red, blue, and green), plumb line, or laser level

Photography subjects: Variety of bloodstained exemplars (animal blood can frequently be found at meat processing sites), mirror, glass surfaces, dry erase markers, permanent markers, white cardstock, phosphorescent kid's toy (glow sticks from a *Dollar Store*)

I. Photographing blood on difficult surfaces:
   A. On a plain sheet of white paper, draw a few small replica bloodstains (or actual bloodstains) onto the paper and photograph.
   B. On a reflective surface, such as a mirror, use a dry erase marker to draw replica bloodstains (or actual bloodstains) on the mirror and photograph.
   C. On a window, use a dry erase marker to draw replica bloodstains (or actual bloodstains) on the window and photograph. Use a scale in this photograph and get the lighting to balance between the background and the foreground (scale and bloodstains).
II. Practice using filtration to increase the contrast in bloodstain photography:
   A. Set the camera to monochrome (B&W) and place a red stain on different colored substrates:
      1. Photograph stained substrates in unfiltered monochrome setting.
      2. Photograph stained substrates using different colored filters (red, green, and blue).
      3. Compare resulting images.
III. Photographing small bloodstains:
   A. Draw a few small (2–4 mm in size) bloodstains (or actual bloodstains) and photograph them by filling the viewfinder. Record images with the camera perpendicular to the subject, filling the viewfinder, and with proper lighting.
IV. Practice photographing Luminol reactions:
   A. Using a phosphorescence kid's toy (glow sticks), photograph the glowing toys and add light to place the toy into context with the environment:
      1. Record one image in a completely dark room.
      2. Record one image in a room with some ambient light.

Additional Readings

Bevel, T. and Gardner, R.M. (2008). *Bloodstain Pattern Analysis with an Introduction to Crime Scene Reconstruction*. 3rd ed. Boca Raton, FL: CRC Press.

Duncan, C.D. (2013). Luminol and Bluestar photography. *Chesapeake Examiner* (Fall), 51(2):6–13.

Duncan, C.D. and Ramirez, C. (2012). Quadrant mapping of bloodstains. *Chesapeake Examiner* (Fall), 50(2).

Gardner, R.M. (2005). *Practical Crime Scene Processing and Investigation*. Boca Raton, FL: CRC Press.

Miller, L.S. (1998). *Police Photography*. Cincinnati, OH: Anderson Publishing Company.

Photography of Shooting Incidents

9

According to the Federal Bureau of Investigation's Uniform Crime Reports, year after year firearms account for approximately 70% of all homicides, and this does not even include the greater number of aggravated assaults and robberies perpetrated by suspects armed with firearms. As a result, the documentation of crime scenes involving weapon discharges is numerous and requires all the skills of a crime scene photographer. Investigators must be able to use all their abilities and artistry in order to record these incidents in an understandable and informational manner. Everything from macrophotography to timed exposures can come into play when documenting the scene of a shooting. Depth of field, perspective, a camera's orientation with the subject, and an understanding of reciprocity are also important concepts that a crime scene photographer must master in order to capture meaningful and valuable crime scene photographs.

General Photographic Concepts When Documenting Shooting Scenes

The proper documentation of shooting incidents begins with a comprehensive photographic portrayal of the overall crime scene. Walking into a crime scene and focusing on the fired bullets and cartridge cases without fully establishing the location with overall photographs will only confuse those who view the images. For example, just because a shooting incident occurs inside a business or residence does not mean the exterior of that property does not need to be fully photographed. The value of any single crime scene photograph is directly related to the ability of the viewer to place it into context with the crime scene or overall location itself. Therefore, the first step in the documentation of any shooting incident is to completely document the overall crime scene with a 360° view of the location. The photographic compositions should also incorporate any viewpoints or perspectives that parties to the shooting or witnesses would have had of the incident. Recording these points of view of a crime scene may become important during the investigation or trial because it could help corroborate or refute an eyewitness' statement. Furthermore, the photographer should be sure to capture enough overall or establishing photographs that show the entire scene from multiple angles and directions. The photographer should also remember the little things that help establish a crime scene's location, such as street signs, business signs, and individual reference points that were used to record measurements for any scene diagrams that were drawn. As a never ending theme, the value of completeness is not outweighed by the cost of film (or storage media).

It bears repeating that understanding and controlling a photograph's depth of field is one of the most valuable tools in the crime scene investigator's arsenal. The difference between a snapshot and a crime scene photograph often comes down to an image's depth of field. Two photographs can have the same views, but the two images may tell entirely different stories because of the information lost or gained by the choice of aperture. When a photographer records images in a *Program* or automatic mode, the camera attempts to find a balance between an acceptable shutter speed and aperture. Automatic cameras tend to have a bias toward faster shutter speeds and larger apertures in order to eliminate camera shake. Therefore, although the *Program* mode may be easier or quicker to work with, the end product may suffer.

Many cameras have what are affectionately known as a *creative zone* but are more commonly known as an *idiot zone*. Creative modes are typically found on the camera's main command dial and have small icons such as a pair of mountain peaks, a person's profile, or the outline of a runner. These icons allow the photographer to tell the camera where to direct the biases, toward either a particular shutter speed or aperture value. However, the camera will only go so far in determining a balance between aperture and shutter speed. By understanding reciprocity and the relationship between ISO values, apertures, and shutter speeds, the photographer can create a much better end product rather than rely on the camera to make all the exposure decisions. For those who are still not comfortable finding the right balance between the exposure variables, using the *Aperture Priority* or *Shutter Priority* mode is an acceptable alternative to using one of the creative modes. *Aperture Priority* allows the photographer the ability to seek a smaller aperture, thus increasing the zone of sharp focus in the image. The camera will determine the proper shutter speed to match the chosen aperture. However, be aware that the camera may not warn the user of the potential for camera shake and the photographer must be cognizant of the shutter speed so that if it slows below a certain point the camera should be stabilized in some manner.

Remember the rule of thumb that one over the lens' focal length is the minimum shutter speed for holding a camera by hand during capture. Regardless of any other bells and whistles cameras may have, all cameras have an audible warning indicating the need for a tripod. The warning is not found in the camera's instruction manual. The warning occurs when a photographer hears the distinct *click–click* of the shutter opening and then closing. At that time, the camera must be supported because those double-click sounds are clear indications of the potential for a distorted photograph due to camera shake.

Whether a crime scene investigator chooses either of the priority modes or operates the camera in a fully *Manual* mode, the goal of any photographic endeavor is to capture an image that is meaningful to the viewer. In order to be meaningful, the photographic image must be in focus and free of distortion and have a desirable zone of sharp focus. The easiest way to ensure an ample zone of sharp focus is by choosing a small aperture. There is no one right answer as far as the best aperture for a particular image is concerned. The decisions concerning focal lengths, apertures, and subject distance (factors affecting depth of field) all depend on the physical constraints of the crime scene and what in particular needs to be recorded. The choice is ultimately determined by the crime scene photographer. The value of having a lens with very small apertures, such as f/22 and smaller, will certainly come into play when it comes time to photograph lasers that simulate the flight paths of fired projectiles. These smaller apertures may cause a softening of the image's periphery, but when needed, the advantage gained in obtaining a better depth of field and longer (time) exposures is worth the trade.

Documenting shooting scenes requires the full gamut of photography, including macrophotography skills. Close-up photography still requires dedication, attention to detail, and a plan toward the recording of these vitally important photographs. In addition, depth of field is just as important in close-up photography as it is in midrange photography. There are evidentiary photographs that can create an impact with the jury that are frequently overlooked because they are deemed *impossible* to capture. As a general school of thought, if an investigator is told that photographing and/or recovering a piece of evidence is impossible, that investigator should analytically examine the problem and devise a plan to do the impossible. Sure, sometimes finding a pubic hair in a haystack is impossible, but as far as crime scene photography goes, if that hair is located, it better well be photographed and documented as it was discovered.

As an example of a difficult composition, fired bullets find their way into every conceivable orifice, nook, and cranny. In addition, fired projectiles can fragment into smaller pieces or mushroom upon striking a surface. They can penetrate, ricochet, or imbed themselves into every imaginable surface. For those bullets that penetrate into or through a surface, the scene's photography frequently ends with the investigator simply recording the hole, which the bullet created and passed through. However, the fired bullet will not always just come to a stop and easily found on the other side of the impacted surface. Fired bullets have amazing penetrating power and can pass through multiple surfaces, including ductwork, insulation, wood studs, and/or framing. The damage these bullets do to the interiors of walls, car doors, and other surfaces, as well as the projectiles themselves, should also be photographed. The first problem lies in getting the camera into these small confines. The second is getting enough light on the subject to make the evidence visible.

When a fired projectile penetrates a building's wall or other confined space, the crime scene investigator must attempt to recover the projectile. This typically entails cutting a hole in the surface large enough that the investigator can fit his or her hand inside to collect the item. A camera lens is approximately the size of a human hand and therefore should easily fit into the opening created by the investigator (Figure 9.1). A small flashlight or flexible head light-emitting diode (LED) light can be used to illuminate the interior of the surface. Obviously, the photograph should be recorded with the camera stabilized in some manner. The value of such an image is priceless. It shows the investigator's skill and commitment to the investigation.

Before causing any additional damage to the impacted surfaces by placing trajectory rods or probes through the bullet holes, the impact sites must be photographed, and in a way that they accurately reflect the subject being documented. As always, perspective, clarity, and filling the viewfinder with the subject are the key components of a quality evidentiary photograph. Ballistic evidence, and specifically impact sites, must be photographed in enough detail and in a manner where crime scene reconstructionists are able to determine angles of impact, directionality, identity, and precise location of the impact site (Figure 9.2). It is not always about making an impression with the image's viewer; valuable information can be garnered from photographic evidence that can help tell the story of an incident even though the individual examining the photographs did not actually respond to the crime scene under scrutiny.

Perspective or subject-to-camera orientation is a key element in any incident reconstruction attempt made through photographs. Just as with the photography of fingerprint or footwear impression evidence, bullet impact sites must be recorded in a perpendicular alignment. Similar to bloodstain evidence and the determination of their impact angles, the angle of impact can possibly be calculated by the length and width of the impact site (inverse sine of the width divided by the length equals the angle of impact). In order for this to be determined from a photograph, the camera's lens must be aligned to the impact site at a 90° angle. Using an ABFO #2 scale with the alignment circles visible in the picture will help confirm that a photograph was aligned properly at the time of capture. Some surfaces may not

Figure 9.1 Photographing small pieces of evidence trapped inside walls, tires, or permanent fixtures is a true test of a photographer's skill. Getting a jury member to think, "Wow, how was that photograph taken?" will go a long way toward supporting a crime scene investigator's credibility and professionalism on the witness stand. This photo was recorded by illuminating the hidden projectile inside the flattened car tire with a small flashlight and a beanbag-mounted camera set at ISO 400, f/5.6, for ½ s.

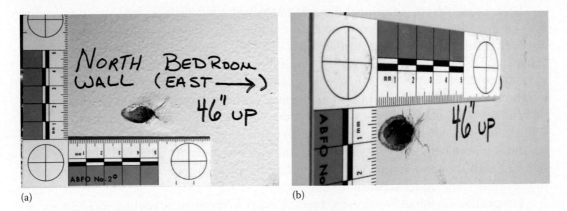

(a)   (b)

Figure 9.2 Impact angles of fired projectiles can be determined from a photograph if the image is recorded in a perpendicular orientation between the camera's lens and subject. Incorporating a scale with circular alignment marks into the image will assist those attempting to reconstruct an incident through the crime scene's photographs. In (a), the width of the printed image measured 32 mm and the length was 52 mm. 32/52 = 0.615. The inverse sine of 0.615 states the angle of impact for this fired bullet was approximately 38°. However, compare (a) with (b) of the same impact site and observe that the alignment circle has more of an elliptical appearance. Calculating the impact angle from (b) reveals an incorrect angle of impact of 71° (impact site measured 35 mm × 37 mm from photograph).

be large enough or conducive to the use of such scales. In those cases, using a template with circles that can be traced onto the impacted surface can act as a substitute for a scale without alignment circles. Unlike footwear and fingerprint evidence, the photograph does not have to be enlarged to an exact one-to-one image. As long as the image is enlarged in correct proportion, the relationship between the impact site's width and length should remain the same and allow for the trigonometric calculations to be completed. In fact, a scale is not even needed for the calculations of impact angles. However, having a scale in the photograph is still a good idea for no other reason than it may help indicate the caliber of firearm that discharged the projectile and because it is expected to be present within the composition.

Another advantage or help to investigators gained by recording quality close-up photographs is the ability to determine the directionality of a fired projectile from the image. Minute fracture lines in the impacted surface and/or pinch points can help investigators determine a fired projectile's direction of travel. On painted surfaces, such as the painted areas of a motor vehicle, fracture lines in the paint form along the edges of acute-angle impacts. These fracture lines radiate back toward the point of origination for the projectile (Figure 9.3). These fracture lines can be enhanced with a little black (or some other contrasting color) fingerprint powder. In order to make these minute fracture lines clearly discernible in a photograph, the impact site should fill the camera's viewfinder. Choosing a quality lighting setup (oblique or side lighting is frequently more beneficial in these images) may also help create a valuable image.

In those scenes that have multiple surfaces impacted or even a single surface struck by multiple projectiles, differentiating between the individual impact sites can be crucial to alleviating confusion among the different locations of evidence (Figure 9.4). Just because an investigator cannot place a plastic evidentiary tent marker on the side of a car or a home's wall does not mean the evidence does not have to be identified in the crime scene photographs. In addition to some sort of identifying number or letter, other information can be incorporated into the image. For example, height and directionality are quite beneficial.

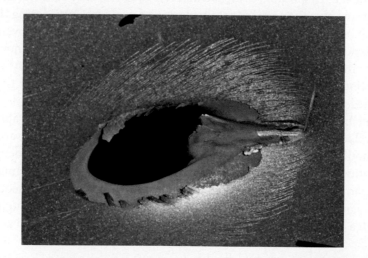

Figure 9.3 The minute fracture lines visible in this figure are created by a fired projectile passing through the painted metal of a motor vehicle. The fracture lines will bend back toward the point of origin and tell investigators from what direction a fired bullet originated. For white or black vehicles, a contrasting fingerprint powder can be brushed onto the impact site in order to highlight the fracture lines in a photograph.

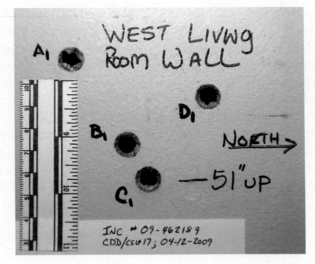

Figure 9.4 Differentiating between multiple impact sites on a surface or multiple surfaces is critical to avoid confusion. Marking the evidence with permanent markers or disposable stickers will go a long way toward alleviating potential areas of confusion between two or more similar appearing bullet impact sites. The photograph can include as much detail as the photographer wishes to include. This figure illustrates several impact sites and this one photograph also provides orientation information, including directionality, height, and the specific wall in which the impacts were found.

Using a permanent marker to draw an *up* arrow will help correctly orient a photograph. The height of a particular impact site can be easily added to an image by extending a collapsible carpenter's ruler between the ground and the bullet hole. Another option is to have the height and even the horizontal distance from the nearest wall written on the surface near the impact site. Disposable evidence markers or labels may be advantageous because they are less destructive than permanently marking a surface. Considering that the projectile will have to be dug out of the surface and the surface itself may be covered with blood spatter, the marking of the surface with an indelible pen is quite likely not the most detrimental factor in the ultimate cleanup or repair of the damaged property. In the end, the more information included in the photograph, the better and the easier that photograph can be identified in court and/or used for reconstruction purposes.

As another hint in the labeling of evidence in crime scene photographs it is recommended that all identifying words visible in a photograph be written out and not abbreviated. A jury should not have to guess what *B.S.* refers to; they may not understand that B.S. is an abbreviation for bullet strike. Because bullets may pass through multiple surfaces before coming to a stop, the labeling of bullet strikes should be labeled sequentially when at all possible. For example, a fired bullet that passes north to south through the front of a home, through a bedroom, and comes to rest in a hallway may be labeled as follows:

- A-1—home's exterior north wall
- A-2—interior bedroom's north wall
- A-3—interior bedroom's south wall
- A-4—interior hallway's north wall
- A-5—interior hallway's south wall from which the fired projectile was recovered

The goal of labeling and marking of any crime scene evidence is to make the scene fully understandable to someone who was not present at the location. Sequentially labeling evidence and being consistent with labeling practices will help improve the overall scene's documentation, from the crime scene photographs to any scale diagrams completed. Every investigator has his or her own techniques and methods of labeling evidence. Because of the complex nature of shooting incidents and the multiple types of surfaces that evidence can be found imbedded into or lying on, the investigator may find that differentiating evidence found on horizontal surfaces (floors, roads, sidewalks, etc.) from vertical surfaces (walls, cars, fences, etc.) may be beneficial. This is most easily completed by labeling evidence found on horizontal surfaces with numbers and on vertical surfaces with letters (or vice versa). Typically, commercially produced evidence markers purchased from crime scene supply businesses come numbered (1, 2, 3...). These numbered evidence placards are perfect for horizontal surfaces. This allows the vertical surfaces to be written upon with indelible markers and identified by lettering (A, B, C...). The sequential lettering needed to track projectiles through multiple surfaces is more easily understood using A-1, A-2, A-3... rather than 1-1, 1-2, 1-3....

In conclusion, the scene documentation through still photography must tell a complete story to those viewing the images. Whether the viewers are investigators who responded to the actual crime scene or jury members deciding between guilt and innocence, the photographs must be true, accurate, and free of distortion and provide a complete understanding of the incident. Crime scene photographers need to strive for more than simply a point-and-shoot style of photography. In order to make an impact on a jury, images must be deliberately recorded, with apertures and shutter speeds specifically selected with an eye toward capturing sharp-focused images and with as much detail as possible. In order to ensure sharp-focused (stable) and perpendicularly aligned images, a tripod is frequently required. Trying to ensure a properly aligned and stable image, even in the daylight, is better accomplished with the help of a tripod or some other stable platform on which to mount the camera. Although a jury or even an investigator may not appreciate the exceptional quality of an image recorded as described earlier, anyone who attempts a reconstruction of the incident based upon the photographs recorded at the scene will most certainly be appreciative.

Examination Quality Photography of Gunfire Incidents

Once an investigator departs the crime scene, the photographic documentation of ballistic and firearms evidence has just begun. Evidence recovered at the crime scene can be photographed in much better detail, with improved lighting and backgrounds in a laboratory setting. Consequently, evidence recovered at crime scenes should be rephotographed at the investigator's laboratory or office and in a controlled environment. These additional photographs not only assist investigators and prosecutors in putting together a criminal case for trial but also have a positive effect on the jury by presenting jurors with professional-looking photographs they can sort through during deliberations without having to handle bloodstained evidence or firearms.

Bloodstain evidence is particularly problematic and needs special attention and photographic documentation. In general, bloodstain evidence is difficult to photograph because of the multiple types of surfaces it can be found on and the many different forms it can exhibit. Shooting incidents are often accompanied by bloodshed from mist patterns to projected bloodstain patterns, such as arterial spurt. Bloodstains found on clothing, weapons, or other recovered items should be fully documented through photography. The importance of bloodstain evidence cannot be overemphasized because bloodstain evidence can be used to position suspects and victims in proximity to each other and identify their actions during or immediately after a bloodletting event. Photographing bloodstains is more thoroughly covered in Chapter 8. However, it does not hurt to review some important concepts typically found when blood is associated with ballistic and firearms evidence.

Photographing bloodstains found on clothing may be a challenge both because of the color and texture of the material and because of the size of the stain. Spatter stains can be less than a millimeter in diameter and especially difficult to image. Fortunately, if a stain can be seen, it can be photographed. Blood typically has a nice red color that is easily distinguishable from the surface on which it is found. However, there are times when additional contrast may be needed in the photograph. When contrast is necessary, contrast filters or a colored light source can be used to improve the difference in density (contrast) between the blood and its background.

As a review, the primary colors of light are red, blue, and green. Attaching a colored filter to the camera lens will lighten that particular color in the image and darken the opposite colors. For example, photographing blood found on blue jeans can be improved by selecting a blue (Wratten #47B) filter to lighten the blue jean's color and darken the blood's red color (Figure 9.5). Do not forget to load the camera with black-and-white film or select the black-and-white (monochrome) setting on the digital camera when working with colored filters or colored light sources. For blood that is on a similarly colored material such as a red shirt, an alternate light source (ALS) may be the preferred method of obtaining better contrast because a good-quality ALS can be fine-tuned in order to find the perfect wavelength in which to create a contrast between two similarly colored subjects (Figure 9.6). Regardless of what Hollywood would like one to believe, blood does not fluoresce under ultraviolet light. However, ultraviolet light may cause clothing to lighten in color while the blood will absorb the radiation and appear darker in comparison to the background.

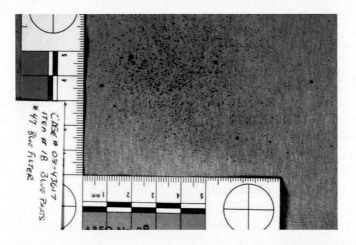

Figure 9.5 Bloodstains found on clothing can be difficult to image because of the small nature of high-energy bloodletting events. Colored filters can be used to improve an image's contrast. Colored filters will lighten similarly colored subjects and darken their opposite colors. This photo was enhanced with a Wratten #47B blue filter in order to darken minute bloodstains and lighten the blue jeans, thus improving contrast.

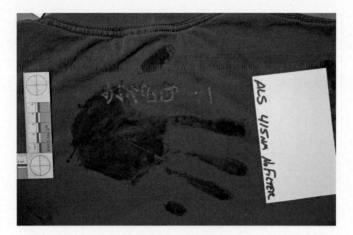

Figure 9.6 Blood impacting dark-colored clothing can be a real challenge to photographers. An ALS can be used to fine-tune the wavelength of light in order to create the greatest contrast between the blood and the material it was found on. Unlike what is seen on television, blood absorbs ultraviolet light. This photo was recorded at ISO 400, f/8, for 1/5th of a second, and an ALS set at 415 nm was used to create the needed contrast to have the bloody handprint visualize against the dark blue background. Photographers should not assume that 415 nm will work on all subjects and there is a trial and error process involved in finding just the right wavelength of light.

Another technique that a photographer may find helpful is shining a white light (including an electronic flash) at different angles across the stained surface. Blood can be a highly reflective property, and if light is shined at just the right angle, the blood may appear lighter than the surface it was found on. Although the contrast is the opposite of what is typically sought in bloodstain photography, ultimately it is about creating contrast between the blood and the surface or object it landed on.

Bloodstains and bloodstain patterns are frequently associated with shooting incidents, and the documentation of blood evidence may require experimentation and the use of different lighting techniques to develop a quality evidentiary photograph. ALS units have a number of applications to the photography of ballistic evidence. Burned gunpowder, soot, and smoke absorb infrared light or that light that is invisible to the human eye and found above 700 nm. Using an infrared light source or an infrared barrier filter over the camera lens can make the residue pattern on clothing more visible. Similar to photography utilizing colored filters, the camera should be loaded with black-and-white film or set to the monochrome setting found on the digital camera. The burned gunpowder and soot will appear as small black particles in the image (Figure 9.7). Placing a scale in the photograph will allow for test fire patterns to be compared with the evidentiary photograph, and an approximate distance between the firearm and target can be determined. Photographing in infrared light is a challenge, especially when using an infrared barrier filter, because of the inability of the camera to focus on its subject. There are digital cameras built specifically for forensic purposes that possess built-in ultraviolet and infrared capabilities, allowing crime scene investigators to have live-view preview screens of their compositions. Although these cameras can produce amazing results with sharp-focused images, the cost of the camera is often cost prohibitive. Instead of spending a couple thousand dollars on a high-end forensic camera, a photographer can opt for the infrared filter (less than $100).

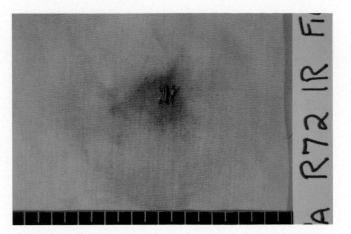

Figure 9.7 Infrared light photography can be utilized to shed light onto gunshot residue patterns present on target surfaces. Soot, smoke, and carbon can be hidden from view on dark-colored clothing, but their presence can be enhanced with infrared light. This photo was captured with a Hoya Infrared #72 filter placed over the camera's lens, which effectively blocks all light wavelengths below 720 nm. The gunshot residue was completely hidden by the black fabric but was made visible by using an IR filter; the image was recorded at ISO 400, f/8, for 61 s.

These inexpensive filters are much less costly than an ALS. The illumination and focusing of infrared subjects is covered in Chapter 10.

On the opposite side of the electromagnetic spectrum is the ultraviolet continuum of light, which is found below 400 nm. Unburned particles of gunpowder may actually fluoresce under ultraviolet light, but the gunpowder itself is not what actually fluoresces (Figure 9.8). Gunpowder manufacturers add a coating to some powders to control the rate

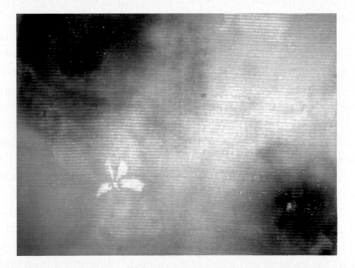

Figure 9.8 Unburned particles of gunpowder can fluoresce in ultraviolet or black light. Expensive light sources are not necessary for this particular photographic technique. This image was created by photographing a piece of clothing in a dark environment with the only light being provided by an inexpensive 4″ fluorescent-tube black light. The image was recorded at ISO 100, f/8, for 8 s. Small particles of unburned propellant can be seen in the smoke ring surrounding the two bullet holes.

of burn, and it is these coatings that fluoresce under ultraviolet light. Wavelengths around the 400 nm mark work quite well and allow investigators to use inexpensive black lights that cost less than $20 to get the unburned particles of gunpowder to fluoresce. Black lights typically operate around the 405–415 nm wavelengths and are an excellent resource for developing such results. The use of a yellow filter oftentimes creates a better contrast and overall image. The presence of these particles, whether burned or unburned, indicates the close proximity of the shooter to the target surface and can corroborate or refute a witness or suspect's statement. Although the manifestation of a fluorescing substance does not conclusively prove gunpowder is present on the surface, the clothing can be marked for further examination by a crime laboratory, and conclusive tests can be performed. In the end, now the crime scene investigator has a piece of demonstrative evidence to testify with at trial, and the jury can *see* what the examiners and investigators are testifying about.

Evidence, especially small pieces of evidence, recovered from a crime scene should be photographed again in the controlled environment of the laboratory using techniques discussed in Chapter 4. Small pieces of evidence found and recovered from a crime scene are not always discovered in an ideal position. One cannot move the evidence so that a better on-scene image can be recorded, but the evidence can be rephotographed in a controlled environment. Specifically related to shooting investigations, the following items commonly found at crime scenes ought to be photographed more than once but are commonly overlooked:

- Headstamps on fired cartridge cases
- Fired bullets (how they expanded or blood, tissue, and other debris attached to the projectile)
- Position of a semiautomatic's safety or the cartridge alignment in a revolver's cylinder
- Serial numbers and other pieces of individualizing information or identification
- Weapon's condition (clean, dusty, oily, damaged, etc.)
- Presence of blood (spatter stains) and tissue

Minute features of a weapon, such as blood or tissue debris found inside a weapon's barrel, are often written about in an offense report, but the photographic documentation of such information is frequently and inexplicably thought to be impossible, too time consuming, and/or unnecessary. Nothing could be further from the truth. Take the extra effort and create meaningful and valuable pieces of photographic evidence. One of the main functions of a crime scene investigator is to fully document the scene of the crime and that includes a complete photographic representation of every aspect of the physical evidence recovered from the crime scene.

The investigator may not see the immediate need to photograph all the evidence a second time, especially fired cartridge cases. Although the headstamp markings and firing pin impressions present on the rear of cartridges and primers will not be used by firearms examiners to make a conclusive identification, having one or two quality photographs for the examiners to show the jurors and explain how they make such comparisons could be of great assistance to them during trial. Not every cartridge case must be rephotographed, but in those instances where multiple guns of the same caliber were fired, these photographs can be very helpful to both the jurors and the investigators. Take as an example a shooting with multiple cartridge cases littering a parking lot in which both shooters fired

Figure 9.9 This cartridge was photographed with light striking the surface of the cartridge case at an oblique angle. The details of the headstamp and firing pin impression were greatly improved by casting oblique light onto the subject, rather than having the light directly projected onto the fired cartridge case from a camera-mounted or built-in flash.

9 mm handguns. If one shooter carried a Beretta and the other fired a Glock, the two firing pin impressions would appear completely different. Having quality, close-focused images of the different cartridge-case headstamps and primer strikes could prove helpful in reconstructing the crime scene. For this reason (possibility of multiple weapons fired), it is recommended that all firearms evidence, including each fired cartridge case, be individually rephotographed after their recovery. Lighting is probably the most difficult part of photographing the backside of a cartridge case. Oblique lighting will likely provide the best result because firing pin impressions and headstamp markings are indented into the cartridge case (Figure 9.9). Therefore, oblique lighting will create the best contrast and shadowing in order to allow the intricate markings to be most visible.

Ejected cartridge cases have partners in crime, and those are the fired bullets or projectiles that they once were attached to. Images of these fired bullets, especially those with blood and tissue attached, make a tremendous impact on their viewers. Just one picture can tell an entire story of pain, loss, and suffering. In addition, information about the bullet can be ascertained from photographing it. For example, what kind of surface did the projectile strike? Was it flattened by impacting concrete, or was it coated with gypsum from penetrating a sheet of drywall? Certainly the paths of fired projectiles will be documented in a number of ways, but macroimages of these small projectiles and even smaller fragments are an important part of the crime scene puzzle that needs to be documented through photography. Depth of field considerations and lighting once again are the keys to a quality macrophotograph.

Because a bullet is round, the subject has a great deal of inherent depth to it. Add in the close-focused nature of a macrophotograph, and a deep depth of field is critical. Photographers should utilize as small an aperture as is available to them. Lighting is another consideration. Fired bullets, especially those that mushroom or expand into multiple directions, illuminated by a single light source, such as from an electronic flash, can leave unwanted shadows on the subject. One benefit of photographing with a very small aperture is that the photographer has more time to illuminate the subject. In addition, selecting a low ISO setting (i.e., ISO 100) will give the photographer additional time to

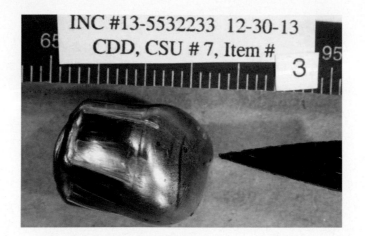

Figure 9.10 The fired bullet shown here was photographed with the camera set at ISO 100, f/22, for 25 s. The longer exposure time allowed the subject to be painted with light. The beam from a small flashlight was projected across the subject from every angle by moving it around the perimeter of the bullet during the 25 s of exposure. This technique eliminated shadows from the image while enabling light to reach all the visible surfaces of the fired projectile.

cast light onto the subject. Regardless of the chosen light source, whether it is an ALS's light guide, a small LED flashlight, or a manually set electronic flash, one can paint the subject with light by moving it around the evidence and projecting light onto the item from all around its perimeter (Figure 9.10). This painting with light technique is discussed in Chapter 4. Painting with light is especially applicable to photographing fired bullets because of the odd shapes and distorted surfaces commonly found with fired projectiles.

Accurately recording a weapon's condition is imperative to a quality investigation. Two examples of abnormalities that result in a weapon's inability to discharge a projectile are a rusty frame or a broken firing pin. These can be reflected through close-up photography. A weapon's inability to fire may also be caused after the firearm has been discharged at least once, rendering it inoperable because a cartridge case became jammed in the ejection port or the weapon broke into pieces because recoil caused the weapon to strike the floor. It is common for jammed actions (stovepipes) to occur during suicides because the person does not have a firm grip on the weapon and a semiautomatic firearm does not have the ability to completely cycle, thereby causing the cartridge case to block the ejection port. Long-barrel firearms tend to have a stronger recoil than pistols, and those committing suicides with long guns are unable to stop the recoil, causing the weapon to recoil forcefully into a nearby surface, such as a floor. This may cause the weapon, especially an older firearm, to fracture. Given enough time, crime scene investigators will see almost every conceivable weapon malfunction and unintentional damage. The photographic documentation of these factors may help provide corroboration or rebuttal to a claim of suicide or an accidental shooting.

Basically, if some condition of the firearm is worth recording in an investigator's report, then it is important enough to document photographically (Figure 9.11). Photographing such things as the position of a semiautomatic weapon's safety can also be extremely important to an investigation. A semiautomatic weapon found at the scene of a suicide with the safety engaged should raise a red flag to investigators. Most all investigators have seen or are aware of these types of investigative questions. However, far too many evidence photographers fail to document such aspects of an investigation with their cameras.

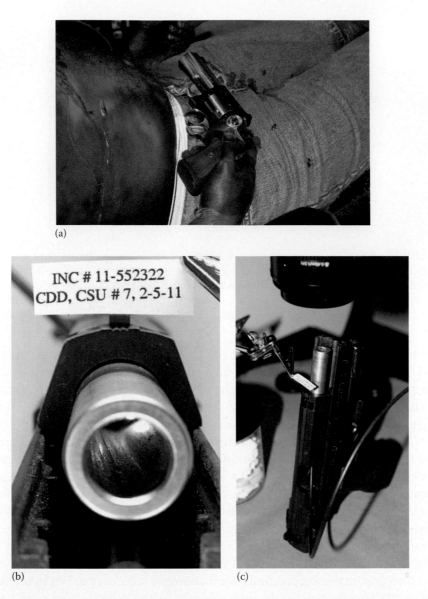

Figure 9.11 The exact condition and precisely how a weapon was found are critical in determining whether a shooting was a suicide or murder and whether a particular weapon was involved in the incident. If an investigator finds a particular facet of a firearm warrants being documented in words, it is significant enough to photograph. The photographic documentation of a weapon begins at the scene. (a) shows the condition of a weapon as it was found at a crime scene. (b) shows the presence of dust and rust inside the barrel of a gun thought to have been involved in a shooting, and (c) shows how image (b) was recorded. Notice the placement of the identification tag, so that it aligns with the area photographed inside the gun's barrel.

It is not merely semiautomatic weapons and long guns that require close examination. Revolvers should be thoroughly documented and photographed as well. For example, if an investigator finds a revolver resting in the hands of a *suicide* victim and there is a live cartridge underneath the hammer and firing pin, an investigator may want to comprehensively document such a condition because the investigation should no longer be limited

Figure 9.12 Documenting the exact chambering condition of the weapon as it was found on the scene is very important. This image was recorded at ISO 100, f/22 (for better depth of field), for 1 s. Observe how the cylinder and the weapon's barrel are aligned to match the position in which the revolver was originally found.

to a suicide. Photographing the cartridges loaded into a revolver's cylinder requires that a pointing device be incorporated into the photograph. When the pistol is mounted underneath the camera and the cylinder is opened, it is a good idea to not only have an arrow pointing to the chamber found underneath the hammer, but that this particular chamber should be rotated so that it is aligned with the hammer's position (Figure 9.12). This will help eliminate any confusion on the part of the image's viewer.

Maintaining chain of custody and being able to identify individual pieces of evidence are both critical to having evidence accepted by the court. Serial numbers, owner applied numbers, and manufacturer's information are commonly imprinted on a weapon, somewhere on the frame and/or barrel of a firearm. These identifying marks are used by investigators to recognize and establish individual pieces of evidence. At times these markings may be concealed by a weapon's grips or tucked underneath a revolver's closed cylinder. Either way, the investigator should photograph the weapon's identifying information, wherever it resides.

Weapons can be chrome-plated or blue steel and the serial numbers are usually stamped into the metal without much inherent contrast. Illuminating the serial numbers is best accomplished by casting an oblique light across the surface. Similar to a cartridge case's headstamp, the shadows created by the oblique lighting will highlight the serial number and make it much clearer in the recorded image. Depth of field is not always an issue, but

Figure 9.13 Serial numbers and/or a weapon's identifying information may be located in hard-to-reach areas. However, with patience and orchestration, a photograph containing all this information can be recorded. Like other indented writings or impressions, oblique lighting helps bring out the fine details of the information sought. This photo shows the weapon's model number tucked under the open cylinder. Electronic flash was projected at an oblique angle across the two surfaces holding the information.

when the weapon's identifying information is found imprinted on the curved barrel of a weapon, then a photographer might consider using a smaller aperture to ensure that the information is legible regardless of its distance from the camera. The ultimate goal of any photographic documentation of a serial number or other piece of written information is to make sure that the subject is clear and legible (Figure 9.13). The subject should fill the viewfinder and the lighting should be cast to ensure the best contrast. With depth of field and compositional issues accurately addressed, there should be no doubt as to which weapon or piece of evidence was recovered from a particular crime scene.

What if there is a question as to whether or not a weapon was even fired during a shooting incident? The fact that a weapon showed signs of discharge or had a dust-filled barrel might be an important piece of information. Some crime scene investigators may desire to give up on obtaining such a photograph because it is deemed *impossible* to photograph the inside of a barrel. However, recording such images is not impossible and should be thought of as a challenge, not as a futile waste of time. After recording the overall photographs of the weapon and the weapon's general condition, including oiled mechanisms, buildup of dust, and/or the presence of soot, gunpowder residue, and impact spatter, the photographer can then seek to capture the more difficult images of the weapon's interior components.

The imaging of small fragments of trace evidence found inside the barrel of a weapon requires thought and planning. To begin with, the camera needs to be in relatively close proximity to the end of the gun's barrel; therefore, the photographer will need a macro-lens or close-focusing attachment to fill the viewfinder with the barrel's interior. Both the camera and the weapon must be anchored in a stable position, with the end of the barrel roughly perpendicular to the camera lens. Sometimes a better picture is possible if the barrel is slightly canted at an angle. Since the length of the barrel will be extending away from the camera lens, the zone of sharp focus should be manually set so that the entire zone of sharp focus is incorporated into the image. Consequently, the camera's aperture should be closed to the smallest possible setting. In addition, focus should be set approximately ⅓–½ of the distance into or through the area being targeted for imaging. For example, if one is focusing into a pistol's 3″ barrel, the point of focus should be approximately one to 1½″ down the length of the barrel. This will ensure that the greatest amount of surface area inside the barrel is in focus. However, if a particular particle, stain, or piece of evidence is visible in the barrel, then the focus should be placed directly upon that object. Many cameras have a depth of field preview button, and this feature can be used to fine-tune the camera's focus with the chosen aperture for the composition.

The final piece of the equation is the lighting and creating illumination inside the interior of the weapon's barrel. A LED single-bulb flashlight with a flexible cable head works wonderfully. Place the end of the LED cable into the opposite end of the barrel, and shine the light back through the barrel and toward the camera. Investigators who do not have an LED light can slide a small dental mirror into the weapon's breach behind the barrel, and using a regular flashlight, they can reflect light up through the barrel. These small flashlights are not extraordinarily brilliant, but they do not have to be. Small inexpensive penlight flashlights work best for such undertakings. Depending on the length of the barrel, a second light may need to be projected down the end of the barrel from the direction of the camera's lens. Photographers should avoid casting too much light on the front end of the barrel so that the details being photographed are not washed out in the recorded image. If careful, a softer secondary light casting a small amount of illumination into the front end of the barrel may help create the best overall image. Figure 4.30, which can be found in Chapter 4, illuminates the value of recording the interior of a weapon's barrel. The crime scene photographer merely has to align the lights so that no hot spots are created inside the barrel and so that the resulting photograph has an overall balanced appearance. Once the lighting is orchestrated, it is simply a matter of recording a series of bracketed exposures. Recording photographs from two stops overexposed to two stops underexposed in half-stop increments is sure to guarantee the best possible result.

Bloodstain evidence found on firearms offers a tremendous amount of information to the investigator. The presence of spatter stains on the weapon can place the firearm in close proximity to the subject, and the photographic documentation of these stains can help determine the course of events that occurred during a shooting incident. In addition, *drawback*, which describes the condition when blood and/or tissue is pulled back into the barrel during its firing, is a good indication that the weapon was in hard contact with the victim at the time of the shooting. This particular bloodstain pattern should always be documented through photography. All these factors discussed here are pieces of the investigative puzzle. They are used to corroborate or refute the statements of complainants, suspects, and witnesses. Having quality photographic documentation of these puzzle pieces makes the job of an investigator and/or prosecutor much easier.

Rods, Strings, and Lasers

Crime scene photography is not only about the documentation of evidence and crime scenes, but quality photographs can also assist with the reconstruction of crime scenes

Figure 9.14 Trajectory rods provide the jury with good demonstrative pieces of photographic evidence. This figure shows a vehicle peppered with multiple bullet strikes. The rods provide an excellent resource for prosecutors to prove the defendant *knowingly and intelligently* attempted to cause serious bodily injury or death.

and be used as demonstrative pieces of evidence for court. Investigators documenting the scene of a shooting incident can go one step beyond just simply documenting the scene of a crime—they can actually photograph the approximate flight paths of fired projectiles. Even if the photographer does not understand tangent and sine trigonometric functions, he or she can still thoroughly document the scene of a shooting so that a clear *picture* of the transpired events is obtained. More specifically, the use of trajectory rods, strings, and lasers can reproduce the approximate flight paths of fired bullets (Figure 9.14). This form of ballistic evidence, the time between when a bullet departs the barrel and when it impacts a surface, is commonly referred to as external ballistics. Reproducing the flight paths of fired bullets creates an intriguing piece of demonstrative evidence, in addition to providing information for those who need to reconstruct a crime scene from photographs.

Trajectory Rods

Trajectory rods provide a graphical representation of a fired projectile's penetration into a surface. Trajectory rods may be purchased commercially from a number of crime scene supply companies or made much more cheaply from inexpensive products that can be purchased at any home improvement store. Trajectory rods are easily created by painting fiberglass or wooden dowel rods with fluorescent paint. Fluorescent paint stands out in the photographs and the paint can be chosen from any number of different colors, including fluorescent orange, yellow, and green. Additionally, the dowel rods can be purchased in several diameters to correspond with the different calibers of bullets.

In addition to trajectory rods, an angle finder and a *zero-edge* protractor will assist photographers in correctly documenting an impact site (Figures 9.15 and 9.16). Angle finders

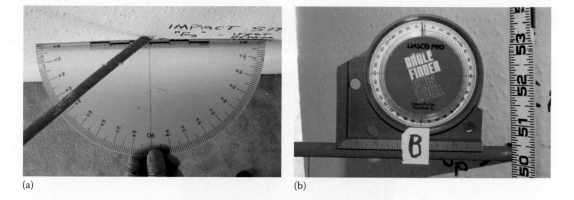

(a)   (b)

Figure 9.15 (a) shows how a forensic protractor and a trajectory rod combine to create an accurate recording of the horizontal impact angle of a fired projectile. The key to an accurate measurement is to use a zero-edge protractor and align the 90° line of the protractor with the bullet hole's center. (b) shows how the vertical angle of a bullet strike can be recorded by attaching an angle finder to the top edge of the trajectory rod. The keys to a quality and valuable photograph include a well-focused and legible angle reading and an identification of the impact site.

can also be purchased at the neighborhood home improvement store and come in two basic forms. One is a simple gravity-controlled pendulum style of angle finder. It is suggested that the angle finder have a *V-grooved* base so that it will rest securely on a trajectory rod as the rod extends from a wall or other impacted surface. Another style of angle finder is a digital version. These are a little more expensive and require batteries but will provide a more accurate reading because they provide more specific angle determinations.

Angle finders are used to determine the vertical impact angle of a projectile that struck a surface. Protractors are most often used to measure the horizontal impact angle, but they can measure both vertical and horizontal angles of impact. Protractors must have a *zero edge* to be useful as a crime scene investigation tool. *Zero edge* means that the zero degree (0°) line will rest flat across the surface that the protractor rests upon. Most protractors found at office supply stores are built for a student's schoolwork and will have a bottom edge that rests below the 0° line. Consequently, the purchase of a 90° and/or a 180° forensic protractor is more adaptable to the crime scene investigator's needs.

One final item that is beneficial for use with trajectory rods is a plumb bob. Although a plumb bob might seem to be a strange tool to carry in a photography kit, it is an alternative to an angle finder and may come in handy when photographing and determining vertical impact angles. This is especially true for those photographs when the trajectory rod cannot support the weight of an angle finder or the location of the impact site prohibits the use of an angle finder. A weighted string (plumb bob) serves as an excellent alternative in these situations (Figure 9.16). There are commercially sold plumb bobs, but something as simple as a hefty fishing weight can be tied to a string and used. The weighted string can be mounted above the trajectory rod and a short distance away from the impacted surface. Once the securely mounted string stops moving, it will provide a perfect vertical line from which to calculate the angle of impact. The intersection between the trajectory rod and string must be photographed in a perpendicular alignment. The printed photograph can then be used to calculate the angle of impact by overlaying a clear plastic protractor on

Figure 9.16 When the use of an angle finder is impractical or the natural weight of the tool causes the trajectory rod to misalign itself, a string and plumb bob can work as a substitute. A weighted string can be mounted above the impact site and the trajectory rod. The intersecting string and trajectory rod can be photographed at a perpendicular angle, and the resulting photograph can then be used to determine the angle of impact. A small clear plastic protractor can be laid across the image and the angle of impact determined from the straight lines created by the trajectory rod and string. The angle of impact shown in this photo is approximately 5° downward.

the visible angle between the trajectory rod and the free-hanging string (plumb line) seen in the picture. The photograph does not have to be printed in a one-to-one relationship to allow accurate calculations of angles from photographic evidence. Enlargements will have the same ratio as the captured image, and therefore the determined angles of impact can be trusted.

Probing bullet impact sites with trajectory rods is most accurate when there is a pair of aligned holes through which to securely position the trajectory rod. Fortunately, fired bullets have a tendency to penetrate multiple surfaces such as the drywall on either side of a wall's wood framing or the exterior and interior sides of a car door. When there is only one impacted surface and a trajectory rod cannot remain securely or snugly in the opening, although not nearly as effective, a little plumber's putty can be used to solidify the trajectory rod's alignment within the center of the impact site. Plumber's putty can be purchased at any home improvement store for just a few dollars and is reusable. One small jar of the putty is more than enough to fulfill the needs of a crime scene investigator for a multitude of scenes. In addition, the putty is an excellent adhesive to use for attaching scales to vertical surfaces during other photographic endeavors. Instead of plumber's putty, most trajectory kits sold by crime scene supply companies come with *centering* or *forcing* cones that help stabilize and find the center of impact sites so that the angle of impact can be more accurately determined.

The angle at which the trajectory rod is positioned and photographed must not be fabricated simply to create a compelling photograph. If the approximate angle of impact cannot be determined by mathematical calculations or by a well-formed impact site, then a photograph should not be recorded showing false angles of impact. Crime scene investigators are not in the business of creating evidence, but rather are tasked with accurately documenting and recovering the physical evidence found at the crime scene. The impact site can still be photographed, just not with any unsupported or inaccurate angle determinations.

Prior to photographing the specific angles of impact using trajectory rods, it is recommended that the photographer capture a well-composed overall image of the surface and trajectory rods, especially if there are multiple impact sites. These overall images should be recorded from different perspectives, especially when the rods jut out in different directions and/or from different surfaces. Remember that smaller apertures will help ensure a better depth of field and if the image is being recorded in the nighttime, an available light photograph should be taken rather than rely on a synchronized flash exposure. Flash compositions are fine for smaller compositions or subjects that are within the same focal plane, but larger or broader compositions will likely benefit from timed exposures versus flash exposures.

Once the scene's overall images are recorded, the more specific and individual photographs can be captured. For well-defined bullet holes, up to six measurements can be recorded. Not every one of these measurements can be ascertained from each and every bullet strike. However, if possible, the following six measurements should be recorded in addition to any photographic documentation:

- Length of bullet hole
- Width of bullet hole
- Vertical height of bullet hole from the floor or ground or triangulation measurement #1
- Horizontal distance along the impacted surface or triangulation measurement #2
- Vertical angle of impact
- Horizontal angle of impact

Photographing the latter two measurements is completed with the use of trajectory rods. As previously stated, the photographic documentation of horizontal impact angles is easily accomplished by placing a zero-edge protractor adjacent to the trajectory rod and aligning the 90° line to the center of the bullet hole. As the trajectory rod extends outward and away from the impacted surface, the circular edge of the protractor where the trajectory rod intersects can be photographed, and the horizontal impact angle will be permanently documented. The bullet hole being photographed should be labeled in the photograph so that it is not mistaken for another similarly appearing impact site. An additional piece of information that can be beneficial is an orientation marker. For example, placing a small arrow indicating north or pointing toward a feature of the environment, such as *front door*, *kitchen*, or *main avenue*, is always a recommendation. The more information included in the photograph, the better.

Once again the trajectory rod can be combined with an angle finder to show the vertical impact angle of a fired projectile (Figure 9.17). Some angle finders are larger than others, and some have a heavy magnetic base that may cause the trajectory rod to flex or bend resulting in an inaccurate angle measurement. To avoid this, investigators should select an angle finder that has a nice balance between visibility and weight. If the weight of the angle

Figure 9.17 Handwritten notes of all scene measurements are important. However, documenting these angles and measurements through photography can be of great assistance during any reconstruction efforts and courtroom testimony.

finder does cause the trajectory rod to bend downward, there would be nothing wrong with holding the rod in a more natural and accurate alignment so that a photograph can be captured. Remember that the photograph's composition should include a legible angle reading and an identification of the projectile strike being examined.

Strings

Trajectory rods can only reach so far in their ability to recreate the flight paths of fired projectiles. However, colored string, purchased from crime scene supply companies or home improvement stores, can be used to recreate longer distances between a shooter and their target. Any product that bears the word *forensic* automatically carries an exponential price increase. Therefore, money can be saved by purchasing colored strings at the hardware store. A variety of colored strings should be kept so that the investigator has options. The choice of colors will be based on the background color. Creating as much contrast as possible is important. A photographer would not want to use a green-colored string, even fluorescent green, when the background is a grass-covered knoll. In addition, different colored strings can represent different shooters or different firing positions of a single shooter. Similar to trajectory rods, fluorescent colors are most effective because they are more visible in the recordings. The surveyor strings that are wound around a revolving drum are also useful because they are easier to unwind and rewind after the reconstruction is complete. Some forensic supply companies offer an elastic type of trajectory string, as well as reflective string. Both of these products are quite valuable and if an investigator can afford the added expense, they are worth consideration. As another way to make the thin string more visible is to photograph the strings with the camera aligned with or parallel to the string (Figure 9.18).

An investigator should also have a supply of thumbtacks, which he or she can use to anchor the strings onto the end of a trajectory rod or impacted surface. If the reconstruction encompasses a greater distance, the photographer can use a staple gun to secure the strings. Staple guns are better for securing strings that will be pulled with more force

(a)   (b)

Figure 9.18 Fluorescent-colored strings are an excellent tool for representing the paths of fired bullets over an extended distance. Stringing reconstructions should be photographed from multiple angles in order to ensure the best possible end result. In these photographs of the same reconstruction, one (a) shows the strings from a parallel orientation and the other (b) shows the strings from a perpendicular orientation.

because they are extended over greater distances. A final way to anchor a string into a bullet hole is to tie the string onto a thin, but sturdy, wire and slide the wire through the bullet hole. When the string is pulled taut, the length of the wire will lay flat across the back of the perforation and create a solid point from which to pull the string taut. Cutting up 2″–3″ sections of a wire coat hanger creates excellent anchors for trajectory lines. Anything can be used to anchor the string. A writing pen might be convenient because it is readily available, but being prepared for such needs is more beneficial.

With the string anchored at one end, the final piece of the puzzle to determine is where the fired shot originated. Witness statements or physical evidence found at the crime scene can help determine the shooter's position. Once determined, investigators can have a partner or an officer represent the shooter's position and pull on the *dummy end* of the anchored string. The representation of fired bullets traveling across hallways or through a vehicle is simply accomplished by having the string pulled straight over the expanse between the two impacted surfaces, and a stand-in for the shooter is not required. Once the trajectory strings are in place and pulled tight, either by a person pulling the strings taut or by having them anchored between two impact sites, the photograph can now be recorded.

Photographing a stringing reconstruction from the side provides an excellent representation of the flight path of a fired projectile. However, trajectory strings are small and narrow. As a result, sometimes the strings are lost in the background of an image, especially in outdoor environments. For this reason, it is important to record photographs from multiple perspectives. When the background overwhelms the colored strings, recording the

Figure 9.19 Flagging tape offers another alternative for those needing to photograph longer trajectories from a perpendicular perspective. The surface area of the tape is broader than string and consequently is more visible in the recorded photograph.

image so that the string extends along the camera's line of sight will increase the intensity and visibility of the string in the final image. The photograph can be captured either from the shooter's position or from the target's perspective. Photographing a strung trajectory from a parallel point of view also helps conceal *string droop*, which is caused by gravity and the natural weight of the string. When string is extended over a long distance, it will curve or droop downward because of gravity. The resulting photograph can be more misleading than enlightening.

A change of perspective may enhance the string's intensity, but the photographer can also use flagging tape (Figure 9.19). Flagging tape is used by surveyors and construction workers to *flag* or mark items of importance. Flagging tape offers an advantage because it has a broader surface than surveyor's string and is more visible in photographs. It can be purchased at home improvement stores and a couple of 100 ft costs just a few dollars. Unfortunately, because flagging tape is made from a stretchable plastic, it is more difficult to pull tight, especially over longer distances. In addition, the stretching effect of flagging tape has a tendency to continue due to the tape's natural weight. Consequently, once the tape is pulled taut, the photograph should be quickly recorded. Another drawback is that the flagging tape's broader surface makes the tape more susceptible to wind. Even a light breeze can cause the tape to move during an exposure. In low-light conditions, this can actually make the tape disappear completely from an exposure, or at best, create a blurry line through the photograph. However, on calm days, flagging tape offers the crime scene investigator another option to make the approximate flight path of a bullet more visible.

Lasers

The effects of gravity and wind can be overcome by using lasers to represent the approximate flight paths of fired bullets. Lasers can be photographed with a little additional effort and patience, and the results will be much more vivid than with surveyor's string or flagging tape. In addition, a laser beam can span hundreds of feet and still provide as straight a trajectory line as if a string were stretched across the width of a hallway. Juries expect and believe that crime scene investigators have the latest and greatest technologies available at their disposal. Investigators and photographers must address and meet this *CSI (Crime Scene Investigator) Effect*, which is easily accomplished with a few impressive laser trajectory photographs. The tools needed to create effective pieces of demonstrative evidence can be purchased for much less than might be expected, and yet the results can be stellar.

As with everything else in a crime scene investigator's arsenal, forensic supply companies sell shooting reconstruction kits and laser trajectory kits. These kits cost up to several hundred dollars and are excellent tools for determining and calculating angles of impact, but the lasers provided with the kits are often powered by small, watch-style batteries. Even with brand new batteries, the power of the lasers is quite low and can only be recorded in very low-light conditions. However, most crime scenes will have some ambient lighting that will cause difficulty in capturing the laser's beam in the photograph. Therefore, it is suggested that a slightly more powerful laser be purchased at a hardware or home improvement store.

Inexpensive lasers can yield a quality photographic image in nighttime and/or low-light conditions. Class IIIA lasers have less than 5 mW of power and include the typical laser pointers used for teaching and laser levels used in construction. The lasers powered by AA or AAA batteries are best, because the beam will be more intense and last much longer than those powered by small watch batteries. Laser pointers found at hardware stores have two additional advantages over the handheld lasers used by instructors. *Torpedo* or laser levels found at the home improvement stores typically have a tripod mount. The threaded-screw hole can be attached to a photographer's tripod. Speaking of tripods, investigators will need two tripods to complete a laser trajectory photograph: one for the camera and one for the laser. The second benefit offered by a carpenter's style laser is that it should have an on–off switch. The on–off switch helps conserve battery power and is a useful feature when multiple trajectories are photographed. Laser pointers designed for teaching and shaped like writing pens can be used, but a homemade housing must be built to hold the laser pen steady during the exposure (Figure 9.20). As will be described, the laser must not move during the exposure or the result will be anything but useful. Homemade housings

Figure 9.20 This photo demonstrates one possible design for a laser pen holder that was adapted for use as a crime scene trajectory laser. Any custom design will work, as long as it allows the device to be mounted to a tripod and allows for the pen's *on* switch to be held down during an exposure.

can be made in several ways. However, follow the steps listed here to construct a very practical laser pen holder, with a tripod mount and on–off switch:

- Start with a block of wood, approximately 4″ × 8″ × 1″ (or one that accommodates the size of the laser pen).
- Drill a ¾″ diameter hole through the length of wood and equal to the length of the laser pen minus about ½″.
- On the bottom of the block of wood, *hammer* in a ¼″ nut for the tripod mounting screw (a small amount of wood glue can be added to secure the nut in place). This will serve as the mounting nut for the tripod.
- Measure the distance between the rear of the laser pen and the *on* button.
- Measure from the back of the previously drilled ¾″ hole and drill a vertical hole completely through the top of the wood block so that it intersects the interior drilled tube.
- Secure a nut (hammer in the nut) with a threaded bolt into this top hole, and this will act as an on–off switch by screwing the bolt down onto the laser pen's on–off switch.
  - To turn off the laser or remove the laser, one simply has to unscrew the bolt.

Investigators will need one more item to make the laser visible to the camera, and that is something to reflect the laser's beam back to the camera. Class IIIa lasers are only visible when they come into contact with an object. They cannot show a visible beam of light without assistance. Crime scene supply companies sell *Photographic Fog* packaged in an aerosol dispenser can for nearly $20 per can. Considering that laser trajectory photographs are rarely captured on the first attempt, the $20 per can expense makes such a product cost prohibitive. Less expensive alternatives have been suggested, ranging from baby powder to cans of compressed air. Even if such a product costs just pennies, dispensing a huge cloud of fog and powder across a crime scene is ludicrous. The only piece of equipment an investigator needs is a scrap piece of paper. Those who wish to be a little more creative can make reflective cards (Figure 9.21). A solid white card, a black card with a smaller white center, and a black card framing a smaller section of translucent material, such as wax paper or a glassine material, can all be useful in shooting reconstructions. Although the use of these materials may be completely befuddling at this point, their uses will be perfectly clear by the end of this chapter.

Typically, laser trajectory photographs are limited to nighttime or low-light conditions. This fact has been a somewhat limiting factor in providing laser trajectory images to juries and investigators. However, daytime laser trajectory photographs can be recorded with the assistance of higher-powered lasers. Daytime laser photographs will be discussed later in this chapter. For now, the basic process of reconstructing shooting incidents with lasers will involve low-light and nighttime environments.

Whether it is daytime or nighttime, photographing laser trajectories is a rewarding experience. In addition to being fun, it is a way to amaze and impress the viewers of these images. A small laser level's beam is merely a small red dot in space. The recording of a laser's beam of light is similar to the photography of a fireworks display (Figure 9.22). A photographer does not set out to photograph a fireworks display by handholding the camera and taking a 1/60 of a second exposure and expect to capture the brilliance and

Figure 9.21 Pictured here are three reflective cards that are useful with different types of lasers and under different ambient lighting conditions. The reflector on the far right has a hole cut into the middle of two pieces of black card stock. Sandwiched between the two cards is wax paper. When the laser's beam strikes the wax paper, the beam of light can be photographed from the front of the laser instead of from behind. The other two reflecting cards are black and white cards, which can be used in different lighting conditions. Although having a variety of reflecting cards available is advantageous, all an investigator needs is a scrap piece of white notebook paper to fulfill the need for a reflective surface.

Figure 9.22 Photographing a shooting reconstruction by lasers is similar to photographing a fireworks display. Recording the light produced by a firework's rocket is accomplished through a time exposure. The time exposure records the entire flight of the rocket as if it occurred in a single moment in time. This photo was recorded at ISO 400, f/19, for 2 s.

magnitude of a rocket's full burst of light. Photographing a fireworks display requires a tripod-mounted camera and a timed-exposure recording, typically, over the course of several seconds depending on the intensity of the display. Capturing a beam of light from a laser is exactly the same. The laser may produce only a bright dot of light on the target, but by reflecting that one dot throughout the entire length of the beam, an entire beam or line

Figure 9.23 Light is additive. Photographers need to imagine the end result or the *big picture*, not just the individual segments that make up a photographic image. This photo is of an instantaneous appearing image that was created letter by letter over time. The exposure was recorded at ISO 100, f/20, for 25 s, and the words were created by spelling out the letters with a laser pointer. (Photographed by Daniel Nunez, Crime Scene Investigator, Houston Police Department, Houston, TX.)

of light will become visible in the recorded image. Light is additive and adding all those dots of light during a timed exposure will create the desired line of trajectory.

Similar to painting a crime scene with light, the *big picture* must be envisioned by the crime scene photographer, not just the incremental steps that create the final image. Light is additive on film or digital media (Figure 9.23). Consequently, any light seen by the camera at any point during the exposure will be visible in the photograph. Obviously, the more intense the illumination source, the more intense that particular light source will be in the recorded photograph. If the light does not move, the size of the light will grow larger and brighter in the image. If the light moves through the image, it will cause a streak to develop within the image. For example, if a car drives through a nighttime crime scene with its headlights on, streaks of light will appear through the image. Photographing a laser is quite similar, but instead of the light source moving through the crime scene, a reflecting card is moved through the scene.

Before starting the photographic process, an investigator must locate the point of impact and the approximate position of the shooter at the time the weapon was fired. The shooter's position can be established by witness statements or mathematical calculations based on the impact site. Either way, once the approximate position of the shooter is determined, the laser can be positioned in the appropriate spot. If the laser is attached to a tripod, the height of the tripod can be fine-tuned to meet the approximate height of the shooter. In addition, tripods have multidirectional adjustments. Consequently, once the laser is turned on, its projected light can be positioned directly onto or into the impact site. Once the laser is positioned, the camera needs to be positioned. The camera can be positioned almost anywhere the photographer desires. However, in regard to the laser beam's light, the background must be taken into consideration. The laser produces a light that is to be made visible in the picture, and that light can be absorbed or overpowered by a background that is too bright or by other distracting light sources. In addition, when a laser is photographed from a perpendicular orientation, the beam will not be as vivid as a beam that is photographed from the

(a)   (b)

Figure 9.24 The exact position of the camera in relation to the approximate flight path of the fired bullet represented by the laser is a decision best made by the photographer based on the environment. If all variables are equal, the intensity of a laser beam photographed from a parallel orientation will be more intense than recorded from a perpendicular orientation. However, the photography of a laser beam from a perpendicular orientation can be improved by a slower tracking of the laser beam, thus giving the light more time to record on film. Here, (a) was recorded at ISO 100, f/22, for 132 s, while (b) was recorded at ISO 400, f/5.6, for 13 s.

same perspective (parallel) as the laser travels. This is the same philosophy as an investigator who is photographing stringing trajectories.

A laser beam photographed from directly behind or directly in front of the laser will produce a much denser line or beam of light in the captured photograph (Figure 9.24). The beam of light records by overlapping itself and therefore is more vivid or dense in the recorded photograph. In contrast, photographing a laser's light from a perpendicular perspective may not be as intense because the particles of light are more spread out and therefore diffused. When the nighttime environment leans toward brighter conditions due to ambient lighting, a more intense beam of light will be needed and can be recorded if the camera is positioned with the laser's beam traveling in the same direction as the camera is pointed; this will offset the bright ambient light. Slowing the speed of tracking or tracing of the laser may also help improve the beam's intensity. *Tracking* the beam is the way in which the laser's beam is recorded and will be described in greater detail in the following.

Now that the camera and laser are positioned, the next step is to determine a starting point for the exposure. Time is on the side of the photographer and an ISO 100 setting is suggested because it will give the investigator more time to complete the reconstruction. Higher ISO values can be chosen. It all depends on the amount of ambient light present in the composition. The investigator next estimates the length of the exposure and matches the shutter speed with the approximate amount of time believed necessary to track the laser beam. The tracking time is the time necessary to slowly, but steadily, walk between the shooter's position and the target and then return. The investigator will be walking with the reflecting card through the composition at this time, thereby creating a line of light or reconstructing a bullet's flight path. This estimation will provide the time or shutter speed value for the exposure equation. The aperture can then be selected with the help of the camera's light meter and based upon the ambient lighting conditions. For example, the investigator believes it will take approximately 30 s to track a particular trajectory. Setting the camera with an ISO value of 100 and a shutter speed of 30 s will allow the camera to determine the third exposure value, the aperture. Most cameras stop metering light at 30 s, and if additional time is required to complete the reconstruction, then investigators will have to use reciprocity and adjust the exposure values to determine the appropriate final settings. Remembering how difficult it is to overexpose when shooting photos at night, photographers should not be overly concerned about overexposing the image as long as harsh light sources are removed from the image's composition. For example, assume that a particular image requires approximately 2 min to complete the trajectory's tracking and the camera shows that a proper exposure of f/11 at 30 s will provide a balanced exposure. Because 30 s is two stops less than 2 min, an increase of two stops of light can be offset by the decrease of two stops of light in the aperture. Therefore, moving the aperture from f/11 to f/22 and a 2 min shutter speed should provide a similar exposure. A one-stop *overexposure* would be equal to a 4 min exposure. As one can imagine, a one-stop overexposure at night leaves plenty of room for error. As repeatedly mentioned, bracketing of the exposures will also ensure that a quality image is recorded.

When completing laser trajectories, the camera's shutter dial should be set to the *bulb* setting, even if the exposure is expected to be less than 30 s. The camera must be allowed to record the entire length of the laser's beam and not unintentionally be turned off before the beam's recording is finished. It is alright if the length of the exposure is a little longer than the amount of time needed to track the laser beam. One just does not want to come up short and record only a partial trajectory. Therefore, a general assessment of the camera's settings will include an ISO 100, a bulb setting for the shutter speed, and an aperture size determined by the camera and based upon the ambient lighting conditions. Typically, the aperture will tend to be toward a smaller opening due to the longer exposure times associated with laser trajectory photographs.

The term *tracking* has been referred to several times in this chapter, but has not yet been fully explained. Basically, the recording of a laser beam is completed by *tracking* or walking along the length of the projected laser beam with a reflective card. The card is not necessarily reflective like a mirror, but just a light-colored surface that causes the dot projected by the laser device to be clearly visible to the camera. The card needs to be angled back toward the camera so that the laser's dot is visible to the camera. This may be a little more difficult for a camera aligned perpendicular to the trajectory. However, it is possible; it just means the investigator must take more care when illuminating the beam so that it does not develop any breaks as it is drawn into the photograph. The physical presence of the photographer should not be visible in the final recorded photograph, because the individual is not illuminated. Additionally, because the photographer is moving throughout the exposure and not stationary for an extended period of time, his or her presence is not likely to be visible in the recorded image. The same theory applies to painting with light, when the photographer must walk through the scene to add flash illumination to various subjects. If visibility of the investigator is an issue, wearing dark clothing will help prevent the visibility of the person.

The individual walking the card through the length of the laser beam must be careful not to place his or her body between the camera and the laser beam, thereby shielding or preventing the camera from recording the beam's light. The actual pace as the investigator walks along the bullet's recreated flight path depends on the power of the laser being used. A typical Class IIIa/5 mW laser can be thoroughly recorded with a steady, smooth walking pace. The investigator does not have to walk heel to toe as if performing a DWI sobriety test, but should not race to complete the trajectory's path either. Taking small strides of about 12″ in length is a way to maintain a smooth, consistent line throughout the length of the trajectory. It is also important to remember that if the photograph is recorded from a side angle, the pace should be slightly slower. This is because the beam's light is not being recorded over itself as when it is photographed from a parallel perspective. Each purchased laser will have different intensities and therefore should be experimented with prior to using the laser on an actual crime scene. Investigators should practice tracking lasers with their personal equipment so that they will have an idea of the best pace that results in the best image.

A sharper or more intense laser beam can be recorded if the tracking of the beam is done in both directions—from point of origination to point of impact and back. This will also help conceal any holes in the illuminated laser's line that may have occurred because the beam fell away from the reflecting card for a step or two. As a result, when estimating the length of one's exposure, the time needed to walk up and back must be factored into the equation. In addition, the photographer should be aware that if the laser beam is left visible for too long on the impact site or at any single point, a large ball of light may form on the image and be very distracting to the overall composition. The recorded beam itself will be straight regardless of how much the reflecting card is bounced around during tracking (Figure 9.25). This occurs because the light's actual beam is stationary. The reflecting surface is moving, but to the camera, the line of trajectory is stationary. Furthermore, the reflecting surface should not be visible in the final image, and so there will be no visible movement in the photograph.

If in the course of tracking the beam, the laser's projected dot falls away from the reflecting card, an investigator can simply back up a short distance before the beam's light was lost and reengage the laser, continuing the tracking process. This action will ensure that there are no unwanted breaks in the recorded beam of light. At worst, there might be a slightly visible increase in the beam's intensity where it was tracked over a second time. However, the increase in intensity is more desirable than having a gap in the recorded line of trajectory. As a review, the following steps should help investigators create excellent results with laser trajectory photographs:

- Position laser to simulate the flight path of a fired projectile.
- Position camera so that the laser's beam is fully within the camera's view and that harsh or distracting light sources are not included in the photograph (as best possible).
- Set camera to ISO 100 unless the scene is extraordinarily dark.
- Estimate length of time investigator expects it will take to walk the length of the laser's beam twice (once up and once back).
- With a time value estimated and an ISO value selected, the camera can select an appropriate aperture value.

Figure 9.25 A laser trajectory photograph, shown here, can be an outstanding piece of demonstrative evidence, as well as graphically representing the flight paths of fired bullets. This exposure was recorded with the following camera settings: ISO 100, at f/16, for 126 s. The more powerful green lasers were allowed to burn into the image for approximately 15 s each, while the two red lasers were tracked with a reflecting card in order to become visible in the photograph.

- Begin trajectory exposure:
  - Turn laser on.
  - Start exposure (turn camera on).
  - Place the reflecting card on the beam of light, and angle the reflected dot back toward the camera.
  - Begin walking between the two points (position of shooter and impacted surface)
  - Return back to starting point and turn off laser.
  - Stop exposure (turn off camera) or allow timed exposure to complete on its own.
- Complete reconstruction photograph and record a series of bracketed exposures by changing the size of the aperture or adjusting the length of the exposure.

For laser trajectory exposures estimated to last longer than 30 s, reciprocity calculations are the solution for the camera's inability to meter light past 30 s. As an example, observe the following composition's dilemma:

- Time estimation of a multiple-shot trajectory will be approximately 4 min of total time.
- ISO set to 100, shutter speed set to 30 s, and an aperture of f/8 is chosen by the camera as an accurate metering of the scene's ambient light.
- A 4 min exposure is three stops of light more than the 30 s chosen by the camera.
  - 30–60–120–240 s (4 min total time)

- Moving the aperture an equal number of stops (–3 stops of light) from f/8–f/22.
  - f/8–f/11–f/16–f/22
- Exposure values are equal:
  - ISO 100, f/8, for 30 s
  - ISO 100, f/22, for 4 min
- Photograph can now be recorded:
  - If tracking lasers ends sooner, allow the camera to complete the exposure of 4 min.
  - If exposure lasts longer than 4 min, simply keep tracking the lasers. Remember an 8 min exposure is only one stop more light than calculated.

A few problems can arise during laser trajectory photography. As stated earlier, light is additive on film. Therefore, if an investigator is carrying a visible radio or cellular telephone that has an illuminated feature, that feature will streak through the exposure. Photographers must also ensure that no unnecessary lights are visible during the exposure, such as a police vehicle's strobe lights. Some nighttime crime scenes have areas of increased light intensity from streetlights or some other illuminating light source. If the person tracking the beam's light is wearing a light-colored uniform, the individual should consider covering his or her uniform with a dark-colored jacket. Dark-colored clothing is less reflective and will help prevent the person tracking the laser from being visible in the recorded photograph.

One of the benefits of photographing crime scenes with digital cameras is the ability to instantly examine the image for lighting and composition. If any ghosting occurs or an unintentional reflection becomes visible in the image, the easiest solution is to close down the aperture and, if necessary, extend the length of the exposure in order to compensate for the smaller aperture (Figure 9.26). In addition, if the photographer can identify the object that is causing the ghosting presence, the photographer should try to cover or otherwise conceal the object. Sometimes the card used to reflect the laser beam causes a halo or ghost to appear along the edges of the laser's recorded beam of light. When this occurs, closing down the aperture might help, but also using a black reflecting card with a small white circle in the

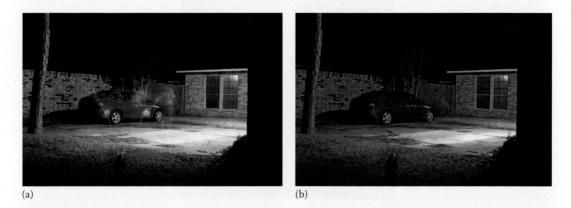

(a)   (b)

Figure 9.26 If an object creates a ghosting presence in a photograph, whether it is the individual tracking the laser's beam or the reflective card itself, the easiest correction is to close down the aperture to a smaller size and/or conceal the particular object creating the ghost impression. (a) was recorded at ISO 100, f/16, for 53 s. (b) shows the corrected image by closing down the aperture and was recorded at ISO 100, f/29, for 112 s.

center will help eliminate or at least minimize the ghosting or halo effect. The individual tracking the laser beam may have to walk more slowly to ensure the laser beam remains in the white center of the reflecting card, but the results are well worth the extra effort.

Reflecting cards can be made in a number of forms for different lighting conditions and different strength lasers. One useful reflecting card is made by taking two pieces of black foam core or poster board and cutting a 3″ or 4″ diameter hole in the middle. The 3″–4″ center of this frame can be covered with wax paper or other translucent material. This new card is not designed to reflect the laser beam, but to cause the beam to become visible along its projection line, which will then allow the camera to be positioned looking toward the actual laser itself. In other words, the laser will be aimed toward the camera, and the photograph will illustrate the trajectory from the target's point of view. Tracking of a laser beam from this unique perspective occurs in the same fashion as if the light were reflected back toward the camera. The laser's beam will strike the translucent material and become visible on the opposite side and therefore visible to the camera. This particular point of view or perspective can be used to show what a victim or complainant observed at the time of a shooting (Figure 9.27).

A majority of shooting incidents involve more than just one shot fired. Multiple trajectories can be photographed in the same image for a piece of demonstrative evidence that will definitely create a lasting impression with the viewer. Recording multiple trajectories in a single photograph requires neither multiple tripods nor additional laser devices. An investigator needs only one laser, but they will need additional time to complete the tracking of additional trajectories. Once again, it is difficult to overexpose nighttime

Figure 9.27 In order to take a photograph from a target's point of view, the standard reflecting card cannot be utilized. Creating a frame with the interior of the frame filled with a translucent material such as wax paper will allow the tracking of the laser beam to occur just as before but will allow the photograph to be captured from the unique perspective of the victim. This photo was recorded at ISO 100, f/25, for 20 s.

photographs, and reciprocity failure (film) allows photographers to capture photographs that require several minutes to record. Even digital cameras have a bit more flexibility during nighttime exposures. Simply be observant of harsh or point light sources, and try and keep them out of the image's composition.

The setup for a multiple-trajectory photograph is orchestrated like a single-trajectory image. The ISO is set to 100, the expected time of tracking all the trajectories is estimated, and an appropriate aperture is selected based on the ambient light conditions. Nothing has changed except that the time estimation has increased. Therefore, some reciprocity calculations will likely be required of the photographer. Bear in mind that a single stop of light is one-half or twice the amount of light added or subtracted from an exposure. Therefore, a photograph calculated to take 2–3 min to complete the exposure will only be a single stop *overexposed* by recording an image of 4–6 min in length. A single stop of light should not be detrimental to the overall composition of an image. However, photographers should do everything possible to keep any point or harsh light sources from being visible in the image. Positioning the camera to keep the physical sources of light from being directly visible will go a long way toward improving the overall appearance of the image.

Multiple trajectories may involve a shooter who remains in relatively the same position and discharges multiple shots or who discharges numerous shots from different firing positions. Consequently, prior planning will prevent any delays in recording the photograph. Investigators should have a solid idea in regard to each shooter's and target's positions within the composition. Having a *game plan* will help prevent any unnecessary delays during the image's actual recording process. Photographers should set up everything for the first trajectory just as described earlier. The next step is to go ahead and photograph the first trajectory.

Once the first trajectory is completed, the camera must not be allowed to continue recording the crime scene. If the camera is allowed to continue recording the scene, then as the laser is being aligned with the next impact site, the beam's light will be reflecting off other surfaces, and the resulting photograph will appear as if a kindergarten child scribbled across the photograph with a pen. There are two basic ways to stop the exposure while the laser is adjusted. One option is to use the camera's multiple exposure capability. Most film cameras are capable of recording two or more exposures on the same frame of film. Digital cameras are just beginning to possess this capability. Using the double exposure feature is the easiest solution because investigators are not rushed to set up for subsequent shots. For cameras that do not have the multiple exposure ability, the photographer can place a black opaque cloth over the lens while the laser is being adjusted to the next impact site. This will prevent light from entering and ruining the photograph. Do not use the plastic lens cover designed to protect the lens when not in use. The physical placement and removal of the lens cover could cause the camera to move ever so slightly, and a blurry exposure may result. One problem with this technique in digital cameras is the creation of *noise* artifacts in the image. Even though the camera cannot *see* the composition, it is still recording and longer exposures can cause these artifacts to develop in the image. Therefore, investigators should be swift in resetting the laser for subsequent trajectories.

Once a photographer has chosen a way to conceal the lens or stop the exposure, the laser can be adjusted to the next impact site, or the entire laser and tripod can be repositioned and adjusted for the next line of flight to be tracked. Once the laser has been positioned, the camera lens can be reopened, the laser turned on, and the next trajectory tracked. Having a partner in laser reconstructions has tremendous value, but is not required. However, the camera and laser adjustments are completed more efficiently when two investigators are working together. Always turn on the laser after the camera's exposure has begun, because the laser should not strike any one surface for a significantly longer period of time than another. If the laser is left striking the impact site or other surface for an extended period of time, that area or dot may mushroom into a large distracting ball of light. Depending on the strength of the laser and the size of the lens' aperture, this distracting increase in the size of the laser's light can occur in just a few seconds. The goal is to create a consistently sized line throughout the length of the trajectory.

Laser pointers come in different colors. They are available in red (650–655 nm), green (532 nm), and blue (470–473 nm). The blue lasers are typically cost prohibitive; however, green lasers have become much more affordable in recent years and are not that much more expensive than a quality red laser pointer. Most affordable green lasers are typically styled like laser pointers and do not have an on–off switch that will automatically remain depressed, much less possess a tripod mount. For these reasons, it will be necessary to build a laser holder as described earlier in this chapter. Having two or three different colored lasers can be especially beneficial when a particular crime scene involves more than one shooter. Each shooter can be represented by a different colored laser (Figure 9.28).

The inexpensive lasers used in low-light conditions typically have a 5 mW maximum power level and are considered Class IIIa lasers. Class IIIb lasers have power levels above 5 mW, and some of these lasers even have enough power to be used in daytime conditions. Laser pens and pointers with 20–30 mW of power can cost less than $40, while pointers with 80–100 mW may cost several hundred dollars for a single laser. There are a number of mail-order/Internet-based companies that sell the more powerful lasers for a number of applications, including astronomy (star pointers), tactical, and forensic purposes. The 20–30 mW lasers have enough power to work in brighter nighttime environments, but not enough to work in the daytime, especially on a cloudless day. However, lasers with at least an 80 mW rating can be photographed in the daytime, even on sunny days. Human eyes, as well as digital cameras, have a greater sensitivity to visible light in the green region. Consequently, green lasers are recorded much easier than red lasers, even red lasers that have an equivalent milliwatt rating.

When investigators have a choice between a 30 mW laser and an 80 mW laser, the decision must be based on its intended use (Figure 9.29). While processing nighttime crime scenes, the 80 mW lasers typically have enough power to be visible without having to track the laser through the composition. However, if the flight path of a fired projectile passes through a highly illuminated part of the crime scene, the beam's light could be overpowered by the ambient light, and the path of the laser may be lost from the photograph. As a result, it will be necessary to track the laser. Furthermore, if the tracking surface that the higher-power laser strikes is reflective or light in color, the resulting explosion of light at the impact site can be detrimental to the photograph. Unfortunately, lasers with a rating of 80 mW or more are actually more difficult to track because of their intensity. Consequently, when using more powerful lasers in low-light conditions, having a black-colored tracking card is a better choice to use. The card will absorb much of the light, but a nice, narrow line of light can still be recorded by the camera. Depending on the power of the laser, the photographer may wish to place a white center on the card to help the beam become more visible. Investigators need to practice with a particular laser after its purchase to learn which reflective materials provide the best results or simply if the laser is powerful enough to be visible without any tracking efforts. Typically, an untracked laser beam is best photographed with the camera aligned with the beam of light's flight path (the lens aimed in the direction of the beam's travel).

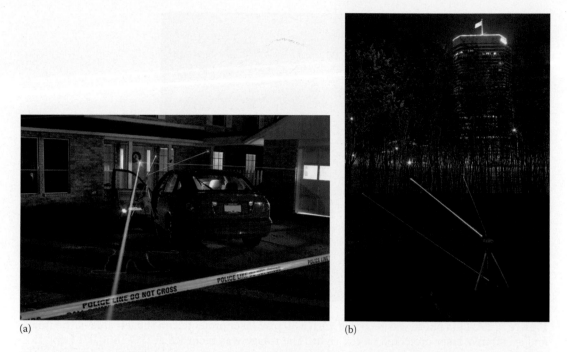

(a)   (b)

Figure 9.28 Multiple trajectories can be indicated by tracking multiple lasers in a single photograph. After one flight path is tracked across the composition, the camera lens can be covered by a black opaque cloth or a multiple exposure recorded through the camera's settings and the laser adjusted to match the next fired shot. The lens can then be reopened and the next laser tracked as necessary. (a) represents the firing of four shots from two firing positions and was recorded at ISO 100, f/8, for 252 s. The lens was covered with a black cloth between the trackings of the individual trajectories. (b) was recorded by combining three individual exposures using a *multiple exposure* feature (one for each trajectory) at ISO 400, f/8, for 10 s. In addition, three colored lasers were used: red, violet, and green.

Another detriment of the stronger lasers is their insatiable appetite for battery power. These lasers chew through fresh batteries at an alarming rate. As the battery power wanes, the beams become dimmer and tracking the beam becomes more necessary. When the power has diminished, the laser's beam can be recorded with a white reflecting card, similar to the recording of a Class IIIa laser. Furthermore, higher-powered lasers will heat up during use, and once they reach approximately 25°C, their intensity will start to fade. This can be problematic for those investigators working in warm environments. Although the stronger-powered lasers are great for photographing without needing to track the beam, occasionally beams recorded by tracking provide a better result than those that are not. Consequently, the less expensive 30 mW lasers still create just as good a photographic image, if not better, than the 80 mW lasers in lower-light conditions. Investigators may find it helpful to possess an assortment of lasers in order to meet the variety of environments faced during crime scene investigations.

Daytime Laser Reconstruction

One major advantage that a strong (80+ mW) green laser pointer possesses over the less expensive versions is that it can be utilized in the daytime. The Class IIIa red lasers commonly sold for forensic and carpentry work just do not have the power to be made visible

Figure 9.29 This photo was recorded with a 30 mW laser projected on the left side of the image and an 80 mW laser projected on the right. The image was recorded at ISO 1600, f/13, for 15 s. Both lasers were recorded without tracking. Observe the increased thickness or density of the 80 mW laser as compared to the 30 mW laser. There are occasions when using less powerful lasers is more effective. For this reason and because of the many different environments where crime scene investigators work, the investigator should possess an assortment of lasers.

during the daylight hours. However, a Class IIIb laser can be used to reconstruct shooting scenes in the daytime. In addition to the green laser pointer, photographers need a selection of neutral density (ND) filters. ND filters lessen the amount of light entering the camera. Basically, they help turn daytime into nighttime for investigators and provide the benefits offered by nighttime photography. ND filters are graded by how many stops of light they remove from an exposure. Examples of ND filters include

- ND.3 = one-stop reduction in light
- ND.6 = stop-stop reduction in light
- ND.9 = three-stop reduction in light

Possessing each of these filters will help photographers fine-tune the amount of light needing removal from a daytime exposure. Lighting conditions vary from scene to scene based upon the time of year, amount of cloud cover, and time of day. Therefore, having a set of variable-stop ND filters is advantageous. These filters can be stacked together, but combining more than two filters may cause a color shift and an overall softening in an image's focus. Consequently, one stronger or denser filter is recommended in order to take an extended time exposure during daylight hours. These more dense filters include, but are not limited to the following:

- ND 3.0 = 10-stop reduction in light (transmits 0.1% of light)
- ND 4.0 = 13⅔-stop reduction in light (transmits 0.01% of light)
- ND 6.0 = 20-stop reduction in light

Figure 9.30 This photo was recorded on a bright sunny day. An ND 3.0 filter (–10 stops of light) was attached to the camera's lens, and an 80 mW laser was used to represent the flight paths of the two fired bullets. The camera settings were ISO 100, f/29, for 73 s. The laser's beam was tracked with a reflecting card during the exposure.

For shooting reconstructions, the ND 3.0 filter is a good compromise, because it limits the amount of sunlight from entering the camera but still allows the laser to be visible (Figure 9.30).

ND filters and a powerful green laser combined allow for the photography of daytime trajectories. The recording of daytime lasers is similar to photographing nighttime trajectories. One difference that will be observed by photographers is the more common presence of ghosting in the recorded image. As a result, photographers with light skin and/or light-colored uniforms should consider covering themselves with dark-colored, but lightweight (in warmer weather) jackets so that light-colored or reflective surfaces are concealed.

In addition, the card used to reflect the laser's beam should be carefully selected. A full sheet of white notebook paper is likely to cause a long white halo around the laser beam to develop in the photograph. In order to prevent this halo/ghosting effect, a black piece of poster or foam core board can be used, and a 2″–3″ diameter white circle can be glued onto the center of the black reflecting board. The investigator will want to walk a little more slowly during daytime reconstructions in order to record a dense laser beam in the photograph. An added benefit to slowing the pace of tracking is that it will help investigators keep the laser point in the center of the reflecting card. Furthermore, when tracking the card up and down the laser's line of flight and when at all possible, the card should be tilted slightly downward so that a small shadow covers the reflecting portion (white circle) on the card. This will also help prevent the white halo from developing along the laser's beam. Tilting the card downward is designed to shade the reflecting surface from the sun.

Another hint to help prevent a ghostly appearance in the photograph is for the person tracking the laser beam to walk on one side of the beam as he or she tracks outward and then walk on the opposite side of the beam upon their return. Splitting the physical presence of the investigator at any one point in the composition will allow the background to burn into the image better and help eliminate any ghosting.

Although these powerful green lasers make trajectory photographs possible in the daytime, the photographer must still contend with the brilliance and intensity of sunlight.

Consequently, the best results are often obtained with the camera positioned behind the laser pointer. The camera can still be offset slightly to show more of the background or scene in the photograph. It does not have to be lined up directly over the laser, unless that particular perspective is desired. Photographing the laser's beam from this parallel position is similar to photographing colored strings or nighttime lasers; the beam's intensity and color will improve because the beam is building (recording) upon itself in the image. On cloudy days, a photographer might be able to get away with a perpendicular orientation to the bullet's flight, but it is important to record an image from the parallel perspective in order to guarantee a useful image.

In order to emphasize this technique, capturing daytime photographs of laser reconstructions is quite similar to nighttime endeavors. The one additional component is the addition of an ND filter (or two) to the end of the camera's lens. To begin the recording of a daytime composition, position the laser as normal, aligning the approximate shooter's position with the impact site, and decide on the best orientation of the camera to the path of the laser's beam. The camera should be focused and the 3.0 (–10 stops) ND filter attached to the camera lens. For daytime/sunny days, a 10-stop ND filter is a good starting point for the photographer (Figure 9.31). The photographer should have a firm grasp on the focus and zoom apparatus when screwing the filter onto the end of the lens, because he or she does not want the camera's focus to change while attaching the filter. If a camera has an autofocus lens, the autofocus feature can remain engaged while screwing on the filter. This will help lock the focus ring in place while the lens is being handled. However, it is important to turn off the autofocus feature before depressing the exposure button. Most likely, the camera will not be able to focus through the ND filter, and when the exposure button is pushed, the autofocus feature will force the photographer to start all over because the focus point may have been changed by the camera.

After the focus is set, the ND filter is attached, the shutter speed is set to bulb (time), and an aperture is chosen to correspond with the scene's lighting, the actual recording can begin. Selecting the appropriate aperture is similar to nighttime compositions. With the ISO value set to 100 and an estimation of time needed to take the picture, the camera can

Figure 9.31 This was recorded on a sunny day and the camera settings were ISO 400, f/18, for 52 s. An ND 3.0 was added to an ND.3 filter for a total of 13 stops of light removed from the composition. The advantage of using lasers as opposed to string and flagging tape is that lasers project a straight line and do not suffer from gravitational forces as the string and flagging tape do.

evaluate the ambient light and select or recommend an aperture. One may also find that a more accurate exposure can be determined by metering the ambient light without the ND filter attached. The next step would be to attach the ND filter to the camera's lens and subtract the matching number of stops of light from the exposure calculation. Here are some examples:

- Ambient daytime light exposure equals ISO 100, f/16, for 1/125th of a second (sunny f/16 rule).
- Place a –10-stop ND filter onto the camera's lens.
- Subtract 10 stops of light from the preceding daytime exposure.
  - 1/125–1/60–1/30–1/15–1/8–1/4–1/2–1″–2″–4″–8″
  - 10-stop change in light 1/125th of a second to 8″
- For added time, f/16 can be changed to f/32 (–2 stops of light).
  - f/16–f/22–f/32
- Add two stops of light to exposure with time (30 s).
  - 8″–15″–30″
- Final exposure is ISO 100, f/32, for 30 s.
  - Exposure is equal to ISO 100, f/16, for 1/125th of a second –10 stops of light.
- A one-stop *overexposure* of 60 s would not be detrimental to the image, but an additional ND filter would be a better choice for a much longer exposure.

For those using digital cameras, a photograph of the scene can be recorded at the selected setting and evaluated in the preview screen before actually tracking the beam. Once confident with a set of exposure values, start the exposure, turn on the laser, and begin tracking the beam slowly and smoothly across the crime scene.

After completing the tracking of the trajectory, turn off the laser, and stop the camera's exposure. The image can be reviewed in the digital camera for any possible adjustments to the aperture or tracking technique. For those photographers still using film cameras, bracket a series of exposures by changing the apertures. As mentioned previously, one should not change two or more variables at once when bracketing, because the best possible image may be passed over by too large of a jump in exposure values or variables.

Conclusion

The photographing of shooting incidents is much more than a point-and-shoot endeavor. Photographs from crime scenes involving the discharge of firearms are useful to investigators and prosecutors by helping them to understand the transpired events. Strong pieces of demonstrative evidence can be created for the jury by utilizing inexpensive tools purchased at the local hardware store. In order to create these quality images, photographers need to be comfortable photographing in the *Manual* mode because apertures and shutter speeds need to be specifically selected in order to achieve the intended results. Furthermore, manual reciprocity calculations must frequently be made. In regard to the crime scene itself, scene orientation, evidence establishing, and accurate perspective images are all vital for any subsequent attempt to reconstruct a crime scene based on the photographic evidence. In conclusion, crime scene photographers are required to slow down their documentation process, envision what the end product should be, and determine or calculate the best way to accomplish this goal. Furthermore, utilizing rods, strings, and lasers while photographing reconstruction efforts at the crime scene will give the crime scene investigator an opportunity to really shine and provide valuable as well as important pieces of demonstrative evidence to viewers. Investigators should strive to leave a lasting impression by recording accurate and informative photographic images of shooting incidents.

End of Chapter Questions

1. How should the camera's lens be oriented toward an impact site when a photograph is recorded?
    a. Perpendicular
    b. Perspective
    c. Parallel
    d. One-to-one

2. What is the goal when using colored filters (red, green, and blue) in photography?
    a. Improving the image's contrast
    b. Improving the image's exposure
    c. Decreasing the image's density
    d. Improving the image's color saturation

3. Gunpowder residues will always absorb light and will never fluoresce.
    a. True
    b. False

4. Which type of lighting works well to illuminate small impression evidence, such as a bullet's headstamp markings or a weapon's serial number?
    a. Ultraviolet lighting
    b. Infrared lighting
    c. Oblique lighting
    d. Reflective lighting

5. What is a disadvantage of utilizing trajectory rods when documenting shooting incidents?
    a. Trajectory rods are inexpensively created
    b. Trajectory rods cannot span great distances
    c. Trajectory rods are limited in their sizes and diameters
    d. Trajectory rods have limited applications in crime scene investigations

6. What is a disadvantage of utilizing trajectory strings when documenting shooting incidents?
    a. Gravity affects strings over greater distances
    b. Strings do not have the diameter size that trajectory rods have
    c. Strings come in only a limited number of colors
    d. Strings cannot be used over short distances

7. What is an advantage of utilizing lasers when documenting shooting incidents?
   a. With a little practice, photographing lasers is relatively easy
   b. Gravity and wind does not affect a laser's light
   c. Fulfill a jury's expectation to see quality laser photographs (*CSI Effect*)
   d. All of the above

8. Which alignment between the laser's light and the camera will provide the densest line of light?
   a. With the camera perpendicular to the line of light
   b. With the camera aimed along the line of light
   c. With the camera at a 45° to the line of light
   d. Any of the above

9. What is best used to make a laser's dot turn into a complete line of light or bullet's flight path?
   a. Atomized baby oil
   b. Baby powder
   c. Fog
   d. An index card

10. In laser reconstruction photography, the composition's exposure length is typically chosen to match what value?
    a. The distance of travel
    b. Aperture × ISO value
    c. Estimated time to walk along the laser's beam and back
    d. 30 s

11. A photographer examines the ambient light conditions of a particular composition and determines that an ISO 400, f/8, for 30 s would create an excellent photograph. However, the photographer anticipates that the time needed to complete the laser's trajectory is 2 min. What would be the proper exposure settings?
    a. ISO 100, f/8, for 2 min
    b. ISO 400, f/16, for 2 min
    c. ISO 400, f/11, for 2 min
    d. ISO 800, f/4, for 2 min

12. A photographer meters the ambient light of a nighttime crime scene and finds that an ISO 400, f/4, for 4 s creates a proper exposure. However, the photographer wishes to have the longest exposure possible, which combination of exposures would reciprocally equal?
    a. ISO 800, f/16, for 8 min
    b. ISO 400, f/2.8, for 2 min
    c. ISO 200, f/8, for 4 min
    d. ISO 100, f/22, for 8 min

13. During the course of completing a laser trajectory photograph, a ghosting image of the photographer walking through the composition appeared in the image. What can be done to remove the ghosting appearance from the composition?
    a. Close down the aperture to a smaller opening and lengthen the exposure's time
    b. Walk faster during the tracking of the laser's beam
    c. Use fog instead of using the tracking technique
    d. None of the above, one cannot remove the ghosts from appearing

14. It is possible to track multiple lasers or multiple flight paths of fired bullets in the same photographic image.
    a. True
    b. False

15. A photographer has calculated a proper exposure to be at ISO 100, f/16, for 2 min. After tracking the full length of the laser's beam, the photographer still has slightly over 30 s left on the exposure. What should the photographer do?
    a. Walk the laser's beam again until the time runs out
    b. Paint the scene with light with the remaining time
    c. Simply let the exposure time continue and turn off the camera at the 2 min mark
    d. Immediately turn off the camera when the tracking has been completed

16. What types of filters are beneficial when completing laser trajectories in brighter or daytime conditions?
    a. Infrared filters
    b. ND filters
    c. Compensating filters
    d. ALS filters

17. A photographer is recording a daytime laser photograph, and the daytime exposure was determined to be ISO 400, f/16, for 1/500th of a second. A −10-stop filter is attached to the camera. What are the new exposure settings?
    a. ISO 100, f/22, for 15 s
    b. ISO 200, f/16, for 30 s
    c. ISO 400, f/16, for 15 s
    d. ISO 800, f/22, for 30 s

Photography Assignments

Required Tools: Trajectory rods (dowel rods), colored surveyor's string, laser (inexpensive laser levels can be found at discount tool supply stores)

Photography Subjects: Bullets, cartridge cases, an object with an indented serial number (simulating a firearm's serial number)

  I. Photograph Ballistic Evidence
     A. Compose projectile in order to fill the frame, include an identification tag, and properly illuminate subject with quality lighting.

    B. Photograph a cartridge case's headstamp markings using the same techniques as the aforementioned (fill the frame, identify the evidence, and use proper lighting).

    C. Photograph a weapon's (or other item's) serial number.

II. Photograph Rods, Strings, and Lasers

    A. Photograph a set of trajectory rod, including the angles of impacts within the images using a protractor, angle finder, or plumb line.

    B. Photograph a set of stringing trajectories:

        1. Photograph strings from different perspectives or angles, and observe the differences in density in the colored strings between the images.

        2. Also photograph the trajectory strings as they are pulled over extended distances (greater than 25 ft), and observe the effect of gravity and wind on the photography of the strings.

    C. Photograph a set of laser trajectories:

        1. Photograph a single laser trajectory.

        2. Photograph a multiple laser trajectory (covering lens or using multiple exposure capability available on some cameras).

        3. If in possession of the necessary equipment (higher-powered laser and ND filter), attempt a daytime laser trajectory photograph.

Additional Readings

Duncan, C.D. (2004). Shooting reconstruction with lasers. *Chesapeake Examiner* (Fall), 42(2):5–7.

Duncan, C.D. (2010). The precise art of daytime laser trajectory photography. *Chesapeake Examiner* (Spring), 48(1):6–12.

Haag, L.C. (2006). *Shooting Incident Reconstruction*. Burlington, MA: Elsevier, Inc.

Hueske, E.E. (2006). *Practical Analysis and Reconstruction of Shooting Incidents*. Boca Raton, FL: CRC Press.

Ultraviolet and Infrared Photography

10

If something can be seen, it can be photographed, and sometimes an image can be recorded that cannot be seen by the naked eye. This basic precept of photography can be extended to the photography of things unseen to the human eye by utilizing ultraviolet (UV) and infrared (IR) radiation (light). The electromagnetic spectrum measures radiation or energy. Energy residing between 400 and 700 nm is detectable by the human eye and is perceived as visible light. A nanometer is one-billionth of a meter in length, a measurable distance, although not to the average person. Residing below 400 nm is UV light or energy, and residing above 700 nm is IR light or energy. Photography in these regions of the electromagnetic spectrum can be accomplished through a number of simple, inexpensive techniques. Focus and exposure difficulties are common with IR and UV photography, but a little practice and experimentation goes a long way toward alleviating those challenges.

Much misunderstanding surrounds UV and IR photography. A number of variables are involved in obtaining a quality result with IR and UV radiation, including but not limited to the following:

- Specific wavelengths and intensity of the individual light source
- The surface upon which the reacting subject rests
- Type of processing completed on substrate, such as dye staining
- The age and condition of subject matter
- The type of camera, the quality of lens, including the amount of protective UV coating on the lens' glass elements
- The selection and use of any barrier filters

The number of UV and IR light sources is seemingly infinite, and each light source has its own specific range of wavelengths in which it transmits energy and light. Investigators should be aware that these wavelengths may change over time as a result of the light source's aging. Furthermore, the intensity of the light can change over time and have a direct bearing on the final result. The age of a particular stain, bite mark, or bruise may also affect the quality of the photograph captured. As the body heals or as a stain begins to fade, less material will be available to enhance through the use of UV or IR light. It is well known that a camera's lens is a determining factor in the quality of photograph ultimately captured. This is even more the case in UV photography, because most lenses have coatings on their elements designed to block UV light. In some cases, this might be advantageous because while the exciting effect of the UV energy is blocked, the visible reaction can still be recorded on film or the digital media. On the other side of the spectrum, digital cameras have IR barrier filters covering their imaging chips. This too will affect the outcome of a photograph. Finally, the use of barrier filters, typically in the colors of yellow, orange, and red, can generate better contrast and improve the overall composition and contrast.

313

Just mentioning these few considerations is meant to illustrate the value of experimentation with one's own equipment in order to gain an idea as to when and how IR and UV photography might be advantageous.

Many of the misunderstandings surrounding alternate light photography involve the tremendous number of previously mentioned variables unique to every photographic endeavor. Because each individual crime scene investigator will have his or her own arsenal of light sources, filters, cameras, and lenses, the ultimate responsibility for determining what works and what does not work is the investigator's responsibility and is based on that investigator's experiences, experiments, and practice with their own equipment and tools.

A long dissertation could be included here on how UV and IR lights travel, how they interact with different substances and surfaces, and how they can be used to the crime scene investigator's benefit. However, what is most important to crime scene investigators and photographers are the techniques necessary to record evidentiary photographs of subjects not easily seen by the naked eye. Some of these techniques are made easier through an expensive alternate light source (ALS) unit, but many crime scene investigators do not have access to such costly ALS systems. The good news is that there are effective, less-expensive alternatives. Although some alternate light techniques discussed in this chapter can produce results in a number of applications, there truly is no single technique that works perfectly for each and every crime scene application. What follows in this chapter is a discussion of the various pieces of equipment, applications, and techniques used to photograph in an energy that exists outside the visible light range of the electromagnetic spectrum.

Ultraviolet Light Photography

UV light encompasses energy or radiation below 400 nm and therefore is outside the range of visible light. In general, the purpose of adding UV light or light below 400 nm is to create or enhance contrast through fluorescence. Fluorescence is created by the excitation of a subject's electrons by the addition of UV energy. Contrast is created because the excitation of the subject's electrons into a higher state of energy or orbit propels the potential evidence into the visible range of the electromagnetic spectrum, while the background is not excited as much. The fluorescing properties of the subject will stop when the exciting energy source is removed. This is in contrast to phosphorescence, which is where the stimulation of electrons into the higher energy orbit continues even after the removal of the light source. Utilizing UV light to create greater contrast and show details unseen in natural light can be an essential tool for investigators in order to properly search and document a crime scene. UV light has a number of applications, including, but not limited to, improving the visibility of the following:

- Forgery and document alterations
- Fibers and other trace evidence
- Semen, blood, and other bodily fluids
- Bruises and bite marks
- Gunpowder residue
- Fingerprint enhancements

Documentation of each of these applications will have its own unique techniques, whether the subjects are photographed with expensive ALS units or with inexpensive black lights. Many times, results can be improved through the use of barrier filters and the use of such barrier filters will also be discussed throughout this chapter.

UV light is present in nearly all light sources. Although its presence cannot be seen by the naked eye, its existence can be felt in a number of ways. For example, UV light can cause a person's skin to tan, skin cancers to form, or glaucoma to develop in one's eyes. Among other detrimental effects, UV radiation can deteriorate photographs and other documentary evidence over time. On the positive side of the spectrum, UV light can be used to make the unseen visible. Common light sources that include UV energy as part of their discharge include the following:

- Sun
- Incandescent light bulbs
- Flashlights (some light-emitting diode [LED] flashlights do not possess UV radiation)
- Electronic flashes (those without a UV blocking filter or coating)
- UV light sources (LED flashlights, black lights, etc.)
- ALSs

In order to use some of these light sources, the photographer needs to prevent wavelengths greater than 400 nm from entering the camera. To do this, an *exciter* or an *excitation* filter is placed over the light source. These filters are commonly available through crime scene or photographic supply companies and allow investigators to utilize existing light sources, typically flashlights and electronic camera flashes, to capture images with only UV radiation. Excitation filters are typically placed over the light source and are used in controlled-lighting (low-light) environments. On the other hand, barrier filters can be used to block unwanted light from entering the camera. Barrier filters are placed on the camera's lens. Obviously a photographer cannot place a filter on the sun, but he or she can use a Wratten 18A or equivalent filter to block the wavelengths of light between 400 and 700 nm. The 18A filter allows radiation between 300 and 400 nm to pass through to the camera lens. It also allows a small amount of IR light between 700 and 800 nm. Photographing with an 18A filter is commonly referred to as reflected UV light photography. Reflected UV light photography can be used in varying degrees of success to enhance the photography of bruises and bite marks. Because IR light is passed by the 18A filter, the use of film cameras is recommended with its use. Digital cameras can record IR light, which can defeat the goal an 18A filter is trying to achieve. Film media is sensitive to UV energy, but not to IR energy. Therefore, film is the preferable recording media for use with the Wratten 18A (UV) filter.

Instead of using filtration to control the light impacting a surface, UV light sources can be utilized. Some inexpensive and some not so inexpensive UV light sources include black lights, long-wave fluorescent-tube lights, or LED lights that pass radiation and light just above and below the 400 nm mark. These lights do produce some visible light in the deep violet region. *Black lights* can commonly be found at department stores, especially around Halloween, and are cheaper than those bought from a crime scene supply vendor. These lights work in varying degrees of success and typically require low-light environments in which to operate.

ALS units can be very expensive and outside the disposable income of most individual photographers and investigators. However, their intensity and versatility make their value in crime scene investigations priceless. The more advanced ALS units have the ability to adjust the color of light by fine-tuning the wavelengths in less than 10 nm increments. Remember, any technique discussed in this chapter using less-expensive alternatives can normally be photographed with a true ALS unit as well. ALS units also have greater intensity than the smaller handheld forensic light sources or battery-powered black lights. The combination of intensity and the ability to fine-tune colored light (wavelengths) make an ALS unit the instrument of choice when it comes to searching and photographing a crime scene with alternate light. However, the cost of such equipment can be cost prohibitive to smaller departments and agencies. Fortunately, there are alternatives. Smaller and less powerful light sources may not work as effortlessly as an ALS, but they can produce the same quality of photographs, especially in small-scale applications such as the photography of individual pieces of evidence.

One example of a low-cost alternative to an ALS is LED flashlights. These flashlights have specific wavelength diodes, are relatively inexpensive, and come in a variety of colors, including

- UV (<405 nm)
- Blue (470 nm)
- Green (532 nm)
- Red (670 nm)
- IR (>700 nm)

Individual crime scene investigators and photographers are urged to conduct their own experiments in order to determine what works for them and what satisfies their particular needs, whether it be working in the controlled environment of a crime lab or working in the field at an actual crime scene. Experimenting with one's own equipment not only provides investigators with a knowledge base of approximate exposure values and circumstances in which the use of any tested technique may apply, but also gives them confidence in knowing how a quality photographic result can be achieved.

In Chapter 7, photographing of evidence utilizing painting techniques was explained as a way to eliminate shadows and cast a more even illumination across an entire subject. When photographing with smaller UV or colored light sources, the same painting-with-light techniques are recommended. Because a smaller ALS may cause a photograph to possess shaded edges and unwanted shadows, moving the light around and across the subject during the exposure will provide a more balanced and evenly illuminated photograph from corner to corner.

Once a subject is composed within the viewfinder, the next step is to find an exposure evaluation, regardless of the chosen light source. Metering an exposure recorded with UV light is similar to metering a composition with a visible light source. Once the subject matter is composed in the camera's viewfinder, hold the ALS so that it shines across the center of the composition. Begin metering the light by first adjusting the aperture and the ISO value to a desirable setting, and let the camera help choose an appropriate shutter speed. Working in the *Manual* mode, the photographer simply has to slide the shutter speed control so that the exposure value reads "0" and predicts a proper exposure. Many photographers find that

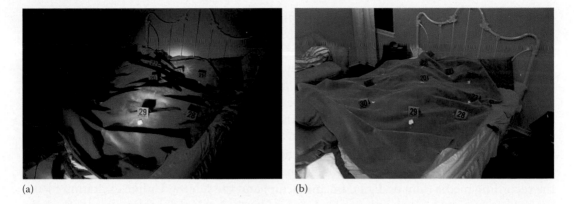

(a)   (b)

Figure 10.1 These figures were recorded with a portable UV light source. When the light source is stationary, subjects with multiple facets, depressions, or crevices can be difficult to illuminate with a stationary light source. The camera did an adequate job of metering the highlights located closest to the light source in (a), requiring an exposure of ISO 400, f/16, for 6 s. However, (b) was one of a series of bracketed exposures that increased the exposure and the duration of the photograph; the UV light was swept across the bed's surface from all angles. The exposure values for (b) were ISO 400, f/7.1, for 10 s. Compare the two photographs, and notice how diffusing and painting the light across the subject is more likely to result in a better photographic image.

an *underexposed* UV light photograph results in a better overall image. However, because the painting with light process will likely produce a better result, this technique will normally cause the light to move off the subject here and there as it is swept across the subject. As a result, a balanced ("0") exposure effectively results in an *underexposure*, because the metered light source will not be striking the entire subject during the entire exposure. In fact, additional light will likely need to be cast onto the subject because the light source will not be stationary during the painting process. The larger the surface area, the greater the increase in exposure may be required, because the light will move in and out of the composition by the natural actions of the painting effort. If the light source covers the entire subject and is merely moved around to avoid shadows, the exposure will be much closer to what the camera evaluated as a proper exposure. However, if the subject is not covered completely by the light source, then an additional stop or two of light may be necessary (Figure 10.1). As with any other critical evidentiary photograph, bracketing exposures will ensure a quality result. Remember not to change multiple variables at the same time when bracketing. Only change the aperture, length of exposure, or the painting with light technique with each subsequent exposure. It is important to not alter more than one variable at a time, because too many alterations from one photograph to the next may pass completely by what would have been the best exposure.

As stated before, the more expensive ALS units can easily be tuned to specific wavelengths. ALS units also have a broad spectrum at which they can output light, typically ranging from 350 to 1000 nm. The intensity or brightness of ALS units is also significantly greater, and because of this, the intensity of light is usually adjustable. Investigators should not be afraid of dialing down the brightness in order to capture a better image. Barrier filters are used to improve a composition's contrast by blocking the radiating energy from reaching the camera, but allowing the excited state of the fluorescing material to pass through the filter. Barrier filters typically come in red, orange, and yellow. Commercially available units are packed with matching eye protection goggles of the same colors. In general, the yellow filters are used with the shorter wavelengths of light, 350–470 nm (violet to blue); the orange filters are used in the midrange of visible light, 470–555 nm (blue to green); and the red filters are used with the longer wavelengths of light above 600 nm (green to red). These wavelengths are approximations and can vary depending on the color of the fluorescing material and the substratum the material rests upon. Therefore, do not be surprised if a red filter creates the best contrast when utilizing a blue (470 nm) wavelength of light. At the least, these cited combinations give investigators a starting point from which to begin their search for the optimal combination of wavelength and barrier filter. A barrier filter is placed between the recording media (film or digital imaging chip) and the subject. Unlike excitation filters, the light source does not pass through a barrier filter before it strikes the subject. The light shining onto the subject reflects back toward the camera and only a specific range of wavelengths passes through the barrier filter and lens on its way to the film or imaging sensor.

Barrier filters come in different shades and densities of color. The basic filters that accompany an ALS unit are yellow, orange, and red. Using a Wratten filter threaded onto the lens can provide an even greater fine-tuning of the final image through the use of varying filter densities. An extended assortment of barrier filters may include the following:

- Wratten #8 (yellow)
- Wratten #15 (deep yellow)
- Wratten #16 (yellow orange)
- Wratten #22 (deep orange)
- Wratten #25 (red)
- Wratten #29 (deep red)

Unfortunately, purchasing a large selection of filters can quickly deplete an agency's financial resources, especially if different filters must be purchased for varying sized lenses. There are adapter rings called step-up and step-down rings that can be fitted onto a filter so that they can be attached to a wider range of lens sizes. It is typically better to purchase the largest sized filter necessary and step down to the smaller lenses. Fortunately, fine-tuning a photograph's contrast through the use of barrier filters is only necessary for the perfectionist, and if one is a perfectionist, he or she probably already has an ample number of filters to choose from. For the majority of crime scene investigators, the basic colors yellow, orange, and red should suffice.

There may be rare times when an unorthodoxed filter color may be needed. Along the same lines as contrast filters, if the color of the fluorescing material needs a little assistance in separating itself from the substrate, selecting the same color of filter as the fluorescence may provide a solution. For example, a photographer attempting to image a fingerprint enhanced with green fluorescent fingerprint powder can lighten the green fluorescence of the powder with a green filter (Figure 10.2). Remember, adding a colored filter to black-and-white (monochrome) photography will lighten the matching color in the recorded image.

One way to save money is to purchase the color-tinted *viewing plates* from crime scene supply companies. These are square pieces of tinted plastic designed specifically for ALS work and can be carefully held between the camera's lens and the subject to act as a filter that is physically attached or threaded onto the end of a lens. Viewing plates also allow the photographer to observe the fluorescing material without being glued to the camera's

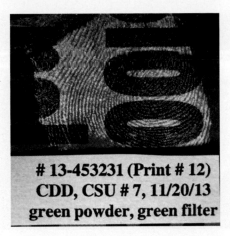

13-453231 (Print # 12)
CDD, CSU # 7, 11/20/13
green powder, green filter

Figure 10.2 A green filter was added to enhance (lighten) the fluorescent green fingerprint powder on the patterned surface. The camera settings were ISO 100, f/11, for 2.5 s. The camera's light meter was used to determine the exposure and the light was painted across surface during the 2.5 s of exposure.

viewfinder. Furthermore, viewing plates offer the photographer more freedom by allowing for the quick interchange of plates to determine the best combination of colored light and colored filter. These viewing plates typically cost less than ten dollars apiece, which is much cheaper than the cost of just three of the Wratten camera filters. The photographer only has to ensure that the light source does not strike the viewing plate between the camera lens and the plate. If light does get in between the two surfaces, distracting lens flair or dust particles on top of the viewing plate may appear in the final image.

As a final reminder, metering or evaluating light from a fluorescing subject is not difficult. Other than those times when the use of an 18A filter and reflected UV light photography is called for, metering of alternate light photographs is fairly straightforward. The majority of photographs will typically require longer exposure times and therefore need a tripod-mounted or otherwise stabilized camera. Since the camera must be stabilized in some manner, high-speed film is not needed. Selecting an ISO of 100–400 will produce sharper images and less noise (or grain) and only require slightly longer exposure times as a compromise. Metering surfaces and subjects that are fluorescing or absorbing UV light is exactly the same as any other photographic endeavor because one is still capturing a subject that is visible to the camera. A photographer will likely still want to bracket his or her exposures by one and/or two stops in each direction for each composition to ensure a quality result. The contrast of an image will change with the amount of light allowed into the camera, and a more favorable result may be captured through an intentional under- or overexposure. UV photographs can be captured in color, but the odd (violet)-colored staining may distract viewers from the actual subject of the photograph. Therefore, capturing photographs using alternate light is probably best accomplished through black-and-white photography (Figure 10.3).

Forgery and Document Alterations

Now armed with a general idea on how to record UV light images, one needs to know what kinds of subjects can benefit from such unique illumination. IR light is frequently

Figure 10.3 The purpose of using UV light is to make unseen properties in a subject visible. In this photo, the unseen property is a fingerprint developed on top of a small drug capsule. The latent print was enhanced with Rhodamine 6G. The light source was a SPEX CrimeScope set to *CSS* and an orange barrier filter was used to capture the image. (Photographed by Laura Tierney, US Immigration and Customs Enforcement, Washington, DC.)

used to distinguish between inks in forgery investigations, and that topic will be discussed later in this chapter. However, there are other ways in which forgers try to defraud victims. Obliterating, washing, erasing, and other methods of obscuring once valid checks and fiduciary instruments are all examples of forgery practices. The use of solvents, alcohols, and cleansing liquids to alter or obliterate ink may be made more visible under UV light (Figure 10.4). Where a forger may get lucky in using the same brand or composition of ink as the original document writer, the minute changes in the paper caused by the solvent

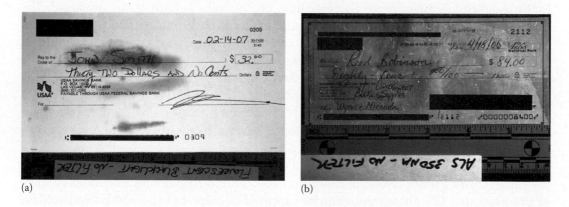

(a)   (b)

Figure 10.4 Obliterations, alterations, and erasures can leave telltale marks and remnants on the paper used for fiduciary instruments. UV light can help bring these illegal changes to light. (a) and (b) are examples of attempted erasures. (a) was photographed using a fluorescent black light and the camera settings were ISO 100, f/8, for 30 s. In (a), it is clear where the solvent was applied to the payee's name and where some of the dissolved ink dripped elsewhere on the check. (b) was photographed using an ALS set to 350 nm and was recorded at ISO 100, f/8, for 13 s. Although the forger did a better job at masking his work in (b), where the ink was dissolved and bled above and below the payee's line on the check is now visible with UV light.

may be seen using UV light. Utilizing UV light between 350 and 415 nm is likely to produce the best visualization of a document's alterations. If filtration is required, a yellow filter is generally best.

Investigators can choose from a variety of light sources, ranging from expensive ALS units to handheld, battery-operated black lights. Because most document photography occurs in the controlled setting of a laboratory, the investigator should choose the best quality light source available. Intensity of the light is not a large factor in selecting a light source, because documents are typically flat (no depth of field issues) and stationary. Therefore, apertures can be set wide open and/or exposure times adjusted in order to meet the requirements necessary to record a quality image. Meter the light as with any other UV photograph and record the composition. Do not forget to bracket a series of exposures.

Fibers and Other Trace Evidence

Small threads, hairs, and fibers can be particularly difficult to see in natural light. However, the visibility of such trace evidence, especially fiber evidence, can be enhanced with UV light. Many fabrics are chemically treated so that their colors remain bright and vibrant. Furthermore, laundry detergents are infused with *brighteners* to enhance the color of clothes and fabrics. Consequently, when fibers and threads fall or tear away from a garment, their detection can be made easier using UV light. These valuable pieces of trace evidence might become the critical link between a suspect and the scene. UV light can be used to increase the intensity of these fibers and their built-in brighteners, especially when they are found on a contrasting colored surface or a substratum that does not fluoresce similarly to the fiber evidence. Once again, UV light assists in creating contrast, causing the trace evidence to stand out against the background (Figure 10.5).

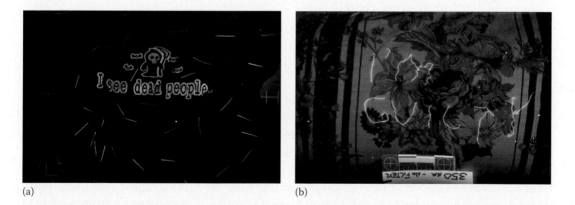

(a)   (b)

Figure 10.5 This illustrates the benefit of utilizing UV lights and black lights in the search and documentation of trace and fiber evidence. (a) was photographed using a 4″ fluorescent-tube black light (ISO 800, f/8, for 15 s) and recorded fluorescing fibers hidden in the folds of the shirt. The UV light source was painted across the shirt in order to have the fibers appear. (b) was captured using an ALS set at 350 nm (ISO 400, f/8, for 10 s) and recorded various pieces of fiber evidence on a multicolored pillow. The ALS recorded a faster image and the end result was just as valuable: locating and permanently documenting the presence of trace evidence.

Oblique lighting is also an excellent way to detect trace evidence present on a surface. The shadows created by the oblique lighting striking the trace evidence can help investigators locate such items. In addition, oblique lighting remains the most effective way to locate hair evidence because hair is not likely to fluoresce like fiber evidence. Textured surfaces such as bedding, carpeting, or grass lawns can pose a problem when utilizing oblique lighting in the search for trace fibers and hairs because of their undulating forms and/or shapes. In this case, a UV light may prove more beneficial than oblique lighting. The UV light will seek to excite the unknown fiber's electrons into a higher state and into the visible range of energy (400–700 nm), thus making it photographable. Since the light source itself is not emitting visible light, it should not compete with the fiber's illumination or intensity. If the photographer finds that a wavelength above 400 nm provides the best fluorescence, then a barrier filter can be utilized to enhance the image's contrast and help remove the illuminating light from the composition. Creating the necessary contrast and allowing the fiber evidence to stand out against the substratum is the ultimate goal, and investigators may have to try an assortment of filters and wavelengths of light to get just the right combination.

The choice of light source is up to the individual investigator or photographer. Some of those choices may be based upon availability, ease of use, and personal experience. As far as fiber and trace evidence is concerned, inexpensive light sources, such as fluorescent-tube black lights or UV LED flashlights, work extremely well in causing fiber evidence to excite, especially over small areas of examination such as clothing. If an entire scene needs to be searched and photographed, a more powerful ALS may have greater value. Filtration is likely not necessary, but may enhance the final result depending on the color of the substratum and/or the fiber evidence itself. If filtration is desired, attempt to match the color of the fiber with the color of the filter. In black-and-white photography, matching the fiber's color with the filter will lighten or brighten the colored fiber in the recorded image, thereby improving the contrast. As a reminder, when conducting a search for unknown fibers, the colored light and filter combinations are as follows:

- Less than 470 nm (violet to blue light) and a yellow filter
- 470–532 nm (blue to green light) and an orange filter
- Greater than 532 nm (green to red light) and a red filter

UV light photography can be recorded in color, but if barrier filters are used, then a black-and-white image capture is best.

As previously stated, a photographer may have to try different combinations of filters and lights. Patience and perseverance are vital. Natural light may be sufficient to photograph some trace evidence, but black lights can enhance the visualization of latent evidence. Furthermore, versatile ALS units can improve the photographic documentation of trace and fiber evidence by providing a greater range of wavelengths from which to choose from and apply to a subject. A crime scene photographer merely has to practice and experiment with his or her unique light source. Practice and experimentation does not and should not necessarily be completed at an actual crime scene. Pick a light source and search the office, the officer's *down room*, or even one's own home. Practice photographing what is found and record notes about how the best exposure was obtained. In this way an investigator will have a general idea as to the best choices of ISO speed, aperture, and shutter speed when it comes time to process an actual crime scene.

Gunpowder Residue

IR and UV light are frequently used to improve the visibility of soot, smoke, and gunpowder residue on targeted surfaces. IR lighting is most commonly utilized for gunpowder residue imaging. (IR techniques will be discussed later in this chapter.) However, UV light can also be employed. Similar to IR light, UV light will cause soot and smoke stains found on a target surface to appear black in the recorded image. Creating a separation or contrast between the substratum and gunpowder residue can help investigators determine distance between the firearm and the target. UV light has one advantage over IR light. Unburned particles of gunpowder that have been forced down the barrel of a firearm may actually fluoresce under UV light. Not all gunpowder will fluoresce because the fluorescing properties are actually the coatings applied to gunpowder by some, but not all, manufacturers. The coatings are designed to control the gunpowder's rate of burn. Finding these fluorescing properties is a clear indication that the firearm was in close proximity to the target when fired (Figure 10.6).

A black light emitting light around 400–415 nm is sufficient to produce results when photographing gunpowder residue on bodies, clothing, or other physical surfaces (Figure 10.7). An ALS unit can be used, and an investigator can tune the light source between 350 and 415 nm in order to create the best results. Additional contrast may be created by placing a yellow barrier filter between the subject and camera. Selecting an ISO of 100 will create the sharpest image. Depth of field may not be an issue if the surface is flat. Consequently, the aperture can be set to a larger aperture. With all else equal, selecting an aperture found approximately in the middle of a lens' range of apertures (f/8 or f/11) will help create the sharpest image from corner to corner. If photographing a victim's body, there will naturally be some depth to the composition. In this instance, the aperture should be closed down to compensate for the body's curvature and composition's depth. Even with large apertures creating quicker exposure times, a tripod-mounted or otherwise stabilized camera will probably be necessary. The final piece of the exposure equation is its length (shutter speed). The camera's light meter can be used to determine the appropriate shutter speed as with any other UV exposure. Do not forget to bracket a set of captured images.

Figure 10.6 The image was recorded at ISO 100, f/11, for 15 s and shows the fluorescing properties of the unburned additive to gunpowder that helps control the rate of burn.

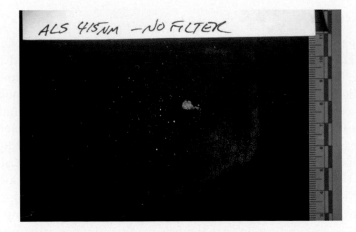

Figure 10.7 This photograph was recorded using an ALS unit set to 415 nm; no filtration was necessary. The image was recorded at ISO 400, f/8, for 2.5 s. The fluorescing properties of the unburned gunpowder coating applied to some manufacturer's propellants to control the rate of burn can be detected with UV light and permanently documented through photography. The white specks of fluorescence found along the left edge of the bullet strike are the small particles of unburned propellant. Burned powder or soot can be seen around the right edge of the bullet hole.

Semen, Blood, and Other Bodily Fluids

In television crime dramas, the presence of semen at a crime scene is portrayed as some miraculously glowing substance that amazingly identifies the suspect in a matter of minutes. It is as if the suspect left his signed confession on the bedsheets next to the seminal deposit. On television, semen always glows bright and strong regardless of the surface on which it is found. Unfortunately, true crime scenes are not always that clean cut. Most investigators would be happy if the crime scene itself was as tidy as those portrayed on television, much less if the trace evidence was so easy to find. In fact, a number of substances fluoresce under UV light so that the mere presence of a fluorescing substance indicates only the *possible* existence of semen. Bleach, milk products, and bodily fluids including saliva and mucus can also fluoresce under UV light. Regardless of what causes the fluorescence, an investigator should seek to collect any unknown substance for further evaluation, and prior to its recovery, the surface should be photographed.

Similar to the photography of other reactions under UV light, photographing semen requires taking into consideration a number of variables. The color of the surface on which a stain is found is of primary importance, but also the stain's age and whether it is mixed with vaginal fluid (a dried mixture fluoresces better than semen alone). Semen found on bedding is the most difficult to photograph, because the two elements (semen and bed linens) may have little contrast. A large percentage of bedding is white in color and dried semen possesses a similar color. Semen can be searched for with a number of different light sources and at a variety of wavelengths. A change in wavelength may assist investigators in creating better contrast between the reaction and the background; thus, the benefit of a true ALS unit is evident in these cases. However, small handheld UV light sources are equally capable of creating a fluorescent reaction (Figure 10.8).

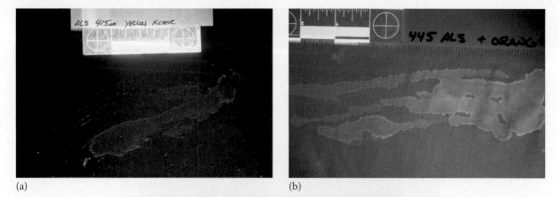

(a)   (b)

(c)

Figure 10.8 Semen stains located on darker surfaces are fairly easy to photograph because there is a natural contrast between the fluorescing stain and the background. (a) was recorded with a handheld LED UV light (415 nm) and at ISO 400, f/8, for 60 s. Creating contrast on light-colored surfaces may require the use of barrier filters. (b) and (c) are images of the same stain on a white bedsheet. (b) was recorded through an orange-colored filter using an ALS set at 445 nm. (b) had an exposure value of ISO 100, f/8, for 1/6 of a second. (c) used an INNOVA 470 nm blue flashlight to create the reaction and was recorded at ISO 100, f/8, for 10 s. These figures make clear that the choices of light source, filter, and length of exposures can vary widely. The investigator's goal is to find the greatest possible contrast between the subject and the surface on which it is found.

Starting with the shorter wavelengths, a 350 nm UV light source will create a reaction and a yellow barrier filter can be beneficial, but may not be necessary. However, as the wavelengths of the light source elongate, barrier filters will more likely be required. Fluorescent-tube lights and LED light sources, peaking at or around 405–415 nm, work quite well at creating an illuminating reaction with semen and other body fluids. A barrier filter may be necessary depending on the color of the substratum, and if a filter is necessary, a yellow filter will likely be called for. As the wavelength elongates, the photographer will need to use a denser barrier filter, such as orange or red. A fluorescent reaction from semen may even be detected with light found in the green region (approximately 532 nm). Once again, the change in color may be advantageous because of the color of the substratum. In the end, photographing semen stains, as well as saliva and mucus, is a matter of trial and error. Regardless of the light's wavelength, investigators can use a permanent marker to delineate the boundaries of the stain under examination, in a similar way as an

Figure 10.9 Bloodstains can be enhanced with UV light by increasing the contrast between the stain and the surface upon which it impacted. Blood absorbs UV and blue light. As a result, blood should appear darker against its background when photographed with an ALS. This figure was enhanced with an ALS set to 350 nm. The image was recorded at ISO 100, aperture of f/13, for 2.5 s.

investigator would circle individual bloodstains to make them more visible in the captured photographs. As a final note, investigators must be flexible in their techniques and patient during their investigation.

For some inexplicable reason, the television crime dramas that indicate semen glows like the Fourth of July are the same shows that mislead the general public into believing that blood fluoresces under UV light. Nothing could be further from the truth. Blood absorbs light in the UV and blue regions of the electromagnetic spectrum. This absorption causes the blood to appear dark and is best photographed in black and white when utilizing UV light. Bloodstains and pattern impressions are easily observed on light-colored surfaces, but the contrast can be greatly enhanced with UV (<400 nm) through blue (470 nm) light. Photographing bloodstains is discussed more thoroughly in Chapter 8, but this section specifically addresses image enhancement through UV light. Photographing bloodstains found on light-colored surfaces and using a light source between 350 and 470 nm will create excellent contrast. The stains and/or stain pattern will absorb the UV (or near UV light), causing the stain to look darker against the lighter background, thereby improving the contrast (Figure 10.9).

Bruises and Bite Marks

The enhancement of bruises and bite marks by UV light is nothing new to crime scene investigators. Bruising, including bite marks, causes the iron in the blood to stain the subcutaneous skin. This staining can be made more visible through UV light, which is able to penetrate through the epidermis layer of the skin and thereby improve the all-important contrast (Figure 10.10). The techniques for improving injury photography are varied. The photographer can utilize either reflected or conventional UV light. Reflected UV light photography requires a Wratten 18A or compatible filter and film photography, while conventional UV light sources require an ALS unit, preferably one with the capability of light production in the 350–415 nm range. The photographer may be able to use the

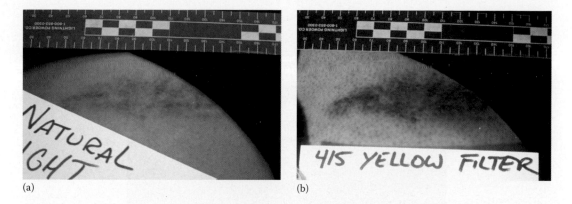

(a)   (b)

Figure 10.10 Bruising can be enhanced and hidden details brought out through the UV light penetrating under the skin and showing the bloodstained tissue. (a) is a 2-day-old bruise photographed in natural light; (b) is of the same bruise photographed with a 415 nm light source and a yellow barrier filter. The exposure was recorded at ISO 800, f/11, for 3.2 s.

less-expensive black lights for fresher injuries, but the intensity and capability of cheaper light sources are not always adequate for older injuries or injuries not yet visible. ALS units typically pass light at very specific wavelengths, thus providing the photographer more control over the subject. Wratten 18A filters are capable of blocking light above 400 nm, allowing most energy to pass at approximately 365 nm. These band-pass filters are much less expensive than ALS units, but their effectiveness is oftentimes hit or miss. In addition, because the filters pass IR light as well as UV light, they are much less effective with digital imaging systems.

If a bruise has fully developed on the victim's body, better results are obtained by using an ALS, whereas the 18A filter is used in reflected UV light photography when the bruising is not visible or only slightly visible to the human eye. Furthermore, reflected UV light techniques work best on the thinner skin of children and infants. Photographing adults with an 18A filter is a hit or miss proposition, but can be attempted if other techniques fail.

To begin with, utilizing a Wratten 18A filter requires the recording media to be film. The 18A filter allows IR light to pass and the digital imaging chips can *see* this radiation. Standard film cannot *see* IR light; therefore, the Wratten 18A filter is effecting with only film recordings. Photographing through an 18A filter requires a shift in the focus. Cameras and their lenses are designed to focus in the visible light spectrum. Therefore, when captured through an 18A filter, subjects will be slightly out of focus. A crime scene photographer will need to test the18A filter along with the camera lens for the focus shift. The easiest method to adjust for the shift in focus caused by UV light is with a lens that possesses an IR indexing mark. The focus shift for UV and IR is relatively the same and focusing the lens with the IR indexing mark should compensate for the shift in focus. Alternatively, the photographer can test their equipment and find the correct focal distance for their lens. The testing protocol begins with the photographer setting the lens to a specific focal length (maybe more than one in order to be useful in different photographic situations) and choosing a specific aperture (e.g., f/8) (Figure 10.11). The last part of the equation is the specific point of focus (distance between lens and subject). Focus should be accomplished by rotating the focus ring all the way over to the macro side of the scale so that there is no doubt as to where the focus is set. Since the infinity focus may place the camera too far away

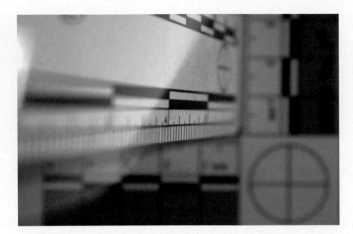

Figure 10.11 This was recorded with an 80 mm lens focused at its closest point. The aperture was set to f/8. The ruler extending away from the lens provided the exact distance to the sharpest point of focus, which was 4.25″. In subsequent crime scene photographs, this distance can be matched to ensure that all images are sharply focused even though the photographer cannot see the subject through the camera's viewfinder.

from the subject for a quality photograph, photographers should consider setting the focus point to the closest possible focus capability of the lens. Setting the focus to one extreme of the focus' range has the added benefit of removing all guesswork about where the focus is on the focus ring, because the focus ring will be as far as possible to the macro side of the focus-distance scale. Next, mount the camera into a fixed position and place a ruler with the zero point immediately adjacent to the lens' front element. Record an image of the ruler as it extends away from the lens. Have the ruler's scale visible in the viewfinder by having the scale canted ever so slightly in the composition. When the recorded photograph is examined, the exact distance for a particular focal length, aperture, and focus point will be known. Investigators need to take notes and make a *cheat sheet* so results can be reproduced. As another option, an aperture of f/16 can frequently compensate for the focus shift of UV filters, but be prepared for lengthy exposure times due to the small aperture.

The individual photographer's focal length and aperture preferences as well as the macro capabilities of the lens will vary. Consequently, every photographer needs to conduct his or her own series of tests. A standard 28–80 mm or a zoom lens may require several test photographs be recorded. For example, a series of tests can be completed at 28, 50, and 80 mm. In this way, a photographer can select the best focal length for the size of the subject being photographed.

Investigators should also decide which type of light source they prefer along with what exposure values they will require when conducting tests and experiments with the 18A filter, taking into consideration the fact that the camera is unable to accurately meter light through a Wratten 18A filter (Figure 10.12). As far as light sources go, the sun is probably the best light source and, with everything being equal, requires the least amount of time to complete an exposure. A second light source would be an ALS, using the white light spectrum that includes UV and visible light waves. Light from an ALS provides greater intensity than other man-made sources, but is not always convenient or available in the field. Furthermore, if the photographer has access to an ALS, he or she may not even need the use of an 18A filter.

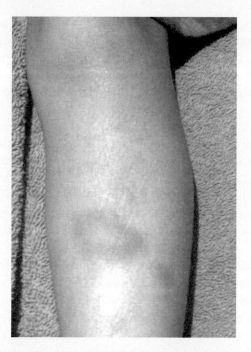

Figure 10.12 Photographers can use a number of different light sources with the Wratten 18A filter. This photo was recorded in sunlight at ISO 400, f/8, for 20 s. The amount of UV light generated by individual light sources can vary dramatically. The following are examples of a variety of light sources and possible exposure settings necessary when using a Wratten 18A filter: 400 watt ALS white light, ISO 400, f/8, for 20 s; electronic flash (144gn), ISO 400, f/8, for eight full-power flashes (the exposure time is inconsequential and depends on the flash's recycling times); and flashlight (Streamlight SL-20), ISO 400, f/8, for 45 s.

Many times, injury photographs are recorded in a hospital when the only convenient light source may be the investigator's duty flashlight. A flashlight can be used with an 18A filter. While the exposures will understandably be longer, if the subject remains stationary, the photograph is recordable. Because the subject must be completely still, living subjects are more difficult to photograph using reflected UV light photography, especially if the injury is on or near the neck and chest regions of the body. Not all flashlights produce light in the UV range. Many LED flashlights do not typically possess UV or IR energy. Therefore, photographers should conduct tests with their equipment in order to ensure quality results in the field.

When using a flashlight as the light source, the light should be painted across the subject so that no hot spots form in the final image. Painting with light is accomplished in a similar manner as painting other subjects with light, as described in Chapters 4 and 7. Recording bracketed exposures will be necessary because of the different variables involved with painting and photographing subjects through an opaque filter.

Another light source available to photographers is their external electronic flash. Some flash heads have a protective UV filter that makes them useless in reflected light photography. However, if the flash does not have a UV filter, it can be used to project light onto a subject and its UV rays recorded through the Wratten 18A filter. Very likely, the recording of the photograph will require multiple flashes. The length of the exposure is not important. It will last as long as it takes to produce the necessary number of flashes required to produce a proper image. The filter is opaque; therefore, indoor ambient light has only a small impact on the overall exposure. Once again, it is important to test the equipment being used. The aperture should already be selected based on the previous testing for focus and a film speed of 400 is adequate for the average flash. Increasing the ISO value may increase the image's grain, but it will reduce the number of flashes required for a proper exposure.

The third variable in reflective UV light photography while using an electronic flash as a light source is the distance between the subject and flash. Since the subjects (bruises and bite marks) are typically not very large, holding the flash a constant 2–3 ft away from the subject should be sufficient. A series of test photographs keeping all three variables constant and changing the number of flashes will provide the investigator with an idea as to the correct number of flashes necessary to project onto a victim's injury. It is important for investigators to create a cheat sheet listing the following photographic variables:

- Particular lens (and focal length if using a zoom lens)
- Particular flash unit and distance from subject
- Film speed and aperture preferences
- Lens' focus (macro or infinity) and the actual distance between subject and lens

A little preparation will prevent a poor performance at the crime scene.

Bruising that is already visible or is fading away can be enhanced with a UV light source such as that provided by an ALS unit (Figure 10.13). Black lights might be able to produce slightly better contrast in some situations, but a light source capable of producing a strong 350–415 nm wavelength of light has a greater potential for positive results (Figure 10.14). The benefit of photographing with energy in the visible range of light is that the camera is better able to meter the composition. Depending on the person's skin color, the exposure may have to be tweaked with a little more or less light in order to capture the best contrast in the image. Here again, remember to bracket exposures to ensure the best evidentiary photograph possible.

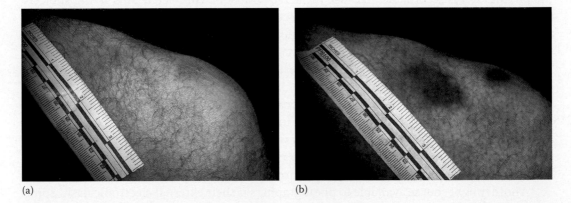

(a)   (b)

Figure 10.13 Even bruising that begins to fade can be photographed because the iron in a person's blood stains the subcutaneous skin. (a) and (b) are of the same 3-week-old bruise. (a) was recorded in natural light and barely shows the injury's location; (b) was recorded with a 415 nm light source and a yellow barrier filter. The exposure was recorded at ISO 800, f/8, for 4 s and the healed injury is made much more visible.

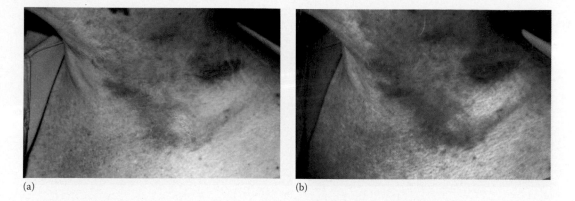

(a) (b)

Figure 10.14 Both images were recorded of a 10-day-old burn caused by a fired cartridge case impacting the victim's skin. (a) was recorded in visible light. (b) was recorded with an ALS light set to 415 nm and a yellow filter was utilized to improve contrast. The exposure settings were ISO 5000, f/16, for 1/2 s.

One should not forget about the benefits offered by barrier filters. The final image can certainly be enhanced with the use of a barrier filter. A yellow filter is best for shorter wavelengths of light, while an orange barrier filter may be necessary if the ALS-produced light rises above 470 nm. The barrier filter can improve the contrast and definition of the region encompassing the bruised area of tissue. However, the addition of a barrier filter may significantly lengthen the time of the exposure, especially with battery-powered UV light sources, so it is important to be sure that the subject and the camera are both completely stabilized before the photograph is recorded. Photographers should be aware that the yellow and orange filters that are built into the camera's menu system are far less effective than the physical *barrier* of a screw-on mounted filter attached to the camera's lens.

Fingerprint Enhancements

Fingerprint enhancement is one of the more common uses for UV light. Anyone processing latent prints will have his or her favorite fluorescent powders and dye stains used to enhance latent prints (Figure 10.15). These fluorescent powders and dyes help eliminate distracting backgrounds, enhance faint latent prints, and are effective on both porous and nonporous surfaces. Regardless of the dye or powder used, the photographer has a choice of light sources. ALS units have the versatility to adjust power and wavelength, and for that reason, they can be very advantageous in the controlled environment of a laboratory. However, they are large and cumbersome for use in the field. In those instances, inexpensive black lights and UV flashlights can be just as effective.

Fingerprint photography requires the camera to be mounted on a tripod or stabilized in some fashion. This stability is necessary not only because of the longer exposure times that result from using UV light but also because of the need to ensure a perpendicular orientation between the camera and subject. When the camera is stabilized, the length of the exposure should not be a major concern. This is especially useful when the latent print is located on a curved or deeply textured surface and a smaller aperture is necessary to ensure the greatest depth of field. During the longer exposure times necessitated by the smaller apertures and UV light, the photographer should move the light source around

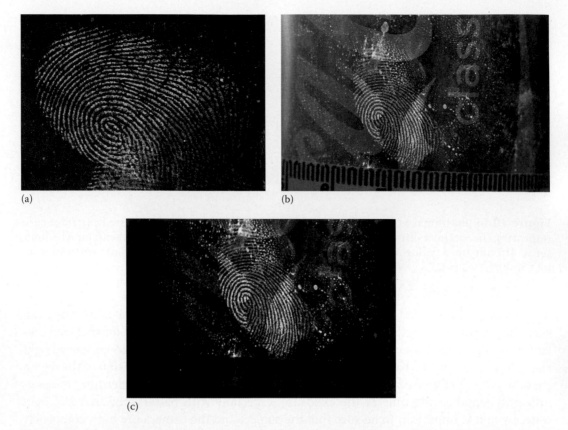

(a)

(b)

(c)

Figure 10.15 Fluorescent powders and dye stains help bring out a fingerprint's ridge detail present on confusing backgrounds or surfaces. The light source exciting the reaction into the visible range of the electromagnetic spectrum can come from a variety of UV light sources without losing valuable detail. These images of fluorescing fingerprints were captured with different light sources and with the camera set to ISO 100, photographed through an orange barrier filter with an aperture of f/8: (a) Optimax CSS 450 nm UV light for 1/6 of a second, (b) LED 415 nm UV light for 2.5 s, and (c) Streamlight Twintask 3C 390 nm UV light for 1/4 of a second. Observe that all three inexpensive light sources enhanced the fluorescent-powdered print. The orange filtration assisted in reducing the distracting nature of the background. (Photographed by Andrew Taravella, Crime Scene Investigator, Houston Police Department, Houston, TX.)

and across the subject to ensure that the edges of the composition receive as much light as the subject's center (Figure 10.16). Information may be lost if the entire composition does not receive adequate light. UV lights, or any light source for that matter, have a stronger illuminated center than the periphery of the projected light. Consequently, the composition and its illumination will be improved by moving or painting the light across the entire subject throughout the length of the exposure. The photographer may decide to add more time, approximately a half to a full stop of light to offset the light lost through the painting process. Additional exposure is required because light will be cast outside the borders of the composition during the painting process and thus not be included in the final exposure.

The choice of dye stain or fluorescent powder will most likely be determined by the investigator's preference and/or what is available. Contrast is the ultimate goal in fingerprint photography, and as such, the color of powder or dye stain should be different or in

Figure 10.16 When using smaller, less powerful UV light sources, the quality of the image will improve if the photographer paints the subject with the light instead of casting the light across it from a stationary position. By painting the subject, light will be more evenly applied to the overall composition and allow light to reach the crevices and perimeter of the composition in equal proportions. This image was recorded using a 40-bulb LED UV black light at ISO 100, f/22, for 20 s. During the 20 s exposure, the light was swept across the shoes so that the light cast onto the subject was even across all the nooks and crannies of the evidence. The camera's light meter correctly evaluated the light for the composition.

contrast from the surface that holds the impression. In black-and-white photography, fluorescing fingerprints produce a white ridge detail and hopefully a darker background; this is the complete opposite of an inked or rolled impression. Remember that the photograph must be reversed to be of value to the latent print examiner.

In conclusion, remember to bracket the exposures because the quality of the latent may change through the intentional under- and overexposure of the composition. There is no hard and fast rule in regard to obtaining the *best* exposure for different UV light compositions. However, slightly underexposed images, more often than not, do tend to provide the best results. Crime scene photographers should experiment with the different powders and dye stains available to them in order to determine which filters and light sources they feel produce the most reproducible and reliable results. And finally, those utilizing digital imaging systems must record their impression evidence in the RAW format and capture the impression at an appropriate pixel-per-inch (ppi) ratio: 1000 ppi for fingerprints and 500 ppi for palm prints.

Osseous Matter

Skeletal material can fluoresce under UV light, and UV light ranging between 350 and 415 nm works particularly well, especially when the bones have entered the dry stage of decomposition. If skin tissue, mud, or other intervening matter covers the

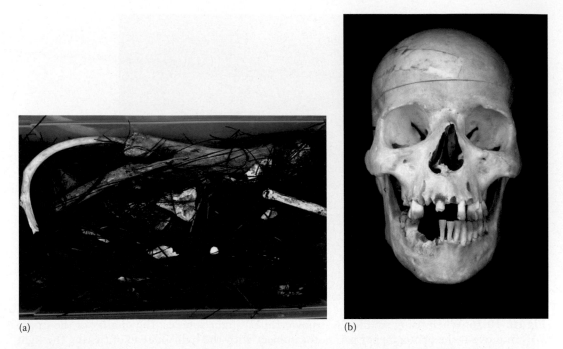

(a)   (b)

Figure 10.17 (a) was captured with an ISO setting of 400, f/8, for 60 s. The image was recorded with a fluorescent black light, which was painted across the subject. Notice that the bones stand out against similar looking items, such as rocks and sticks, commonly found in a scattered-skeletal recovery. (b) illustrates the benefits of using UV light to distinguish details on skeletal material. The image was captured using an LED UV flashlight. The captured image was recorded at ISO 100, f/8, for 30 s. The light was painted across the subject during the exposure and a barrier filter was not utilized.

skeletal material, the fluorescing properties of the osseous matter will be concealed (Figure 10.17). Using UV light to search for skeletal material can be problematic with AC-powered ALS units, because it may be difficult to obtain electrical power in the field. Portable, battery-powered UV light sources are better adapted to searching actual crime scenes, and when osseous material is located, portable light sources are better suited to photographing this material in its natural environment. The use of barrier filters can further suppress the background and increase the contrast between the bones and the landscape, leaf litter, or other debris. A yellow filter is typically the best choice for UV light residing around 400 nm and will help create greater contrast between the bones and the surface it lies upon.

Since UV light requires dark environments to be of value, the search for skeletal material must be completed after the sun sets. This, of course, does not preclude searching for human remains during the daytime. The search for osseous matter may also be required in indoor environments. It is not uncommon for nervous criminals to attempt at cleaning up crime scenes, but miss small skull and other bone fragments. Turning out the lights and using a UV light source to search for bone fragments may prove extremely rewarding. When the fragments are found, photographing such evidence with the UV light can be quite valuable when it comes time to testify in court. A crime scene photographer should always strive to bring the crime scene to the courtroom through photographic documentation.

Infrared Photography

The techniques used for UV light photography are similar to those used for IR photography. Photographers are merely dealing with a different area and the longer wavelengths of the electromagnetic spectrum. Investigators can use IR light in a number of applications, including

- Enhancement of tattoos (obscured by blood, soot, or decomposition or *removed*)
- Document examinations and forgery investigations
- Gunshot residue
- Bloodstain evidence

Investigators have several options in which to restrict non-IR light from entering the camera or cast IR light onto a subject. IR light resides above 700 nm on the electromagnetic scale. Reflected IR photography can be completed by using filters to block all visible light waves from entering the camera and only allowing IR light through the lens. A crime scene investigator may also choose to produce IR light by using an ALS or other IR light source. The results may vary slightly between the two techniques, but IR photography techniques can produce evidentiary photographs of tremendous value. The choice of technique to be utilized may be dictated by the environment. If the photographs need to be recorded at an outdoor-daytime crime scene, a reflected IR light photograph will be required because these images can be recorded in a well-illuminated environment. However, when the investigator is working in a laboratory where the lights can be completely subdued, the increased speed and convenience of using an IR light source to illuminate an image may be more advantageous. The decision is up to the individual photographer and based upon experience, experimentation, and the available resources.

In reflected UV light photography, a film photographer uses a Wratten 18A filter to block visible light waves. In reflected IR photography, an equivalent Wratten filter is used, but one designed to admit only IR light. Film photographers will have to use specific IR film to record these images. However, digital cameras are able to record IR radiation. Digital imaging chips are receptive to IR energy all the way up to approximately 1200 nm. However, the imaging chips have a barrier or *hot mirror* resting in front of them, which acts as an IR-blocking filter. Fortunately, this IR-blocking filter only slows down the recording of IR energy and does not completely stop one from recording images with IR light. In conclusion, photographers are absolutely able to use their digital cameras to record all types of images discussed in this chapter. Investigators can have their camera's hot mirror removed, thereby making IR photography much easier. However, removing the hot mirror may have some drawbacks in regard to visible light photography and is not necessary.

IR filters come in different densities that pass various wavelengths of light into the camera. All of them are designed to block visible light between 400 and 700 nm. Different manufacturers may identify their filters by alternate numbering or labeling taxonomy. Investigators should check the specifications of their filters as to the wavelengths of blocked energy. A list of common Wratten IR filters includes the following:

- #89B—blocks light below approximately 675 nm
- #88A—block light below approximately 720 nm
- #87A—blocks light below approximately 750 nm
- #87C—blocks light below 850 nm

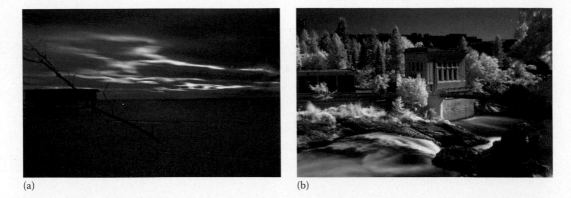

(a)   (b)

Figure 10.18 A series of test photographs should be recorded before working an actual crime scene so that investigators will have an approximate idea as to the length of the exposures for various light sources. Even after completing the test photographs, the investigator will only have a starting point to begin a bracketed series of exposures, because the variables of light intensity are just too numerous. Both figures (a) and (b) were recorded with the sun as the light source. Figure (a) was recorded at ISO 800, f/16, for 30 s and needed less exposure due to the photograph having been taken in the late afternoon when the sun's light produces a large amount of IR light. Figure (b) was recorded earlier in the day and needed more exposure, having been recorded at ISO 400, f/16, for 5 min.

The 87A (720 nm) filter is the most common IR filter used by crime scene investigators and is fully capable of producing results in all of the areas discussed in this chapter. A number of different manufacturers produce IR filters and they will have alternate numbering systems. Therefore, investigators need to check with the manufacturer to know the exact wavelengths of light passed by a particular filter. Some filters block all energy or light below the 900–1000 nm wavelength range, while others only block energy below 720 nm. The use of higher-valued filters is limited in crime scene work, and they are expensive, which often prohibits their use by the average investigator who has to purchase his or her own equipment.

As with the Wratten 18A filter, a focus shift occurs when photographing through an IR filter. The photographer needs to complete a series of experiments to determine the correct relationship between the lens and the IR filter chosen, as well as exposure variables (Figure 10.18). In exactly the same procedure as the 18A filter, the photographer should set the camera lens to a specific focal length, adjust the focus ring to the closest possible focal point, and then record an image of a ruler extending from the end of the lens. Next, the photographer should examine the recorded image and note the values for focal lengths, apertures, and subject-to-camera distances so that the results can be reproduced when photographing an actual piece of evidence. A much easier way to compensate for the shift in focus is by choosing a smaller aperture, such as an f/16. Realize that the length of the exposure may be rather long depending upon the light source and the camera's ISO setting. Consequently, the camera will need to be stabilized on a tripod or copy stand. An aperture of f/16 is typically capable of compensating for any focus shifts because it allows for a greater depth of field.

In addition to testing the equipment for the exact point of focus, the photographer must ascertain the type and amount of light necessary to produce a quality image (Figure 10.19). One benefit of using IR filters is the ability to work in illuminated environments. The number of potential light sources is nearly infinite and can include the sun, tungsten or halogen

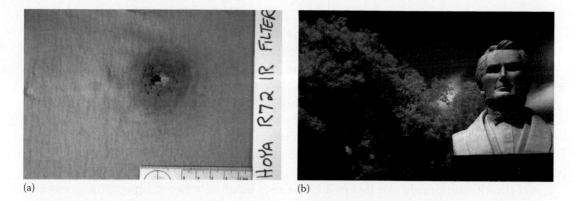

(a)   (b)

Figure 10.19 As an example of how divergent exposures can be using IR filters, (a) and (b) were both recorded using a Hoya 72R IR filter. (a) was recorded at ISO 400, f/8, for 45 s and used four 100 W lights mounted to a copy stand. (b) utilized the sun as its light source and was recorded at ISO 100, f/22, for 30 s. With a little practice and experience, investigators will at least become familiar with where to start an exposure with different light sources.

lights, flashlights, electronic flash, and even standard incandescent light bulbs. LED and fluorescent lights are typically not a great source of IR illumination. Obviously, the stronger the light source, the shorter the exposure time. The sun is the best light source because of its intensity, but may not be practical if the subject is in the hospital or the morgue. If the investigator maintains a consistency in the aperture and ISO settings, for example, f/16 at ISO 400, then the combination of the light source and exposure length is the only variable that must be dealt with when working in an actual crime scene. Remember that when working with smaller light sources, such as a flashlight, the light should be moved or painted onto the subject to eliminate hot spots.

When an investigator chooses to use an IR light source such as an ALS unit, he or she needs to control the ambient lighting because there will be no barrier filter on the camera's lens. The investigator cannot record an IR image when the IR light competes with the ambient light or at least that is true when barrier filters are not employed. ALS units can be expensive, but they do produce a consistent beam of light that can be used to enhance the presence of hidden evidence. Investigators can also use IR spotting scopes designed for hunters and police officers working surveillance. The spotting scopes are less expensive than an ALS unit but can be challenging to find, and their strength or intensity can vary widely. The Internet is a good resource to research and purchase IR light sources. However, a homemade IR light source can be made out of an old, discarded flash unit, exposed and developed color-print film, and black duct or electrical tape. The steps to build one's own IR flash unit are as follows:

- Expose a roll of color-print film to light and develop the exposed film.
- Cut two lengths of the developed film long enough to fully cover the head of the flash.
- Lay the two strips of film on top of each other so that a double-thick barrier is created.
- Place the two-piece barrier across the flash head.
- Use black tape to secure the film barrier to the flash head and to seal off any areas where visible light may escape.

When the white light projected from the flash passes through the two overlaid sections of film, it produces IR light. In addition to being inexpensive, this technique can produce excellent results. This homemade IR flash technique must be utilized in a dark environment, in contrast to reflected IR photography. The basic theory is that barrier filters block visible light and can be used in daylight conditions. In contrast, dark environments allow photographers to use IR light sources without a barrier filter. Either technique can be used with today's digital cameras.

Before attempting to utilize the IR flash technique on an actual crime scene, investigators need to experiment with it in order to determine the correct relationship between ISO value, aperture, and the number of full-power flash exposures necessary to produce a well-illuminated image. An ISO of 400 is a nice balance between image sharpness and the amount of light necessary to produce an image. The aperture can be adjusted to the investigator's personal choice, but for the sake of argument, an aperture of f/16 is a good choice because it compensates for the IR-focus shift. The length of the exposure is not important, because the darkened environment does not allow visible light to impact the image. As a result, the exposure will depend solely on the number of flashes needed to record an image and the length of the exposure will be determined by the recycle time of the flash. Therefore, the final part of the equation is to take test exposures and determine how many full-power flashes are required to capture an IR image. Since these photographs are typically of smaller subjects, the flash does not have to be held very far from the subject. Two to three feet between the subject and flash should be adequate. Remember to keep this same distance when photographing an actual subject. Take notes of the test results in regard to ISO, aperture, and the number of flashes cast in order to obtain a quality result.

Obviously, digital cameras have a great advantage in IR photography because the image can be examined immediately and compensations made if necessary. Film photographers must bracket their exposures. Remember to change only one variable at a time while bracketing. For example, add or subtract the number of IR flashes projected onto the subject or change the ISO or aperture settings, but do not make multiple changes all at once. Too many changes could cause the picture to move from well underexposed to well overexposed without any middle ground.

Tattoo Evidence

The identification of deceased persons is an important responsibility for both crime scene and death investigators. Frequently, investigators must comb through missing persons reports in order to match up common features, such as scars, marks, and tattoos, or pathologists may have to rely on such distinctions in order to identify a body. However, environmental and time factors often make the identification of bodies difficult at best. As the body begins to putrefy and decompose, unique identifiers such as tattoos may go completely unnoticed. As the body passes through the various stages of decomposition, tattoos may become less and less visible. Fortunately, investigators can photograph these hidden or latent tattoos using IR lighting techniques and create sharp-focused photographic images of tattoos.

Photographing with IR light can be accomplished through a number of methods. Each method will have its own set of positive and negative attributes. The various techniques that may be employed for documenting tattoos on decomposing bodies include

- The use of an IR camera (or camera converted to record with IR light)
- The use of IR filters (also known as reflected IR photography)
- The use of an IR light source, including a homemade IR flash

The choice of a specific technique is up to the individual investigator and typically will be guided by an analysis and/or compromise of available resources, the environment in which the subject rests, and the desired quality of the final recorded image.

Reflected IR photography was commonly employed by both artistic photographers and crime scene investigators when film was the recording media of choice. The switch to digital imaging has not created a detrimental effect on the abilities of photographers to capture images in light found above 700 nm. In fact, digital imaging chips are highly sensitive to IR light and digital cameras can be used in a number of crime scene investigative applications. Digital cameras are sensitive to IR light up to approximately 1200 nm. To prevent the IR light from spoiling the average photographer's composition, a *hot-mirror* or IR filter is placed over the imaging chip or sensor in order to limit the amount of IR light from striking it. Fortunately, IR light can penetrate through the hot mirror over time and allow investigators the ability to record images with IR light. One application for IR photography is in the area of tattoo documentation. It is not uncommon to find potentially important tattoo details concealed by blood, putrefaction, and/or the decomposition process. It is completely possible to enhance the visualization of these tattoos with an investigator's current camera, simply by adding an IR filter to the end of the camera's lens and recording a timed exposure.

There is no need to have the IR hot mirror removed from any investigator's camera. Given enough time and allowing enough light to pass through the hot mirror and to the imaging sensor, any digital camera can record a photograph in IR light. The trade-off between paying for a camera converted to record IR light and using IR filters is simply exposure time. One may be able to handhold an IR-converted camera for an exposure lasting only a fraction of a second. However, basically, the same IR image can be recorded with any digital camera, although the exposure might last minutes instead of a fraction of a second. Compare Figure 10.20a and b. Figure 10.20a was recorded with a Fuji IS-1 UV/IR camera and was recorded at ISO 100, f/3.7, for 1/60th of a second. Figure 10.20b was recorded with a Canon 40D at ISO 400, f/16, but required 170 s of exposure using the sun as a light source.

Reflected IR light photography does have a few issues that must be addressed by the photographer in order to record a sharp-focused image. Because the filters attached to the camera's lens are opaque, the camera is unable to give a preview or *live view* of the image. This is simply overcome by focusing the image in the viewfinder using ambient light, attaching the IR filter, and then turning the camera's autofocus feature off. The camera is now focused for light ranging between 400 and 700 nm, even though the image is recorded in wavelengths somewhere between 700 and 1000 nm depending on one's choice of filter. The change in wavelengths causes a shift in the focus. Focus is simply a matter of distance between subject and camera and a photographer could conduct a set of easily designed experiments to determine the exact distance or point of focus for their particular lens. However, the easiest method is simply to select a small aperture to increase the image's depth of field so that it incorporates the shift in focus. An aperture of f/16 should be adequate to compensate for a shift in focus between 700 and 850 nm. Once again, the trade-off is simply time. All things being equal, smaller apertures will require longer

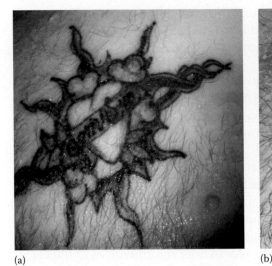
(a)

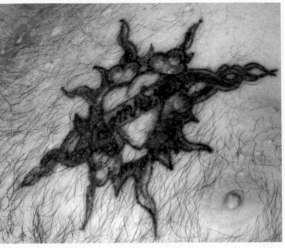
(b)

Figure 10.20 (a) was recorded with a Fujifilm IS-1 digital camera and the exposure values were ISO 100, f/3.7, 1/60th of a second. (b) was recorded with a Canon 40D digital camera and the exposure values were ISO 400, f/16, 170 s.

exposures. Fortunately, deceased bodies are unlikely to move on the photographer and a lengthy exposure should not be a major concern.

Lengthy exposures and digital cameras do not always go well together. The increase in exposure time allows for noise (random generation of pixel information) to develop in the image. As digital technology continues to progress, the amount of noise seen in recorded images continues to lessen and overall compositions continue to improve over time, especially with full-frame (36 × 24 mm) imaging chips. In addition, many cameras now have built-in *noise-reduction* features. This feature does a fairly good job at removing unwanted noise from long exposures. Photographers simply need to be patient and allow for the extra time the camera needs to work its magic. As a side note, investigators should ensure they have spare batteries on hand for extensive crime scene work. Another *possible* unwanted result of long exposures in the daytime is caused by light leaking into camera through the viewfinder. Figure 10.21 shows what light leakage may look like. The easy fix to this is to cover the eyepiece with a specially designed cover or simply throw a black cloth, such as a lens cleaning cloth, over the eyepiece in order to prevent such a distraction to occur.

Another distraction that might occur when utilizing reflected IR photography techniques occurs when light bounces between the hot mirror and lens elements, creating a hot spot in the image. Using a lens hood or shade will help reduce the amount of extraneous light from entering the camera. In addition, hot spots are greatly diminished by using a longer focal length lens rather than a wide-angle lens. Figure 10.22 illustrates what a hot spot will look like in an image. If this distraction develops, use a lens hood and/or a longer focal length to eliminate the anomaly.

A barrier filter is the key to reflected IR photographs, and investigators have a number of manufacturers to choose from in order to find a filter that fits their needs. Photographers are likely to find that two IR filters should be more than adequate to image difficult to see tattoos. First, a Wratten 89B filter that prevents light below 720 nm from entering the camera will work in a majority of situations. Equivalent 720 nm filters include Hoya R72,

Figure 10.21 Light can leak into an image through the camera's viewfinder. This usually causes a fog to appear, similar to what is seen in this image.

Figure 10.22 The hot spot visible in this image was created by light bouncing between the hot mirror and lens elements. Using a longer focal length lens and lens hood helps eliminate this unwanted distraction.

B&W 092, and a Peca 914 filters. For those tattoos that may be concealed due to severe decomposition or charring (burning), a filter that prevents light at approximately 850 nm may be more useful. A Wratten 87C prevents light at 850 nm from entering the camera. Equivalent 850 nm filters include Hoya IR85, B&W 093, and a Peca 910. If a photographer still cannot image a tattoo with an 850 nm equivalent filter, one could try a denser filter, such as a 930 nm or a 1050 nm filter. The great benefit of IR photography is that it is not invasive; it will not cause further harm to the subject or investigation by recording multiple photographs of a subject. Consequently, photographers should possess at least one or two IR filters in their photography gear.

Cameras not converted for photographing with IR light by having their hot-mirror filters removed cannot provide an accurate exposure metering. Once again, investigators will have to conduct some test exposures. The variables involved in almost any exposure are ISO value, aperture, shutter speed, and the source of light. In order to limit the number of variables, photographers may find it easier to maintain similar ISO values and apertures for all their compositions, and in that way, only the length of the exposure and the particular light source need to be tested for. IR light sources can include copy stand lights, flashlights, and electronic flashes, but the best source of IR light is the sun. When a photographer conducts their test exposures with the sun, they should also conduct test exposures on a cloudy day, because there is no guarantee that the sun will be shining when a tattooed body is discovered. Photographers can record a series of test exposures under varying conditions in order to obtain the approximate length of an exposure. The time a photograph takes to record will not always be the same, even under similar lighting circumstances. However, experimenting with exposures will provide photographers with at least a starting point for their own images. Photographers can create a small *cheat sheet* with their findings, which can be referenced when working a crime scene. The sun's and a flashlight's intensity can vary quite a bit. Therefore, except for the controlled atmosphere of the photographic laboratory, one must be flexible in calculating exposure times. Bracketing an image's capture is still an excellent way to ensure that a quality image is captured. As an additional note on using flashlights, the photographer should cast the light by sweeping it back and forth across the subject. This will create a more even lighting across the entire composition and will prevent a hot spot from forming in the image.

Sometimes tattoos are obscured from view because of blood flowing from one or more wounds. Recording a blood-covered tattoo with IR light can help reveal tattoos and injuries beneath the staining blood due to the fact that IR light can easily pass through blood and reveals what is beneath. Obviously, blood can be washed off during autopsy. However, sometimes the identification of a subject might be facilitated while still investigating the crime scene prior to the victim being transported to the medical examiner's or coroner's office for autopsy. Compare figures found in Figure 10.23. Figure 10.23a was recorded with visible light and the tattoo present on the stomach of the individual was partially concealed by the presence of blood. Figure 10.24b was recorded with reflected IR photography techniques, using a 720 nm filter to block the visible light. The camera's settings for

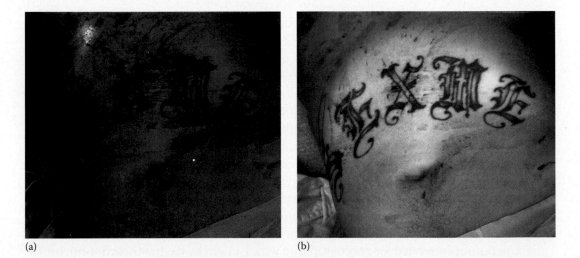

(a)   (b)

Figure 10.23 (a) was recorded in visible light. The exposure values were ISO 400, f/8, for 1/125th of a second. (b) was recorded at ISO 800, f/16, for 2 min and a Streamlight SL-20 flashlight was cast across the subject during the entire exposure's length.

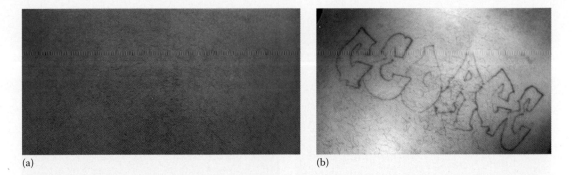

(a)

(b)

Figure 10.24 (a) was recorded in visible light and shows a light and faded tattoo. (b) is an image of the same tattoo but was recorded through a 720 nm filter, and the exposure settings were ISO 400, f/16, for 80 s. The sun was the light source.

Figure 10.23b were ISO 800, f/16, for 2 min. The composition was photographed inside a residence. Additional light was provided by a Streamlight® SL-20 flashlight and the light was swept across the subject during the entire length of the exposure.

Tattoos can fade over time, especially with darker-skinned subjects. IR light photography is an excellent resource to make faded tattoos much more visible and identifiable. Once again, an IR filter blocking light just above the visible spectrum is all that is needed to produce superior results. Compare Figure 10.24a and b. Figure 10.24a is a photograph of a faded tattoo that was recorded in sunlight. Figure 10.24b was also recorded in sunlight using a Hoya R72 IR filter. The camera settings for Figure 10.24b were ISO 400, f/16, for 80 s. Simply as a reminder, an aperture of f/16 was selected to increase the composition's depth of field in order to compensate for the focus shift due to IR light, and an ISO of 400 was selected as a compromise between the light-gathering ability of the recording media and the amount of digital noise that can be created with higher ISO values. The exposure time of 80 s was slightly less than expected, but the sun's rays were strong and directly over the subject.

Putrefaction and the decomposition of a human body can truly play havoc with the visibility of tattoos and make the job of an investigator or medical examiner much more difficult by obscuring the unique and identifying information that can be obtained from an individual's tattoos. Fortunately, IR light can shed illumination and clarity onto tattoo evidence and assist in the identification of a decomposed body. What follows are examples of reflected IR light photography techniques in the imaging of a human body as it decomposed over the course of 6 months at Sam Houston State University's Southeast Texas Applied Forensic Science (STAFS) facility. The STAFS anthropological research facility is a unique facility in Texas that allows researchers to study the decomposition of human remains. Dr. Joan Bytheway is a forensic anthropologist and the current director of the facility. Dr. Bytheway granted access to the facility to the author and provided subjects to study and document as they transitioned through the decomposition process.

The primary donation and photographic subject was a white male who had multiple tattoos, including one on each arm, each leg, and each side of the upper chest. The subject was placed out onto the grounds of the STAFS facility in December of 2009. Huntsville (Texas) had a particularly cold winter, including a couple of snowfalls, which was quite unique to Southeast Texas. As a result, insect activity was not as destructive as may have occurred during the summer months, and the decomposition process was also slowed greatly by the

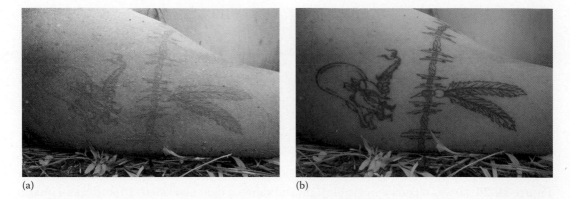

(a)   (b)

Figure 10.25 (a) is a visible light image of a faded tattoo. (b) is an IR image (720 nm) of the same tattoo. The exposure settings were ISO 800, f/16, for 118 s and the sun was the source of light.

cooler temperatures. Both factors provided the author with the added benefit or luxury of time, allowing the opportunity to record photographs over the course of 6 months. Figure 10.25a and b show one of the tattoos on the subject's upper arm as it appeared the first day of exposure to the elements. The body's overall appearance was pale and the tattoo did not have a great deal of brilliance or intensity in visible light (as depicted in Figure 10.25a). Even with a light-skinned person, the details brought out in Figure 10.25b by the use of a 720 nm IR filter are superior to what was obtained through photographing in visible light. When the tattoo is simply faded or covered in blood, an IR filter blocking only visible light (up to approximately 720 nm) is fully capable of capturing a quality image. Figure 10.25b was recorded at ISO 800, f/16, for 118 s and was captured in sunlight.

After a couple of weeks of exposure and as one would expect, the top layer of the skin begins to slough off the body. Certainly, the peeling back of the sloughed skin would allow the tattoo to become more visible. However, IR light can also cut through the epidermis layer of the skin and reveal what is just beneath the surface. Figure 10.26a and b was recorded 1 week into the study. Figure 10.26a was recorded in visible light and Figure 10.26b was recorded through a 720 nm IR filter (ISO 400, f/16, for 62 s).

(a)   (b)

Figure 10.26 (a) was recorded in visible light after 1 week of exposure to the elements. (b) is of the same tattooed area, but recorded with a 720 nm filter. The exposure values were ISO 400, f/16, for 62 s and the sun was the light source.

Skin continued to slough off during the first month of decomposition and after a month of exposure to the elements, the subject began to putrefy and turn black. Figure 10.27 shows a star-shaped tattoo on the subject's ankle. Figure 10.27a was recorded in visible light, and a small portion of the tattoo can be seen in the upper right-hand corner, protruding from beneath the separating skin. Figure 10.27b was recorded through a 720 nm IR filter and the entire tattoo could be seen (ISO 400, f/16, for 30 s). On the opposite leg, a tribal band style of tattoo was present, but due to a bit more putrefaction, this tattoo was less visible when viewed on the same day. Figure 10.28a was recorded in visible light, and Figure 10.28b was recorded through a 720 nm IR filter at ISO 400, f/16, for 94 s. The additional time required in Figure 10.28b as compared to Figure 10.27b was due to the fact that Figure 10.28b's tattoo was shaded by pine trees.

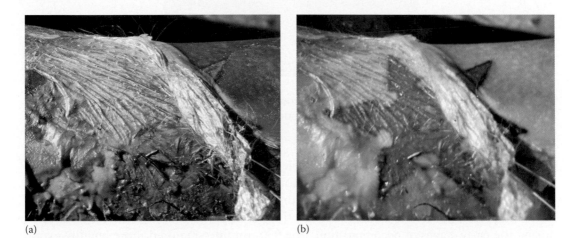

(a)   (b)

Figure 10.27 (a) was recorded in visible light after 1 month of exposure to the elements. (b) was recorded in IR light, utilizing a 720 nm filter. The exposure values were ISO 400, f/16, for 30 s.

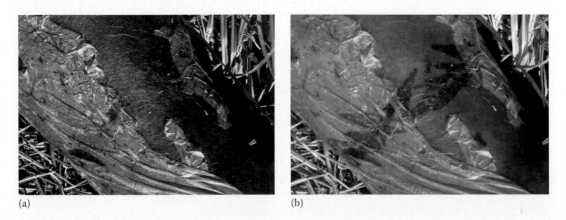

(a)   (b)

Figure 10.28 (a) was recorded in visible light after 1 month of exposure to the elements. (b) was recorded in IR light, utilizing a 720 nm filter. The exposure values were ISO 400, f/16, for 94 s. The extra exposure time was required because the tattoo was shaded by trees.

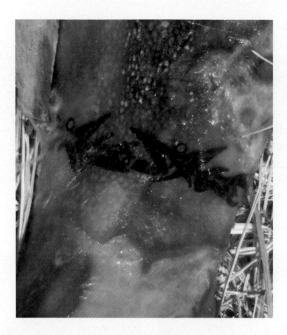

Figure 10.29 This figure was recorded of a completely hidden tattoo due to decomposition and putrefaction. The image was recorded in sunlight and through an 850 nm IR filter. The exposure values were ISO 400, f/16, for 8 min.

After 2 months of decomposition, the subject began to turn so black that the 720 nm IR filter stopped having a desirable effect. The photographer moved up the IR scale to approximately 850 nm, utilizing a B&W 093 filter. For lack of a better word, the stronger 850 nm filter was just as successful cutting through the decomposition as was the 720 nm filter during the early stages of decomposition. The 850 nm filter required more lengthy exposures in order to let the IR light penetrate the camera's hot mirror. Subsidizing the sunlight with a flashlight may keep the exposure lengths manageable, especially on cloudy days. The second suggestion to anyone imaging subjects requiring lengthy exposures is to utilize the digital camera's noise-reduction filter. There is far less digital noise or artifacts visible in the final image if the noise-reduction filter is used. Figure 10.29 was recorded of the tribal band tattoo observed back in Figure 10.28b. However, due to the discoloration of the skin, the tattoo was completely hidden from the human eye. Figure 10.29 was recorded using the 850 nm IR filter and the image was recorded at ISO 400, f/16, for 8 min.

An interesting growth of mold formed on one of the tattoos found on the subject's chest. Two circular and black-colored fungal growths appeared on the chest's tattoo approximately 5 months after the body was exposed to the environment. The 850 nm IR filter was able to record most of the detail obstructed by the mold growing on top of the tattoo. Figure 10.30a was recorded in visible light, while Figure 10.30b was recorded with the B&W 093 IR filter (ISO 400, f/16, for 8 min). Once again, if an investigator expects that a tattoo is hidden beneath the skin and concealed by the process of putrefaction and decomposition, the ability for IR light to penetrate through the skin and capture a quality photographic image of the tattoo is of unquestionable value.

Another subject became available at the STAFS facility who had died after receiving severe burns to his body and had skin grafts attempted in an effort to save the person's life. Figure 10.31a and b show the same area of burning and skin grafting on the individual's

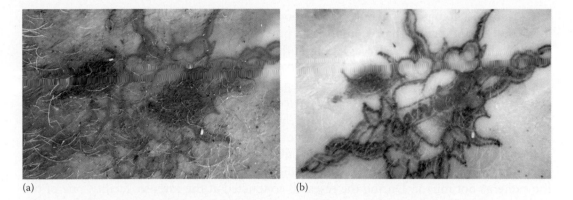

(a)   (b)

Figure 10.30 (a) is a visible light photograph of a tattoo concealed by black mold. (b) is an image of the same tattoo and was recorded through an 850 nm IR filter. The exposure settings were ISO 400, f/16, for 8 min. The sun was the light source.

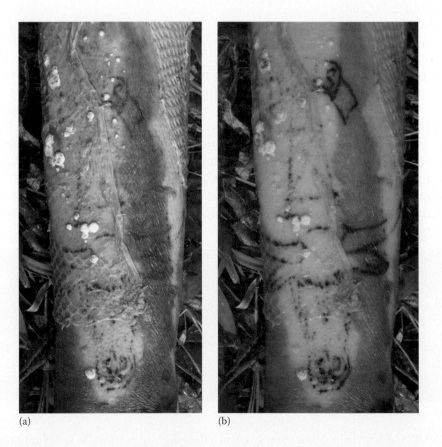

(a)   (b)

Figure 10.31 (a) was recorded in visible light and shows a skin graft repair after a severe third-degree burn injury. (b) was recorded of the same injury site but was recorded through a 720 nm IR filter. The exposure settings were ISO 400, f/16, for 2 min.

arm. The two photographs were recorded soon after the subject was placed onto the facility's grounds and before the decomposition process began. Figure 10.31a was recorded in visible light and Figure 10.31b was recorded through a 720 nm IR filter (ISO 400, f/16, for 2 min).

Instead of film, digital cameras are equipped with a complementary metal-oxide semiconductor (CMOS) or a charge-coupled device (CCD) imaging chip. For a very simplified explanation, the digital sensor acts like silver-halide film in the camera. When the shutter is opened, the sensor collects the incoming light and converts it into a charge, which is then converted into an image. A fairly recent advent of the digital age is the *IR camera*. This type of camera is specifically designed to capture digital images in the IR spectrum by removing the camera's hot mirror. During the research conducted at the forensic facility, one of the cameras utilized was the Fujifilm IS1. The Fujifilm's *Super CCD* is sensitive to both visible and IR light, approximately 400–900 nm. Unfortunately, Fujifilm no longer manufactures a camera designed specifically for IR or UV photography. However, investigators can have their own digital cameras converted for IR photography by having the hot mirror replaced with an IR filter. Photographers can go to a number of companies to have the conversion completed. As a beginning point, investigators can view one of the following websites in order to see what is involved in the conversion process and the cost:

- www.lifepixel.com
- www.precisioncamera.com
- www.maxmax.com

As previously mentioned, when performing IR photography, one needs to limit visible light from becoming part of the exposure. Most often this is accomplished by fitting IR filters over the camera's lens, thereby blocking the visible light from entering the camera. The benefit gained by using a specifically designed or converted-IR camera is that the exposure can be recorded handheld, eliminating the need for a tripod-mounted camera and lengthy exposure times. With this type of camera, photographers can also utilize an IR flash, which entails filtering the light source instead of the camera lens.

Figure 10.32 depicts a tattoo on the test subject's right arm. As is evident from the photo, he is in an advanced state of decomposition. In addition, mummification or the

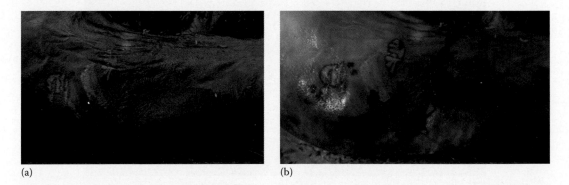

(a)   (b)

Figure 10.32 (a) is a visible light photograph of a decomposing tattoo. (b) is a photograph of the same tattoo but was recorded with an dedicated IR camera and IR flash unit. The exposure was recorded at f/11 and 1/60th of a second. (Photographed by Curtis Klingle, Retired Crime Scene Investigator, Bryan Police Department, Bryan, TX.)

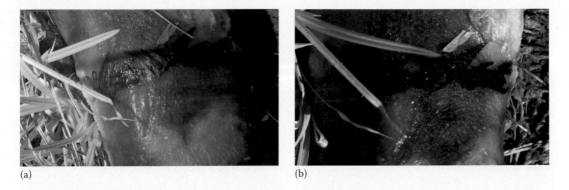

(a) (b)

Figure 10.33 (a) was recorded with a dedicated IR camera and flash. The exposure settings were f/5.6 for 1/60th of a second. (b) was recorded with a standard digital camera and a 720 nm IR filter. The exposure settings were ISO 400, f/16, for 4 min. (Photographed by Curtis Klingle, Retired Crime Scene Investigator, Bryan Police Department, Bryan, TX.)

dehydration of the subject's skin is present. Parts of the tattoo are visible but not clear enough for identification. Figure 10.32b is a photograph of the same tattoo taken with the Fuji IS-1 using a flash unit modified for IR photography. The aperture was set at f/11 and the shutter speed was 1/60th of a second.

Figure 10.33a and b were recorded of the same tribal band tattoo depicted in Figure 10.29. The tattoo's features were not visible to the human eye. Figure 10.33a was photographed using the Fuji IS-1 and an IR flash. Figure 10.33b was captured using a Canon Rebel. The 18–55 mm lens was equipped with an 87A (720 nm) filter. The aperture was set at f/16 and the shutter was allowed to stay open for 240 s (4 min).

Whatever an investigator's personal choice of IR equipment may be, the value such equipment can provide to those needing to identify the remains of a deceased person cannot be overstated. Tattoos are frequently used to help identify a person's remains, and with the assistance of IR light, investigators are no longer limited by the decomposition process. IR-converted digital cameras and/or the use of IR light sources can bring out tattoo details found on decomposed bodies. In addition, any standard digital camera, preferably a single-lens reflex (SLR) camera because of its versatility, and a set of IR filters can record quality sharp-focused images. Two basic filters, a 720 nm and an 850 nm IR filter, are all that are necessary to record quality IR photographs. In conclusion, IR light is just another tool to put into an investigator's arsenal that can be used to help identify the unidentified through tattoos.

Forgeries and Document Alterations

Documents and fiduciary instruments are frequently altered by forgers. These alterations can be detected with IR light. The various inks used to create documents are produced differently and, as a result, absorb IR light differently. For example, writings from two black ink pens may appear identical under visible light; however, when viewed under IR light, their differences become obvious (Figure 10.34). With that said, when dissimilar inks are detected through the use of IR light, the investigator can rightfully suspect that the document has been altered. Document examiners typically have access to light sources that produce narrow bandwidths of IR light so that minute changes in the absorption ability of different inks can be detected. Crime scene photographers may not have the fine-tuning

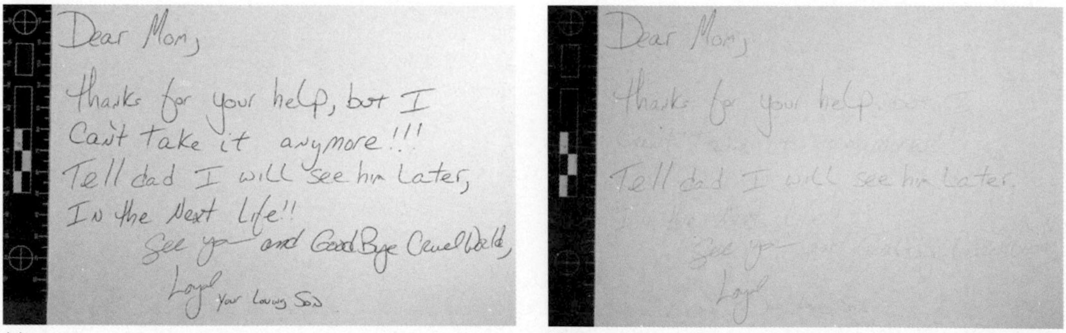

(a)   (b)

Figure 10.34 These images are of an altered document. (a) shows the letter photographed in natural light; (b) was recorded through a Hoya 72R IR filter, with the camera set to ISO 400, f/8, and for 30 s. Although two black ink pens may appear similar, IR light can differentiate between different ink types.

ability of a document examiner's equipment, but they do have filters and light sources available that will enable them to detect some forged documents.

Changes detected in forged documents can be photographed utilizing reflective IR photography techniques or utilizing an IR light source. Although the depth of field for flat pieces of paper does not require a small aperture, the size of the aperture should match the test photographs previously taken by the photographer so that the exposures are accurately recorded. The photographer could feasibly open the size of the aperture to shorten the exposure time. However, if a photographer has not produced a series of test exposures with the larger apertures, there is the risk of taking a poorly focused and/or exposed image. Unfortunately, exact reciprocity between exposure values cannot be guaranteed when working with the longer exposures required while working outside of the 400–700 nm span of visible light. Similarly, illuminated subjects may have slightly different exposure results because of the physical makeup or composition of the subject. Like almost everything else, bracketing the recorded images will help guarantee a more-valuable result.

Bloodstain Documentation

Bloodstain evidence is sometimes overlooked by investigators, especially when found on dark-colored fabrics or surfaces. IR light can help bring out the hidden information and evidence that latent bloodstains can provide to investigators. IR light can be used to greatly improve the contrast between blood and the substratum it rests upon. This contrast can be the difference in being able to identify a stain pattern or never even detecting its presence. Photographing blood on black surfaces so that it is visible is an excellent way to create a lasting impression with a jury (Figure 10.35). Furthermore, locating, identifying, and illustrating to the jury through photographs all of one's findings is a basic duty of all crime scene investigators.

Not only can IR light create better contrast with bloodstained evidence, but IR light also has the ability to see behind bloodstained surfaces. Traumatic injuries concealed by draining or dispersed blood may be photographed using IR light so that the actual wound cavity or substrate can be documented. Obviously, lethal wounds are cleaned during the autopsy process, but the nature of the wound may be a valuable piece of information to

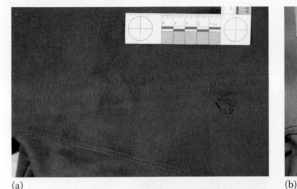

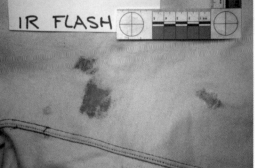

(a)   (b)

(c)

Figure 10.35 These images are of bloodstains found on a black clothing. As demonstrated in (a), the bloodstains are nearly invisible in natural light due to the fabric's color. (b) was recorded using a homemade IR flash. The flash was fired 10 times from approximately 18″ away, the camera was set to ISO 100, f/8, and the exposure required 76 s to allow the flash to fully recharge between each burst of light. (c) was recorded of a black-colored sock using an IR 720 filter, and the exposure settings were ISO 800, f/11, for 4 min. Not only was the blood not visible on the sock, the stripes were also not visible in natural light, both of which were made visible through IR light. The arrow indicates where a bullet passed through the sock.

have while investigating the actual crime scene. Furthermore, when equipped with a digital camera that provides an immediate review of images, investigators do not have to wait for the autopsy to obtain an idea of the type of weapon or cutting instrument that caused the lethal wound. In other cases, blood may stain a piece of paper or other surface containing valuable information that cannot be cleaned without damaging it (Figure 10.36). In those cases, an investigator should photograph the object using IR light. Results are not guaranteed, but once again, it is better to try than to ignore the opportunity to recover a potential piece of information or evidence.

Gunshot Residue

Gunshot residue, powder burns, and propellant projected onto a target are extremely valuable to crime scene investigators. Such evidence can place a gun in close proximity to the victim and may have a huge bearing on a case, because knowing how close a weapon was to the target can limit a suspect's justification for or description of how the shooting occurred. IR light is the perfect platform with which to record such photographic pieces of evidence, especially when the color of the target's surface is dark or has a distracting pattern (Figure 10.37). The substratum can be human skin and even skin covered by blood.

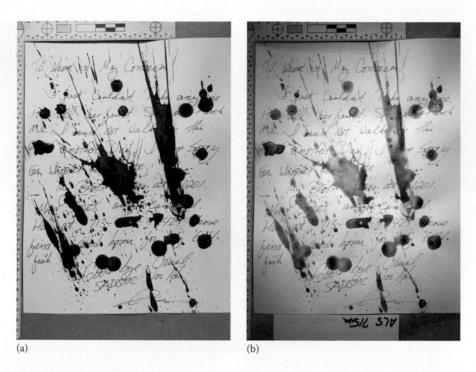

(a)   (b)

Figure 10.36 IR light can penetrate thin layers of skin, blood, and debris and document the underlying surface. (a) was recorded in natural light, while (b) was recorded with the assistance of an ALS set to 715 nm. The exposure was captured at ISO 400, f/4.8, for 77 s. Note that additional information was gained by photographing the suicide note with IR light.

(a)   (b)

Figure 10.37 Frequently, the crime scene investigator may need to photograph gunshot residue, powder burns, and burned propellant on targeted surfaces. IR light will aid in recording these valuable pieces of evidence. The bullet holes photographed in (a) and (b) were both found on black-colored fabric. (a) was recorded using a homemade IR flash unit, which was fired 10 times from approximately 18″. The camera was set to ISO 800, f/8, for 50 s. (b) was recorded through a Wratten 87A filter. The camera's settings were ISO 800, f/22, for 30 s.

Burned propellant absorbs IR light and will photograph as a definitively black color. IR light is also likely to lighten the background, thus increasing the contrast between the gunpowder residue and the surface it rests on. Any of the IR photographic techniques described earlier in this chapter can be used in the documentation of gunshot residue.

Conclusion

The documentation of evidence unseen by the human eye is an important aspect of crime scene investigation. The utilization of UV and/or IR light provides a method for recording these valuable pieces of evidence. There are specific applications in which photography with UV or IR light will produce results. Both forms of photography require investigators to practice techniques and conduct tests with their equipment so that results can be reproduced consistently, especially when it comes time to work an actual crime scene. Reflected IR photography is a little easier in the way in which a photographer applies IR light or limits visible light onto a subject. Any of the IR light techniques will work in most applications, other than in discriminating between inks in forgery investigations. This is because different inks may require narrower bands of IR wavelengths to reveal any distinctions. However, for all the other applications, an investigator may choose his or her favorite IR technique.

Unfortunately, UV light photography is not as simple. Many different UV light sources are available and each light source emits its own particular range of wavelengths. Furthermore, these light sources peak at different wavelengths and that too can alter the photographic outcome. Compounding those variables is the necessity of sometimes adding barrier filters to the composition. Consequently, when utilizing UV light in the photography and search of crime scenes, crime scene photographers must be flexible. However, once a reaction is observed, it can be photographed. Conducting personal experiments with test photographs will enable the investigator to determine the techniques most effective in correctly documenting crime scenes utilizing UV light photography. There is no substitute for experience, even if that experience is conducted in an experimental process.

Photographers are required to produce pieces of photographic evidence that will be of value to investigators, prosecutors, and jurors. Ultimately, photographs may end up being viewed by jurors and the images must meet with their expectations. More often than not, investigators must educate the jury on crime scene investigation realities. For example, this may entail explaining that blood does not fluoresce and that Luminol reactions cannot be seen in daylight conditions. Consequently, becoming familiar with UV and IR light sources and the way they enhance crime scene photography evidence is paramount to becoming both a premier crime scene photographer and a credible witness in court.

End of Chapter Questions

1. Where is UV light found along the electromagnetic spectrum?
    a. Greater than 1000 nm
    b. Less than 700 nm
    c. Greater than 532 nm
    d. Less than 400 nm

2. Where is IR light found along the electromagnetic spectrum?
   a. Greater than 700 nm
   b. Less than 720 nm
   c. Between 532 and 700 nm
   d. Greater than 400 nm

3. When imaging semen stains, which is a better source of light?
   a. UV light
   b. IR light
   c. Visible light
   d. None of the above

4. Which is a source of UV light?
   a. Sun
   b. ALS
   c. Incandescent light
   d. All of the above

5. When imaging fluorescent fingerprints, which is a better source of light?
   a. UV light
   b. IR light
   c. Visible light
   d. None of the above

6. Reflected UV light photography through the use of a Wratten 18A filter is better recorded with digital imaging.
   a. True
   b. False

7. What is the color of 532 nm light?
   a. Violet
   b. Blue
   c. Green
   d. Red

8. What is the nanometer wavelength of blue light?
   a. 365 nm
   b. 470 nm
   c. 600 nm
   d. 720 nm

9. Which colored filter typically works best with UV and violet lighting?
   a. Orange
   b. Red
   c. Yellow
   d. Green

10. Which colored filter typically works best with blue-colored lighting?
    a. Orange
    b. Red
    c. Yellow
    d. Blue

11. The visibility of gunpowder residue can be enhanced with both UV and IR light.
    a. True
    b. False

12. Which ALS is better when imaging obliterated or dissolved writings?
    a. Green light
    b. UV light
    c. IR light
    d. Incandescent light

13. Blood _____ UV light.
    a. Reflects
    b. Absorbs
    c. Fluoresces with
    d. Refracts

14. When correcting for the focus shift with UV light, one can utilize the IR index mark available on some lenses.
    a. True
    b. False

15. Which light source is a better choice for imaging faded or obscured tattoos?
    a. Green light
    b. Fluorescent light
    c. UV light
    d. IR light

16. Digital cameras must have their *hot mirrors* removed in order to have standard digital cameras made capable of recording IR light photographs.
    a. True
    b. False

17. IR filters used for reflected IR photography block what type of light from being used to create an image?
    a. Incandescent light
    b. Visible light
    c. Alternate light
    d. IR light

18. Which aperture is most likely capable of compensating for the shift in focus caused by IR light?
    a. f/2.8
    b. f/5.6
    c. f/11
    d. f/16

19. What can cause a *hot spot* to develop in the center of a reflected IR photograph?
    a. Wide-angle lenses
    b. UV bleed-over
    c. Noise (artifacts)
    d. Focus shift

20. In order to record images with reflected IR or reflected UV light, the ISO value must be greater (faster) than ISO 1600.
    a. True
    b. False

Photography Assignments

Required Tools: UV light source, IR filter, colored barrier filters (yellow, orange, and red)

Photography Subjects: fluorescent fingerprint powder, fluorescent markers, bruises and/or tattoos, altered documents, gunshot residue targets, fibers, body fluids, bloodstained fabric exemplars

   I. UV light exercises, using a black light or similar UV light
       A. Photograph a fluorescent fingerprint:
           1. If fingerprint is not available, use a fluorescent highlighter (marker) and photograph a drawn subject with the highlighter.
       B. Photograph an overall image of a bathroom using the UV light source (painting with light may be necessary).
       C. Photograph close-up images of fluorescing surfaces within the bathroom (fill the viewfinder, use a scale, quality lighting).
       D. If available, photograph a person having a bruise. Photograph the injury with visible light and UV light. Compare the results.
       E. If available, attempt other photography subjects discussed in the chapter, such as altered documents, fibers, and/or body fluids.
  II. IR light exercise, using reflected IR photography techniques:
       A. In the daytime, photograph outdoor landscapes with IR filters.
       B. Photograph smaller subjects, such as
           1. Altered documents
           2. Bloodstained targets
           3. Gunshot residue targets
           4. A person with a tattoo
           5. Charred or soot stained documents
       C. If available, photograph the same subjects listed with an IR light source, such as an ALS, IR light flashlight, or a homemade IR flash unit.

Additional Readings

Cochran, P. Use of reflective ultraviolet photography to photo-document bruising to children. Retrieved August 22, 2014, from http://www.crime-scene investigator.net/uvchildphoto.html.

Dorion, R. (2004). *Bite Mark Evidence*. Boca Raton, FL. CRC Press.

Duncan, C.D. and Klingle, C. (2011). Using reflected infrared photography to enhance the visibility of tattoos. *Journal of Forensic Identification*, 61(5), 495–519.

Finney, A. Infrared photography. Retrieved April 25, 2009, from http://encyclopedia.jrank.org/articles/pages/1148/infrared-photography.html.

Klingle, C. (2008). Photography—Ultraviolet and infrared injury photography. *Lone Star Forensic Journal*, 62(4), 9–15.

Morgan, W.D. and Lester, H.M. (1951). *The New Leica Manual: A Complete Book for the Leica Photographer*. 12th ed. New York: Morgan & Lester, Publishers.

Pex, J.O. Domestic violence photography. Retrieved April 25, 2009, from http://www.crime-scene-investigator.net/dv-photo.html.

Saferstein, R. (2004). *Criminalistics: An Introduction to Forensic Science*. 8th ed. Upper Saddle River, NJ: Pearson Education, Inc.

WWW.LIFEPIXEL.COM. Retrieved August 22, 2014, from www.lifepixel.com.

WWW.MAXMAX.COM. Retrieved August 22, 2014, from www.maxmax.com.

WWW.PRECISIONCAMERA.COM. Retrieved August 22, 2014, from www.precisioncamera.com.

Photographing Fire Scenes

Some of the more challenging environments to photograph, especially at night, are fire scenes. Accurately recording the scene of a fire requires all the skills and talents of the crime scene photographer. Fire and arson scenes offer a large variety of photographic challenges to the investigator. In addition to the dangerous conditions often found in burned-out structures, the photographic challenges are abundant. To begin with, many times these scenes lack any ambient lighting or possess significant contrast between the highlights and shadows. Examples of these challenges may include

- Poor lighting
  - Daytime fire scenes oftentimes have backlit compositions.
  - Nighttime fire scenes oftentimes lack any ambient lighting.
- Lack of contrast
  - In regard to color
  - In regard to depth (char patterns)
  - Presence of haze, smoke, and falling water

As with many perplexing photographic endeavors, getting a proper light exposure is oftentimes the greatest challenge, and that is no different in the photography of fire scenes. Fire and arson photographers must be able to adapt to a variety of difficult conditions by identifying the lighting problems and developing solutions or plans to overcome the photographic dilemmas. Once again, digital photography is a true blessing because of the ability to immediately review one's images on the back of the camera. Arson investigators, as well as all digital photographers, can immediately evaluate an image and identify areas needing improved lighting, focus, and composition. Photographers can then adjust and correct for any observed deficiencies. As with all photographic endeavors, the goal is to be confident that an outstanding piece of photographic evidence is recorded and available for others to view.

In order to record any photograph, one needs to have light. Working fire scenes present a number of potential lighting challenges. One of the more common challenges is simply working in near-blackout or extremely dark conditions. In addition to the lack of electrical power and lights, the walls and ceilings of burned-out structures are frequently covered in black soot or char, which only serves to absorb any ambient light that might be available. When faced with these extremely dark environments, recording an image with a combination of ambient light and supplemental light is most likely going to produce the best results (Figure 11.1). As a reminder, in order to record the small amount of ambient light present, the photographer must stabilize his or her camera on a tripod. As a general rule, hand-holding the camera in these low-light conditions will not likely result in a quality image, and therefore, investigators should have their tripod available. If the subject is small, such as a damaged electrical outlet, certainly a handheld flash photograph will be effective. However, photographing an entire soot-covered and smoke-stained room should

Figure 11.1 This composition was metered for light and recorded at ISO 400, f/11, for 20 s. Supplemental light was added with an external flash to cast additional light into the shadows.

not be recorded in the same manner. The light produced solely by an electronic flash just may not do the scene justice, because the light can be largely absorbed by all the soot- and smoke-stained surfaces.

In regard to the overall type of photographs, whether the composition be an individual room or an overall structure, and where ambient lighting is limited, the camera's light metering can be fooled or inaccurate. For example, one may be faced with one extreme, in which the scene is basically void of ambient light. The camera will not likely be able to meter the light and unable to come up with a proper exposure. Certainly in this case supplemental light must be added to the composition in order to record an image. At the other extreme, the scene will have adequate ambient light to record an image, but because the scene is mostly black in color, the camera will overexpose the composition. The overexposure occurs because the camera wants to turn the black, soot-stained surfaces the color of 18% gray, thereby overexposing the composition. Consequently, fire photographers must be able to adjust for both extremes, and recognizing how one's personal camera interprets light in these situations will assist them in making the appropriate corrections to the camera's exposure evaluations. Not all cameras are equal, and although they all are searching for 18% gray, they do not always arrive at that value in the same manner. Therefore, those photographing fire scenes should definitely practice with their equipment and obtain a general idea how their equipment reacts to different photographic challenges found at fire scenes.

In situations where a photographer's camera cannot meter enough ambient light to find a proper exposure, the photographer has a couple of options. If there is some ambient light, one can increase the camera's sensitivity to light by raising the ISO value and attempt to record the image with only ambient light. Of course, if the ISO value is so high that the photographer is unhappy with the noise or grain generated, then reciprocal changes can be made to the composition (i.e., extend the length of the exposure and lower the ISO value in equal increments). If this technique is chosen, recording a set of bracketed exposures would be advisable, so that if there is a slight overexposure or underexposures of the image due to the subject matter's color, the most accurate photograph is still recorded. In addition to a proper light exposure, fire investigators benefit from having the scene's proper color recorded, so that fire and smoke lines of demarcation are clearly discernable. Photographs recorded with just ambient light, even in dim illumination that is uniformly cast onto the surfaces contained within the composition, frequently produce better results than flash-sync exposures. However, if shadows are visible, there is significant contrast, or the ambient light is pretty much void in the composition, then supplemental light will be required.

In regard to ambient light photography, especially in the nighttime, oftentimes the evaluation of lighting can be complicated by the light sources that are brought into the scene by fire and arson investigators. These light sources have a tendency to cast hot spots into a composition. The hot spots can cause the difference between the image's shadows and highlights to be too great in order to record a quality photograph. It is recommended to set these lights into the scene's background (behind the camera, not into the composition's background). The physically closer these lights are to the actual composition seen in the camera's viewfinder, the greater the chance that the lights will cause hot spots to develop. If at all possible, these lights should be diffused in some manner or pulled further away in order to allow the light to spread out and soften a bit. Another option that will be discussed later is the idea of using the lights to paint the fire scene with light.

It is common for investigators to find themselves inside a burned structure, where the walls and ceilings are still standing, but the power has been cut inside the residence. In these situations, the room can be completely void of light. In those situations, no matter how long one leaves the shutter open or how high one sets the ISO value, there is no light available to record an image. In those situations, supplemental light must be added to the composition. Investigators have a number of options, from flash photography to painting with light. Just like any other composition, the photographer should be conscious of the subject's primary color and the idea that the camera is trying to balance the exposure for 18% gray (Figure 11.2). Therefore, if the walls and furniture in the room are charred or stained black, the camera may try to turn the black-colored surfaces 18% gray or unintentionally overexpose the composition. Photographers should just keep this idea in mind when recording their images.

Another challenge to fire investigators occurs at fire scenes that are investigated during daytime hours. One might believe that the additional light provided by daytime investigations is a benefit to photographers. However, backlit compositions are frequently encountered during daytime investigations. Backlit compositions are always a challenge and frequently present themselves when photographing a burned structure's interior where a broken-out window or doorway is part of the composition. The light entering the scene through these openings causes a drastic difference between the highlights (outdoor lighting) and the shadows (soot-stained indoor surfaces). One must try and balance the lighting by adding light to the areas of shadow. Examine Figure 11.3 and observe how the light is relatively even between the indoor and outdoor portions of the composition. The image was recorded by metering the outdoor lighting and using an external flash unit to illuminate the indoor surfaces. An external flash was chosen because of the bright conditions outside and the short exposure time (1/125th of a second) needed for a proper exposure. If the scene's exterior lighting is not as intense (nighttime fire scenes), photographers may be able to have longer exposures, and longer exposures allow for the option of painting the interior with light (Figure 11.4). Fire investigators can use their external flashes to paint with light or even use the portable lights that are brought into the scene to illuminate the scene for investigators.

Figure 11.2 This composition was recorded of a smoke-damaged, poorly illuminated room. A flash exposure was recorded, and the flash was set to –1 stop of exposure so that the black-stained walls would be recorded accurately for color. Setting the flash for an *underexposure* prevents the camera from attempting to turn the black-colored walls an 18% gray color.

Figure 11.3 This image was recorded at ISO 400, f/4, for 1/60th of a second, which was determined by metering the light found on the exterior part of the burned home. However, the indoor portion of the scene, which did not have sunlight striking it, was illuminated with an external flash set to automatic (TTL) mode.

Similar to nighttime crime scenes, nighttime fire scenes actually offer the photographer much more flexibility in their choices on how to best illuminate a crime scene. When a nighttime fire scene is encountered, the scene can be painted with light like any other crime scene described in Chapter 7. Figure 11.5 illustrates a nighttime arson investigation. The ambient light was only provided by a couple of streetlights set approximately

Figure 11.4 This image was recorded at ISO 400, f/8, for 20 s. The exposure was determined by metering the scene's exterior, which can be seen through the burned-out window. The scene's interior was painted with light by a Pelican® 9430B remote area lighting system. The Pelican light output is approximately 3000 lm.

Figure 11.5 This photograph was recorded at ISO 400, f/11, for 83 s. Light was cast across the scene with a flashlight during the entire exposure in order to get light onto and into all the multilevel surfaces found in the composition.

100 ft from the home. As a result, light was cast into the scene by a Streamlight® SL-20 flashlight during the lengthy (4 min) exposure. The length of the exposure was simply the amount of time needed to paint the scene with light. Once the photographer had cast two coats of painted light across the scene, the exposure was allowed to conclude. Low-light conditions and painting with light techniques are beneficial to fire investigations, because the photographer has time to cast light into and across the burned surfaces, illuminating difficult to reach areas. The key to a successful painting with light photograph is to cast an even amount of light across the entire composition. Light can be cast with an electronic flash, a flashlight, or almost any light source. Photographers should practice with their particular light source prior to working an actual crime scene, so that they have an idea as to a proper ISO value and aperture combination that provides the best result.

The third variable is of course time, and the length of the exposure is simply that amount of time needed to cast the light evenly and thoroughly across the entire composition. Photographers in possession of smaller flashlights should be prepared for lengthy (several minutes) exposures, while a 3000 lm light source may only take 20–30 s to record in a similar environment.

When adding light to the scene of a fire, creating contrast and depth to the compositions is extremely important. Contrast comes in two forms, one is contrast in color and one is contrast in depth or texture. Color is likely the more problematic challenge faced by photographers, because there is oftentimes a lack of natural color in fire scenes. If not completely gutted, many scenes will be largely soot or smoke stained and black in color. However, recording the accurate color of a fire scene can be quite important because the sometimes minor variations in color within a fire scene can provide information to the investigator in regard to the movement of the fire while it burned. Identifying the minor variations in the color of soot- or smoke-stained walls may be critical in identifying the area of origin for a fire or height at which smoke reached down into a room. As a result, photographers should be cautious, especially when utilizing a flash, so that the image is not washed out and that the image is accurately recorded for color, as well as subject matter (Figure 11.6).

Since burned-out structures are likely to be void of actual color, that is, more of a grayscale composition, and the fact that the camera is attempting to reach an 18% gray value, it is possible for the camera to under- or overexpose the composition. If the scene is largely black stained, the camera may overexpose the image. If the scene is largely white or light gray colored, the camera may underexpose the image. Therefore, fire photographers should keep this in mind when metering light inside burned environments (Figure 11.7).

The utilization of a camera's flash can also wash out valuable information found at fire scenes. Attempting to record overall orientation (fire) photographs through the use of a pop-up flash is just as ineffective as trying to illuminate a large crime scene with such a small flash unit. Even using a quality external flash can cause exposure issues when the

Figure 11.6 This image was recorded at ISO 100, f/11, for 30 s. The ambient light was combined with electronic flash in order to obtain the best possible image. The flash was set to –1 stop of compensation so as to not wash out the color of the composition.

Figure 11.7 This fire scene had two distinct colors: the black, soot-stained foreground and the white-tiled bathroom. The exposure was recorded at ISO 400, f/11, for 1.3 s. One electronic flash was cast across the foreground, while another flash illuminated the bathroom. The flash positioned inside the bathroom was set to overexpose the room by ⅔ of a stop, so that the white surfaces came out properly exposed.

Figure 11.8 This fire scene was exposed at ISO 400, f/4, for 1/60th of a second. A Sto-Fen® flash diffuser was placed on the external flash, which was pulled back from the subject and cast downward across the composition.

flash is attached to the camera's hot shoe. Like reflective surfaces, the composition will be better served with the flash pulled away from the camera and cast at an angle across the surface. In addition, using a diffuser on the flash may also help the flash's light filter across the scene, thereby avoiding the vignetting (darkened corners) that may appear with a flash cast directly into the center of the composition (Figure 11.8).

The second type of contrast that can present difficulties to photographers involves the texture patterns or charring patterns that are frequently found at fire scenes. Similar to any indented or textured subject, such as footwear impressions or serial numbers, the photographic documentation of char patterns will benefit from oblique lighting. Oblique lighting will help bring out the details in the texture by creating shadows within the composition so that the char pattern's definition is improved (Figure 11.9). In fire investigations, it is oftentimes just as important to get a good angle of light cast into the scene as it is getting enough total light into the scene. In addition, because fire scenes have a tendency to absorb a lot of light, painting with light frequently produces far better results than casting just a single flash into a crime scene. Figure 11.10 was recorded at ISO 400, f/11, for 30 s, and during the exposure, a flashlight was painted across the charred surface.

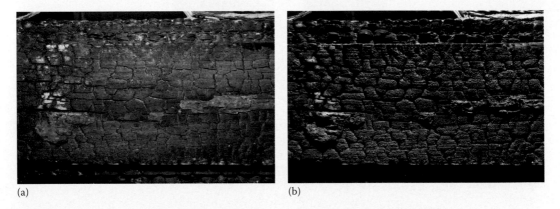

(a)   (b)

Figure 11.9 Both images were recorded with flash. (a) was photographed with the external flash attached to the camera's hot shoe. (b) was recorded with the flash attached by a sync cord and cast obliquely across the charred surface. Notice how the texture of the subject was greatly improved by the oblique lighting.

Figure 11.10 This char pattern was recorded at ISO 100, f/8, for 30 s, and during the exposure, a flashlight was painted obliquely across the charred surface. Casting light obliquely across charred surfaces is more likely to result in quality images.

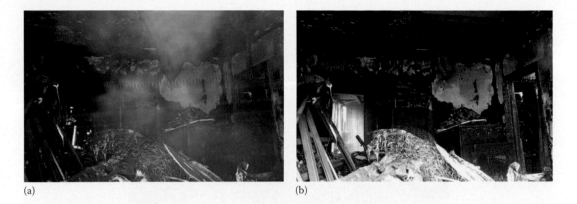

(a)   (b)

Figure 11.11 (a) is a flash photograph of a still smoldering fire. The flash reflects off the smoke, similar to what fire investigators face in their fire scenes. When faced with such environments, a time exposure without any flash is a better option. (b) was recorded at ISO 400, f/13, for 20 s.

When fire investigators begin their work, many times smoke and steam are still wafting across the scene. In addition to the steam and smoke, investigators are also confronted with water dripping down from overhead surfaces. When using flash photography, the flash can reflect off all the smoke and water droplets, causing a very distracting haze or glare across the composition. It is similar to driving a car on a foggy night. If one uses their high-beamed headlights, the driver is nearly blinded by the light bouncing back off the fine water droplets and into the driver's eyes. Flash photography is not much different. Consequently, time exposures are definitely advantageous. Allowing the exposure to extend past a couple of seconds allows the subject behind the moving smoke, steam, and water to record while allowing the moving particles of water and smoke to blur and possibly disappear completely from the image (Figure 11.11). Removing unwanted smoke and water from appearing in the image can be compared to an investigator that physically walks through their composition while painting the scene with light. As long as the photographer does not illuminate themselves while walking through the scene, they will not appear in the final image. Photographing through water or smoke is quite similar, leave the flash in the camera bag and record an ambient light photograph. The length of the exposure does not have to be minutes long, just a few seconds. It is quite easy to record such exposures in low light. If the scene is being photographed in bright daytime, the photographer should choose smaller apertures and lower ISO values in order to record longer exposures. Of course, if the fire is still raging and the smoke is billowing from the scene, even time exposures will not be able to cut through a dense cloud of smoke. Recording images over the course of a few seconds will be beneficial for those scenes where only remnants of steam and smoke are wafting through the composition (Figure 11.12). Even a small amount of steam and smoke can cause severe and unwanted reflections when a flash exposure is recorded. Therefore, leave the flash in the camera case and instead utilize a tripod.

Understandably, setting up a tripod in the muck and guck of a fire scene is not always easy or conducive for preserving one's equipment. However, the benefit gained by recording quality fire and arson photographs is well worth the effort. Investigators

Figure 11.12 This photograph shows the scene of a fire's aftermath. Smoke was still fairly thick inside the store after the fire, but a time exposure instead of a flash exposure was used to record a better image. (Photographed by Matt Milam, Arson Investigator, Houston Fire Department, Houston, TX.)

can protect their equipment by wrapping the tripod's legs with plastic bags if they so wish. Regardless of the conditions one is working in, a tripod-mounted camera and recording time exposures are highly recommended in any fire investigation. A tripod is an absolute necessity whether one is recording ambient light only photographs or is combining ambient light with supplemental light. Fire investigators that are only taking handheld flash exposures are not recording the best possible photograph. As with all crime scene photography, it is important to be patient, thoughtfully compose the image, and orchestrate the subject's lighting so that a valuable, true, and accurate photograph is recorded.

Conclusion

The photography of fire scenes is not always the easiest of endeavors. In addition to the natural hazards of working in scenes decimated by fire, the photographic challenges are all around. Lighting is the primary issue in regard to photographing fire scenes. Many times the burned-out structures being searched and photographed lack any ambient light, because the power has been disrupted. Although investigators will bring in their own portable light sources, the available lighting is typically very subdued, unbalanced, and/or uneven. As a result, fire photographers have to be able to examine the scene for lighting, recognize where the highlights and shadows are located, and decide on how best to record the image, supplementing the poorly illuminated areas with additional light. All the skills and techniques discussed throughout this book can all be utilized during fire investigations, from ambient light time photography to painting with light methods. Experience is certainly a valuable commodity in any photographic situation. However, the ability to diagnose the photographic challenges faced by fire and arson investigators and record quality images is within the grasp of all photographers and investigators.

End of Chapter Questions

1. What kind of difficult photographic compositions is commonly found at fire scenes?
   a. Backlit compositions
   b. Lack of color
   c. Extremely dark environments
   d. All of the above

2. When dealing with falling water being present across a composition, what is the method best to record the photograph?
   a. Use a flash unit
   b. Lengthen the exposure's time
   c. Use an infrared filter
   d. All of the above

3. It is a good idea to bracket a set of exposures when dealing with difficult exposures caused by primarily black (or white) surfaces.
   a. True
   b. False

4. When recording char patterns, what type of lighting would be advantageous?
   a. Ultraviolet lighting
   b. Infrared lighting
   c. Direct lighting
   d. Oblique lighting

5. When photographing a black, soot-stained surface, what is the camera likely going to do with the exposure?
   a. Overexpose the photograph
   b. Underexpose the photograph
   c. Force the flash to fire
   d. Choose a small aperture

6. Because lighting is oftentimes quite limited at fire scenes, photographers should utilize flash-sync speed exposures when possible.
   a. True
   b. False

7. An arson investigator accurately meters a fire scene to record at ISO 400, f/4.0, for ½ s. However, the composition has some area of shadows that need highlighting, and extra time is needed to paint the scene with light. What would be an equal or reciprocal exposure that allows more time for the photograph?
   a. ISO 800, f/22, for 15 s
   b. ISO 200, f/1.4, for 4 s
   c. ISO 100, f/16, for 30 s
   d. ISO 50, f/8, for 60 s

8. When faced with a backlit composition, setting the light meter for the brightest part of the composition and adding supplemental light to the areas of shadow are likely to result in the best image.
   a. True
   b. False

9. Fire investigators frequently bring in portable lights to assist with examining the scene of a fire. When photographing a burned room with those lights, what is the best recommendation for placement of those lights?
   a. Place them close to the photograph's subject
   b. Pull them back and/or away from the photograph's subject
   c. Be sure to include their visibility in the image so that viewers know what light source was used to record the image
   d. Always turn them off prior to recording the image

10. If a photograph is taken that lasts no more than 2 s in length and as long as the photographer is careful, the camera can be handheld when the picture is taken.
    a. True
    b. False

Photography Assignments

Required Tools: General photography equipment

Photography Subjects: General photographic subjects and if available a fire training exercise

  I. Photographing through rain, steam, exhaust, or smoke
   - A. Record a flash exposure and a timed exposure of falling rain.
   - B. Record a flash exposure and a timed exposure of rising steam from a boiling pot, vehicle's exhaust, or similar subject matter.
   - C. Record a flash exposure and a timed exposure of rising smoke from a camp fire, barbeque grill, or similar subject matter.
   - D. Compare the result of the aforementioned recorded images.

  II. Photograph a poorly illuminated room or area, preferably with dark-colored walls.
   - A. Photograph the room with accurate color and quality light balance.

  III. If one has access to a training exercise for firefighters, photograph the actual fire exercise and then the resulting destruction.

Additional Readings

Gardner, R.M. (2005). *Practical Crime Scene Processing and Investigation*. Boca Raton, FL: CRC Press.
Robinson, E. (2007). *Police Photography*. Burlington, MA: Academic Press.

Answer Key to Chapter End Questions

Chapter 1

1. c
2. d
3. d
4. b
5. b
6. d
7. c
8. c
9. b
10. b
11. a
12. a
13. b
14. b
15. c
16. a
17. d
18. a
19. b
20. d
21. d
22. c
23. a
24. d
25. a
26. a
27. b

Chapter 2

1. b
2. c
3. a
4. b
5. d
6. d
7. b

8. c
9. d
10. b
11. b
12. c
13. a
14. b
15. b
16. c
17. d
18. c
19. b
20. d
21. b

Chapter 3

1. d
2. d
3. b
4. c
5. d
6. b
7. b
8. d
9. a
10. b
11. d
12. a
13. d
14. c
15. b
16. a
17. b
18. d
19. b
20. c
21. c
22. d
23. a

Chapter 4

1. d
2. c
3. b

4. a
5. c
6. a
7. c
8. b
9. b
10. d
11. a
12. c
13. a
14. c
15. b
16. d
17. a

Chapter 5

1. c
2. d
3. b
4. a
5. d
6. c
7. a
8. d
9. b
10. c
11. d
12. a
13. c
14. a
15. b
16. d
17. d
18. c
19. b
20. a
21. c
22. d
23. c

Chapter 6

1. b
2. c
3. d

4. b
5. b
6. d
7. c
8. b
9. c
10. a
11. a
12. b
13. b
14. d
15. c
16. b
17. a
18. c
19. b
20. a
21. d
22. d

Chapter 7

1. d
2. b
3. c
4. a
5. c
6. c
7. d
8. a
9. c
10. c
11. a
12. b
13. c
14. d
15. b

Chapter 8

1. c
2. a
3. b
4. d
5. b

6. b
7. c
8. a
9. d
10. b
11. d
12. a

Chapter 9

1. a
2. a
3. b
4. c
5. b
6. a
7. d
8. b
9. d
10. c
11. b
12. d
13. a
14. a
15. c
16. b
17. a

Chapter 10

1. d
2. a
3. a
4. d
5. a
6. b
7. c
8. b
9. c
10. a
11. a
12. b
13. b
14. a
15. d

16. b
17. b
18. d
19. a
20. b

Chapter 11

1.   d
2.   b
3.   a
4.   d
5.   a
6.   b
7.   c
8.   a
9.   b
10. b

Index